The law can only exert its normative, regulatory and justice-administering functions if there is equal access to the law by all groups of the population. The collection of chapters offered in this volume is a most welcome addition to the growth of the discipline. The book deals with real-life, concrete, and specific types of barriers to such access on the African continent. Most importantly, the analyses are carried out by scholars from the very same area with relevant inside knowledge. These "regional" aspects put the book in a class of works with the same aspects of "regional" orientation as *Manual of Romance Forensic Linguistics* (Guillen Nieto and Stein; Walter DeGruyter). This is a timely publication from Africa.

Professor Dieter A. Stein
Heinrich-Heine-University Düsseldorf GERMANY

This book is ground-breaking and provides practical research insights needed to ensure African legal systems are linguistically inclusive and non-discriminatory. This book focusses on vulnerable witnesses making it an important contribution to the ongoing research in forensic linguistics. The chapter contributions expose the legal and linguistic inequalities within various legal systems, while offering practical solutions. This is a must-read for forensic and legal linguists, students, legal practitioners and judicial officers interested in language and the law.

Zakeera Docrat (PhD)
University of the Western Cape SOUTH AFRICA

The variety of themes covered by this book demonstrate the extent forensic linguistics is firmly establishing itself as a field of scientific inquiry in multilingual sub-Saharan Africa. This is a must-read contribution in the field, in its broadest meaning, and the engaged scholars from the various Southern and Eastern African countries have managed to bring to the general readers a clear picture of the challenges posed by language issues in the justice system.

Associate Professor Eliseu Mabasso
Eduardo Mondlane University MOZAMBIQUE

Discrimination and Access to Justice in Africa

There are different forms of discrimination. Among others, people can be discriminated against on the basis of their ethnic grouping, political affiliation, race, gender, age, and language. This book focuses on linguistic discrimination in Africa, acknowledging that language plays a key role in the delivery of justice and much of what transpires in justice systems deals with language use. It argues that to achieve fairness, the state has a responsibility to put in place accommodations aimed at reducing linguistic vulnerability. The collection interrogates some of the issues that are common in Africa, which is arguably one of the most linguistically diverse continents in the world, bringing together a collection of case studies from Malawi, South Africa, Zimbabwe, Tanzania, Kenya, and Zambia. It presents practical insights from academics, legal professionals, and social scientists. Divided into five thematic parts, the first addresses communication linguistic challenges faced by children in the legal system. Theme 2 examines the position of witnesses with physical challenges. The third theme focuses on language as a barrier in access to justice. Theme 4 looks at the language of the court as a major barrier to the poor and the illiterate. The fifth and final theme examines the position of women in sexual assault cases. The collection will be of interest to academics, researchers, and policymakers working in the areas of law and language, human rights law, criminology, linguistics, and African studies.

Wellman Kondowe is a senior lecturer in the Department of Language, Cultural and Creative Studies at Mzuzu University in Malawi.

Paul Svongoro is a senior lecturer in the Faculty of Education at the University of Botswana and a research fellow in the Africa Languages Department of the University of South Africa.

Law, Language and Communication

Series Editors

Anne Wagner is Professor of Legal Semiotics and Research Professor at Centre de Recherche Droits & Perspectives du Droit, équipe René Demogue, Lille University, France. She is the Editor-in-Chief of the International Journal for the Semiotics of Law (Springer) and President of the International Roundtables for the Semiotics of Law. She has been awarded the National Research Grant for her research career. Her main research interests include semiotics, verbal and non-verbal sign system analyses, language and law, legal culture and heritage, legal translation, legal terminology, and legal discourse studies.

Vijay K. Bhatia, formerly Professor of English, City University of Hong Kong, is now Adjunct Professor at Chinese University of Hong Kong, and Visiting Professor at the Hellenic American University, Athens (Greece). He is also the founding President of the Languages for Specific Purposes and Professional Communication Association for Asia-Pacific. His research interests include Critical Genre Analysis, academic and professional discourses in legal, business, newspaper, and promotional contexts; ESP and Professional Communication; simplification of legal and other public documents; intercultural and cross-disciplinary variations in professional genres.

This series encourages innovative and integrated perspectives within and across the boundaries of law, language and communication, with particular emphasis on issues of communication in specialized socio-legal and professional contexts. It seeks to bring together a range of diverse yet cumulative research traditions in order to identify and encourage interdisciplinary research.

The series welcomes proposals – both edited collections as well as single-authored monographs – emphasizing critical approaches to law, language and communication, identifying and discussing issues, proposing solutions to problems, offering analyses in areas such as legal construction, interpretation, translation and de-codification.

Titles in the series

Human Rights Discourse
Linguistics, Genre and Translation at the European Court of Human Rights
Jekaterina Nikitina

Discrimination and Access to Justice in Africa
Language, Vulnerability and Social Inclusion in Southern and Eastern Africa
Edited by Wellman Kondowe and Paul Svongoro

For more information about this series, please visit: www.routledge.com/Law-Language-and-Communication/book-series/LAWLANGCOMM

Discrimination and Access to Justice in Africa

Language, Vulnerability and Social Inclusion in Southern and Eastern Africa

Edited by Wellman Kondowe and Paul Svongoro

Routledge
Taylor & Francis Group
LONDON AND NEW YORK

First published 2025
by Routledge
4 Park Square, Milton Park, Abingdon, Oxon OX14 4RN

and by Routledge
605 Third Avenue, New York, NY 10158

Routledge is an imprint of the Taylor & Francis Group, an informa business

British Library Cataloguing-in-Publication Data
A catalogue record for this book is available from the British Library

ISBN: 978-1-032-94208-7 (hbk)
ISBN: 978-1-032-94211-7 (pbk)
ISBN: 978-1-003-56943-5 (ebk)

DOI: 10.4324/9781003569435

Typeset in Galliard
by Apex CoVantage, LLC

Contents

Foreword *x*
List of Contributors *xii*

Discrimination and access to justice in Africa 1
WELLMAN KONDOWE AND PAUL SVONGORO

THEME 1
Children in the legal system 11

1 Child witness protection during criminal proceedings: The law, practice, and challenges in Zambia 13
KAMO MSIMUKO SIMFUKWE

2 Linguistic barriers to access to justice by child victims and witnesses of sexual assault in Malawi's justice system 28
SHYREEN ODALA CHIRWA

3 Silent victims of the law: Children and the legal system in postcolonial Zimbabwe 44
VINCENT CHENZI

4 The application of language and procedural entitlements of children in detention in Malawi 60
DOROTHY NYAKAUNDA KAMANGA

THEME 2
Witnesses with disability 77

5 **Whose access to justice? Civil procedure rules and the right of access to justice for persons with disability in the High Court of Malawi** 79
THOKOZANI SOKO AND WELLMAN KONDOWE

6 **Intoxication, memory, and credibility: Intoxicated suspects and witnesses as a vulnerable group in Zimbabwe's justice system** 95
PAUL SVONGORO AND STANLEY MADONSELA

7 **Vulnerability of girls with communication disorders in the Malawian criminal justice system** 113
WELLMAN KONDOWE, EVANS LWARA, AND HAJIRA BLAMU MITUMBA

8 **Communication barriers faced by deaf citizens when accessing police services in Zimbabwe** 130
TAWANDA MATENDE, PATSON KUFAKUNESU, AND VICTOR MUGARI

THEME 3
Language as a barrier in access to justice 147

9 **Sign Language and the law in Zambia: Promoting equal access to justice for a linguistic and cultural minority** 149
GABRIEL SIMUNGALA AND HUMPHREY M. KAPAU

10 **Challenges of foreign language and migrant workers in South African courts: A critical examination of linguistic justice** 165
JOSEPHAT MUTANGADURA AND TEBOGO J. RAKGOGO

11 **Foreign language speakers, migrants, and refugees in Kenyan courts** 184
JOYCE KASILI AND LYDIA ANYONJE

12 **Legal status of Malawi Sign Language: Implications on language rights and access to justice for the hearing impaired** 202
MARTIN ZOLONI AND DEBORAH NDALAMA-MTAWALI

THEME 4
The poor and the illiterate before the courts of law 217

13 Courtroom interpretation and the dilemma of the poor and illiterate as accused and witnesses in court 219
JONES HAMBURU MAWERENGA AND GODWINS LWINGA

14 Access to justice by unrepresented litigants in Zimbabwe's courtrooms 236
PAUL SVONGORO AND EVENTHOUGH NDLOVU

15 The impact of litigants' socio-economic status on the delivery of justice: The plight of the poor and illiterate in Zimbabwe's rural magistrate courts 254
JOSEPHAT MUTANGADURA AND FELISTUS TAFADZWA MAKUMBE

THEME 5
Women in sexual assault cases 273

16 Rape myths in written judicial opinions from the Tanzanian Court of Appeal 275
PATRICIA MURAGURI, EMMANUEL SATIA, AND SIMON NGANGA

17 Ethical journalism practice in Zvinoyera, zvinotyisa uye zvinoda kufumurwa's coverage of allegations of abuse of women and children against Madzibaba Ishmael 293
WITNESS ROYA

Index *309*

Foreword

In recent years, forensic linguistics – a subject of study that is currently thriving in Africa – has emerged as a very striking and motivating phenomena among academics, notably in the fields of law and linguistics. What may characterise and exemplify this phenomenal development is this volume, *Discrimination and Access to Justice in Africa: Language, Vulnerability and Social Inclusion in Southern and Eastern Africa*, co-edited by Wellman Kondowe and Paul Svongoro, two prolific and enterprising authors in the field of forensic linguistics in Africa.

Admittedly, although forensic linguistics is relatively a new development of applied linguistics, much has been done about language and law. Therefore, the question which naturally arises is: what is new, special, or unique about this volume?

Firstly, the book is deeply rooted in the land of Africa, its unique political, social, and economic conditions and particularly its urgent and critical but often neglected problems. The authors, including linguists, attorneys, judges, and language activists, were chosen from the representative African countries. So, the research and studies in the volume are focused and offer a true, in-depth, and comprehensive picture of forensic linguistics studies in Africa.

Secondly, the volume is committed to addressing real, urgent, critical, and representative problems challenging Africa, particularly the underprivileged people of the continent represented by the five keen and key themes, namely, 'children in the legal system', dealing with such often neglected issues as child protection in criminal proceedings and linguistic barriers for child victims and witnesses of sexual assault in the Malawian justice system; 'witnesses with physical challenges', addressing the question of how persons with physical disabilities have their access to justice; 'language as a barrier in access to justice'; 'the poor and the illiterate before the court of law'; and finally 'women in sexual assault cases'. The devoted studies on these problems will certainly contribute to their solution so as to achieve better social justice.

Thirdly, because forensic linguistics is multidisciplinary in nature, cutting across linguistics, human rights, and law, the linguistic approach to legal problems was highlighted. Language or linguistic perspectives in solving legal problems were emphasised throughout the entire volume as well as in each individual contribution. It was clearly shown that even the most complex legal system may be directly impacted by the study of language and law.

At one level, the answer is simple: if the legal system absorbs some of the learning from the studies that address the basic questions, it is bound to improve.

Fourthly, the authors were not contented with a mere analysis of the cases, the data, or the problems, but went one step further and offered their remedies or ways to improve the situation or solve the problems.

Finally, the insightful research findings and conclusions will definitely provide important implications for other researchers in the same area situated in other parts or jurisdictions or legal systems and facing the same problems.

The contributing authors' approach to research resonates very well with the current practice in the field in helping us move away from naïve assumptions of universality that induce us to think of our own socially and culturally constricted experiences of language use (whether institutional of not) as maximally representative of a supposedly corresponding universal experience.

Meizhen Liao (PhD)
Professor Emeritus
Central China Normal University
Wuhan, People's Republic of China

Contributors

Lydia Anyonje holds a PhD in communication studies from Moi University and a master of arts degree in communication studies from the University of Nairobi. She is a senior lecturer with academic grounding and expertise in communication training and management, community mobilisation, and advocacy. Dr Anyonje teaches at the Department of Journalism and Mass Communication at Masinde Muliro University of Science & Technology (MMUST). Her research interests include media training, development communication, mass media trends, political communication and advocacy, indigenous knowledge and practice, health and environmental communication, and gender and conflict studies.

Vincent Chenzi is a lecturer of disaster management, conflict, peacebuilding, and strategic studies at the University of Zimbabwe (UZ). He holds a BA and MA in war and strategic studies from the University of Zimbabwe. Currently he is studying for his PhD in conflict, peace, and governance at the University of Zimbabwe. His areas of interest include African politics, disaster management, digital media, conflict resolution, human rights, and non-violence.

Shyreen Odala Chirwa is a PhD candidate and tutor for the Master of Laws in Human Rights and Democratisation in Africa programme, at the Centre for Human Rights, University of Pretoria. She holds a master of laws in human rights and democratisation in Africa from the University of Pretoria (2022), a bachelor of laws (honours) from the University of Malawi (2014), and a bachelor of education from the University of Livingstonia, Malawi (2009). Professionally, her career spans over nine years working as a professional magistrate and assistant registrar for the High Court (Civil Division), in the Malawi Judiciary.

Dorothy nyaKaunda Kamanga serves as a Justice of Appeal in Malawi's Judiciary and lectures in criminal litigation at Malawi Institute of Legal Education. She holds a master of arts (Rutgers), a master of laws (UCT), and is currently a PhD candidate at the University of Cape Town. She co-authored *Dispossessing the Widow: Gender-Based Violence in Malawi*

(2002) and contributed a chapter on 'The Role of the Judiciary in Safeguarding and Ensuring Access to Criminal Justice during the Pretrial Stage' in *Goal 16 of the Sustainable Development Goals: Perspectives from Judges and Lawyers in Southern Africa on Promoting Rule of Law and Equal Access to Justice* (2016).

Humphrey M. Kapau holds a PhD in linguistics from the University of the Western Cape (South Africa) and a master of arts in linguistic science from the University of Zambia. He is currently a lecturer and researcher at the University of Zambia. His research interests oscillate within the frontiers of forensic linguistics, systemic functional linguistics, psycholinguistics, discourse analysis, African linguistics, and literature. He is a published scholar with publications in the mentioned areas of interest.

Joyce Kasili holds a PhD in French studies from Masinde Muliro University of Science and Technology in collaboration with Prélude Doctoral School, Indian Ocean, under the AUF (Agency of Francophone Universities), and a master's degree in French as a foreign language from Rouen University, France. She teaches in the Department of Language and Literature Education at Masinde Muliro University of Science and Technology (MMUST). Her research areas are in teaching and learning of languages in general and of the French language in particular. She has widely published in the area of teaching and learning of the French language.

Wellman Kondowe is a senior lecturer in the department of Language, Cultural and Creative studies at Mzuzu University in Malawi. He holds a master's degree and a PhD in applied linguistics from Central China Normal University, obtained in 2014 and 2020, respectively. His research interests include language and law, political discourse analysis, and applied language studies. He has published edited and authored books, journal articles, and book chapters.

Patson Kufakunesu holds a PhD in literature and philosophy from the University of South Africa. He is currently a lecturer in the Department of Languages, Literature and Culture of the University of Zimbabwe. He also holds an MA degree in applied linguistics as well as a graduate certificate in education from the University of Zimbabwe. Some of his research interests are in minority language studies, corporate communication, language and the law, sociolinguistics, and discourse studies.

Evans Lwara is a lecturer in African languages and linguistics at Mzuzu University, Malawi. His main research areas of interest include applied linguistics – lexicography, translation, language rights – and theoretical and practical aspects of the grammar of Malawian languages. He is also an established language consultant, running one of Malawi's leading translation agencies. Evans received both his first degree in African languages and linguistics and a master's degree in applied linguistics from the University of Malawi, in 2008 and 2021, respectively. This contribution is his second book chapter publication.

Godwins Lwinga is a lecturer at the University of Livingstonia. He holds a BA from African Bible College, an MA from Mzuzu University, and PhD from Evangelische Theologische Faculteit (ETF), Belgium. His research interests are in environmental ethics and anti-corruption studies. He has published in the *Evangelical Review of Theology* and *MAGU Ethene Journal*. He is finalising editing his books *Christianity and the Ndali* and *The Ethics of uMunthu and of Dietrich Bonhoeffer as Resources for a New Responsibility-Based Anti-Corruption Approach in Malawi*.

Stanley Madonsela is a professor and chair of the Department of African Languages at the University of South Africa (Unisa). His research focus includes general linguistics, translation studies, and forensic linguistics. He is a co-manager of Unisa's research node of the South African Centre for Digital Language Resources (SADiLaR). In addition to editorial work in DHET accredited journals, Professor Madonsela is a distinguished scholar in his own right with published articles and book chapters in the areas of general linguistics, sociolinguistics, forensic linguistics, translation studies, and language policy in higher education. Professor Madonsela is Unisa's representative in the Community of Practice for the Teaching and Learning of African Languages (CoPAL).

Felistus Tafadzwa Makumbe holds a master's in applied linguistics, and a bachelor of arts degree with dual honours in linguistics and Ndebele from the University of Zimbabwe. Felistus is an experienced lecturer in communication skills, English language for academic purposes, court interpreting, court intermediary, translation, forensic linguistics, corpus linguistics, and sociolinguistics. Her research interests include various fields of applied linguistics and theoretical linguistics. Currently, Felistus is a lecturer and the communication skills coordinator in the Department of Language and Communication at the Women's University in Africa.

Tawanda Matende is a Canon Collins Trust Scholarship Alumni and a lecturer in the department of Languages Literature and Culture at the University of Zimbabwe. He is in his final year of his PhD research at the University of Venda in South Africa. His research interests are in the areas of Sign Language, language policy and planning, language and sustainable development, linguistic human rights advocacy, interpretation and translating studies, language editing and transcription, audiology, and speech therapy. He has published peer-reviewed articles and chapters in various regional and international journals.

Jones Hamburu Mawerenga is a senior lecturer in systematic theology and Christian ethics at the University of Malawi. He earned a PhD from Mzuzu University in 2016. He is also a research fellow in the Department of Practical Theology and Mission Studies, Faculty of Theology and Religion, University of Pretoria, RSA. His research interests and publications include religion and sexuality, albinism, theological education in Africa, the COVID-19 pandemic in Africa, religious violence, and African feminist epistemology (AFE). The current chapter was inspired by the quest to understand how the Malawian poor-illiterate are disenfranchised by courtroom interpretation when accessing justice.

Hajira Blamu Mitumba holds a master's degree in special education from Volda University, Norway, obtained in 2012. She also holds a bachelor's degree in education humanities from the University of Malawi, obtained in 2006. She is a lecturer in inclusive education in the Department of Education Foundations of the Faculty of Education at Mzuzu University in Malawi. She published a paper with East African Journal of Education and Social Sciences about 'Experiences of Learners with Mathematics Learning Difficulties in Regular Classrooms in Malawian Secondary Schools'.

Victor Mugari is an associate professor of linguistics at the University of Zimbabwe. He is also the deputy dean of the Faculty of Arts and Humanities. He graduated with a doctoral degree in linguistics and applied linguistics from the Beijing Language and Culture University (China, 2012). His research interests include syntax and its interfaces with semantics, morphology, sociolinguistics, strategic communication, bilingualism, and second language learning. He is currently working on Sign Language research, and language and ICT research.

Patricia Muraguri is an assistant lecturer at Mbeya University of Science and Technology (Tanzania) and a PhD candidate at Moi University (Kenya). She holds a BEd (honours) in linguistics and literature from Kenyatta University (Kenya), and an MA in linguistics from the University of Dar es Salaam. Her interests include forensic linguistics, discourse analysis, sociolinguistics, and morphology. She is a member of the Language Association of Eastern Africa (LAEA).

Josephat Mutangadura holds a PhD in communication science (UNISA) and a doctor of technology, language practice (TUT), and master in language for specific purposes. He is a senior lecturer in language for academic purposes, interpreting, editing and translation, media and communication studies, forensic linguistics, and African literature. He is an accomplished research supervisor in the aforementioned areas. He has published, individually and with fellow researchers, over 30 journal articles and book chapters.

Deborah Ndalama-Mtawali is a linguistics lecturer with a master's degree in applied linguistics from the University of Malawi. She currently teaches courses in Bantu languages and language rights in the Department of Language, Cultural and Creative Studies at Mzuzu University, Malawi. Her research interests lie in the areas of language use, with a particular focus on Bantu languages and language rights. She has published and presented papers on the usage of local languages in the attainment of Sustainable Development Goals (SDGs), language use in committing financial crimes, and language use in meaning-making encounters.

Eventhough Ndlovu is an associate professor in the Department of Languages, Literature and Culture at University of Zimbabwe. He holds a PhD in linguistics from the University of the Free State, South Africa, and a master of arts degree in African languages and literature. He is also a research fellow in the Department of African Languages at the University of the Free State. He has published extensively and teaches undergraduate and postgraduate courses in language planning, policy and management, human rights, terminography, lexicography, translation, and interpreting.

Simon Nganga holds a PhD in general linguistics from Bayreuth University, Germany. He is a lecturer in the Department of Literature, Linguistics, Foreign Languages and Film Studies, Moi University, Kenya. He has a special interest in contextual uses of language as understood under the areas of pragmatics, phonology, semantics, and discourse analysis.

Tebogo J. Rakgogo obtained his PhD in onomastics from the University of Witwatersrand, Johannesburg. Presently, he is the head of the Department of Applied Languages at Tshwane University of Technology. His research interests span onomastics, sociolinguistics, dialectology, historiography, and language planning and policy. He contributes to language authorities as a member of the Sesotho sa Leboa NLU and NLB. He is an active participant in TUT's governance structures, being a member of the Senate, Campus Management Committee (CMC), and Institutional Forum.

Witness Roya is a postdoctoral fellow at the Department of Digital Transformation and Supply Chain Management within the School of Business Leadership at University of South Africa (Unisa) and holds a PhD in Communication from University of Fort Hare, MSc in Media and Society Studies from Midlands State University among other qualifications. Witness has lectured in English, media, and communication in Zimbabwe and South Africa. Witness is a prolific writer who has co-authored several research papers and has a few single-authored publications.

Emmanuel Satia is a professor and Commonwealth Scholar. He teaches in the Department of Literature, Linguistics, Foreign Languages and Film Studies at Moi University (Kenya). He holds an MA in linguistics and African languages from the University of Nairobi (Kenya), and a PhD in forensic linguistics (Moi University and University of Leeds). His research interests include forensic linguistics, corpus linguistics, discourse analysis, and sociolinguistics. He serves as a member of the editorial board of *The University of Nairobi Journal of Language and Linguistics*, and of the journal *MwangawaLugha* of Moi University's Department of Kiswahili and other African Languages.

Kamo Msimuko Simfukwe (LLM, LLB, AHCZ) is a lecturer of law at Mulungushi University, a Council member of the Zambia Institute of Legal Education, and an Advocate of the High Court of Zambia. Since her admission to the bar she has served as senior legal aid counsel, Counsel in charge of Central Province Legal Aid Board office, and State Advocate with the Director of Public Prosecutions Chambers as it was called then. She has participated in provision of consultancy services involving the training of paralegal officers to enhance access to justice. Her research interests include criminal law and access to justice.

Gabriel Simungala is a PhD candidate in the Department of Linguistics at the University of the Western in South Africa. He holds a teaching position in the Department of Arts, Languages and Literary Studies at the University of Zambia, Lusaka-Zambia. He has published in language education, youth and pop culture, critical and multimodal discourse analysis, globalisation and mobility, linguistic/semiotic landscapes, Bantu linguistics, and the sociolinguistics of language contact. His recent publications include 'Critical Insights into Language Policy and Planning in Zambia' and 'Translanguaging as Means to Optimising Multilingual Education: A Zambian Perspective' (Routledge).

Thokozani Soko holds a master of laws degree in international and comparative disability law and policy from the University of Galway in Ireland. Soko is also the deputy chairperson of the Industrial Relations Court at Malawi Judiciary. She graduated from Chancellor College in 2014 with a degree in law. Before her current role, she held positions as a senior resident magistrate, principal resident magistrate, and assistant registrar. She is an early career researcher interested in doing studies that promote the rights of persons with disabilities.

Paul Svongoro is a senior lecturer in the Faculty of Education at the University of Botswana and a research fellow in the Department of African Languages at the University of South Africa (UNISA). He holds a PhD in applied linguistics from the University of the Witwatersrand, South Africa. Paul Svongoro has over 15 years of university teaching and research experience obtained from different universities in Zimbabwe, South Africa, and Botswana. He conducts research and publishes in the areas of corpus-based translation studies, court interpretation, forensic linguistics, academic literacy, and professional communication skills. To date, Paul Svongoro has over 30 publications in internationally accredited journals and book projects.

Martin Zoloni is a lecturer in linguistics and African languages at Domasi College of Education in Malawi. He is currently pursuing postgraduate studies in applied linguistics (law enforcement discourse) at Mzuzu University in Malawi. His research interests are in language and law, language rights, forensic linguistics, discourse analysis, and Bantu linguistics. His chapter contribution in this book is Martin's first academic publication.

Discrimination and access to justice in Africa

Wellman Kondowe and Paul Svongoro

Setting the scene

Discrimination and Access to Justice in Africa: Language, Vulnerability, and Social Inclusion in Southern and Eastern Africa is a collection of 17 innovative chapters which report on the experiences, insights, and evaluations of linguists, legal experts, and language activists on three interrelated subjects: linguistic discrimination, vulnerability, and access to justice in the southern and eastern regions of Africa.

In contrast to earlier works (Lawson et al., 2020; Malik & Maghani, 2023), which address vulnerability and access to justice in selected parts of Africa from gendered and legal perspectives, this book examines how vulnerable people of the community from six southern and eastern African countries encounter difficulties while attempting to enter the formal justice system. To achieve this objective, the book utilises a forensic linguistics viewpoint that focuses on linguistic discrimination. Using case studies, the book shares the experiences and perspectives of linguists, attorneys, judges, and language activists about how children, women, illiterate people, the poor, people with limited English proficiency (LEP), people with disabilities, migrant workers, and other marginalised groups encounter various forms of discrimination when they access justice particularly when they interact with law enforcement, courts, and prisons.

According to the United Nations for Human Rights Office of the High Commissioner (2016), traditional justice systems rooted in the cultural and historical roots of the African people served as the basis for conflict resolution in Africa prior to the arrival of colonisation. As a result, everyone could understand the traditional leadership and members of the community practicing traditional justice. Because of this, one of the justifications frequently offered for traditional and informal justice systems is that they offer more access to the legal system.

However, from the onset of colonialism, African countries notably those from southern and eastern Africa adopted formal or state judicial systems based on Western customs. Since formal legal systems are products of colonialism, this westernised method of resolving disputes is unknown by the majority of African citizens resulting in various forms of discrimination when citizens

DOI: 10.4324/9781003569435-1

participate in the justice system. For instance, because of the large volume of cases heard by a small number of courts, most processes have significant delays at every level.

In addition, the majority of individuals find the laws, rules, and processes followed in formal courts to be both foreign and complex (Tiersma, 1999; Gibbons, 2003). In a similar vein, linguistic discrimination is further fuelled when proceedings are frequently conducted in a language that common people do not comprehend. Despite the fact that interpreters are usually available, it is still unclear if substantive justice is served in every instance. Thus, only people with adequate legal expertise can comprehend how the formal justice system operates. However, on a daily basis, common people – including the underprivileged – frequently find themselves as witnesses or accused parties in police stations and courtrooms.

With the overall aim of enhancing access to justice by vulnerable members of the society, the chapters on which this book is based suggest further accommodations which governments, those who work in the justice system, and policymakers can adopt to reduce instances of linguistic discrimination and, hence, increase access to justice by all citizens regardless of their social, economic, and physical status.

Language, discrimination, and social inclusion

Broadly, discrimination can be either fair or unfair. Fair discrimination, on the one hand, is based on reasonable and justifiable grounds. Unfair discrimination, on the other hand, is based on factors that are not relevant to a particular context such as a job, a sport activity, a hearing at a workplace or an appearance in a court of law. In the context of the justice system, unfair discrimination may take various forms. One example could be being denied the right to fair representation through the use of language in speech, written characters, or sign language. Another could be being expected to speak in sexually explicit language which goes against your cultural norms, or being expected to wait for a trial for long periods because the court is unable to provide an interpreter who understands your language. While previous research has shown that speakers of African languages and speakers of minority and foreign languages often face prejudice when they make encounters with westernised courtrooms and justice systems (Aldridge, 2010; Powell, 2020; Dissake, 2021; Namakula, 2023; Docrat, 2024), to date, language rights activists, human rights groups, and ordinary citizens further raise concerns that even children, women, illiterate people, people with LEP, people with communication and other forms of disabilities, and foreign or migrant workers, just to mention a few, continue to face instances of unfair language discrimination in the justice system. These concerns are a clear call for research and action to address issues related to the widespread but under-researched problem of 'language-based disadvantage in polities whose law is administered in an elite medium that most citizens lack proficiency in' (Powel, 2020, p. vii). Because we perceive most of the mentioned forms of unfair language discrimination as avoidable, this book, therefore, explores the various forms of unfair discrimination southern and eastern African citizens face. In the interests of enhanced access to justice, the book also provides practical solutions for social inclusion to cater for the language needs of the various vulnerable populations.

Nearly every chapter in this book addresses the idea of social inclusion by offering decision-makers and policy-makers workable solutions that can help them recognise the importance and contribution of the vulnerable and enable them to engage in the legal system in a meaningful way. Having a fair justice system in Africa will ensure that all people realise the future they want regardless of their condition. The proposed book therefore aims at breaking down linguistic barriers limiting vulnerable persons' participation in the justice system and work to drive equal access to justice, fair trial, and equal outcomes in the justice system. Our goal for social inclusion is to ensure that individuals, groups, and communities participate fully in meaningful ways in society.

Vulnerability

As mentioned earlier in the background section, this book also examines the connections between vulnerability and access to justice in southern and eastern African nations, taking into account the communication or language barriers that vulnerable people encounter when trying to access the legal system. Through this investigation, the book sheds light on some of the language obstacles that, in their different contexts, women, children, the uneducated, migrants, foreign language speakers, the impoverished, and the disabled, for example, have while trying to access justice.

Vulnerability has gained prominence in human rights law over the past decade (see Manzoni & Timmer, 2013; Timmer et al., 2021; Limantė & Tereškinas, 2022). Determining the ideas of vulnerability and vulnerable groups is difficult for all these vulnerability experts, because vulnerability is a multifaceted term that can be seen from several angles and is used in a range of fields with both specific and general meanings. Although there are many different viewpoints on vulnerability, this book takes a straightforward sociological and legal approach to it. The sociological and legal approach, on which this book is also based, is borrowed from Limantė and Tereškinas (2022). The concept of vulnerability and vulnerable groups is developed in this book because all people are inherently susceptible, but certain groups are more vulnerable than others.

Thus, from a sociological standpoint, this book sees society as made up of disparate, frequently hostile communities, of which only a tiny percentage have access to sufficient social assistance and services. There is little chance that the surviving people will ever reach their full potential. They are frequently referred to as marginalised, vulnerable, or at-risk groups for social exclusion. Vulnerable people encounter profound discrimination in several domains of life, which has an adverse impact on their standard of living, overall health, and prospects for the future: hence the need for social inclusion.

Furthermore, socially disadvantaged and vulnerable groups (e.g., migrants) are subjected to a dominating discursive tradition that places a heavy load of guilt, shame, and even greater vulnerability on them (see Docrat, 2024). Sociologists have shifted their focus from embracing this discursive heritage to studying social exclusion, social suffering, and everyday hardship, making the experiences of vulnerable individuals with injustice, injury, and damage into important sociological topics.

The book's chapters address legal issues by identifying and analysing the principal international, regional, and local human rights treaties, as well as theoretical discussions of vulnerability and relevant case law that safeguards vulnerable individuals and groups. In this way, the chapters describe the framework of international legal instruments that link national and regional laws.

There are a number of studies that have documented vulnerable groups which face linguistic discrimination before the law (Aldridge, 2010; Ehrlich, 2010; Dissake, 2021; Svongoro & Ralarala, 2023; Namakula, 2023; Docrat, 2024). Such groups include children, second language and minority language speakers, accused persons and witnesses with disability, women in sexual assault trials, the deaf, and the poorly educated (Aldridge, 2010). For instance, children are said to have serious challenges to respond to lawyers' questions. They can easily be threatened, and their stories can easily be destroyed. Second language speakers express serious linguistic challenges during courtroom interactions, and they demonstrate very limited linguistic comprehension and production skills. Furthermore, the sign language system used by the deaf, for example, does not match with the ordinary spoken language in many ways because it is considered a stand-alone language in its own right (Gibbons, 2003; Svongoro & Ralarala, 2023). It is also noted that, as victims of sexual assault cases, women are publicly re-victimised once their complaints of rape enter the legal system (Svongoro et al., 2012). Some legal critics have referred to rape trials as 'judicial rape' or 'rape of the second kind' (Lees, 1996). As a result, the questioning techniques and the demand that the courts use sexually explicit language frequently cause re-traumatisation for women who have experienced various types of sexual assault (Liebes-Plesner, 1994). Sexually explicit language demanded by courts is therefore considered to be unfair discrimination on women witnesses who are victims of sexual assault.

Therefore, the vulnerability framework used in this book offers a fresh perspective on being, seeing, and knowing as well as, ideally, a better means to address the suffering of the entire life order but most importantly for the vulnerable groups just mentioned. Thinking in terms of marginalised groups creates a variety of opportunities, chief among them the chance to advance towards a more comprehensive conception of equality in which discrimination is always guarded against. However, there are also certain inherent problems within the notion.

Access to justice

Another concept the book explores is access to justice. In most contexts, access to justice remains a highly contested issue. In Africa, limited access to justice is often seen as the root cause of underdevelopment, social unrest, and conflict (Malik & Maghani, 2023). This is so because women, girls, and marginalised groups face discriminatory laws and systemic barriers to accessing justice, and are under-represented in decision-making processes and roles. In addition, protracted conflicts, rising levels of political violence, and the weakening of key rule of law and justice institutions are contributing to discrimination, injustices and inequalities, pervasive impunity, and undermining of the social contract.

To address concerns related to access to justice, this book assumes the stance that increasing access for everyone is vital for a peaceful and successful continent, especially for vulnerable populations including women, children, the uneducated, the impoverished, and the disabled. While justice may mean different things to different people, for the vulnerable groups this book is based on those who suffer the most when justice fails. Justice means learning more and making better decisions by investigating the views of those who are most vulnerable, helping to better enable them to access justice.

As shall be seen in the chapters in this book, for example, one of the greatest challenges that poor and vulnerable groups in Africa face in accessing justice is a lack of confidence in the quality of the justice systems in their respective countries. Chapters 13, 14, and 15 of this book, for example, lament the use of foreign languages in courtroom recordings of statements and trials and urge justice systems in Africa to stop the unfair discrimination of speakers of 'less-heard' languages (Namakula, 2023). Others, for example Chapters 8 and 9, bemoan the quality of court interpreting and the lack of interpreters proficient in Sign Language interpreting, yet others, for example, Chapters 10 and 11, explore the language challenges migrant workers and refugees face in the legal systems of their host countries.

Thus, the book contends that in order for vulnerable groups to have equal access to justice, governments and state actors must provide accommodations to reduce language, environmental, and structural obstacles which cause discrimination. A key component of Goal 16 of the 2030 Agenda for Sustainable Development, for example, is universal access to justice. The 2030 Agenda's main goal of leaving no one behind and the equality criterion are fundamentally based on legal assistance. For example, the poor, the marginalised, and the disadvantaged, who may be detained, jailed, or imprisoned, as well as the witnesses and victims, have access to justice when they have access to legal help.

In order to help disadvantaged populations traverse the unfamiliar, convoluted, and daunting African legal systems, access to justice also entails providing them with assistance. The chapters in this book make the case that providing accommodations for vulnerable groups will help lower the number of wrongful convictions, the length of time suspects are held in custody, the frequency of torture, bribery, and justice mismanagement, and eventually the rates of re-offending and re-victimisation.

The book is based on case studies from various regions of eastern and southern Africa, and advocates for just and responsible judicial systems, services, and institutions that can provide high-quality legal services to everyone, including the most marginalised and disadvantaged. The researchers agree with the United Nations for Human Rights Office of the High Commissioner (2016), that improving access to justice necessitates changing the legal system in accordance with Nancy Fraser's Transformative Justice Approach. In order to increase the vulnerable persons' access to justice, attempts to reform the legal system must be informed by and be sensitive to the causes of injustice as well as the everyday demands of individuals for both criminal and civil justice.

The transformative justice approach recognises that formal justice institutions are but one means of pursuing justice and places focus on the effectiveness and calibre of all state and non-state (customary and informal) justice service providers.

A forensic linguistics approach and the need for the book

The subject of forensic linguistics, which is a sub-discipline of applied linguistics, provides the foundation for this book. Although there is no single definition of forensic linguistics because forensic linguistics itself has many sub-disciplines and applications, the primary scope of forensic linguistics is the analysis of language and language-related matters in legal processes. As a scientific field, forensic linguistics for example, helps in combating prejudice, unfairness, and unethical legal processes based on language (Heydon, 2019; Guillén-Nieto & Stein, 2022). This book, therefore, challenges the reader's perception of communication features that many in the legal profession (and other people) would take for granted, illuminating the reasons why linguistic knowledge may be lacking among individuals in the legal profession. The book aims to demonstrate the significance of language analysis for the legal system and, in the end, increase access to justice.

To achieve its objectives, some of the chapters in this book conceptualise forensic linguistics as an interdisciplinary field of research to analyse the difficulties experienced by various vulnerable groups when they attempt to access the legal systems in southern and eastern African nations. Others, for example, the last two chapters of the book, adopt a gendered approach to investigate some of the linguistic discrimination of women and children in Africa's justice systems, yet others assume language advocacy and lexicographic approaches in their examination of vulnerability and linguistic discrimination in Africa's justice system.

The book, therefore, builds on previous research produced in the Americas, Europe, Asia, and Africa (Gibbons, 2003; Aldridge, 2010; Heydon, 2019; Powell, 2020; Dissake, 2021; Namakula, 2023; Docrat, 2024) to further interrogate some of the issues that continue to bedevil Africa, which is arguably one of the most linguistically diverse continents in the world (Kasonde, 2016). The book offers both seasoned and novice researchers pertinent instruments for carrying out forensic linguistics investigations. The research presented in this book shows how language-related social justice issues and legal procedures may be addressed to improve access to justice for all people, regardless of socio-economic status.

Thus, each chapter is framed by a language problem arising from either forensic linguistic cases, courtroom observation, or a major issue in language and the law. The chapters comprise the book's current research methods in forensic linguistics, using case studies from various countries. The chapters' data were drawn from a variety of forensic and legal language sources, including police statements and interviews, magistrates' and judges' questioning of accused parties and witnesses, accused parties' witnesses' cross-examination and chief examination, and reports of sexual assault, to name a few.

This book is, therefore, a perfect resource for linguists who wish to use their expertise in a forensic context, legal and justice professionals who want to know how linguistic analysis can help them in their work, and any student doing research in forensic linguistics within the fields of English language, linguistics, applied linguistics, legal education, gender studies, and all organisations interested in social inclusion. Being one of the first few books in Africa to examine the ideas of vulnerability and access to justice, the book's novelty makes it a vital and important addition to evidence-based strategies for resolving language-related injustices in the continent's legal systems. Additionally, the book also raises awareness among legal professionals of the role forensic linguists may play in the legal domain.

Organisation of the book

The book is structured around five themes that are interrelated. The scholars provide their provocative observations on *Children in the legal system*, which is the first theme of the book. The researchers in this section cover a variety of problems, including the degree of protection afforded to child witnesses during criminal processes and the language and cultural hurdles that young victims encounter during legal procedures. Researchers also offer their perspectives on children being the silent victims of the legal system. To put it briefly, this theme explores the mutually reinforcing link between vulnerability and access to justice via the lenses of children's testimony in court, their linguistic abilities, and the challenges they encounter throughout legal proceedings. The theme also unravels the accommodations the justice system provides for children as a vulnerable group and the extent to which these accommodations work.

The theme of *Witnesses with disability* is covered in the book's second part. For individuals who are interested in how people with disabilities access the legal system, this section is very pertinent. Thus, readers should anticipate reading about whether or not people with impairments can access the court system in this section. This theme also examines how court procedures help or accommodate people with physical disabilities as hearing impairments when they access the justice system. Under this theme, Chapter 6 also examines access to justice by intoxicated suspects and witnesses who appear in court. This part is intriguing since some of the writers support transformational equality in the legal systems of southern and eastern African nations to improve everyone's access to the courts. Other issues covered in this section include the concepts of memory and credibility when courts deal with intoxicated witnesses and suspects as a vulnerable group.

The third section of the book deals with the theme *Language as a barrier in access to justice*. Chapters in this section address topics like translanguaging as a substitute for effective communication to accommodate speakers of minority languages during trials and the hotly debated topic of the language of record in Africa's justice systems because forensic linguistics studies the interface between language and the law (Gibbons, 2003). Additional chapters address the discrimination suffered by speakers of indigenous languages, some of which are considered less-heard languages, during the recording of witness testimonies at police stations, as well as the problem of migratory workers and refugees from other countries finding themselves in foreign courts where their native tongues are unknown (Namakula, 2023).

In section 4, the book delves into the theme *The poor and the illiterate before the courts of law*. While the previous sections of the book pay particular attention to other vulnerable groups such as children, women, and persons living with various forms of disability and the various forms of unfair discriminations they face in the justice system, this section is dedicated to a vulnerable group which forms the majority of participants in African courtrooms, that is, the poor and the illiterate. The section's goal is to increase this vulnerable group's access to justice – the impoverished and the illiterate. This section's chapters pose important questions on how the underprivileged and the uneducated deal with the 'weird' legal systems of their own nations. Researchers in this subject, for example, doubt how well the impoverished and uneducated can understand and interpret legal writings. Furthermore, the three chapters under this theme also take a closer look on access to justice by poor unrepresented litigants who cannot afford legal representation in their countries, and the plight of poor and illiterate villagers who make encounters with formal justice systems in their countries.

The last section of the book comprising of two chapters adopts a gendered approach and addresses the theme *Women in sexual assault cases*. The chapters in this section examine the linguistics difficulties African women encounter while providing evidence in rape and other sexual assault cases. As reported in previous research, for example, African women face linguistic barriers due to formal courts' need that sexually explicit language be used while presenting evidence (Svongoro et al., 2012). This is due to the taboo nature of sexually explicit language among Africans, especially among women. As a result, the chapters in this section offer fresh perspectives on women's legal access when they come forward in court as sexual assault victims. The chapters in this section address a number of topics, such as the problem of rape myths in written judicial opinions and the way women experience 'judicial rape', a term used by Ehrlich (2010, 2016) to describe another type of rape that occurs when they are confronted with cultural, psychological, and emotional obstacles while testifying in sexual assault cases.

Conclusion

This interdisciplinary book which draws insights from language, law, human rights, gender, and African studies is therefore a must-read for linguists, legal professionals, language activists, policymakers, and many other people who seek to expand their knowledge on forensic linguistics and how vulnerability affects access to justice in the developing world. The knowledge one gains from this book can improve decision-making by exploring the perspectives of what justice means to the most vulnerable members of society and how access to justice can be enhanced for this group.

References

Aldridge, M. (2010). Vulnerable witnesses in the criminal justice system. In M. Coulthard & A. Johnson (Eds.), *The Routledge handbook of forensic linguistics* (pp. 296–314). Routledge.

Dissake, E. M. (2021). *Language and legal proceedings: Analysing courtroom discourse in Cameroon*. Palgrave Macmillan.

Docrat, Z. (2024). The discriminatory practice of language testing for authenticating citizenship: An analysis of operation Dudula through a forensic linguistics lens. *Potchefstroom Electronic Law Journal/Potchefstroomse Elektroniese Regsblad*, *7*(1), 1–28.

Ehrlich, S. (2010). Rape victims: The discourse of rape trials. In M. Coulthard & A. Johnson (Eds.), *The Routledge handbook of forensic linguistics* (pp. 265–280). Routledge.

Ehrlich, S. (2016). Post-penetration rape: Coercion or freely-given consent? In S. Ehrlich, D. Eades, & J. Ainsworth (Eds.), *Discursive constructions of consent in the legal process*. Oxford University Press.

Gibbons, J. P. (2003). *Forensic linguistics: An introduction to language in the justice system*. Wiley-Blackwell.

Guillén-Nieto, V., & Stein, D. (2022). Introduction: Theory and practice in forensic linguistics. In V. Guillén-Nieto & D. Stein (Eds.), *Language as evidence*. Palgrave Macmillan. https://doi.org/10.1007/978-3-030-84330-4_1

Heydon, G. (2019). *Researching forensic linguistics: Approaches and applications*. Routledge.

Kasonde, A. (2016). The changing role of the court interpreter-translator in Africa. *Comparative Legilinguistics*, *27*(2), 22–32. https://doi.org/10.14746/cl.2016.27.2

Lawson, D., Dubin, A., & Mwambene, L. (2020). *Gender, poverty and access to justice: Policy implementation in Sub-Saharan Africa*. Routledge.

Lees, S. (1996). *Carnal knowledge: Rape on trial*. Penguin.

Liebes-Plesner, T. (1994). Rhetoric in the service of justice: The sociolinguistic construction of stereotypes in an Israeli rape trial. *Text*, *4*(1–3), 173–192.

Limantė, A., & Tereškinas, A. (2022). Definition of vulnerable groups. In A. Limantė & D. Pūraitė Andrikienė (Eds.), *Legal protection of vulnerable groups in Lithuania,*

Latvia, Estonia and Poland: European Union and its neighbours in a globalized world (Vol. 8). Springer. https://doi.org/10.1007/978-3-031-06998-7_1

Malik, W. H., & Maghani, C. L. (2023). *Voices of the vulnerable: Promoting access to justice in Sub-Saharan Africa*. The World Bank.

Manzoni, M. P., & Timmer, A. (2013). Vulnerable groups: The promise of an emerging concept in European Human Rights Convention law. *ICON-I nternational Journal of Constitutional Law, 11*(4), 1056–1085. h ttp://hdl.handle.net/1854/LU-4430710

Namakula, C. S. (2023). *Fair trial rights and multilingualism in Africa: Perspectives from comparable jurisdictions*. Routledge. ISBN: 9781003325819 (ebook)

Powell, R. (2020). *Language choice in postcolonial law: Lessons from Malaysia's bilingual legal system*. Springer Nature.

Svongoro, P., Mutangadura, J., Gonzo, L., & Mavunga, G. (2012). Language and the legal process: An investigation into the linguistic features used in courtroom discourse involving rape in Zimbabwe. *The South African Journal of African Languages, 32*(2), 117–128.

Svongoro, P., & Ralarala, M. K. (2023). Zimbabwe's constitutional safeguards for persons with communication disabilities: Implications for access to justice. In R. H. Kaschula, M. K. Ralarala, & G. Heydon (Eds.), *Language, crime and the courts in South Africa and beyond* (pp. 51–71). African Sun Press.

Tiersma, P. M. (1999). *Legal language*. University of Chicago Press.

Timmer, A., Baumgärtel, M., Kotzé, L., & Slingenberg, L. (2021). The potential and pitfalls of the vulnerability concept for human rights. *Netherlands Quarterly of Human Rights, 39*(3), 190–197. https://doi.org/10.1177/09240519211048009

United Nations for Human Rights Office of the High Commissioner. (2016). *Human rights and traditional justice systems in Africa*. https://doi.org/10.18356/e4202da6-en

Theme 1

Children in the legal system

1 Child witness protection during criminal proceedings

The law, practice, and challenges in Zambia

Kamo Msimuko Simfukwe

Introduction

One of the most vulnerable groups in society is children. The vulnerability of children stems from a number of factors, including discrimination, poverty, and inherent qualities such as emotional, psychological, and physical weakness. Due to these factors, children are solely dependent on adults to meet their needs and to make decisions for and in their best interest. This dependence and vulnerability permeates all facets of their lives. In relation to the subject matter at hand, the ability of children to access the criminal justice system either as a victim of a crime or an alleged perpetrator of a criminal offence and obtain a just remedy largely depends on the will of their guardians, accommodations by law enforcement officers and the courts at the various stages leading to the determination of the matters involving the affected children. Additionally, children must contend with the challenges of presenting their case in an environment and in accordance with procedures designed for adults that often do not take into account their delicate nature or respect their autonomy. In view of this, the Zambian legal system has incorporated provisions that seek to enhance and safeguard a child's right to access justice through the court system. The law governing the receipt of evidence from children that are victims of crime and/or in conflict with the law in Zambia is largely set out in the Constitution 1996 and the Children's Code Act (hereinafter referred to as the CC Act 2022).

This chapter will explore how these laws seek to ensure access to justice and protection for children that engage with the criminal justice system as victims or alleged perpetrators of a crime. Its focus will be restricted to the child witness (encapsulating both the child victim and the child in conflict with the law) in the Zambian courtroom.

Who is a child witness?

The phrase 'child witness' is not defined in the CC Act 2022. However, reference is made in the CC Act 2022 to the definition of a child, which is premised on Article 266 of the Constitution 2016 which provides that a child is

DOI: 10.4324/9781003569435-3

'a person who has attained, or is below, the age of eighteen years'. Thus, a child witness is a person that is 18 years old or less, that is a victim or alleged perpetrator of a crime or has witnessed the circumstances leading to or related to the commission of a crime. Regardless of the perspective, a child witness is entitled to access justice freely and with the necessary support afforded by law.

Access to justice for children in Zambia

Definition of 'access to justice'

There is no universally accepted definition of the phrase 'access to justice'. However, a number of definitions assist in identifying the key elements of this concept. The Organisation for Economic Co-operation and Development (OECD, 2019) defines access to justice as: 'the ability of individuals . . . to seek and obtain a just resolution of legal problems through a wide range of legal and justice services'.

Thus, access to justice in its most basic form entails the right that every individual has to take a matter to court and expect that court to determine it on its merits without discrimination. It further entails in the immediate context that access to justice is not only an entitlement for child victims of crime but for alleged perpetrators of crime.

Another description of the concept of 'access to justice' is the right that an individual has to litigate or defend one's case (Alberta Civil Liberties Research Centre [ACLRC], n.d.). While this right is open to all, it is difficult for a child to exercise it without the help of an adult, preferably a legal practitioner or other qualified person. Litigation in an adversarial system, as is the case in Zambia, is particularly complex and characterised by a wide range of procedures. Notable among these rules and procedures are the manner in which opponents are permitted to examine the opposing parties' witnesses and the strict adherence to procedure and rules of evidence. This chapter will consider some procedures that are of particular concern for children and could be a hindrance to their ability to access justice.

Additionally, access to justice, refers to the importance of securing counsel for the indigent and identifying the challenges they face in securing affordable legal services through legal aid schemes (ACLRC, n.d.). This perspective of access to justice is of particular importance in the Zambian context where over 60 percent of the population live below the poverty datum line (World Bank, n.d.). Consequently, the majority of the population cannot afford to engage a lawyer to help protect their interests or the services that they offer.

In assessing the extent to which Zambian law accommodates the notion of 'access to justice' for children, it is important to appreciate the respective components of this concept. Kerigan et al. (2012, p. 22) outlines these components by identifying the following aspects:

> Effectiveness and efficiency of justice delivery agencies – the delivery of quality services within a reasonable time; Physical access – how close the

users are to justice and law enforcement agencies; Financial terms – how affordable legal services are to the users; how comfortable users are with legal language and procedural requirements; the treatment of users by law enforcement and justice personnel; their representation by experts in law; the techniques and procedures of the system and the user's ability to afford them i.e. cost (including opportunity cost, as in time spent away from economic and family activity).

Securing access to justice as just described is essential for children 'for protection from discrimination, violence, abuse and exploitation and for ensuring children's best interests in all actions involving or having an impact on them' (Beqiraj & McNamara, 2016).

The legal framework governing access to justice and protection of child witnesses in Zambia

The legal framework governing access to justice and the protection of child witnesses in Zambia is set out in the Constitution 1996, Constitution 2016, and the CC Act 2022.

The legal status of the Zambian Constitution

The Constitution is the supreme law of the land and legitimises or invalidates Acts of parliament that are consistent or inconsistent with it respectively (Constitution, Art.1, 2016). It is also the law from which all pieces of legislation derive their existence.

This position is supported by a plethora of judicial precedents including *Mumba v The People* (1984) in which Justice Chirwa observed that:

> In countries like Zambia where there is a written constitution, the Constitution is the supreme law, any other laws are made because the Constitution provides for their being made; and are therefore subject to it. It follows therefore that unless the Constitution is specifically amended, any Act that is in contravention of the Constitution is null and void.

The centrality of the Constitution to the Zambian legal system makes it imperative that this discussion begins with the interrogation of the Constitution.

The child witness and the Constitution

The Zambian Constitution does not have a distinct set of rights for child witnesses. However, it enshrines the bill of rights, which is a set of civil and political rights that are applicable to all persons in Zambia regardless of their age, sex, status, race, political and religious affiliations, etc. (Constitution, Art. 11, 1996). Among the rights that are of particular interest and cardinal in the discharge of their duties as witnesses are freedom of expression, the right to be heard, the right to legal advice and or representation, the right to information, the right to participate and to be present in criminal proceedings that concern them, and the right to confront the accuser if they are standing trial (Constitution, Arts. 20 & 18, 1996). A number of these rights are replicated in the CC Act 2022 and are skewed to incorporate the peculiar needs of a child witness.

Article 18 of the Constitution 1996 is particularly dedicated to ensuring that a person (this includes children) that is alleged or in conflict with the law is able to access justice through the guarantee of a fair trial. Key components of this provision are the following:

Firstly, the recognition that a person accused of a crime is innocent until proven guilty unless he or she voluntarily admits to his guilt.

Secondly, it entitles the accused to information regarding the allegations that have been made out against them. This is essential in ensuring that the accused person is able to effectively defend him or herself. One of the challenges in relation to children is that information is not always available in a language that is accessible to them. There is no legal requirement for this information to be shared in an age-appropriate manner.

Thirdly it affords the accused person the opportunity to confront the accuser(s) regarding the allegations that have been brought against them. This is done through cross-examination of the opponent's witnesses and calling witnesses in opposition.

Fourthly, it gives the accused person the right to access legal services including legal advice, assistance, and representation provided by the State if they are unable to afford it. This is of particular importance in a developing country where the majority of citizens live below the poverty datum line. These services are available under the Legal Aid Board. Further, more often than not, accused persons are unfamiliar with the court rules and systems consequently, ensuring a fair trial entails representation that protects them from a failed defence based solely on technicalities of court process that they may not be aware of.

Fifthly the Constitution entitles the accused person to be present throughout the court hearing.

It is noteworthy that the Constitution 1996 and Constitution 2016 do not expressly use the phrase 'access to justice' even though it clearly incorporates some of its constituent elements as highlighted previously.

The Children's Code Act

The CC Act was enacted in 2022. It was enacted to reform and consolidate the law relating to children. It has domesticated provisions from the Convention on the Rights of the Child which are particularly relevant to this discourse. It also repealed the Juveniles Act whose main objective was to 'make provision for the custody and protection of juveniles in need of care; to provide for the correction of juvenile delinquents; and to provide for matters incidental to or connected with the foregoing'.

The CC Act 2022 does not expressly use the phrase 'access to justice'; neither does it expressly classify children as vulnerable persons. However, the special treatment of child witnesses as distinguished from adult witnesses clearly suggests incorporation of the notion that children are not only vulnerable but in need of special protection of the law.

The CC Act 2022 has introduced a number of innovations that seek to ensure that children, regardless of their age and cognitive development, are not only able to access the court system but are able to actively participate in it in a manner that considers not only their level of development but also makes the process of testifying less traumatic for the child witness.

The CC Act 2022 also sets out a number of provisions that if implemented will enhance access to justice for children; key among them is the right children have to express themselves in matters that affect them.

Section 6 of CC Act 2022 states that:

> A child who is capable of forming that child's own views shall be informed of, and be accorded an opportunity to express that child's opinion in a decision or a matter of procedure affecting the child, and that opinion shall be taken into account, as may be appropriate, having regard to the age and maturity of the child and the nature of the decision.

A number of observations emanate from this provision, namely that this right is not restricted to a particular age. Any child may express their views provided they are capable of forming an opinion of their own. However, it does afford the court the right to ignore or limit the weight it attaches to the evidence of a child based on their age, maturity, and the nature of the decision. No guidance is provided to the court on the determination of the age, level of maturity or the nature of the decision that could form the basis for the exclusion of a child's opinion, nor are there any Zambian reported judicial precedents that exist in relation to this provision that explain the parameters of the courts' discretion on this matter. Thus, there is a real danger that a child's evidence may be ignored altogether or received with apprehension. This concern is amplified by the traditional perception which the Zambian legal system possesses that views children as suspect witnesses whose evidence must be received with caution. The writer takes cognisance of the fact that the provision highlighted earlier raises concerns about decisions in a general sense rather than in the specific context of the court system. Provisions directed particularly at the rights and procedures pertaining to participation in the courtroom will be discussed in subsequent sections of this chapter.

The practical outworking of access to justice for children in Zambia

Physical access to the court system

The Zambian court system has seven courts that are listed here in descending order: the Supreme Court and Constitutional Court, which are equal in status; the Court of Appeal; High Court; Magistrates (Subordinate)

Court; Small claims court; and the Local Court (Constitution Art.120, 2016). Criminal matters are instituted in the Magistrates and High courts. The Court of Appeal and the Supreme Court are appellate courts in this respect.

Article 133 of the Constitution 2016 created the Children's Court (a specialised division of the High Court) and the Juveniles Court (a specialised division of the Magistrates Court) to determine matters involving children that are in conflict with the law (CC Act, sec 65, 2022). The Juveniles Court is authorised to hear any charge involving a child except charges of murder, treason, allegations that a child has committed an offence with an adult, and offences that can only be heard by the High Court (CC Act, sec 65, 2022). This means that most of the cases involving children in conflict with the law will be determined by the Juveniles Court. Even though the Juveniles Court has such wide jurisdiction to hear criminal matters, Juvenile's Courts are only located in 64 out of 117 districts in Zambia (The Zambian Judiciary, n.d.). This is a significant impediment to the administration of justice.

Further, the Juveniles Courts' geographical jurisdiction is limited to the district in which the offence is committed. Section 4 of the Subordinate Courts Act states: 'Each Subordinate Court shall have the jurisdiction and powers provided by this Act and any other written law for the time being in force and shall ordinarily exercise such jurisdiction only within the limits of the District for which each such court is constituted'. Thus, hearing matters in another district for administrative convenience other than the district in which the offence took place could result in a challenge to the decision made in a matter thereby denying a child victim the justice they deserve or subjecting a child suspected to be in conflict with the law to another trial.

Unlike the Juveniles Court, the Children's Court enjoys unlimited jurisdiction not only in terms of the types of cases it can hear but also the geographical area that falls within its jurisdiction (Constitution, Art.134, 2016). However, the Children's Court division as a specialised court has not been fully rolled out in all the High Courts in the country even though they have presence at all High Court registries. This means that matters pertaining to children are handled alongside other matters in the High Court rather than in a distinct court dedicated to this specific purpose and supported by its own staff. The High Court is present in each of the provincial capitals in Zambia's ten provinces. The absence of Children's Courts as a specialised court solely dedicated to determining criminal matters involving children at provincial and district level means that these cases cannot be attended to expeditiously and with the urgency that they deserve because they are one of the many cases that the court presiding over the matter will have to attend to. However, the progressive implementation of the clauses of the Constitution 2016 in Article 120 (4) targeted at devolution will see the extension of the High Court and or the Children's Court beyond the provincial headquarters into the remaining 107 districts in need of these facilities.

Efficacy of justice delivery agencies

Both the Constitution and the CC Act 2022 identify the timely disposal of court cases as an essential element in securing justice. The Constitution 2016 reiterates this in Article 118 (b), which provides that 'In exercising judicial authority, the courts shall be guided by the following principles: (b) justice shall not be delayed.'

Similarly, Article 18 of the Constitution 1996 entitles an accused person to a fair trial within a reasonable time before an independent and impartial tribunal.

However, there is no indication in the Constitution 2016 regarding what time frame must be observed before court proceedings are deemed to be delayed except in regard to the hearing of cases involving petitions against the loss of local government, parliamentary, and presidential elections. On the other hand, section 79 (7) of the CC Act 2022 provides that both Juvenile and Children Courts are expected to dispose of criminal matters within six months of the first appearance of the child in court. In the event that this is not achieved, the court may discharge the child immediately. However, a discharge does not amount to an acquittal even though it releases the child from the proceedings. The implication of this is that the entire process of prosecution could be recommenced after the child has been discharged.

Access to legal services for children

Children that are victims of a crime are represented by counsel from the National Prosecutions Authority who prosecutes the matter on their behalf. However, access to legal services was not guaranteed for children in conflict with the law until the enactment of section 72 (2) of the CC Act 2022. Thus, the ability of children to access legal services largely depended on the willingness and financial capacity of their parents or guardians. Consequently, most children in conflict with law had no legal representation due to the high levels of poverty exacerbated by the high legal fees required to engage a private lawyer.

Article 18 (2) of the Constitution 1996 guarantees an accused person's right to defend himself in person or by a lawyer. It also recognises the possibility of legal representation from the State for accused persons' that cannot afford it. Notwithstanding, in practice persons appearing before the High Court and on appeal, before the Court of Appeal and Supreme Court in criminal proceedings are more or less guaranteed legal representation from Legal Aid Board unless they are financially able to acquire alternative representation or opt to represent themselves in person. On the other hand, most accused persons do not have legal representation in the Magistrates Court because they cannot afford it coupled with the limited capacity of Legal Aid Board to provide an equivalent degree of representation compared to that which is offered to accused persons in superior courts (Chanda, 2011). Although this may be the case, the Legal Aid Act, sec 43, 2021 empowers courts to order the provision of legal aid services including representation in cases where the court is of the view that the accused person cannot afford legal services or because it is in the interest of justice.

Despite the limitations noted previously, special consideration is made for children in conflict with the law. Section 72 of the CC Act 2022 guarantees legal representation or assistance from a child welfare inspector from the State for indigent children in conflict with the law.

Even with this guarantee, the availability of counsel from Legal Aid Board is limited by the number of counsel available to handle criminal matters in general. The government of Zambia through the Legal Aid Board has created at least one office per province located in the provincial headquarters to mitigate this. Further, due to the limited number of legal aid counsel, cases that may be assumed by counsel in districts outside their stations are likely to take longer due to the heavy workload borne by counsel at their respective stations. On the other hand, access to private legal practitioners is limited by the high cost of legal services and the limited availability of advocates to attend to court matter (Kaaba, 2015). Most of Zambia's legal practitioners are located along the line of rail leaving vast portions of the country with limited or without legal services other than those offered by the Legal Aid Board and other institutions offering paralegal services. Outside government efforts, the Law Association of Zambia has developed a pro bono scheme to facilitate legal representation for the indigent (LAZ, 2022). This will most certainly contribute to enhancing access to justice for vulnerable groups like children.

The child witness in the Zambian courts

The traditional perception of the child witness

The traditional perception of the child witness has been a significant barrier to children's ability to access justice in criminal matters. For a long time now, the child witness had been perceived as a suspect witness whose evidence is received with much caution due to the belief that they were easily influenced by third parties, highly suggestible, and living in a world of their own. This inevitably raised questions concerning the credibility and reliability of their evidence. The reluctance to embrace child witness testimony is clearly demonstrated in a number of authorities including excerpts of various court decisions used in determining the case of *Benard Chisha v The People* (1980) in which Justice Silungwe stated,

> Although children may be less likely to be fraudulent or acting from improper motives than adults yet they are, (sic) as Atkin, J., observed in R.v Dossi (4), at, p. 161: 'possibly more under the influence of third persons – sometimes their parents – than are adults, and they are apt to allow their imaginations to run away with them and to invent untrue stories'.

In support of his position Justice Silungwe also quoted the words of Lord Morris of Borth-Y-Gest in *D.P.P. v Hester* (3), at p. 1059 who stated:

> The accumulated experience of courts of law, reflecting accepted general knowledge of the ways of the world, has shown that there are many circumstances and situations in which it is unwise to found settled conclusions on the testimony of one person alone. The reasons for this are diverse. There are some suggestions which can readily be made but which are only with more difficulty rebutted. There may in some cases be motives of self-interest; or of self-exculpation; or of vindictiveness. In some situations the straight line of truth is diverted by the influence of emotion or of hysteria or of alarm or of remorse. Sometimes it may be that owing to immaturity or perhaps to lively imaginative gifts there is no true appreciation of the gulf that separates truth from falsehood. It must, therefore, be sound policy to have rules of law or of practice which are designed to avert the peril that findings of guilt may be insecurely based.

The conclusion of this case was that the evidence of children required corroboration otherwise it was redundant. This was intended to confirm the evidence of the child witness due to the perceived dangers of receiving unsupported evidence from them.

Consequently, the legal position before the enactment of the CC Act was that the evidence of children could only be received after a child had been subjected to a competence test and passed it, and could only be effective against an accused person if it was corroborated. This approach indirectly hindered effective access to justice for child witnesses because it meant that a child could be prevented from testifying if they failed the competence test or their evidence could be rendered redundant for lack of corroboration.

Despite these challenges, section 78 of the CC Act 2022 has maintained the requirement to subject children to the competence test to determine whether or not a child understands the duty to speak the truth and is possessed with sufficient intelligence to testify in court proceedings. However, it permits children that fail the competence test to testify in court. The implication of this is that a child that does not understand the duty of telling the truth and/or is not possessed of sufficient intelligence to testify will be allowed to do so. However, testimony received in these circumstances will not carry as much weight as that attached to a child witness who passes the competence test. Even though this is a positive development for a child witness that is a victim of a crime, it is questionable whether or not it is a positive development in the administration of justice, whose concern is to ensure that criminal matters are concluded fairly and on the basis of the truth. Corroboration of a child witness's testimony is also no longer mandatory; this means that an accused person can be convicted based solely on a child's testimony (CC Act, sec 78 (9), 2022). This is significant progress in obtaining justice for child victims, particularly in relation to sexual offences such as defilement, indecent assault, offences against the order of nature, and incest, which are often committed in private, and as such their determination relies heavily on the testimony of the child victim who may be the only other person that was present when the offence was committed.

The child as a witness in the Zambian adversarial system

Courts of law are formal platforms created for the resolution of legal disputes. The formality of these platforms finds expression in the rules and procedures that must be observed to facilitate the administration of justice. The adversarial system is characterised by the right that parties to the dispute have to confront their opponent and the opponent's witnesses through cross-examination. Also common to this system is the insistence that parties observe clearly stipulated rules in adducing evidence before court. It is contended by some that this kind of legal system exposes children to trauma because it does not consider their delicate and unique intrinsic qualities.

Section 78 of the CC Act 2022 is an attempt to reduce the stress and trauma that child victims would otherwise experience as a result of this system. It addresses a number of concerns, such as the environment in which trial is being conducted, communication in the courtroom, rules on cross-examination, mode of communication, the right to be heard in camera, and the right not to interact with the accused person in the court room

COURTROOM ENVIRONMENT

The inability of some children to effectively participate in the administration of justice as witnesses has been attributed to the 'unfriendly' environment in the courtroom. The courtroom environment referred to includes the courtroom infrastructure, court room layout and décor, and the formal procedures that must be adhered to by all participants (Committee of Ministers of the Council of Europe, 2011). The European Council holds that 'cases involving children should be dealt with in unintimidating and child-sensitive settings where they feel safe and can speak freely'. The EC Guidelines set out the need for child-friendly waiting rooms for children; interview rooms where there are no disturbances or interruptions; avoiding direct contact between the child victim and alleged perpetrators; and having staff who are not in uniform' (Sheahan, 2021). The importance of this kind of environment in facilitating participation is confirmed by Ngulube (n.d.) who observes 'access to justice does not exist if poor or marginalised groups, such as persons with disabilities, are afraid of the justice system or see it as complex and unusable'. In order to mitigate this 'incapacitating environment' for child witnesses, section 78 (4) and (5) of the CC Act provides that:

> (4) A child that is giving evidence in a court shall –
>
> (a) be questioned in an environment that is child friendly;
> (b) be questioned in camera;

(d) not interact or be in the same room with a person the child is testifying against;

(5) Subject to subsection (4) (d), a person the child is testifying against or that person's legal practitioner shall cross examine a child witness through –

(a) a child welfare inspector, an authorised officer or a child's next friend, acting as an intermediary; or
(b) the use of a video link.

Although the CC Act 2022 is silent on what constitutes a child-friendly environment, it is arguable that aspects of subsection 4 and 5 cited previously are directed at making it easier for the child witness to acclimatise to the court set up and carry out their mandate with greater ease. For instance, separating the child victim witness from the accused person so that the child witness and victim do not have to interact face to face with him or her certainly makes it easier for the witness to testify. The innovation and inclusion of intermediaries who can speak to the child on behalf of the accused or the accused's advocate at a level that considers their age and emotional and psychological development contributes significantly to improving the courtroom environment. Also, it has been a practice since time immemorial to soften formality in the courtroom by requiring judges and lawyers to abstain from the use of wigs and gowns to make the environment less intimidating for children. However, the design and layout of the courtrooms in Zambia have not been altered to accommodate children by, for instance, the acquisition of child-sized furniture or repainting or redecoration of court rooms designated for court cases involving children.

LANGUAGE AND COMMUNICATION IN THE COURTROOM

Muller and Hollely (2000) ably note a key component regarding a child's ability to participate in the court system as a witness. They observe:

> In order to participate in the legal process, a child must have the ability to communicate in a manner that is understood by the adult listeners. Communication in this context, according to Saywitz (1990, p. 345), is an interaction between what the speaker (child) and the listener (adult) bring to the context (courtroom) in which the interchange occurs. To give evidence successfully, a child must have reached a certain level of intelligence, vocabulary and conversational skill.

They further contend that the ability of a child to communicate is dependent on the level of their general development, and cognitive and language abilities. Consequently, when a lawyer makes use of his 'well developed verbal skills without taking cognisance of the level of development of the child witnesses, the use of their own skills may pose a barrier to effective communication with the child witness' (Muller & Hollely, 2000). This invariably means that the child witness may not be able to provide the information that is required to assist in the determination of the matter before court.

The CC Act 2022 has included some provisions that are meant to accommodate these concerns. Thus, section 78 (4) of the CC Act 2022 provides that: 'A child that is giving evidence in a court shall – (c) Be questioned in a manner that is proportional to the child's age and maturity of the child; and (e) not be questioned more than twice'.

However, while the inclusion of these sections is commendable, the preceding section assumes that the person interrogating the child during the proceedings has the relevant skills and expertise to make a determination as to the kind of questions that are appropriate for a child of a particular age and level of maturity, which may not necessarily be the case.

CONTROLS ON CROSS-EXAMINATION

Cross-examination is a very important tool used in the adversarial system to test the veracity of the testimony of an opponent's witness and to elicit evidence that is favourable to the cross-examiners' case. This aspect is often the most intense segment of the witnesses' examination because the opposing counsel or the accused person if unrepresented often wants to prove that the witness is not credible or reliable and, as such, they suggest that their evidence be discounted. If this approach is taken in conducting cross-examination, the child witness is likely to feel overwhelmed and or intimidated. Muller and Hollely (2000) use various authorities to show that cross-examination can negatively affect children. For instance, they refer to Key (1988) who described the experience of a 12-year-old boy who had been sodomised by his father that was subjected to what was described as 'persistent and detailed cross examination' about the abuse he underwent in the hands of his father. He was emotionally broken by the cross-examination and could not understand why the defence counsel could not believe him (Muller & Hollely, 2000). They argue that cross-examination does not produce accurate information from child witnesses because of the techniques that are adopted and the language used are not appropriate for children (Muller & Hollely, 2000). They further identify a number of techniques associated with cross-examination that are not appropriate or at least undermine the child witness's ability to comprehend the proceedings and respond to them appropriately. These include the use of leading questions, hypothetical questions, inappropriate vocabulary, complex syntax, general ambiguity, and a focus on peripheral detail (Muller & Hollely, 2000). These challenges can be an impediment to full participation of the child witness resulting in an outcome that limits or obstructs the course of justice. Despite these challenges, a failure by the accused person to challenge the witness's evidence in chief can have very serious repercussions for his or her case. This was observed in the Derrick Kunaka (2017) case, which referred to the case of *Joseph Mulenga, Albert Joseph Phiri v The People*, where the Supreme Court of Zambia stated:

> We stated that during trial parties have the opportunity to challenge evidence by cross-examining witnesses. Cross-examination must be done on every material particular of the case. When prosecution witnesses are narrating actual occurrences, the accused persons must challenge those facts which are disputed. Leaving assertions which are incriminating to go unchallenged, diminishes the efficacy of any ground of appeal based on those very assertions which were not challenged during trial. In this case, the evidence of gunshots, recovery of ammunition and spent cartridges was not challenged.

It is this position that 'justifies' and sometimes prompts detailed, excessive cross-examination that is counterproductive when applied to children. In view of these conflicting interests there is need for the law to protect children who are victims of crime so that the procedural techniques applied do not result in their being denied justice whilst ensuring that an accused person receives a fair trial – this is at the heart of advocacy for access to justice.

It is clear from the preceding discussion that child witnesses are not like adult witnesses; they are vulnerable and immature. They require an approach that enhances communication rather than one that is an obstruction to communication. Recognising the nature of children will assist in arriving at the best techniques to enhance their ability to freely testify in court. However, arriving at a balance that promotes effective cross-examination that takes into account the special qualities of children is not easy. Stone (2009) describes child witnesses and the challenges in cross-examining them in the following words:

> The first difficulty for advocates and the court is that child witnesses are so often inarticulate and tongue tied, especially in the sensitive areas of their testimony, that it is difficult to extract any coherent evidence from them at all. Despite all the steps taken by the court and advocates to put children at their ease and the presence of a parent, frequently they are subdued and inaudible and they may not even answer some questions at all . . . the defence have to conduct a cross examination in these difficult conditions and usually in an atmosphere which is unsympathetic to any possibility of harassing or upsetting the child and perhaps hostility to the defendant.

Section 78 (4) and (5) of the CC Act 2022 attempts to reduce the aggressiveness associated with cross-examination by limiting the right of counsel to ask a particular question to two attempts. Also allowing children to speak through and be spoken to through an intermediary.

LIMITING EXPOSURE TO ACCUSED PERSON

Section 78 (4) (d) of the CC Act 2022 prohibits children from being physically exposed to the accused person. However, the legal system requires that the victim identifies the alleged perpetrator of the crime and also entitles the accused to challenge the evidence of the child victim through cross-examination. The CC Act, sec 78 (5) (b) 2022 assumes identification and testimony could be given through the use of a video link. However, the vast majority of Zambian courtrooms do not have these facilities, thus a child witness will invariably be required to physically confirm the identity of the accused person and be present to testify in matters concerning them.

Conclusion and recommendations

The enactment of the Children's Code Act has laid a necessary foundation for securing access to justice for child witnesses, including child victims and children in conflict with the law. However, unless practical steps are taken to make the provisions discussed in this chapter effective, access to justice for children will remain a pipeline dream. The following recommendations are made:

Firstly, there is need to adapt court infrastructure and procedure to the needs of children to create an environmental that is friendly rather than intimidating to facilitate the effective. Court infrastructure must make it possible for children to testify remotely to avoid re-traumatisation of child victims.

Secondly, the government through its relevant ministries should ensure mandatory training for legal and judicial officers that handle children's cases to facilitate appropriate handling of child witnesses.

Lastly, government must embark on programmes that increase the number of courthouses per district and availability legal aid services to ensure access to justice for all.

References

Alberta Civil Liberties Research Centre (ACLRC). (n.d.). *What is access to justice?* Retrieved August 17, 2024, from https://www.aclrc.com/what-is-access-to-justice

Beqiraj, J., & McNamara, L. (2016). *Children and access to justice: National practices, international challenges* (Bingham Centre for the Rule of Law Report 02/2016). International Bar Association.

Chanda, A. W. (2011). *Human rights law in Zambia cases and materials* (p. 248). UNZA Press.

Council of Europe. (2011). *Guidelines for the committee of ministers of the council of Europe on child friendly justice and explanatory memorandum.* Council of Europe.

Kaaba, O. B. (2015). *The challenges of accessing justice in Zambia.* https://www.researchgate.net/publication/328830127_The_Challenges_of_Accessing_Justice_in_Zambia

Kerigan, F., Matakala, L., Mwenya, W., Dinda, C., & Moller, M. (2012). *Situation analysis – access to justice in Zambia.* The Danish Institute of Human Rights.

Key, J. J. A. (1988). *The child witness and the battle for justice.* De Rebus.

LAZ. (2022). *Framework for the provision of pro bono legal services.* Retrieved August 29, 2024, from https://www.moj.gov.zm/wp-content/uploads/2022/12/framework-for-the-provision-of-pro-bono-legal-services-1.pdf

Muller, K., & Hollely, K. (2000). *Introducing the child witness*. Print-Rite.
Ngulube, A. (n.d.). *The role of the judiciary in safeguarding and ensuring access to criminal justice: The case of Zambia*. Retrieved July 31, 2024, from https://www.southernafricalitigationcentre.org/wp-content/uploads/2017/08/GOAL-16-Book-Ngulube.pdf
OECD. (2019). *Equal access to justice for inclusive growth: Putting people at the centre*. OECD Publishing. https://doi.org/10.1787/597f5b7f-en
Sheahan, F. (2021). *Child friendly courthouses in Turkey guidance on international and regional law standards and implementation*. Retrieved August 6, 2024, from https://www.unicef.org/turkiye/media/12836/file/CHILD-FRIENDLY%20COURTHOUSES%20IN%20TURKEY.pdf
Stone, M. (2009). *Cross examination in criminal trials* (3rd ed.). Tottel Publishing.
World Bank. (n.d.). *Zambia*. Retrieved April 9, 2024, from https://www.worldbank.org/en/country/zambia/overview#:~:text=Zambia%20ranks%20among%20the%20countries,creation%20and%20declining%20labor%20earnings
The Zambian Judiciary. (n.d.). *The subordinate court*. Retrieved July 16, 2024, from https://judiciaryzambia.com/subordinate-courts/

Judicial precedents

Benard Chisha v The People (1980) Z.R. 36 (S.C.) SCZ Judgement No. 4 of 1980.
Derrick Kunaka v The People Supreme Court of Zambia Appeal No. 95 of 2017.
Thomas Mumba v The People [1984] ZMHC 4.

2 Linguistic barriers to access to justice by child victims and witnesses of sexual assault in Malawi's justice system

Shyreen Odala Chirwa

Introduction

The justice system in Malawi operates within a complex framework shaped by historical, social, and linguistic factors (Zeze, 2015). As a former British colony, Malawi inherited English as the official language of governance and legal proceedings. While this choice aims to maintain a uniform legal standard, it inadvertently creates significant barriers for a substantial portion of the Malawian population, particularly children who are victims and witnesses of sexual assault (Schärf et al., 2015). The children find themselves navigating a system that operates in a language they do not fully understand, thereby having profound implications for their ability to participate in legal processes and receive justice (Makanje, 2020).

Although Malawi's legal framework includes provisions aimed at protecting the rights of child victims and witnesses, the execution of these measures is marred by inadequate resources, lack of specialised training for judicial personnel, and the daunting reality of English as the court's language (Makanje, 2020; Bande, 2020). Consequently, the emotional and psychological trauma of recounting their experiences is exacerbated by linguistic barriers, leading to misinterpretations and incomplete testimonies (Snow et al., 2012).

This chapter, therefore, critically examines how the use of English in the Malawi justice system impacts the experiences of child victims and witnesses, highlighting the need for more accessible language practices within legal contexts. The relevance of this study extends beyond academic inquiry; it speaks to the urgent need for reform in Malawi's legal practices to better protect the most vulnerable members of society. By understanding the implications of the English language use in Malawi's justice system, the study advocates for policies that prioritise child-friendly practices, ensuring that the voices of the child victims and witnesses of sexual assault are not only heard, but are understood and given the necessary weight.

The Malawi linguistic landscape

Malawi is a culturally diverse country with multiple ethnic groups and languages (Zeze, 2015). The primary languages spoken include Chichewa,

DOI: 10.4324/9781003569435-4

Chitumbuka, Chiyao, and Chilomwe, among others. While Chichewa is the most dominant and national language, not all Malawians are proficient in it, especially those from rural areas where other languages dominate. Additionally, cultural norms and practices of different ethnic groups vary significantly, influencing communication styles and perceptions in different contexts (Zeze, 2015). For Malawi, these cultural and linguistic varieties present challenges in the justice system, which are exacerbated by the designation of English as the official language of the court (Schärf et al., 2015). For many Malawians, particularly children, English is, unfortunately, not their first language, resulting in difficulties to understand it and participate in court processes (Schärf et al., 2015).

Structural overview of the Malawi justice system

The Malawi justice system is a product of its colonial past under British rule, which established a framework modelled after the English common law system (Bande, 2020). After Malawi gained independence in 1964, the British court structure was retained, and it has since evolved into a hierarchical three-tiered court system (Bande, 2020). All courts in Malawi are established, composed, and mandated by the Constitution of the Republic of Malawi, 1994 (hereinafter 'the Constitution'). At the top of the judicial hierarchy is the Supreme Court of Appeal, the highest court of record in the country. This court has appellate jurisdiction over decisions from the High Court and other courts and tribunals as prescribed by law. Coming second, is the High Court of Malawi, which has unlimited original jurisdiction to hear and determine any civil and criminal cases under any law. At the base of the judicial system are the subordinate courts, which include the Industrial Relations Court (IRC) and the Magistrate Courts. The IRC has original jurisdiction over labour disputes and other employment-related issues, whilst the Magistrate Courts have limited jurisdiction over both civil and criminal matters as defined by law (the Constitution 1994).

In Malawi, Magistrate Courts are foundational to the country's judicial system (Schärf et al., 2015). Among the many cases that they handle, sexual assault cases involving children such as having sexual intercourse with a child and indecent assault, are particularly prominent (Penal Code of Malawi). The Magistrate Courts are often the first point of contact for such cases, making them crucial in the initial stages of the judicial process (Chanda, 2001). The predominance of sexual assault cases involving children in Magistrate Courts is attributed to the fact that these courts are more accessible to the general population compared to higher courts (Schärf et al., 2015). They are strategically located in various districts, making it easier for victims and their families to have their cases heard and seek justice without travelling long distances. Despite their importance, Magistrate Courts in Malawi face numerous challenges that impact their effectiveness, including limited resources and capacity, and lack of specialised training and support for magistrates and court staff in handling cases involving child victims and witnesses (Makanje, 2020).

Legislative frameworks for child victims and witnesses of sexual assault

According to the United Nations Economic and Social Council Resolution 2005/20: Guidelines on Justice in Matters involving Child Victims and Witnesses of Crime 2005, (hereinafter Guidelines on Justice in Matters Involving Child Victims and Witnesses of Crime, 2005), child victims and witnesses denote individuals under the age of 18 who have either experienced a crime or have witnessed one, regardless of their involvement in the crime or the legal proceedings against the accused person. In Malawi's justice system, child victims and witnesses are among the most vulnerable participants (Malunga et al., 2017). Their unique needs and susceptibilities necessitate a specialised legislative framework to ensure their protection and to facilitate their effective participation in legal processes (Malunga et al., 2017).

Nationally, the Constitution of Malawi, by virtue of its supremacy, provides a foundational framework for the protection of child victims and witnesses. Under Section 23, the Constitution guarantees the rights of children, including the right to protection from exploitation or any treatment that is, or is likely, to be detrimental to their health or physical, mental, spiritual or social development. This broad constitutional provision sets the stage for more specific legislative measures targeting child victims and witnesses.

Supplementary to the constitutional provisions is the Child Care, Protection and Justice Act (CCPJA), which serves as the most significant legislation for child protection in Malawi. Despite being the specific law on children's matters, when it comes to court proceedings, the CCPJA only focuses on children in conflict with the law, leaving out provisions on children as victims or witnesses (Makanje, 2020). The CCPJA is, however, commended for providing comprehensive guidelines for the care and protection of children broadly. It further mandates the establishment of child-friendly courts and procedures that minimise the trauma of legal processes on children. The Act also outlines the responsibilities of various stakeholders, including parents, guardians, social workers, and the judiciary in safeguarding the interests of children.

Additionally, the Malawi Criminal Procedure and Evidence Code Act 36 of 1967 (CP&EC) includes provisions aimed at protecting and supporting the well-being of victims of sexual offenses during court proceedings. The CP&EC provides for measures, such as closing the court to the public while the victim is giving evidence to reduce anxiety and fear, using screens or partitions to prevent the victim from seeing the accused to minimise trauma, and allowing a relative or friend to accompany the victim for emotional support, thereby enhancing the victim's ability to provide a coherent and complete testimony.

These legal provisions for child victims and witnesses in Malawi are significant in establishing a robust protective framework. The provisions are further in alignment with international and regional frameworks, such as the United Nations Economic and Social Council Resolution 2005/20: Guidelines on

Justice in Matters involving Child Victims and Witnesses of Crime 2005, the United Nations Standard Minimum Rules for the Administration of Juvenile Justice 1985, the African Commission on Human and Peoples' Rights' Principles and Guidelines on the Right to a Fair Trial and Legal Assistance in Africa 2003, and the United Nations Guidelines for Action on Children in the Criminal Justice System 1997. Collectively, these frameworks not only guarantee that the rights and welfare of child victims and witnesses are safeguarded but also facilitate children's effective participation in the justice system.

The use of English in the Malawi justice system and its implication on child victims and witnesses of sexual assault

In the Malawi justice system, English is used as a mode of communication in court proceedings and records (Kishindo, 2001). This practice has deep historical roots, tracing back to the colonial era when Malawi was under the British rule (Kamwangamalu & Moyo, 2003). During that period, English was designated as the official language of administration, governance, and the legal system. The colonial authorities introduced English to standardise communication and facilitate the implementation of British legal principles and administrative processes, thereby entrenching English in the legal framework of the country (Service of Process and Execution of Judgments Act 1957).

Today, English remains the language of legal documentation, court records, and formal proceedings in Malawi, adopted by professionals in the justice system as the formal legal language (Kishindo, 2001). Despite being a convenient language, the use of English in the Malawi justice system poses significant challenges mainly because the majority of the Malawi's population are not proficient in English (Kishindo, 2001). The use of English, therefore, impedes their ability to fully understand legal and court proceedings, effectively communicate, and actively participate in proceedings during one's own defence or prosecution (Schärf et al., 2015).

For child victims and witnesses, who are still developing their cognitive and language skills, navigating the justice system in English is particularly challenging (Snow et al., 2012). The complexities of the English language hinder the child victims and witnesses' ability to participate meaningfully in court proceedings and communicate effectively (Wilson & Powell, 2001). To remedy the language challenges, interpreters are deployed to interpret the court proceedings (Schärf et al., 2015). Despite this intervention, however, challenges emanating from the use of English in the justice system still persist to a great disadvantage of child victims and witnesses. This is further discussed later in the chapter.

Comprehension, participation, and articulation of experiences

The use of English presents a profound challenge in the justice system for child victims and witnesses in sexual assault cases (Westcott & Page, 2002).

Owing to their developmental stage, their vocabulary and understanding of complex judicial processes is limited, resulting in difficulties in expressing themselves clearly (Gal, 2011). This is pronounced, for instance, during cross-examination, where the child victims and witnesses are particularly vulnerable to the insincere and controlling questioning techniques applied by lawyers in courtrooms (Kondowe, 2023). The nature of questions imposed by defence lawyers intimidate and confuse child witnesses, leading to incomplete or inaccurate testimonies. Given that many child victims and witnesses in Malawi may not have advanced language skills or only speak local dialects, the linguistic complexity and insincerity of lawyer's questions pose significant comprehension challenges (Kondowe, 2023).

For child victims and witnesses of sexual assault, the ability to communicate effectively is paramount in ensuring that their experiences are accurately conveyed and understood by the court and other legal authorities (Plotnikoff & Woolfson, 2015). According to the Guidelines on Justice in Matters Involving Child Victims and Witnesses of Crime 2005, child victims and witnesses have the right to be heard and to express views or opinions. This right is infringed upon if they fail to express themselves owing to language-related constraints. Child victims and witnesses who lack proficiency in English face considerable difficulties in expressing their experiences and communicating their thoughts effectively. As a result, their testimonies may be incomplete or inaccurate, as they often struggle to find the appropriate words or fully comprehend the questions posed during the proceedings (Gal, 2011).

The trauma associated with sexual assault further complicates this as child victims and witnesses already find it challenging to recount their experiences even in their native language (Robinson, 2015). For example, in the case of the *State v Benjamin Kayembe*, Criminal Case No. 1456 of 2018, the child victim fainted in court during cross-examination by the defence lawyer, overwhelmed by the trauma of having to recount her ordeal once more after the defence successfully applied for her to be recalled to testify. Therefore, the added layer of a foreign or less familiar language exacerbates this difficulty, leading to omissions or incomplete testimonies (Klemfuss & Ceci, 2012).

It is, therefore, essential to ensure that children have the necessary language support, such as interpreters or language services at the cost of the court, to help them fully express themselves and ensure their voices are heard accurately in legal proceedings (Krähenbühl, 2011). It is also incumbent upon all professionals involved in court proceedings to devise and implement measures that would make it easier for child victims and witnesses to give evidence in a way that improves their comprehension and communication (Krähenbühl, 2011).

Misinterpretation of crucial details in court proceedings

The language barrier in court proceedings leads to the misinterpretation of crucial details, particularly, when child victims and witnesses are involved (Berk-Seligson, 2017). Legal professionals, including judges, lawyers, and court interpreters may at times misinterpret child victims and witnesses' statements, miss essential details or else misunderstand the context and nuance of their testimony (Saywitz et al., 2002).

The complexities of legal language pose a challenge even for adults, and it gets heightened when child victims and witnesses are involved (Saywitz et al., 2002). Often, child victims and witnesses do not possess the necessary vocabulary or comprehension to express their experiences clearly (Lamb et al., 2011). Their testimonies may be fragmented, filled with ambiguities, and influenced by their limited understanding of the world (Lamb et al., 2011). For example, in the Malawian case *Republic v Limbikani Cosmas Mpokosa*, Criminal Review No. 30 of 2022, a four-year-old victim used the phrase 'gave me a wound' to refer to the penetration of her vagina by the accused person who was her neighbour, when giving evidence in court. The court corroborated her evidence with the testimony of her father and a medical doctor who examined her genitalia, to prove penetration and found the accused person guilty of the offence of defilement.

As noted from the preceding case, children might describe an incident using simplistic language or omit details they perceive as unimportant, which could be crucial for understanding the full context of their experience (Eisen et al., 2021). They may even convey important information in a manner that seems trivial or irrelevant to an adult, resulting in potential misinterpretation (Lamb et al., 2011).

The implications of misinterpreting are profound. In criminal cases, where the stakes are incredibly high, the inability to accurately interpret child victims and witnesses' words undermines the credibility of their testimony (Robinson, 2015). It may potentially result in a decision that is not in their favour, such as the wrongful acquittal of perpetrators (Robinson, 2015). If a child victim or witness' statement is not accurately communicated or understood, crucial evidence could be overlooked by the court, resulting in a failure of justice (Burrows & Powell, 2014).

In circumstances like these, the deployment of court interpreters becomes crucial as they serve as a vital link between child victims and witnesses and the justice system (Berk-Seligson, 2017). Through court interpreters, child witnesses and victims are guaranteed that their voices will be heard. For interpreters to be effective, they must possess not only linguistic expertise but also an understanding of the cultural and psychological context of child victims and witnesses, as this significantly influences their testimony (Powell et al., 2017). The interpreters must be skilled in conveying child victims and witnesses' emotions, intentions, and the nuances of their speech, given that inadequate interpretation potentially distorts the child victim and witness' testimony, leading to severe consequences on court proceedings (Berk-Seligson, 2017).

Emotional distress

For child victims and witnesses of sexual assault, recounting their traumatic experiences is inherently stressful and painful (Quas & Goodman, 2012). When they are unable to express themselves in a familiar language, this distress becomes amplified (Troxel et al., 2009). The frustration and anxiety that arise from linguistic barriers create an additional layer of emotional strain, making it even more challenging for them to communicate effectively in legal proceedings (Cavett, 2015).

The child victims and witness' compounded stress manifests itself in various ways, including increased feelings of helplessness, isolation, and fear. They often struggle to convey their thoughts and emotions accurately, thereby impacting their ability to give evidence and have their voices heard (Caprioli & Crenshaw, 2017). Furthermore, their inability to articulate their experiences in a familiar language leads to a sense of disconnection from the courtroom environment and the people around them (Barry et al., 2006). It diminishes their confidence and self-esteem as they may feel inadequate or incapable of expressing themselves (Quas et al., 2005).

The traumatic nature of sexual assault results in inconsistencies in a child's testimony, not due to intentional insincerity, but because of the psychological impact, which might be perceived as a lack of credibility (Kondowe et al., 2022). When the child victim and witness experiences such a profound and distressing event, their ability to recall and recount details accurately is severely affected. This is often due to the intense emotional and psychological turmoil they endure, which disrupts memory formation and retrieval (Kensinger & Ford, 2020). Consequently, the child victims and witnesses provide fragmented or varying accounts of the incident over time, remembering certain aspects vividly while other details remain obscured or distorted (Kensinger, 2009). These inconsistencies, when misunderstood by other parties in court, lead to doubts about the child victims and witnesses' honesty and reliability (Pichler et al., 2021). It is, therefore, crucial to approach such testimonies with sensitivity and an understanding of the psychological effects of trauma to avoid unjustly discrediting the child's account (Kondowe, 2022).

According to the Guidelines on Justice in Matters involving Child Victims and Witnesses of Crime 2005, child victims and witnesses are especially vulnerable and require tailored protection, assistance, and support suited to their age, maturity, and specific needs. This is crucial in preventing additional hardship and trauma that arise from their involvement in the criminal justice process (Cossins, 2006). It is, therefore, important to provide these child victims and witnesses with a safe and supportive environment, where they can express themselves freely to mitigate the negative impact of language barriers and support their emotional recovery (Barry et al., 2006).

Court interpreters' inadequacies

Court interpreters play a crucial role in ensuring that a child's testimony is accurately translated and understood (Berk-Seligson, 2017). However, in dealing with child victims and witnesses of sexual assault, many interpreters face significant obstacles, including insufficient training on the unique needs of child witnesses, overwhelming caseloads, and a lack of specialised knowledge about child psychology and trauma (Tribe, 2005). These create a dangerous gap between the child victim and witness' experiences and how they are communicated to the court (Tribe, 2005).

The child victims and witnesses of sexual assault face emotional and psychological challenges that make it difficult for them to articulate their experiences clearly (Snow et al., 2012). For interpreters who are untrained in child-specific trauma, capturing the emotional and linguistic nuances of such children's testimony becomes particularly difficult (Sibirsky & Taylor, 2017). As a result, interpreters unintentionally distort or oversimplify the testimony, leading to miscommunication or misrepresentation of key details. In some cases, important elements of the children's account are lost or altered, which severely affect the outcome of the trial (Eads, 2007).

Moreover, court interpreters are often burdened with heavy caseloads, which exacerbates the problem (Mason, 2008). The need to handle multiple cases within tight timelines pressures interpreters to abbreviate or condense testimonies in an effort to expedite court proceedings (Svongoro & Kadenge, 2015). While this might be seen as a way to manage workload and court efficiency, it risks compromising the depth and accuracy of a child's testimony (Matthias & Zaal, 2002).

The compression also weakens the court's capacity to make informed decisions based on comprehensive evidence, since the child victims and witnesses' testimony is distorted or rushed through due to interpreter inefficiencies (Marsil et al., 2002). It is therefore imperative that court interpreters receive specialised training on how to interact with and interpret for child victims and witnesses (Powell et al., 2017). Additionally, providing interpreters with the necessary resources to handle these cases with care and attention is crucial in ensuring that child victims and witnesses receive the justice they deserve (Quas & Goodman, 2012).

Factors exacerbating the linguistic barriers for child victims and witnesses of sexual assault in Malawi

The linguistic barriers faced by child victims and witnesses of sexual assault in Malawi are deeply intertwined with sociocultural and systemic factors. These barriers impede the justice process and the provision of adequate support services to child victims and witnesses of sexual assault as discussed later.

Cultural stigmas and taboos

The cultural stigmas surrounding sexual assault in Malawian communities create an environment where discussing sexual matters is taboo because sexual matters are considered private and shameful (Sage, 2016). Such cultural norms significantly impair child victims and witnesses' ability to provide complete and accurate testimony in court (Sepúlveda & Donald, 2015). Their participation in court proceedings is marred by the fear of the negative social repercussions of their testimony, such as being ostracised, blamed, or disbelieved (Caprioli & Crenshaw, 2017). This fear and silence are especially detrimental in the criminal justice system, where the credibility and completeness of a victim's testimony are vital (Bottoms et al., 2009).

This intersection of cultural stigmas that are deeply embedded in the Malawi cultural and societal fabric and linguistic barriers create a compounded effect that severely impedes children's access to justice (Grandjean, 2010). As discussed earlier, the cultural taboo against discussing sexual matters instils fear and shame in victims, discouraging them from speaking out (Ullman, 2002). Sadly, when these child victims and witnesses do muster the courage to come forward, linguistic barriers further complicate their ability to communicate effectively in court (Snow et al., 2012). Child victims and witnesses struggle to provide detailed accounts, either providing too little information due to fear or too much irrelevant information due to lack of understanding of what is pertinent (Kondowe et al., 2022). This potentially results in incomplete or inaccurate testimonies, which may lead to unjust outcomes, such as the dismissal of cases or the acquittal of perpetrators (Burrows & Powell, 2014).

In the Guidelines on Justice in Matters Involving Child Victims and Witnesses of Crime 2005, the United Nation's Economic and Social Council takes cognisance of the cultural and other factors that affect child victims and witnesses. The Council urges countries to implement the Guidelines in accordance with their national legislation and judicial procedures, while also considering their legal, social, economic, cultural, and geographical conditions. In the present context, the United Nation's Economic and Social Council's resolution underscores the significance of cultural sensitivity in the justice system when handling sexual assault cases involving child victims and witnesses. It further acknowledges and considers the interconnected circumstances of child victims and witnesses which influence the extent, quality and depth of their testimony in court (Guidelines on Justice in Matters Involving Child Victims and Witnesses of Crime 2005).

Insufficient personnel capacity within the justice system

Malawi's justice system falls short of specialised personnel to address the specific needs of child victims and witnesses during court proceedings (Mulambia et al., 2018). Owing to their vulnerability, child victims and witnesses require special consideration and a child-friendly approach in legal proceedings (Liefaard, 2016). Knowledge on children's cognitive, emotional, and social development is crucial as it has a bearing on how they perceive, process, and communicate information (Alzahrani et al., 2019). Judicial officers and legal professionals, for example, need to be aware of these developmental differences to interact effectively with child witnesses and victims (Thumma & Braddock, 2019).

Specialised training enables judicial and legal professionals to create a supportive environment that encourages effective participation from children

(Powell et al., 2017). The participation of child victims and witnesses in the criminal justice process is essential for effective prosecutions, especially when the child victim may be the sole witness (Guidelines on Justice in Matters Involving Child Victims and Witnesses of Crime, 2005). Judicial officers, for instance, must understand the unique memory characteristics and suggestibility of child victims and witnesses, which heighten their vulnerability, to improve their participation in court and ensure a child-friendly justice system.

Child-friendly justice strives to create justice systems that prioritise children's rights, considers their best interests, and encourages their active participation in both formal and informal decision-making processes that affect them (Liefaard, 2016). International and regional frameworks, such as the UNCRC and the ACRWC which have been duly domesticated in Malawi outline the rights and protections afforded to children. These frameworks emphasise the best interests of the child, and also guarantee their rights to protection and participation. Professionals in the justice system must be well-versed in these frameworks to effectively advocate for children's rights and further act when children's rights are at risk of being compromised (Eastwood & Patton, 2002).

In the absence of specialised training, there is a danger that judicial officers and legal professionals might overlook or misapply children's critical protections, leading to outcomes that do not serve the best interests of the child (Skelton, 2008). The United Nations' Economic and Social Council underscores the importance of specialised training by emphasising the necessity of guiding professionals who work with child victims and witnesses of crime. Such guidance is essential for the daily practice of judicial and legal professionals in the justice system and guarantees the child victims and witnesses a fair trial.

Procedural inefficiencies

Procedural inefficiencies within the Malawi justice system represent a significant challenge, affecting the efficacy, fairness, and perception of judicial processes (Chawinga et al., 2020). Lengthy court procedures, bureaucratic delays, and cumbersome legal formalities often result in extended case durations (Tyler, 2003). These inefficiencies are particularly detrimental in cases involving child victims and witnesses who, owing to their vulnerability, require prompt handling to safeguard their rights and well-being (Whittam & Ehrat, 2003).

The aforementioned lengthy court processes are often attributed to several factors, including overloaded court dockets, insufficient judicial resources, and complex legal requirements (Cossins, 2006). When cases drag on for months or even years, the child victims and witnesses are left in a state of uncertainty and distress, which is especially damaging to them. The prolonged exposure to legal proceedings exacerbates the trauma experienced by child victims, impeding their emotional recovery and overall development (Whittam & Ehrat, 2003).

Additionally, bureaucratic delays further compound the inefficiencies within Malawi's justice system that impact child victims and witnesses (Chawinga et al.,

2020). The complex process of paperwork, approvals, and procedural steps slow down the progression of cases. This bureaucratic sluggishness means that a lot of cases get stuck in unnecessary steps, causing delays (Cossins, 2006). For child victims and witnesses, these delays are particularly detrimental, as they have a bearing on the temporality of their testimony (Kondowe, 2022). In sexual assault cases, some evidence, such as the availability of sperms and evidence of physical struggle can be easily destroyed with the passage of time (Kondowe, 2022). The degradation of physical evidence and the fading of memories, affect the credibility of the children's evidence, especially when they fail to provide crucial details about the time and dates of occurrence of the alleged offence (Kondowe, 2022).

Malawi's cumbersome legal procedures are another significant barrier to the timely resolution of cases (Chawinga et al., 2020). The complexity of legal protocols and the requirement for meticulous adherence to procedural rules creates bottlenecks in the judicial process (Eastwood, 2003). Lawyers and judges are expected to navigate these complexities carefully to ensure that cases are handled correctly. However, this often results in slower case progression (Rhode, 2001). For child victims and witnesses, the convoluted legal procedures are confusing and intimidating, as they have to interact with documents, such as affidavits, medical reports, and witness statements and go through processes that are done in a language that they are not familiar with (Cyr, 2022). Simplifying legal procedures and streamlining court processes could significantly alleviate the stress experienced by these vulnerable child victims and witnesses, and facilitate swifter justice (Richter et al., 2004).

The detrimental impact of procedural inefficiencies is starkly evident in cases involving child victims and witnesses. Children, due to their age and developmental stage, are more susceptible to the negative effects of prolonged legal proceedings (Burman & Brooks-Hay, 2020). As children, the victims and witnesses of sexual assault require expedited handling to make sure that their rights and well-being are protected and prioritised. Delays in the judicial process result in prolonged exposure to stress and trauma, which have lasting psychological and social consequences (Whittam & Ehrat, 2003). The child victims and witnesses risk suffering from increased anxiety and depression. Additionally, the social stigma and disruption to their daily lives affect their academic performance and relationships with peers (Burman & Brooks-Hay, 2020).

The slow pace of justice also undermines public confidence in the judicial system in handling sexual assault cases (Bibas, 2006). Delays create a perception that the system is ineffective and incapable of delivering timely justice to the victims (Eastwood, 2003). This erosion of public trust has broader implications on child victims and witnesses, resulting in their reduced willingness to report sexual and other assaults that they may have been subjected to. It is, therefore, imperative to address the procedural inefficiencies that contribute to these delays and ensure that cases are handled with the urgency they deserve, considering that child victims and witnesses are involved (Burman & Brooks-Hay, 2020).

Conclusion

This chapter has illuminated the multifaceted barriers faced by child victims and witnesses of sexual assault in the Malawi justice system, emphasising the profound impact of linguistic challenges on their access to justice. The use of the English language in judicial proceedings, coupled with complex legal terminologies and procedures, creates significant obstacles for child victims and witnesses, undermining the accuracy and credibility of their testimonies. Cultural taboos surrounding discussions of sexual assault further silence these vulnerable victims and witnesses, compounding their reluctance to engage with the legal and judicial processes. Additionally, the procedural inefficiencies within the Malawi judicial system exacerbate these challenges, highlighting the urgent need for systemic reforms. Simplifying court procedures, enhancing cultural sensitivity, and implementing specialised training for judicial and legal professionals are critical steps towards creating a more inclusive and responsive justice system. By effectively addressing these barriers, Malawi's justice system can ensure that the voices of child victims and witnesses are heard, respected, and given the appropriate consideration in court and legal proceedings.

References

Alzahrani, M., Alharbi, M., & Alodwani, A. (2019). The effect of social-emotional competence on children academic achievement and behavioral development. *International Education Studies*, *12*(12), 141–149.

Bande, L. C. (2020). A history of Malawi's criminal justice system: From pre-colonial to democratic periods. *Fundamina: A Journal of Legal History*, *26*(2), 288–336.

Barry, L., Nixon, K., Tutty, L. M., Wyllie, K., & Mackenzie, J. (2006). A review of the Calgary child witness court preparation program: Issues and implications for child witnesses and the criminal justice system. *The Canadian Society for the Investigation of Child Abuse*, 1–127.

Berk-Seligson, S. (2017). *The bilingual courtroom: Court interpreters in the judicial process*. University of Chicago Press.

Bibas, S. (2006). Transparency and participation in criminal procedure. *New York University Law Review*, *81*(3), 911–966.

Bottoms, B. L., Najdowski, C. J., & Goodman, G. S. (Eds.). (2009). *Children as victims, witnesses and offenders: Psychological, science and the law*. The Guilford Press.

Burman, M., & Brooks-Hay, O. (2020). Delays in trials: The implication for victim-survivors of rape and serious sexual assault. *The Scottish Centre for Crime and Justice Research*, *7*(3), 1–7.

Burrows, K. S., & Powell, M. (2014). Prosecutors' recommendations for improving child witness statements about sexual abuse. *Policing and Society*, *24*(2), 189–207.

Caprioli, S., & Crenshaw, D. A. (2017). The culture of silencing child victims of sexual abuse: Implications for child witnesses in court. *Journal of Humanistic Psychology*, *57*(2), 190–209.

Cavett, A. M. (2015). Cognitive-behavioural play therapy. In D. A. Crenshaw & A. L. Stewart (Eds.), *Play therapy: A comprehensive guide to theory and* practice (pp. 83–98). Guilford.

Chanda, A. W. (2001). The role of lower courts in the domestic implementation of human rights. *Zambia Law Journal*, *33*, 1–17.

Chawinga, W. D., Chawinga, C., Kapondera, S. K., Chipeta, G. T., Majawa, F., & Nyasulu, C. (2020). Towards e-judicial services in Malawi: Implications for justice delivery. *The Electronic Journal of Information Systems in Developing Countries, 86*(2), e12121.

Cossins, A. (2006). Prosecuting child sexual assault cases: Are vulnerable witness protections enough? *Current Issues in Criminal Justice, 18*(2), 299–317. Routledge.

Cyr, M. (2022). *Conducting interviews with child victims of abuse and witnesses of crime: A practical guide*. Routledge.

Eads, D. (2007). Telling and retelling your story in court: Questions, assumptions, and intercultural implications. *Current Issues in Criminal Justice, 20*(2), 209–230.

Eastwood, C. (2003). The experiences of child complainants of sexual abuse in the criminal justice system. Trends and issues in crime and criminal justice. *Australian Institute of Criminology, 250*, 1–6.

Eastwood, C., & Patton, W. (2002). *The experiences of child complainants of sexual abuse in the criminal justice system*. Criminology Research Council.

Eisen, M. L., Goodman, G. S., Diep, J., Lacsamana, M., Ristrom, L. J., & Qin, J. J. (2021). Disclosures of sexual and physical abuse across repeated interviews. *Journal of Child Sexual Abuse, 30*(8), 932–952.

Gal, T. (2011). *Child victims and restorative justice: A needs-rights model*. Oxford University Press.

Grandjean, A. (2010). No rights without accountability: Promoting access to justice for children. In S. Golub & T. McInerney (Eds.), *Legal empowerment: Practitioners' perspectives* (pp. 265–283). International Development Law Organization.

Kamwangamalu, N., & Moyo, T. (2003). Some characteristic features of Englishes in Lesotho, Malawi and Swaziland. *Journal for Language Learning, 19*(1–2), 39–54.

Kensinger, E. A. (2009). Remembering the details: Effects of emotion. *Emotion Review, 1*(2), 99–113.

Kensinger, E. A., & Ford, J. H. (2020). Retrieval of emotional events from memory. *Annual Review of Psychology, 71*(1), 251–272.

Kishindo, P. (2001). Language and the law in Malawi: A case for the use of indigenous languages in the legal system. *Language Matters, 32*(1), 1–27.

Klemfuss, J. Z., & Ceci, S. J. (2012). Legal and psychological perspectives on children's competence to testify in court. *Developmental Review, 32*(3), 268–286.

Kondowe, W. (2022). Towards the principle of believability: A new socio-pragmatic model in forensic settings. In M. K. Ralarala, R. H. Kaschula, & G. Heydon (Eds.), *Language and the law* (pp. 261–278). African Sun Media.

Kondowe, W. (2023). Insincerity in lawyers' questioning strategies in Malawian criminal courtroom discourse. *Text & Talk, 44*(6), 763–786. https://doi.org/10.1515/text-2022-0083

Kondowe, W., Liao, M., & Ngwira, F. F. (2022). A study of intentional insincerity in Malawian criminal justice: Witnesses discursive strategies. In M. K. Ralarala, R. H. Kaschula, & G. Heydon (Eds.), *Language and the law: Global perspectives in Forensic Linguistics from Africa and beyond* (pp. 241–260). African Sun Media.

Krähenbühl, S. (2011). Effective and appropriate communication with children in legal proceedings according to lawyers and intermediaries. *Child Abuse Review, 20*(6), 407–420.

Lamb, M. E., Hershkowitz, I., Orbach, Y., & Esplin, P. W. (2011). *Tell me what happened: Structured investigative interviews of child victims and witnesses* (Vol. 56). John Wiley & Sons.

Liefaard, T. (2016). Child-friendly justice: Protection and participation of children in the justice system. *Temple Law Review, 88*(4), 905–928.

Makanje, G. D. (2020). The protection of vulnerable witnesses during criminal trials in Malawi: Addressing resource challenges. *African Human Rights Law Journal, 20*(1), 206–232.

Malunga, B., Kanyongolo, N. R., & Mbano-Mweso, N. (2017). Access to justice of children with disabilities in defilement cases in Malawi. *African Disability Rights Yearbook, 5*, 25–39.

Marsil, D. F., Montoya, J., Ross, D., & Graham, L. (2002). Child witness policy: Law interfacing with social science. *Law and Contemporary Problems*, *65*(1), 209–242.
Mason, M. (2008). *Courtroom interpreting*. University Press of America.
Matthias, C., & Zaal, N. (2002). Hearing only a faint echo? Interpreters and children in court. *South African Journal on Human Rights*, *18*(3), 350–371.
Mulambia, Y., Miller, A. J., MacDonald, G., & Kennedy, N. (2018). Are one-stop centres an appropriate model to deliver services to sexually abused children in urban Malawi? *BMC Pediatrics*, *18*, 1–7.
Pichler, A. S., Powell, M., Sharman, S. J., Zydervelt, S., Westera, N., & Goodman-Delahunty, J. (2021). Inconsistencies in complainant's accounts of child sexual abuse arising in their cross-examination. *Psychology, Crime & Law*, *27*(4), 341–356.
Plotnikoff, J., & Woolfson, R. (2015). *Intermediaries in the criminal justice system: Improving communication for vulnerable witnesses and defendants*. Policy Press, University of Bristol.
Powell, M. B., Manger, B., Dion, J., & Sharman, S. J. (2017). Professionals' perspectives about the challenges of using interpreters in child sexual abuse interviews. *Psychiatry, Psychology and Law*, *24*(1), 90–101.
Quas, J. A., & Goodman, G. S. (2012). Consequences of criminal court involvement for child victims. *Psychology, Public Policy and Law*, *18*(3), 392–414.
Quas, J. A., Goodman, G. S., Ghetti, S., Alexander, K. W., Edelstein, R., Redlich, A. D., & Haugaard, J. J. (2005). Childhood sexual assault victims: Long-term outcomes after testifying in criminal court. *Monographs of the Society for Research in Child Development*, *70*(2), 1–139.
Rhode, D. L. (2001). Access to justice. *Fordham Law Review*, *69*(5), 1785–1820.
Richter, L. M., Dawes, A., & Higson-Smith, C. (Eds.). (2004). *Sexual abuse of young children in Southern Africa*. Human Sciences Research Council Press.
Robinson, J. (2015). The experience of the child witness: Legal and psychological issues. *International Journal of Law and Psychiatry*, *42*, 168–176.
Sage, E. O. M. (2016). *Sexual violence against children in Malawi: Understanding protective factors and gender norms aimed at reducing victimization* [Doctoral thesis, The University of Georgia].
Saywitz, K. J., Goodman, G. S., & Lyon, T. D. (2002). Interviewing children in and out of court: Current research and practice implications. In J. Myers, L. Berliner, J. Briere, C. J. Hendrix, & T. Reid (Eds.), *The American psychological association handbook on child maltreatment* (2nd ed., pp. 349–377). Sage.
Schärf, W., Banda, C., Röntsch, R., Kaunda, D., & Shapiro, R. (2015). *Access to justice for the poor of Malawi? An appraisal of access to justice provided to the poor of Malawi by the lower subordinate courts and the customary justice forums*. Retrieved June 27, 2024, from https://dullahomarinstitute.org.za/acjr/resource-centre/access-to-justice-for-the-poor-of-malawi-an-appraisal-of-the-access-to-justice-provided-to-the-poor-of-malawi-by-the-lower-subordinate-courts-and-the-customary-justice-forums
Sepúlveda, C. M., & Donald, K. (2015). Beyond legal empowerment: Improving access to justice from the human rights perspective. *The International Journal of Human Rights*, *19*(3), 242–259.
Sibirsky, S., & Taylor, M. C. (2017). *Language into language: Cultural, legal and linguistic issues for interpreters and translators*. McFarland & Company, Inc.
Skelton, A. (2008). *Justice for child victims and witnesses of crimes*. Centre for Child Law, Pretoria University Law Press.
Snow, P. C., Powell, M. B., & Sanger, D. D. (2012). Oral language competence, young speakers and the law. *Language, Speech, and Hearing Services in Schools*, *43*, 496–506.
Svongoro, P., & Kadenge, M. (2015). From language to society: An analysis of interpreting quality and the linguistic rights of the accused in selected Zimbabwean courtroom. *Southern African Linguistics and Applied Language Studies*, *33*(1), 47–62.

Thumma, S. A., & Braddock, C. (2019). Ten tips for how judges can more effectively communicate with children in court. *Judges' Journal, 58*(1), 12–17.
Tribe, R. (2005). Working with interpreters. In K. Barret & W. George (Eds.), *Race, culture, psychology and law* (pp. 163–176). Sage Publication.
Troxel, N. R., Ogle, C. M., Cordon, I. M., Lawler, M. J., & Goodman, G. S. (2009). Child witnesses in criminal court. In B. L. Bottoms, C. J. Najdowski & G. S. Goodman (Eds.), *Children as victims, witnesses, and offenders: Psychological science and the law* (pp. 150–166). Guilford Press.
Tyler, T. R. (2003). Procedural justice, legitimacy, and the effective rule of law. *Crime and Justice, 30*, 283–357.
Ullman, S. E. (2002). Social reactions to child sexual abuse disclosures: A critical review. *Journal of Child Sexual Abuse, 12*(1), 89–121.
Westcott, H. L., & Page, M. (2002). Cross-examination, sexual abuse and child witness identity. *Child Abuse Review: Journal of the British Association for the Study and Prevention of Child Abuse and Neglect, 11*(3), 137–152.
Whittam, A., & Ehrat, H. (2003, May 1–2). *Child witnesses in the criminal justice system: The issue of vulnerability.* Paper presented at the Child Sexual Abuse: Justice Response or Alternative Resolution Conference convened by the Australian Institute of Criminology and held in Adelaide.
Wilson, C., & Powell, M. (2001). *A guide to interviewing children: Essential skills for counsellors, police, lawyers and social workers.* Routledge.
Zeze, W. (2015). Democratic constitution and ethnic organisation in Malawi: Preserving good traditional practices or promoting nepotism and tribalism. *History Research, 5*(3), 169–187.

Constitutions, statutes, and international law

African Charter on the Rights and Welfare of the Child (ACRWC), Adopted on 1 July 1990, and entered into force on 29 November 1999.
African Commission on Human and Peoples' Rights, Principles and Guidelines on the Right to a Fair Trial and Legal Assistance in Africa, adopted and entered into force on 29 May 2003.
Child Care, Protection and Justice Act 7 of 2010.
Constitution of the Republic of Malawi.
Criminal Procedure and Evidence Code Act 36 of 1967.
Guidelines for Action on Children in the Criminal Justice System, recommended by Economic and Social Council resolution 1997/30 of 21 July 1997.
Penal Code of Malawi, Chapter 7:01 Laws of Malawi.
Service of Process and Execution of Judgments Act Paper 4:04 Commenced on 1 February 1957. Retrieved 27 June 2024, from https://malawilii.org/akn/mw/act/1956/4/eng@2014-12-31
United Nations Convention on the Rights of the Child, adopted by General Assembly resolution 44/25 of 20 November 1989, entry into force 2 September 1990.
United Nations Guidelines on Justice in Matters involving Child Victims and Witnesses of Crime, adopted by the United Nations' Economic and Social Council ECOSOC Resolution 2005/20 on 22 July 2005.

United Nations Standard Minimum Rules for the Administration of Juvenile Justice, adopted by General Assembly resolution 40/33 of 29 November 1985.

Cases

Republic v Limbikani Cosmas Mpokosa, Criminal Review No. 30 of 2022, High Court of Malawi, Lilongwe Registry Criminal Division.

State v Benjamin Kayembe, Criminal Case No. 1456 of 2018, in the Senior Resident Magistrate Court Sitting at Lilongwe.

3 Silent victims of the law

Children and the legal system in postcolonial Zimbabwe

Vincent Chenzi

Introduction

This chapter examines the drivers, manifestation, and possible measures for mitigating the vulnerability of children before legal institutions of Zimbabwe. It argues that children in Zimbabwe suffer as silent victims at the hands of its legal system that not only fails to protect them but is also complicit in denying them their rights as citizens. In order to articulate the children's vulnerability, the study focused on three categories of children. In particular, the girl child; children living with disabilities, especially those with speech and hearing impairment; and children of members of African Initiated Churches (AICs).

Zimbabwe's Constitution is the supreme law of the land. It is the principal act for any other legislation in the country. Nevertheless, the country's legal system consists of a hybrid body. Laws that are currently utilised in the country were drawn from foreign territories and adopted into the country by the white minority settlers during the colonial period (Saki et al., 2014). This hotchpotch legal corpus consists of the common law (non-statutory or unwritten Anglo Roman Dutch Law), legislation, case law (precedent), and customary law. However, with the exception of the criminal law, which is codified, the rest of Zimbabwe's law is not codified (Saki et al., 2014). This is the primary precedent within which vulnerable groups are exploited, abused, and denied justice because of the legal convolution.

Globally, at least 800 million children live in fragile and conflict-ridden communities where their rights are frequently negated and wholesale childhoods are taken by exploitation, slavery, and abuse (World Vision, 2024). These anomalies manifest despite commendable advancement in mainstreaming child rights in recent decades. Consequently, millions of children continue to live in appalling conditions without their basic rights. At present, more children's lives are being touched by violence, conflict, and the effects of climate change.

In Zimbabwe, the depiction of children as 'property' is pervasive throughout the society. This manifests in the manner in which the state, society, and family conceptualise childhood as nothing but a phase of paternalistic socialisation. Thus, children are seldom consulted even when decisions impacting

DOI: 10.4324/9781003569435-5

them are made. They are regarded as inept to make logical choices that are in their best interests or conformable with adult choices (Fambasayi & Moyo, 2020). This reasoning is profoundly established in Zimbabwe's social, cultural, and educational praxis. Consequently, children's agency is tacitly undervalued, inhibiting them from making independent rational decisions (Fambasayi & Moyo, 2020).

Zimbabwe's Mashonaland East and Mashonaland Central provinces were selected as case studies. Apart from having high cases of child victimisation, these two provinces are also dominated by African Initiated Churches (AICs). These churches are widely responsible for perpetuating crimes against children and minors. Examples of dominant AICs in Zimbabwe include the Africa Apostolic Church (AAC), Johane Marange Apostolic Church (JMAC), and Johane Masowe weChishanu Apostolic Church (JMCAC). The AICs in Zimbabwe were formed by indigenous Africans during the colonial period to resist settler religious influence (Hove & Chenzi, 2017). Hence, they were strongly linked to the nationalist political parties, especially the Zimbabwe African National Union–Patriotic Front (ZANU–PF).

In post-independence Zimbabwe, AIC's have been at the centre of politics since they support the ruling ZANU–PF party. In return, the ZANU–PF offers them protection from prosecution when they commit human rights abuses through their abusive practices, including child marriages and denial of medical and education provision to members. Cases of abuse of children by AIC members have recently been on the rise due to widespread poverty in the rural communities, primarily driven by historical, political, and religious injustices. This is further compounded by the fact that most rural communities where AICs are predominant depend on subsistence agrarian livelihoods (Chenzi, Chivasa, et al., 2025; Chenzi, Mateyisi, et al., 2024). Hence, out of the 70 percent Christian population in Zimbabwe, AICs comprise the highest percentage of Christians (34 percent), followed by Pentecostal (20 percent) and Protestant (16 percent) churches (Zimbabwe National Statistical Agency, 2017).

The chapter is divided into four broad sections excluding the introduction. The methodological segment marks the first segment followed by the literature review section. The literature review section adopts a thematic approach by first examining developments on the concept of vulnerability and legality in the global north before narrowing down to Africa. The third section is the findings section. It explores the drivers and effects of child vulnerability and victimisation by Zimbabwe's legal and law enforcement organs. The fourth and final portion of the research summarises the study's findings and it also provides possible recommendations that can be adopted in mitigating the vulnerability of children and minors in Zimbabwe.

Materials and methods

The methodology for the research was qualitative with data being mainly drawn from in-depth interviews. Data for the study was gathered from two case studies in Mashonaland East and Mashonaland Central provinces between November 2022 and April 2024. Four key informants were interviewed from each of the two provinces. Furthermore, four Focus Group Discussions (FDGs) were also conducted in the two case study areas (Yulianti & Sulistyawati, 2021; Hennink & Kaiser, 2022). Two were held in Mashonaland Central province on 29 November 2022 at a church hall in Tsakare resettlement community and on 20 April 2023 at Tabex community hall. The other two FGDs were held on 23 February 2024 at Musami Arupe Jesuit School of the Deaf and at St Paul Musami Mission Hospital.

Each FGD for the study lasted an average of 1 hour 30 minutes to 2 hours. The participants in the FGDs included village heads, AIC church members, medical personnel, law enforcement, and elderly community members. Each FGD consisted of eight members, including the researcher. The use of a total of eight key informants and four FDGs was most appropriate for this study in order to avoid data redundancy and saturation (Mwita, 2022).

The study was also guided by the Convention on the Rights of the Child (CRC), which is the most widely sanctioned human rights pact in history. It establishes the rights of children in 54 articles and is guided by four core principles, namely:

- Children should not suffer discrimination (Article 2).
- In all decisions affecting children, their best interests should be the main concern (Article 3).
- Children have the right to survive and develop healthily (Article 6).
- Children have the right to have their views taken into account in matters that affect them (Article 12) (World Vision, 2024).

By referring to these four central values, the study was able to clearly identify the causes and manifestation of the child rights violations by both law enforcement and judiciary systems. These values also provided possible guidelines to buttress and uphold children's rights.

In order to clearly pronounce the objectives of the chapter, the study was primarily guided by the following three research questions: What are the major drivers of child victimisation in Zimbabwe's legal system? How exactly are children being victimised by Zimbabwe's legal system? And what are the possible measures that can be adopted to address child legal victimisation? These questions were critical in identifying the causes, manifestations, and possible remedies of child victimisation by the legal system.

All ethical considerations were followed during the data gathering process. All the informants who were interviewed gave their consent to agree to participate in the research. Furthermore, all participants were above 18 years of age, despite the fact that the research was focusing on children, so as to avoid the ethical minefield of interviewing minors (Brooker, 2020). Furthermore, some of the informants gave very sensitive information during the in-depth interviews and, therefore, their real names were replaced with pseudonyms to protect their identity (Lahman et al., 2023).

Vulnerability and the law: a global perspective

There is a steadily growing body of literature on vulnerability and the law. However, this corpus mainly focuses on communities outside the African continent. Furthermore, it has largely focused on commercial and international human rights law (Herring, 2016; Nifosi-Sutton, 2017; Malgieri & Niklas, 2020; Macioce, 2022). However, Africa and the developing world has in recent times witnessed a perpetual increase in its vulnerability due to climate induced disasters, which have increased poverty and hardships across the globe (Birkmann et al., 2022). These developments have also increased interest on vulnerability and its relationship to environmental and national security law (Nevitt, 2020; Peel & Osofsky, 2020).

Studies in the European continent mainly focus on the nexus between vulnerability, human rights, and European law. Malgieri and Niklas' (2020) study, for example, examined how the proliferation of digital data technologies can lead to the emergence of digital data subjects. By using the framework of vulnerability, they were able to develop an alternative language to clarify challenges of social injustice, power imbalances, and inequality (Malgieri & Niklas, 2020).

On a similar note, Nifosi-Sutton's (2017) book examines the general scope of the protection of vulnerable groups under international human rights law. Nifosi-Sutton (2017) was able to demonstrate how international human rights law instruments and relevant practice of regional human rights monitoring bodies vary in their protection of vulnerable groups under international human rights law. This endeavour was attained by conceptualising how the protection of vulnerable groups acts as an underlying and indispensable element of international human rights law. This study is of import because it sheds light in understanding the nuances that influence how some vulnerable members and their groups remain vulnerable because of the failure to apply the law equally.

Likewise, Macioce (2022) also utilised the legal concept of group vulnerability. Special focus was placed on how it is applied by the UN legal framework and the Council of Europe in developing the notion of vulnerable groups in the European Union (EU) law. Macioce's (2022) study concluded that despite being widely used, the notion of vulnerable group is not precisely defined in the system of international law. This can potentially create challenges in protecting the rights of vulnerable groups and members by legal bodies.

Building on Macioce's (2022) findings, Limantė and Tereškinas's (2022) study sought to define the concepts of 'vulnerability' and 'vulnerable groups' from a legal sociological perspective. They came to the conclusion that unpacking the concepts of 'vulnerability' and 'vulnerable groups' is very difficult because vulnerability is a multidimensional concept used in referring to both specific and universal meanings in several fields, and can also be investigated from different positions (Limantė & Tereškinas, 2022).

In order to provide a working definition, Limantė and Tereškinas (2022) forwarded the view that although all humans are vulnerable, some groups are more vulnerable than others. This working definition is also critical for this study which explains why children or minors, young girls, and children living with disabilities were selected as the study's subjects. These groups are more vulnerable than other groups especially in terms of applying the law in protecting them in Zimbabwe. Again, Limantė (2022) also assessed the legal safeguard accessible to vulnerable groups and their members under the European Convention on Human Rights (ECHR), through the auspices of the European Court of Human Rights (ECHR).

Despite these visible strides, experienced in the developed world especially in the EU region in the field of vulnerability and the legal framework, very little has been done in expunging similar developments in the developing world. Heikkilà and Mustaniemi-Laakso (2020) for example adopted a comparative approach between the judicial bodies in Africa and the EU. They focused on how vulnerability is interpreted as a human rights variable in the two regions. They discovered that the concept of vulnerability especially its nature and function can influence the idea of special protection which is inherent in the vulnerability paradigm. This can be considered as a subsidiary safety mechanism, which can be utilised in deepening and widening the ambit of measures of protection in scenarios where 'regular' protection is insufficient to guaranteeing the effective realisation of rights (Heikkilà & Mustaniemi-Laakso, 2020).

Handmer and Monson (2004) used the case study of South Africa to demonstrate how mitigating the consequences of climate-related disasters can be conceptualised as being about minimising or addressing 'vulnerability'. They discovered that studies on the nexus between vulnerability and human rights have mainly focused on international law rather than national law. This is despite the fact that national law is generally more convenient and enforceable than international law especially in developing communities. Hence, they recommended that citizens in developing nations can potentially mobilise public law to lessen their own vulnerability rather than depend on international law (Handmer & Monson, 2004).

In the same vein, Wily (2011) also examined the recent surge in vulnerability in rural parts of the African continent. Wily (2011) was primarily focused on the wholesale land acquisition by both local and foreign investors for livestock, palm oil, commercial food, and carbon trading functions. By examining over 20 African land laws, Wily (2011) came to the conclusion that legal vulnerability was the primary driver of land rights. That is, despite several factors being identified behind the subject of involuntary loss of rural lands, fragile legal position of communal rights was identified as the primary driver. Legal fragility enabled governments to take excessive liberties with their citizens' lands rights, particularly those which are unfarmed and by tradition held in common.

This observation by Wily (2011) is also critical in understanding the manifestation of vulnerability in rural Zimbabwe. The state is the sole owner of all communal and rural land in rural Zimbabwe. This government privilege has frequently been used by the incumbent government to pressure the electorate to vote for it or risk eviction (Marewo et al., 2021).

Gloppen and Kanyongolo (2007) examined the reasons behind the failure to develop a pro-poor jurisprudence in Malawi. This is despite Malawi's 1994 democratic constitution which resulted in the emergence of an astonishingly strong judiciary establishment in an otherwise weak political system. These developments usually point towards a pro-poor direction which has however not materialised in Malawi. Several factors were identified behind the anomaly and they included the nature of Malawi's legal culture, high access barriers, deficiency of litigation resources, and the propulsion of alternative institutions (Gloppen & Kanyongolo, 2007). These findings also shed light on why children and minors remain vulnerable in Zimbabwe despite the existence of legal regulations and institutional safeguards.

In Zimbabwe, there are very few works that have explored the plight of vulnerable groups at the hands of law enforcement and the prosecuting authorities. One such work is by Dudzai et al. (2023). They examined the perspective of the Johanne Marange Apostolic Church (JMAC) regarding the rights of women and girls. Their study was primarily motivated by the fact that women and girls' rights are consistently violated in religious settings and these cases are never reported (Dudzai et al., 2023).

Findings from the study demonstrated that the JMAC's doctrine creates a conducive environment within which the maltreatment of girls and women is permitted under the guise of 'sacredness' of the religious sect. This situation has been taking place since the inception of the church and continues unchecked. The research concluded that abuse cases in the JMAC manifest through forced teen marriages to older men and these are expedited by adult congregants and is highly safeguarded within religious cultism (Dudzai et al., 2023). This study is of import to the current research because it helps in situating the role that religion plays in perpetuating the violation of rights of girls and women.

Research findings

Major drivers of child victimisation in Zimbabwe's legal system

This section of the study was guided by the first question regarding the major drivers of child victimisation in Zimbabwe's legal system. It draws upon several reasons behind the victimisation of children by the legal system. These reasons range from political interference, mental and physical condition of the children, role of the community, lack of adequate expertise in dealing with children, cultural and religious practices. In order to clearly articulate the vulnerability of children, this section was guided by the four core principles of the CRC. In attempting to understand the drivers of child discrimination, it became clear that the causes of discrimination directly contravened Article 2 of the CRC which posits that, 'Children should not suffer discrimination' (World Vision, 2024).

There are several causes which can assist in explaining why children fall victim to the legal system in Zimbabwe. Chief among these causes is political interference. In Mashonaland East province, child marriages are rife, especially among members of AICs (Zondo, 2022). Families and communities where child marriages are practised are also complicit in the abusive acts. Consequently, thousands of children in Zimbabwe fall victim to statutory rape and some of them succumb to death whilst giving birth in the 'church shrines' since these AICs forbid their members from going to hospitals (Zondo, 2022). This also contravenes CRC Article 6 that, 'Children have the right to survive and develop healthily' (World Vision, 2024).

The reproductive organs of the minors require specialised medical attention which they are denied by the church leaders under the guise of preventing western influence. However, the reality is that they will be attempting to conceal the criminal acts (Chiremba, 2024). Some of these AICs also believe in acquiring healing and deliverance from family challenges by committing sexual intercourse with minors (Zondo, 2022). This has encouraged the increase in rape cases against minors in these communities. Furthermore, in the event that the perpetrators of these heinous crimes are arrested, the state through the presidential pardon releases them. They are usually released before they even serve half of their sentence.

For example, Bobby Makaza, a 61-year-old AIC member from Mashonaland East was sentenced to 16 years in jail for raping his then ten-year-old niece in 2018. However, he was released after only serving four years of his sentence (Bwanya, 2023). After his release from prison journalists interviewed him about how he felt towards president Mnangagwa and he replied that, 'Mnangagwa *huchi* and ZANU PF *huchi*!' This meant that, 'president Mnangagwa was honey and ZANU PF was honey' (Bwanya, 2023). His confession became a slogan for ZANU PF during the 2023 harmonised elections such that his face and statement was printed on ZANU PF regalia. Furthermore, he received many presents including cash, a house, and a car from elite ZANU PF supporters who rewarded him for his support towards the political party (Harris, 2023). This attitude towards criminality not only encourages such acts but also silences victims from speaking out.

A child's physical and mental condition which includes age, gender, mental and physical capabilities are also determinants of child victimisation by the law. Children with disabilities are the ones mainly disadvantaged by the court system. This is largely because of their disabilities which makes them vulnerable to the legal system either as victims or witnesses to crime. Findings from Musami school of the deaf revealed that children who have hearing and speech impairment are seriously affected by their disabilities. Consequently, court cases involving them are usually 'swept under the carpet' (Kamucha,

2024). Again, this attitude towards children with disabilities contravenes the CRC Article 2 that, 'Children should not suffer discrimination' (World Vision, 2024).

Corruption also acts as another driver of victimisation of children by the courts and law enforcement. It has been a pervasive social pathology in Zimbabwe that has characterised the country since the turn of the millennium (Reliefweb, 2007; Chenzi, 2021). In Zimbabwe, civil servants including police, medical professionals, judges, and public prosecutors are paid very low wages. This situation has gotten even worse under Zimbabwe's Second republic after it introduced austerity measures that reduced salaries of civil servants to less than 10 percent of what they were getting under the Mugabe regime (Chenzi & Ndamba, 2023).

Discussion

Repertoires of child victimisation under Zimbabwe's legal system

This section of the chapter focused on the second question of the study that sought to identify the actual processes which children are being victimised by Zimbabwe's legal system. Most children affiliated with the AICs continue to be victims of statutory rape. The courts and law enforcement are usually unwilling to pursue these cases because of the strong ties of the AICs with the ruling government (Chiremba, 2024). Statutory rape is also encouraged by lack of agency from the community and families of the victims. Parents and guardians marry their minor daughters to the older men who rape them. In the event that those cases are reported, guardians and parents of the victims are usually unwilling to cooperate with law enforcement and courts. The fear of embarrassing the church or being excommunicated by the church and community is usually the main reason (Chiremba, 2024).

Statutory rape in Zimbabwe refers to the act of committing sexual intercourse with a minor or a person below the age of 18 years (*The Herald*, 2024). Under Statutory Instrument (SI) 2 of January 2024, any person found guilty of committing sexual intercourse with a person below the age of 18 years will face a maximum jail sentence of ten years. Prior to the institutionalisation of SI 2 of January 2024, the government of Zimbabwe had been typically ignoring the practice of child marriage. More so, the child marriage proceedings are carried out without the consent of the minors. This contravenes Article 3 of the CRC that, 'In all decisions affecting children, their best interests should be the main concern.' (World Vision, 2024).

Zimbabwe has two types of marriage laws – the Customary Marriages Act and the Marriage Act. Neither of the two laws provided a minimum age for marriage consent, whilst the customary law permits polygamy (Chingono, 2021). That is why this new law was a welcome development. However, in most parts of rural Zimbabwe, including in the provinces of Mashonaland East and Mashonaland Central where there is a strong presence of AICs, this law is disregarded by members of these churches. For example, between January and June 2023, 680 minors aged between 10 and 14 were impregnated and some of them were found to be HIV positive (Machivenyika, 2024; Moyo, 2024). What is more worrying is that these children should be in school, but their entire future and career prospects are jeopardised by adults who are protected by the state.

Zimbabwe's rural areas are not only havens of AICs, but they are also the political stronghold of the incumbent ZANU PF party (Tarusarira & Humbe, 2022). Therefore, leaders of the ZANU PF party which has ruled postcolonial Zimbabwe since independence consider themselves members of these churches (Chiremba, 2024). This is driven by the desire to gain political clout from the rural electorate during elections. In return, the government of Zimbabwe run by the ZANU PF regime casts a blind eye to the criminal practices of these churches in order to maintain their *quid pro quo* relationship.

Interview with informants from the Mashonaland East province also revealed that ZANU PF officials frequently threaten police, medical, and Non-Governmental Organisation (NGO) personnel. The threats are directed on personnel who attempt to prosecute members of the AICs for statutory rape. Consequently, some have been dismissed from work, threatened with death or assaulted for attempting to prosecute suspected offenders (Zondo, 2022; Chiremba, 2024). These sentiments were also echoed by Kenneth Mtata, General Secretary of the Zimbabwe Council of Churches (ZCC) who stated that, 'At the moment, we have many cases where sentencing seems not to be happening, and many people get away with it' (Chingono, 2021).

Although this study was mainly focusing on minors, it has to be understood that religious induced structural vulnerabilities are not only experienced by minors. Women also experience similar challenges. Mr Chiremba (pseudonym), a doctor at Musami mission hospital, revealed that a monthly average of 20 women are found with either cervical or breast cancer. These cancer cases will usually be at advanced stages. The patients usually claim that they were denied access to treatment by their churches until it is too late (Chiremba, 2024). Consequently, most of the patients succumb to the diseases.

Most children who use sign language are at a great disadvantage with law enforcement and in the courts because sign language is not universal. Sign language depends on how the child was taught. Therefore, those that are taught at home informally develop a 'new' language different from the one taught in schools. This informal language will have signs and expressions that can only be understood by very few people. However, most children in Zimbabwe who have speech and hearing impairment do not have access to formal education due to economic hardships and scarcity of schools with facilities to carter for them (Majoko, 2019; Dube et al., 2021; Chataika & Hlatywayo, 2022). This means that they communicate using 'homegrown' sign language which can only be understood by those who taught them.

This situation creates serious legal challenges when they fall victim to a crime or witness one. This is because law enforcement and court interpreters cannot understand the sign language which they were taught at home and may require those who taught them to act as interpreters (Kamucha, 2024). This situation usually creates a conflict of interest since the very people capable of understanding the language are usually the perpetrators of those crimes and will be the ones under investigation. Consequently, most cases involving children with speech and hearing impairment never reach the courts. If these cases manage to reach the courts, they are usually dismissed for lack of clear evidence to implicate the perpetrators. This tacitly encourages further abuse since courts and law enforcement cannot effectively prosecute the offenders. This further undermines CRC Article 2 that, 'Children should not suffer discrimination' (World Vision, 2024).

This failure by the law enforcement to assist minors in the event of their victimisation or acting as witnesses to crime is not limited to children with disabilities. Normal children are also not an exception. For example, in the event of a rape case against a minor and the minor reports the case to the police they will require the plaintiff to narrate the details of the event on paper (Mashayamombe, 2022). However, most of these minors come from underprivileged backgrounds. Hence, the majority are not provided with decent education to enable them to read and write properly. Consequently, most cases involving these children usually fall apart since they cannot clearly articulate the details of their ordeal.

Mrs Mashayamombe (pseudonym) also lamented how her 14-year-old daughter was raped numerous times by a close relative. However, since her daughter could not read nor write down her experience so as to prosecute the suspect, the charges were dropped for lack of evidence (Mashayamombe, 2022). This situation reinforces the plight of children as silent victims of the law in Zimbabwe. Consequently, Article 3 of the CRC – 'In all decisions affecting children, their best interests should be the main concern' – is utterly disregarded.

Corruption of is perpetuated by public officials who subsist on bribes especially from the accused persons. Hence, most cases against minors never reach the courts and if they manage to do so they are usually written off from the books on the pretext of lacking evidence. However, these cases are usually deliberately removed due to bribes given to the judges and prosecutors by the suspects to evade prosecution (Chiremba, 2024). Similar sentiments were echoed by Mr Chimanikire the village head for Tsakare resettlement community who lamented that:

> We no longer report any cases to the local police because as soon as you report your case there, the suspect will quickly be released such that by the time you arrive back home, the suspect will have arrived ahead of you. . . . We know that they pay-off the police money ranging from USD $10–USD $50 depending with the nature of their offense . . . as soon as they make the payment, they are released.
>
> (Chimanikire, 2023)

What this situation means is that a lot of cases are never prosecuted. This further discourages community members from reporting any new cases due to the corruption that has come to characterise Zimbabwe's legal system. Mr Mutumbame, a resident of Tsakare resettlement area, also further highlighted the vented frustration by members of the community by stating that:

> The law enforcement do not just request bribes from the suspects but also from the complainants as well. . . . If you want the police and courts to take your case seriously you have to pay a lot of money to receive proper justice. If you do not have the money then your case will most likely fall apart despite the amount of evidence you provide.
>
> (Mutumbame, 2023)

This issue of bribing law enforcement has not only denied victims the right to receive the justice they deserve. It has also led to the prosecution and incarceration of innocent suspects by overzealous law enforcement and prosecutors. This is usually done in an attempt to please their 'clients' who would have given them bribes (Kugarakuripi, 2023).

Furthermore, it was also discovered that there are corruption syndicates in Zimbabwe consisting of police personnel, prosecutors, and magistrates. These reportedly solicit bribes from suspects before organising acquittals via sloppy investigations and prosecution (Nemukuyu, 2021). According to Nemukuyu (2021), this process begins at the local police station where the report would have been made. The suspects are discouraged by the rogue police officers from engaging lawyers. The suspects are assured of acquittals in exchange for bribes.

Both the bribes and acquittals will be irresistible to the suspect since the bribes will be lower than what a lawyer would charge in any case, without the same degree of acquittal. Afterwards, lackadaisical investigations are conducted by the bribed investigating officer. The sloppy findings will then be handed over to a rogue prosecutor who will also be part of the syndicate, for vetting. During the trial there is under prosecution such that the magistrate is left without any option but to clear the suspect of any wrong doing (Nemukuyu, 2021). This is a direct infringement of CRC Article 12 that, 'Children have the right to have their views taken into account in matters that affect them' (World Vision, 2024).

However, this situation is not unique to Zimbabwe alone but has been identified in most African states. A survey conducted by the Global Corruption Barometer (GCB)-Africa in 2020 revealed that 28 percent or 13,160 people out of 47,000 citizens from 35 African countries paid bribes to police in 2019 alone (Mutowekuziva, 2020). On the other hand, Zimbabwe has a 24 percent bribery rate for the police. Also, 25 percent of the country's general public believe that the judges and magistrates are corrupt (Mutowekuziva, 2020).

Measures to address child victimisation

This segment of the chapter focused on the third research question, which sought to identify the possible measures that can be adopted to address child legal victimisation.

In order to address these challenges against children, a number of measures urgently need to be adopted. These measures should target regional, national, provincial, and local institutions. This can engender inclusive transformation that can address the plight of children at all levels. Furthermore, efforts to address these challenges affecting children can promote the realisation of the CRC Articles 2, 3, 6, and 12.

The first measure should emanate from the Southern Africa Development Community (SADC) within which Zimbabwe is a member. That is, SADC must exert sustained pressure on the government of Zimbabwe in the areas of human rights, rule of law, and upholding of children's rights. SADC must also guarantee that the Zimbabwean government makes clear progress towards addressing human rights abuses. This will be carried out by prosecuting those who perpetrate such acts, strengthening the rule of law, implementing judicial reforms, and ensuring the rights of children across all communities in the country. These measures can go a long way in deterring corrupt dealings by the state and public authorities who deny the upholding of justice for children and other vulnerable groups. This can also address the core values under Article 2 that, 'Children should not suffer discrimination' (World Vision, 2024).

Another measure is to increase the number of social workers in all local communities in Zimbabwe. At present, there is a dearth of social workers especially in Zimbabwe's rural villages (Dudzai et al., 2023). This situation compounds the challenge because it is within rural communities where the abuse of the minors by both religious sects and community members is a common occurrence. Unfortunately, social workers assigned to prevent such acts from happening are stationed at district level and the district offices are far away from the villages where these abuses happen.

Therefore, there is urgent need for Zimbabwe's Department of Social Development (DSD) to recruit and station more social workers at village level. This will enable social workers to monitor and operate alongside traditional local authorities in addressing possible cases of abuse of minors (Dudzai et al., 2023). This scenario will also enable social workers to assist in investigating reports of child abuse, which can potentially reduce tempering of evidence by law enforcement officials. The social workers can also operate with village authorities in educating villagers about the rights of minors and children. This intervention will uphold CRC Article 12 which posits that, 'Children have the right to have their views taken into account in matters that affect them' (World Vision, 2024).

There is need to introduce programmes to train officials who deal with cases involving the abuse of children. These officials will be able to communicate and get detailed information that can be admissible in court. This can directly address the demands of CRC Article 3 that, 'In all decisions affecting children, their best interests should be the main concern' (World Vision, 2024). The failure of social workers, law enforcement, and judiciary personnel to communicate properly with minors who would have either been abused or witnessed abuse taking place has resulted in most cases being dismissed for lack of evidence. As a result, perpetrators have been able to avoid prosecution which encourages further abuse.

Furthermore, the Government of Zimbabwe (GoZ) can operate together with the Zimbabwe Human Rights Commission (ZHRC) to enforce the constitutional provision under section 26 (b). This section posits that it is requisite for the government to adopt befitting measures to guarantee that children are not committed into marriage. Moreover, the ZHRC should also participate in investigating and exposing cases and perpetrators of child abuse within communities and religious organisations (Muchacha & Mthetwa, 2015; Muridzo & Malianga, 2015). Such an approach can uphold CRC Article 3 that, 'In all decisions affecting children, their best interests should be the main concern' (World Vision, 2024).

In order to deter any future practices, crimes against minors including rape, forced marriages and denial to seek education and medical support should be reprimanded in accordance with the law. This approach may force perpetrators to desist from such harmful practices. This measure can also be buttressed by establishing a legislation that regards child abuse in religious settings as a crime against humanity. There is also a need to establish a policy that interdicts religious sects that abuse vulnerable members such as children. Empowering Zimbabwe's child welfare ministry with the authority to investigate, suspend, and prosecute religious organisations found guilty of sanctioning the abuse of vulnerable groups is also necessary. This will go a long way in saving the lives of many children which upholds CRC Article 6 that, 'Children have the right to survive and develop healthily' (World Vision, 2024).

Conclusion

In the final analysis, evidence from the study indicates that children in Zimbabwe's Mashonaland Central and Mashonaland East provinces are indeed silent victims of the law. This situation is driven by a plethora of reasons ranging from corruption by law enforcement and judiciary personnel, political interference, cultural and religious beliefs, and widespread poverty. This has undermined the four core principles of the CRC for minors living in Zimbabwe's AIC dominated rural communities. However, the adoption of several measures including working with the SADC, ZHRC, and other religious organisations in the country can go a long way in exposing, prosecuting, and imprisoning of offenders. This may gradually lead to the realisation of the CRC Articles 2, 3, 6, and 12.

References

Birkmann, J., Jamshed, A., McMillan, J. M., Feldmeyer, D., Totin, E., Solecki, W., Ibrahim, Z. Z., Roberts, D., Kerr, R. B., Poertner, H. O., & Pelling, M. (2022). Understanding human vulnerability to climate change: A global perspective on index validation for adaptation planning. *Science of the Total Environment*, *803*, 150065.

Brooker, L. (2020). Interviewing children. In *Doing early childhood research* (pp. 162–177). Routledge.

Bwanya, M. (2023, August 8). Prison authorities defend 'Mnangagwa huchi' rape convict's premature release. *Zimlive*. Retrieved from June 19, 2024, from https://www.zimlive.com/prison-authorities-defend-mnangagwa-huchi-rape-convicts-premature-release/

Chataika, T., & Hlatywayo, L. (2022). Examining the implementation of inclusive education in Zimbabwe. In *Disability rights and inclusiveness in Africa: The convention on the rights of persons with disabilities, challenges and change* (Vol. 44, p. 79). Boydell & Brewer.

Chenzi, V. (2021). Fake news, corruption, human rights, and the Mnangagwa regime, 2017–2021. *Whitehead Journal of Diplomacy and International Relations*, *22*, 97.

Chenzi, V., Chivasa, N., & Murau, N. T. (2025). Climate change, religion, health and structural violence in post-colonial Zimbabwe. In E. Chitando & S. M. Kilonzo (Eds.), *Palgrave handbook on health, religion and climate change in Africa*. Palgrave Macmillan.

Chenzi, V., Mateyisi, M., Nangombe, S., & Maoela, M. A. (2024). Emerging adaptation constrains in Mount Darwin District, Zimbabwe. In M. Matsa, L. Chapungu, & G. Nhamo (Eds.), *Climate change resilience in rural Southern Africa: The dynamics, prospects & challenges*. Springer Nature.

Chenzi, V., & Ndamba, A. (2023). Surviving the Covid-19 lockdown: Zimbabwe's informal sector, 2020–2021. *Review of African Political Economy*, *50*(176), 261–271.

Chingono, N. (2021, October 11). Death of a 15-year-old girl while giving birth exposes dark practice of child marriage in Zimbabwe. *CNN*. Retrieved June 30, 2024, from https://edition.cnn.com/2021/10/11/africa/zimbabwe-church-abuse-intl/index.html

Dube, T., Ncube, S. B., Mapuvire, C. C., Ndlovu, S., Ncube, C., & Mlotshwa, S. (2021). Interventions to reduce the exclusion of children with disabilities from education: A Zimbabwean perspective from the field. *Cogent Social Sciences*, *7*(1), 1913848.

Dudzai, C., Zvokuomba, K., & Mboko, T. G. (2023). Religion, women, and girls' rights in Zimbabwe: The case of Zimbabwe's Johanne Marange Apostolic Church. *Journal of Human Rights and Social Work*, *8*(4), 376–388.

Fambasayi, R., & Moyo, A. (2020). The best interests of the child offender in the context of detention as a measure of last resort: A comparative analysis of legal developments in South Africa, Kenya and Zimbabwe. *South African Journal on Human Rights*, *36*(1), 25–48.

Gloppen, S., & Kanyongolo, F. E. (2007). Courts and the poor in Malawi: Economic marginalization, vulnerability, and the law. *International Journal of Constitutional Law*, *5*(2), 258–293.

Handmer, J., & Monson, R. (2004). Does a rights based approach make a difference? The role of public law in vulnerability reduction. *International Journal of Mass Emergencies & Disasters*, *22*(3), 43–59.

Harris, L. B. (2023, August 7). Zanu PF glorification of convicted rapist Bobby Makaza sparks outrage. *Cite*. Retrieved June 19, 2024, from https://cite.org.zw/zanu-pf-glorification-of-convicted-rapist-bobby-makaza-sparks-outrage/

Heikkilà, M., & Mustaniemi-Laakso, M. (2020). Vulnerability as a human rights variable: African and European developments. *African Human Rights Law Journal*, *20*(2), 777–798.

Hennink, M., & Kaiser, B. N. (2022). Sample sizes for saturation in qualitative research: A systematic review of empirical tests. *Social Science & Medicine*, *292*, 114523.

The Herald. (2024, January 13). Age of consent gazetted, offenders face a maximum sentence of 10 years. *The Herald*. Retrieved June 19, 2024, from https://www.herald.co.zw/age-of-consent-law-gazetted-offenders-face-maximum-of-10-years-jail/

Herring, J. (2016). *Vulnerable adults and the law*. Oxford University Press.

Hove, M., & Chenzi, V. (2017). 'Prophets of doom': The Zimbabwean Christian community and contemporary politics. *Insight on Africa*, *9*(2), 173–195.

Kugarakuripi. (2023, March 31). *AD625: Zimbabweans see their police as lacking in integrity, professionalism*. Afro Barometer. Retrieved June 30, 2024, from https://www.afrobarometer.org/publication/ad625-zimbabweans-see-their-police-as-lacking-in-integrity-professionalism/

Lahman, M. K., Thomas, R., & Teman, E. D. (2023). A good name: Pseudonyms in research. *Qualitative Inquiry*, *29*(6), 678–685.

Limantė, A., & Tereškinas, A. (2022). Definition of vulnerable groups. In *Legal protection of vulnerable groups in Lithuania, Latvia, Estonia and Poland: Trends and perspectives* (pp. 3–27). Springer International Publishing.

Machivenyika, F. (2024, June 14). Children mark international day of the African child. *The Herald*. Retrieved June 30, 2024, from https://www.herald.co.zw/children-mark-international-day-of-the-african-child/

Macioce, F. (2022). The vulnerable groups and their legal value. In The Politics of Vulnerable Groups (Eds.), *Critical political theory and radical practice*. Palgrave Macmillan. https://doi.org/10.1007/978-3-031-07547-6_3

Majoko, T. (2019). Inclusion of children with disabilities in physical education in Zimbabwean primary schools. *Sage Open*, *9*(1). https://doi.org/10.1177/2158244018820387

Malgieri, G., & Niklas, J. (2020). Vulnerable data subjects. *Computer Law & Security Review*, *37*, 105415.

Marewo, M. K., Ncube, S., & Chitonge, H. (2021). Land governance and displacement in Zimbabwe: The case of Chilonga communal area, Chiredzi district. *The Africa Governance Papers*, *1*(1).

Moyo, A. (2024, June 22). 680 minors impregnated in six months. *The Herald*. Retrieved June 30, 2024, from https://www.herald.co.zw/680-minors-impregnated-in-six-months/

Muchacha, M., & Mthetwa, E. (2015). Dynamics of child sexual abuse in Zimbabwe: Towards a socio-ecological framework of prevention. *Southern African Journal of Social Work and Social Development*, *27*(1), 118–136.

Muridzo, N. G., & Malianga, E. (2015). Child sexual abuse in Zimbabwe: Prevention strategies for social workers. *African Journal of Social Work*, *5*(2), 41–64.

Mutowekuziva, T. (2020, June 10). Delivering justice in Zimbabwe's courts. *The Herald*. Retrieved June 30, 2024, from https://www.transparency.org/en/blog/delivering-justice-in-zimbabwes-courts

Mwita, K. (2022). Factors influencing data saturation in qualitative studies. *International Journal of Research in Business and Social Science*, *11*(4), 414–420, 2147–4478.

Nemukuyu, D. (2021, May 28). Cops, prosecutors in acquittals storm. *The Herald*. Retrieved June 30, 2024, from https://www.herald.co.zw/cops-prosecutors-in-acquittals-storm/

Nevitt, M. P. (2020). On environmental law, climate change, & national security law. *Harvard Environmental Law Review*, *44*, 321.

Nifosi-Sutton, I. (2017). *The protection of vulnerable groups under international human rights law*. Routledge.

Peel, J., & Osofsky, H. M. (2020). Climate change litigation. *Annual Review of Law and Social Science*, *16*(1), 21–38.

Reliefweb. (2007, January 29). Hungry Zimbabwean police officers turn to corruption for survival. *Reliefweb*. Retrieved June 30, 2024, from https://reliefweb.int/report/zimbabwe/hungry-zimbabwean-police-officers-turn-corruption-survival
Saki, O., Chiware, T., Pfumorodze, J., & Chitsove, E. (2014). *Update: The law in Zimbabwe*. Hauser Global Law School Program. New York University. (GlobaLex). Updated April. http://www.nyulawglobal.org/globalex/Zimbabwe1.html
Statutory Instrument 2 of 2024, Presidential Temporary Powers (Temporary Measures) (Criminal Laws) (Protection of Children and young Persons) Regulations 2024.
Tarusarira, J., & Humbe, B. P. (2022). The ambivalence of African independent/initiated Churches in colonial and postcolonial politics. In *Religion in rebellions, revolutions, and social movements* (pp. 158–172). Routledge.
Wily, L. A. (2011). 'The law is to blame': The vulnerable status of common property rights in sub-Saharan Africa. *Development and Change*, *42*(3), 733–757.
World Vision. (2024). *Child rights: History, facts & how to protect them*. https://www.worldvision.com.au/child-rights
Yulianti, T., & Sulistyawati, A. (2021). Enhancing public speaking ability through focus group discussion. *Jurnal Pajar (Pendidikan Dan Pengajaran)*, *5*(2), 287–295.
Zimbabwe National Statistical Agency. (2017). *Inter censal demography survey 2017 report*. https://zimbabwe.unfpa.org/sites/default/files/pub-pdf/Inter%20Censal%20Demography%20Survey%202017%20Report.pdf

Interviews

Chimanikire (Mr) a village head for Tsakare resettlement community in Mashonaland Central, 19 April, 2023.
Chiremba (Mr) (pseudonym) ST. Paul Musami hospital doctor, 23 February, 2024.
Kamucha, (Mrs) ST. Paul Musami School of the deaf teacher and matron, 23 February, 2024.
Mashayamombe (Mrs) (pseudonym), local villager whose daughter was raped, 21 November, 2022.
Mutumbame, (Mr) local villager from Tsakare resettlement area, 19 April 2023.
Zondo (Mr) (Pseudonym), community Pentecostal pastor, 21 November, 2022.

4 The application of language and procedural entitlements of children in detention in Malawi

Dorothy nyaKaunda Kamanga

Introduction

Children under the age of 18 who are legally capable of violating the law have been extensively researched, highlighting children's experiences within the legal context and profoundly impacting reforms to promote children's access to justice (Coppins et al., 2011; Kilkelly et al., 2023; Kaime, 2009). Various countries have recognised the unique vulnerability of children that result from their physical and mental immaturity, thus necessitating specialised protection and support throughout their engagement with criminal justice stakeholders (Suri, 2019; Deuchar & Bhopal, 2017). Studies have indicated that 'children in conflict with the law' (Kilkelly et al., 2023) may experience prolonged periods of detention, either in police custody or prisons, until they are released by a court or transferred to child detention facilities, usually following a motion (Van den Brink, 2019; Kanyuka, 1989; Haydon, 2020; Hodgson, 2024; Moraa & Gor, 2023). The term 'children in conflict with the law' refers to children who are criminal suspects or have infringed the law (Kirkelly et al., 2023). Children's linguistic and procedural rights may be compromised during interactions with law enforcement and detention in adult correctional facilities, exposing them to potential punishment and degrading treatment (Rap, 2016; Kupchik, 2003; Peeler et al., 2020).

Existing research highlights that children involved in criminal proceedings often encounter difficulties appreciating the formal courtroom arrangement and are constrained from fully participating in legal processes because of the technical language used by legal professionals (Fernández-Molina et al., 2021; Lount et al., 2018; Kilkelly, 2023). Nevertheless, there remains a gap in knowledge regarding how duty-bearers, such as police, prosecutors, corrections officials, and judicial officers, implement language and procedural rights for children in detention.

This chapter examines how duty bearers in Malawi potentially violate the language and procedural rights of children detained in police cells and prisons. The chapter raises the following questions: What terminology is utilised by duty bearers during criminal proceedings that could lead to the detention of a child? What factors determine the selection of a detention facility for a

DOI: 10.4324/9781003569435-6

child facing criminal proceedings? Who is authorised to adjudicate criminal cases involving children? The chapter contends that appellate court decisions reveal a miscarriage of justice and failure by duty-bearers to promote 'the principle of the best interests of the child' (Chitha, 2024; Japharidze, 2023) in safeguarding the linguistic and procedural rights of children facing criminal proceedings.

The chapter is structured to approach the study questions as follows: After this introductory overview of the vulnerability of detained children in the legal system, an examination of the existing literature is presented. It highlights the legal and conceptual framework for children facing criminal proceedings. An exposition of the research findings from the court cases forming the basis of the study will follow afterwards, along with a description of the methodology. The chapter will also discuss the common themes emerging from the data before concluding.

Literature review

The legal framework

Constitutions serve as a paramount legal framework of most nations and represent the highest source of power, enabling recourse to international law (Hansen, 2002; Chirwa, 2007; Chitha, 2024). Concerning the area of criminal justice, the Malawian Constitution provides for children's rights during arrest, detention, and trial. Malawi has ratified several international and regional conventions and treaties, which impact its national laws and judicial decisions concerning and impacting children (Chirwa & Kaime, 2008; Mwambene & Mawondza, 2017; Chitha, 2024). The main international instruments the country adheres to in order to protect and promote children's access to justice include 'The United Nations Convention on the Rights of the Child' (CRC) (1989), 'The African Charter on the Rights and Welfare of the Child' (ACRWC) (1990), and the 'United Nations Standard Minimum Rules for the Administration of Juvenile Justice (the Beijing Rules)' (1985). The CRC is a seminal and highly respected international treaty in the realm of child law as it recognises children as individuals with distinct rights and entitlements (Acconciamessa, 2020; Chirwa & Kaime, 2008; Kaime, 2005). It serves as a benchmark for evaluating Malawi's child justice system and its alignment with international standards (Chirwa & Kaime, 2008; Kilkelly & Pleysier, 2023).

'Children in conflict with the law'

According to the Malawian Constitution (1994), the CRC, the ACRWC, and The Child Care Protection and Justice Act (CCJPA) (2010), children are individuals below the age of 18 (Odala, 2012; Banda & Carlson, 2022; Kaime, 2005). The Malawian Penal Code designates 14 years as the threshold age for criminal liability, indicating the nation's assumed level of maturity at which a child can be answerable for criminal offences (Chirwa, 2022; Kilkelly & Pleysier, 2023). Children undergoing criminal proceedings are also known as 'juvenile delinquents' (Kadilu, 2017) in the Beijing Rules. However, Malawi has adopted the person-centred term 'children in conflict with the law' (Chirwa, 2022; Kilkelly et al., 2023). The term encompasses all young individuals engaged at any phase of the criminal justice system, whether as suspects, defendants, or offenders (Kilkelly et al., 2023; Coppins et al., 2011).

To uphold children's best interest and ensure non-discrimination as mandated by articles 2, 3, and 40 of the CRC, children in conflict with the law must not be classified as 'accused or convicted individuals' or labelled with criminal suspect terminology (Kilkelly & Pleysier, 2023; Odala, 2012; Bedell et al., 2019). Children involved in legal proceedings must be treated with concern for their rights, humanity, and dignity following both domestic and international standards (Kilkelly & Pleysier, 2023; Odala, 2012).

Children in detention

This study discusses the handling of children in Malawi's criminal justice system where there is no resort to the effective approach of shielding them from general criminal laws, institutions, and processes and averting their detention during legal proceedings (Kadilu, 2017; Coppins et al., 2011; Kupchik, 2003). Personal liberty is guaranteed in s.18 of the Malawian Constitution, but it can be deprived through detention. In criminal proceedings, detention is the act of confining individuals, leading to reduced autonomy and increased dependency on authorities for basic needs, making them vulnerable (Marwandana et al., 2022). The state is legally mandated to ensure that any individual arrested and detained on suspicion of committing a crime is promptly presented before a court to face criminal charges or to be informed of the reasons for their continuing detention (s.42(2)(b) of the Constitution). Otherwise, failing to do so could warrant release.

Frackson, Chikalamba and Jabes v Republic, the *Frackson* case, which will be discussed later, emphasises the importance of courts in promptly examining the reasons for depriving someone of liberty due to alleged criminal acts, ensuring that freedom is potentially restored. If detained individuals appear in court and are not released from custody, they can assert their entitlement unless justice demands otherwise (s.42(2)(e) of the Constitution).

Article 37 of the CRC and sections 95, 96, and 97 of the CCPJA are important in the context of this research as the provisions lay down fundamental principles, which should be applied for detaining children. These include ensuring rights, such as separation from adults, limited detention periods, respectful treatment, legal assistance, and rehabilitation programmes (Moraa & Gor, 2023). Stalford and Hollingsworth (2020) emphasise the significance of these rights for detained children, particularly in police custody where the risks of coercion, false admissions, and maltreatment are high. The challenges encountered by children in 'conflict with the law' regarding the protection of their linguistic and procedural rights will be highlighted by utilising these principles.

Conceptual framework

'Best interests of the child'

Section 23 (1) of the Constitution, section 88 of the CCJPA and Article 3 of the CRC collectively prioritise the 'child's best interests' as a primary consideration in all matters concerning or impacting children, mandating public and private institutions to guarantee their welfare and protection (Chitha, 2024; Odala, 2012). The 'child's best interests' represent a multifaceted three-fold concept involving a substantive right, a fundamental interpretive guideline and a rule of procedure (Chitha, 2024; Moraa & Gor, 2023; Lonardo, 2022).

Child defendants are particularly vulnerable due to their developmental immaturity, underscoring the fundamental legal principle that the 'best interests of the child' must be accorded paramount consideration in the courts and across all legal proceedings (Moraa & Gor, 2023). Additionally, a strong focus exists on integrating and applying this universal principle in all legal proceedings to promote social rehabilitation through appropriate child-friendly procedures. When dealing with children involved in criminal activities the aim is to emphasise the child's best interests by promoting reform and reintegration into society (Moraa & Gor, 2023).

As noted by Moraa and Gor (2023) and Chitha (2024), the principle of the 'child's best interests' is important for determining or reviewing orders for the detention of children. In instances where language and procedural rights of detained children are challenged, court orders are issued to ensure the integration of appropriate language and procedures as well as the relocation of children from any undesirable surroundings or environments to conducive settings that facilitate their access to nutrition, education, and recreational activities (Tosouni, 2014; Thompson, 2018).

The cultural lag

William F. Ogburn is known for introducing the concept of cultural lag, a theoretical framework valuable for analysing social and cultural transformations and maladjustment during transition (Ruggiero, 2018). This phenomenon manifests when material components of society change faster than non-material cultural elements, causing challenges for institutions in addressing the resulting discrepancies (Ruggiero, 2018). The Cultural Lag theory explains the challenges that government officials face in implementing language and procedural rights for detained children due to delayed adaptation to societal changes. It may explain the rapid progressions in child justice policy and the challenges in implementing these changes in the legal system, particularly in terms of child-friendly terminology, procedural rights, and prohibition of imprisonment of children (Kamwendo, 2009). Ame's (2011) findings of adverse societal perceptions and governmental officials' perceptions towards children in conflict with the law in Ghana may similarly impede the implementation of children's rights in Malawi. This chapter demonstrates the relevance of the Cultural Lag, as legislative changes do not prevent the labelling and treatment of children as adult criminal suspects.

Procedural justice

A fundamental principle of Malawian criminal procedural law underscores the significance of ensuring substantial justice while minimising emphasis on the importance of technicalities (s.3 of the Criminal Procedure and Evidence Code – CPEC). For children facing criminal proceedings, the child justice system fundamentally departs from this doctrine of harmless error by advancing procedural justice as a crucial principle to be adhered to (Kilkelly & Pleysier, 2023; Acconciamessa, 2020; Sormunen, 2020; Enujioke et al., 2023). This means that in instances where a trial court's decision leads to a miscarriage of justice, prompt correction is imperative as specified in section 5 of the CPEC. The Supreme Court of Appeal stated the importance of procedural justice in *Ngwira & Chiumia v Ngwira*, in which it underscored that procedural justice is necessary for substantive justice and that non-compliance with procedural requirements constitutes an infringement of the judicial process.

The Procedural Justice Theory explains the rationale underlying the courts' prioritisation of informality and due process protections for children in legal proceedings (Suri, 2019; Braun, 2022; Birckhead, 2009; Matczak, 2018). This theoretical framework is implemented through the utilisation of simple, plain, and person-centred language in child justice proceedings to prevent the exposure of children to harsh treatment within the legal system (Tran et al., 2018; Bedell et al., 2019; Bedell et al., 2018; Harney et al., 2022).

The Malawi Constitution and the CCJPA mandate the courts to inform children of the criminal accusations so that they know the offence and how to defend themselves; the entitlement to legal representation will safeguard the child's rights and ensure adherence to due process while awareness of the right to appeal will afford the child an opportunity to challenge errors that might have transpired during the proceedings of the trial court.

Procedural justice is crucial in the process of legal socialisation. Academics and legislators have deemed it necessary for officials interacting with children in legal proceedings to use person-first language and avoid legalese as well as dehumanising language, such as 'convicts', that could stigmatise or judge a child (Harney et al., 2022; Reid, 2022; Cox, 2020; Bedell et al., 2019). The preference is to use respectful simple language that children can understand and one that fits the cognitive capacities of the children (Tran et al., 2018). Child justice proceedings heavily depend on the judge's exercise of discretion, the informal nature of the process, and the demonstration of empathy (Braun, 2022).

The limited understanding children have of law enforcement and criminal justice underscores the necessity for established fair and unbiased systems (Kilkelly & Pleysier, 2023; Ervo, 2016). *Republic v Balala* exemplifies the challenges children encounter in legal proceedings, from arrest to prosecution and case disposal. The case pertains to a child who was tried by a Magistrate, convicted, and sentenced as a rogue and vagabond after being observed loitering at a trading centre by police on patrol. The High Court reversed the judgment, citing the ambiguous evidence surrounding the child's purpose. The Court noted that the child might have been homeless and vulnerable. The court expressed concern regarding the potential misuse of nuisance-related offences to target destitute individuals without criminal intent. The case reveals that a child's predicament stemmed from three elements: abuse of prosecutorial discretion, poor judicial interpretation by the magistrate, and the unrepresented child's inability to defend himself and appeal.

Methodology

The study used case law to investigate and describe possible violations of detained children's language and procedural rights in Malawi. The focus of the study is on content analysis, emphasising the following keywords: child, police cell, detention, best interest and prison. Regarding data collection, the cases under study are few and include eight judgments from the High Court of Malawi and two judgments from the Malawi Supreme Court of Appeal. Due to the qualitative nature of the study, a sample of ten cases was purposively selected based on the relevance of the text in the judgment to the subject matter, to provide evidence to support the arguments presented. The limited data and methodology present a shortcoming in generalising the results. If an empirical study was done on a greater scale to include magistrates' court judgments, it would give a broader foundation for analysing how children are handled in the criminal justice system.

The primary sources for this study are largely unreported cases from Malawi's Judiciary. The cases were obtained from the High Court Library in Blantyre and accessed online at www.malawilii.org. Additional relevant documentation includes international and regional conventions as well as domestic laws. Academic articles are also used as secondary sources.

Findings

In matters relating to children in legal proceedings and subjected to detention, the courts possess the authority and capability to significantly promote children's rights through judicial decisions (Khamari, 2023; Lonardo, 2022; Japharidze, 2023). The courts in Malawi have addressed various issues involving how duty bearers handle linguistic and procedural rights concerning or impacting detained children. This section reviews selected judgments to understand the court's interpretation and application of linguistic and procedural entitlements for these children within specified thematic areas. These thematic areas include the use of appropriate terminology, placement in appropriate detention facilities, the appointment of suitable magistrates to preside over child justice matters, and the adherence to the child's best interest principle.

Use of appropriate terminology

Four cases will demonstrate how courts have addressed the requirement to use appropriate terminology for children facing criminal proceedings. In *Republic v Children in Detention at Bvumbwe and Kachere Prisons, the Prisons Case*, the court found that inappropriate use of terms, like 'prison' and 'conviction', during legal proceedings can result in children being placed in adult prisons instead of safety homes. *The Prisons Case* involved children detained at Bvumbwe and Kachere Prisons, some of whom were on remand while others were serving sentences. The children challenged the legality of being sentenced and incarcerated in the prisons. The court established that detaining or imprisoning children in facilities not designated as safety homes or reformatory centres is unlawful and violates the rights of children, which prioritise the 'best interests of the child' (Moraa & Gor, 2023; Fambasayi & Moyo, 2020). Child justice courts are prohibited from imposing sentences or detaining children in prison before or following a finding of liability.

The crucial linguistic aspects of the decision appear on page 3 of the judgment where the High Court articulated that child detention before a finding of responsibility in Malawi is restricted to exceptional circumstances and the appropriate facilities under the children's law are a 'safety home' or a 'reformatory centre'. The court noted that under the Prisons Act, the facilities at Bvumbwe and Kachere are classified as 'prisons' and children should not be detained there. The court scrutinised the statutory definitions of safety homes and reformatory centres and concluded that they do not fall under the category of prisons. The court ordered that all detained children be transferred to safety homes or reformatory centres within 30 days.

The second linguistic facet in the preceding case pertains to the court's emphasis that in a court trial, the terms 'finding of guilty', 'conviction', and 'sentence' should not be used to refer to a child (*The Prisons Case*). Instead, upon pronouncing a conviction, the court should 'record that the child is found "responsible" for the offence charged' (*The Prisons Case*).

In *Republic v Michael Khonje*, a 17-year-old was tried before a jury and convicted of murder and a sentence of capital punishment was imposed on him. The High Court reheard the case and recognised the illegality of imposing a death penalty on the juvenile. The judge ordered the child's release from prison since the terms 'sentence' and 'death' were inappropriately used. The court also acknowledged the deplorable conditions within Malawi prisons, highlighting that when an individual is incarcerated, the substandard prison conditions serve as an additional form of punishment. Prisons are, therefore, not appropriate facilities for holding children.

In *Republic v MC*, a teenage boy was convicted of the offence of murder by a jury and sentenced to death. The child 'convict' was detained on death row at Zomba Central Prison until the State President commuted the death sentence to life imprisonment after the judgment in *Francis Kafantayeni v Attorney General* allowed for individualised sentence rehearing. MC was referred to by various stigmatising names while incarcerated, including 'convict', 'lifer', and 'condemned prisoner'. The High Court ordered that any child should not face conviction for any offence and expressions and terms, such as 'finding of guilty', 'convicted', and 'sentence', should never be used in relation to them.

In *Blackson Nkhonjera v Republic*, *The Nkhonjera Case*, the High Court criticised the use of adult terminology and procedures for a 17-year-old child who was convicted and sentenced to a 96-month prison term for defilement. The appeal court substituted inappropriate terms used by the magistrate, such as 'conviction' with 'responsible for the offence charged'. Additionally, the Court replaced the term 'sentence' with an order for the child to be admitted to a 'Reformatory School'.

These decisions show that judicial officers are not integrating child justice linguistic principles in proceedings and judgments. The cases demonstrate the failure of the first-instance courts to promote the child's best interests by complying with the legal requirement to use appropriate child-friendly terminology and not adult language when handling children in conflict with the law. This is an aspect where judicial officers have control, and with continuous judicial training, they may improve in adjusting the language to accommodate children.

Placement of children in (in)appropriate detention facilities

A series of four cases will demonstrate the importance of designating and utilising appropriate terminology and infrastructure for the facility intended for detaining minors involved in legal proceedings. One instrumental case, establishing the unlawfulness of imprisoning children is *Evans Moyo v Attorney General*, *The Moyo Case*. The case illustrates the various challenges experienced by children during legal proceedings. Evance Moyo was arrested for murder at 16 and was remanded in the adult section of Chichiri Maximum Prison for five years before being sentenced to detention at Chilwa Approved School. The High Court released Moyo from the reformatory centre, finding his ten-year detention and imprisonment illegal. The Court emphasised his status as a minor at the time of his arrest and that detaining him with adults before and after his trial was a violation of his rights. The Court underscored the importance of safeguarding a child's welfare and development through regular reviews.

In *The Prisons Case*, however, the Court did not release the children, but instead directed that those detained in inappropriate facilities at Bvumbwe and Kachere Prisons be transferred to safety homes or reformatory centres. In *The*

Frackson Case, three murder suspects, including a 15-year-old child, appealed against the denial of bail by the High Court of Malawi during pre-trial detention at Ntcheu Prison. The Supreme Court of Appeal was concerned with the belated transfer of the child from prison to remand custody at a reformatory centre after nine months of unmonitored unlawful incarceration. The panel of justices highlighted the harmful effects that might have been caused by the prolonged pre-trial detention and the State's negligence in expediting the trial process. Consequently, the court ordered the appellants' release on bail subject to specific conditions.

In *Francis Kapu and Seven Others v The State*, *The Police Cell Case*, eight children who were facing various offences before a child justice court were detained in police custody pending trial. The High Court found that legislation only permitted the detention of children in a safety home and that their detention at Limbe Police Station for periods ranging from two weeks to four months without provision of necessities was not an appropriate environment or in the 'children's best interests'.

These cases serve as palpable manifestations of the 'gap between the law in the books and the law in practice' in the enforcement of children's rights (Ame, 2011, at 272). This study reveals the inadequacies exhibited by prisons and detention facilities in accommodating children in appropriate facilities to the cultural lag phenomenon. As Ame (2011) contends, negative social perceptions obstruct the implementation of rights to children in conflict with the law. Such children are often viewed as undeserving of humane treatment.

Appointment of suitable magistrates to preside over children's cases

The following two cases illustrate the courts' commitment to the standards of magistrates appointed and authorised to preside over criminal cases involving children. In *The State, the Second Grade Magistrate's Court (Thyolo) and Malawi Prison Service, ex parte Stanford Kashuga*, *The Kashuga Case*, a visually impaired boy, who was an accomplice with a 20-year-old suspect, was convicted for the crime of burglary. The boy was sentenced to 48 months' imprisonment by a Child Justice Court and sent to Bvumbwe Prison. He challenged the decision, contending that the magistrate lacked jurisdiction and protective safeguards to try him. Specifically, he objected to being sentenced to imprisonment instead of being directed to a reformatory centre. The High Court ruled that only professional and lay magistrates of the First Grade were conferred with jurisdiction over child justice courts, not the Second Grade Magistrate.

In the *Prisons Case,* the court also determined that magistrates of the Second and Third Grades lacked authority over child justice courts unless specifically designated by the appointing authority. Their orders concerning children were nullified and the court directed retrials before properly constituted child justice courts. Legal errors may adversely impact children by prolonging case resolution and increasing their exposure to the CJS. Further, unsuitable magistrates may have capacity deficiencies that detrimentally influence the quality of proceedings and outcomes.

Application of the principle of 'the best interests of the child'

The notion of prioritising the 'child's best interests' in child detention cases is also a recurring theme across the cases under consideration (Thompson, 2018). The following two cases demonstrate the implementation of this conceptual framework as a procedural standard. The *Kaudzu and four others v Republic, The Kaudzu Case,* pertains to the detention in prison of two children and three adults beyond the statutory prescribed pre-trial custody time limits. The apex court held that the High Court had failed to consider the welfare of the children when denying them bail. A court must evaluate specific factors, such as the children's welfare, separation from negative influences and the potential impact on the justice system from the possible release of the children. Moreover, alternative measures, like supervision, care, family placement, or educational settings should be explored before detention is used 'as a measure of last resort and for the shortest appropriate period of time' (Moraa & Gor, 2023, at 38).

The *Moyo Case* is significant for child justice because it recognises children's entitlements and emphasises the essential premise of prioritising a 'child's best interests'. This includes finding the detention of children in facilities like prisons or police cells illegal. Implementation challenges may arise from magistrates' incapability and resource limitations for alternative measures.

Discussion

The examination of policy documents, reveals that compliance with the global norms in terms of enacting provisions for appropriate language and procedure rights for addressing children facing criminal proceedings has been observed by the State through ratifying conventions. This has been demonstrated in various cases under study, such as *The Kashuga Case, The Kaudzu Case,* and *The Republic v MC* where the judges highlighted the applicable laws and the binding status and applicability of the relevant conventions. Although the idea of children's best interests applies to all legal proceedings, upon closer scrutiny of the legislative implementation of the treaties and laws through the cases under review, discrepancies come to light.

Prohibited and inappropriate terminology in legal proceedings violates the legal entitlements of children

The law requires and underscores the significance of using simple, plain, and person-centred language in legal proceedings involving children in criminal proceedings to cultivate a less stigmatising approach (McLernon, 2017; Bedell et al., 2018). Further, legalese is difficult to comprehend for children; it hinders their effective participation in court proceedings (Smith, 1985; Ashipu & Umukoro, 2014). In addition, the official language of the courts is English, implying that a child undergoing criminal proceedings is entitled to accurate and simple interpretation in a local language he understands (Mphasha & Mutele, 2014; Steytler, 1993; Bakibinga-Gaswaga, 2018). The use of English within a multilingual Malawi presents several challenges, notably the existence of several local languages, alongside the reality that English is not a mother tongue for most children who are also illiterate, necessitating their dependence on proficient interpretation to comprehend the charges and proceedings.

The *Prisons Case, The Republic v MC,* and *The Nkhonjera Case* illustrate the prevalent use of inappropriate terms that label and stigmatise children during criminal proceedings. The statutory law and procedure, in addition to stipulating the necessities for informalities in child justice proceedings, specifically mandate that terms, such as 'convict', 'sentence', and 'guilty', used in adult criminal proceedings are prohibited. In *Republic v MC* and *The Nkhonjera* cases, during the sentence rehearing, the judges pinpointed legal errors in both the substantive and procedural dimensions of the trial, judges' management of the case, particularly in a finding of 'guilt', entering a 'conviction' and subsequently 'sentencing' the child defendants to 'death'. Regarding nomenclature, terms like 'responsible' and 'order' are more appropriate for children who may be detained, as explained in *The Nkhonjera Case.* The study reveals that some judges, magistrates and other justice system officials have flouted this linguistic legal provision, with the appeal and review processes being instrumental in upholding children's language rights.

The findings show that the transformation towards language that is person-first and empowers children has been gradual in judicial proceedings. While some errors may be rectified during the appeal stage, it is difficult to eliminate some harm that might already have affected children, as observed in *The Frackson Case.* Further, the cases under examination demonstrate that interpretation was not an issue before the courts, which could be a potential topic for future research.

Children detained in prisons and police cells

A fundamental child justice concept dictates that before deciding on the detention of a child, the judicial officer or duty-bearer must evaluate alternative options as outlined in *The Kaudzu Case.* The case emphasises that detaining a child in an appropriate facility, such as a safety home or reformatory centre, distinct from the facilities for accused and offenders, such as police custody or prison, should only be considered as a last resort (Fambasayi & Moyo, 2020; Kilkelly & Pleysier, 2023; Du Toit, 2006). Moreover, the decision ought to be informed by the age and vulnerability of the child, ensuring that the chosen placement corresponds with the 'child's best interests' (Moraa & Gor, 2023).

The Police Cell Case and *The Moyo Case* illuminate the interplay between linguistic aspects and procedural obstacles faced by prosecutors and judicial officers when deciding the detention arrangements for children. The legislation prohibits the imposition of sentences or detention of children in prison before or following a finding of liability, instead directing that children found responsible may only be detained in a 'safety home' or a 'reformatory centre' as a last resort. It is imperative to provide special consideration to children, as prisons are inappropriate environments for detaining children. The Court in *Gable Masangano v Attorney General* determined that prison congestion falls short of minimum international standards and breaches human rights.

The reviewed cases highlight situations where children were improperly detained in unsuitable facilities like police cells, as evidenced in the legal proceedings in *The Police Cell Case* and prisons, as demonstrated in *The Moyo Case* and *The Prisons Case*. The court ruled that Moyo's detention at Chichiri Prison before and during his trial was illegal, as the law regards prison facilities as inappropriate environments for children. The series of three cases challenging the detention of children in prisons and police cells, which include the *Moyo Case* of 2009, *The Prisons Case* of 2018 and *The Police Cell Case* of 2021 exposes systemic inefficiencies in managing children in the justice system. It is characterised by recurrent non-compliance with court orders prohibiting the detention of children in prisons. The attempt in *The Police Cell Case* to detain children in police cells, possibly due to a lack of appropriate facilities, was likewise found illegal, as the law explicitly states that children can only be detained in safety homes or reformatory centres.

Cultural lag is most pronounced under the third thematic area on placement in appropriate detention facilities. In *The Police Cell Case*, the court found that the Minister for children's welfare as a duty bearer, neglected her statutory duty by failing to designate or establish facilities or institutions as public safety homes for children. The High Court directed the Minister to fulfil this requirement within 30 days, along with ordering the release of the children. Failure by duty bearers to discharge their responsibilities, such as designating or establishing safety homes or reformatory centres several years after the statutes and treaties became operational, signifies a lack of accountability among these officials.

Procedural injustice

The research findings reveal that conducting a jury trial in *Republic v MC* and *Republic v Khonje* was procedurally improper, leading to a miscarriage of justice by imposing a death penalty on the children. *The Kaudzu Case* and *The Frackson Case* also demonstrate procedural violations of children's entitlements by indeterminately imprisoning children and housing children with adult offenders, highlighting the importance of legal assistance for children in criminal proceedings which is often lacking in magistrates' courts. Legal representation is crucial in defending children's rights although it was not an issue in these cases and could be a topic for further research.

'The best interests of the child'

The chapter endeavoured to investigate the research questions by focusing on thematic areas. However, the results indicate that issues, such as appropriate terminology, detention in proper facilities, and the magistrates handling child justice cases are interconnected and mutually reinforce each other to promote 'the child's best interests' (Sormunen, 2020). The High Court's adoption of a rights-based approach in *The Prisons Case* demonstrates the advancement of detained children's rights by establishing that magistrates of the Second or Third Grades lack jurisdiction over child justice courts. The Case also discusses the importance of appropriate detention facilities for children, utilising child-friendly language in judicial proceedings, and prioritising 'the best interests of the child' (Fambasayi & Moyo, 2020) by restricting the duration a child spends in a facility to prevent indefinite stays.

Conclusion

The chapter aimed to investigate how duty-bearers in Malawi might breach the language and procedural entitlements of children involved in criminal proceedings and detained in police cells and prisons. An analysis of court decisions indicates that initial duty bearers manage these children in a manner that deviates from the requirements of the relevant statutes and processes. The results reveal unauthorised magistrates adjudicating child justice cases, the use of prohibited and inappropriate terminology, and the detention of children in prohibited and inappropriate facilities. These infringe upon the rights of these children and fail to promote their best interests. Consequently, the interpretation and meaning of the international conventions and domestic legal texts do not correspond with the actual practices. The practices within the criminal justice sector do not meet the established international benchmarks that the country has ratified and incorporated into its legal framework (Kilkelly & Pleysier, 2023).

To transform the system, it is important for justice sector duty bearers to be knowledgeable of the linguistic provisions and adopt comprehensible plain language for children's understanding and participation in legal proceedings, while also employing person-centred language to eliminate stigma for children facing criminal proceedings (Van der Houwen & Jol, 2017; van Domselaar, 2022). Applying inclusive and child-friendly language is crucial for dismantling barriers and enhancing the welfare of children involved in legal proceedings (Berrick et al., 2018). Further, the UN Committee on the Rights of the Child should urge Malawi policymakers to fulfil its obligations under the CRC and CCPJA.

References

Acconciamessa, L. (2020). Bringing the child's procedural rights before the ECtHR through interpretative tools: Access to justice, participation and representation. In P.

Czech, L. Heschl, K. Lukas, M. Nowak, & G. Oberleitner (Eds.), *European yearbook on human rights 2020* (pp. 49–78). Intersentia.
Ame, R. K. (2011). The rights of children in conflict with the law in Ghana. *The International Journal of Children's Rights*, *19*(2), 271–293.
Ashipu, K. B. C., & Umukoro, G. M. (2014). A critique of the language of law in selected court cases in Nigeria. *Mediterranean Journal of Social Sciences*, *5*(8), 622–626.
Bakibinga-Gaswaga, E. (2018). Unpacking legal pluralism in commonwealth Africa–towards strengthening methods for rule of law programming for development. *Law and Development Review*, *11*(2), 277–332.
Banda, L. C. G., & Carlson, J. (2022). Malawi's Marriage Law (2015) and Constitutional Amendment (2017): Human rights based analysis of policy solutions to increase girls' rights. *The Journal of Sociology & Social Welfare*, *49*, 4.
Bedell, P. S., So, M., Morse, D. S., Kinner, S. A., Ferguson, W. J., & Spaulding, A. C. (2019). Corrections for academic medicine: The importance of using person-first language for individuals who have experienced incarceration. *Academic Medicine*, *94*(2), 172–175.
Bedell, P. S., Spaulding, A. C., So, M., & Sarrett, J. C. (2018). The names have been changed to protect the . . . humanity: Person-first language in correctional health epidemiology. *American Journal of Epidemiology*, *187*(6), 1140–1142.
Berrick, J. D., Dickens, J., Pösö, T., & Skivenes, M. (2018). International perspectives on child-responsive courts. *The International Journal of Children's Rights*, *26*(2), 251–277.
Birckhead, T. R. (2009). Toward a theory of procedural justice for juveniles. *Buffalo Law Review*, *57*, 1447–1513.
Braun, M. (2022). The transition towards child-friendly communication in the justice system: And you, are you listening to me? In M. Paré, M. Bruning, T. Moreau, & C. Siffrein-Blanc (Eds.), *Children's access to justice: A critical assessment* (pp. 183–196). Intersentia.
Chirwa, D. M. (2007). Upholding the sanctity of rights: A principled approach to limitations and derogations under the Malawian constitution. *Malawi Law Journal*, *1*(1), 3–32.
Chirwa, D. M., & Kaime, T. (2008). Where are the missing pieces? Constructing a mosaic of the CRC and the African children's charter in Malawi's law and policy. *Malawi Law Journal*, *2*(1), 85–114.
Chirwa, S. O. (2022). *The other child: The plight of the boy child in the context of defilement in Malawi* [Master's dissertation, University of Pretoria].
Chitha, M. F. (2024). Malawi's legislative integration and the court's interpretation and application of 'the best interests of the child' principle vis-à-vis international and regional standards. *Kenyatta University Journal of Children's Rights*, *1*(1), 84–111.
Coppins, V., Casey, S., & Campbell, A. (2011). The child's best interest: A review of Australian juvenile justice legislation. *The Open Criminology Journal*, *4*(Suppl 1-M1), 23–31.
Cox, A. (2020). The language of incarceration. *Incarceration*, *1*(1), 1–13.
Deuchar, R., &Bhopal, K. (2017). The judiciary, system processing and youth (in) justice. In *Young people and social control: Problems and prospects from the margins* (pp. 99–123). Palgrave Macmillan.
Du Toit, C. (2006). A measure of last resort? Child offenders and life imprisonment. *SA Crime Quarterly*, *17*, 13–18.
Enujioke, S. C., Aalsma, M. C., Meagher, C. G., Hunt, A., Hensley, M. M., & Ott, M. A. (2023). Perception of procedural justice amongst previously incarcerated youth: Procedural justice in incarcerated youth. *International Journal of Offender Therapy and Comparative Criminology*, 0, 1–16. doi: 10.1177/0306624X231159878 Published online March 9, 2023.
Ervo, L. (2016). Facing people through language use–linguistic tools to make proceedings fair. *International Journal of Legal Discourse*, *1*(2), 277–293.

Fambasayi, R., & Moyo, A. (2020). The best interests of the child offender in the context of detention as a measure of last resort: A comparative analysis of legal developments in South Africa, Kenya and Zimbabwe. *South African Journal on Human Rights, 36*(1), 25–48.
Fernández-Molina, E., Bermejo, M., & Baz, O. (2021). Observing juvenile courtrooms: Testing the implementation of guidelines on child-friendly justice in Spain. *Youth Justice, 21*(2), 192–209.
Hansen, T. T. (2002). Implementation of international human rights standards through the national courts in Malawi. *Journal of African Law, 46*(1), 31–42.
Harney, B. L., Korchinski, M., Young, P., Scow, M., Jack, K., Linsley, P., Bodkin, C., Brothers, T. D., Curtis, M., Higgs, P., Mead, T. S., Hart, A., Kilroy, D., Bonn, M., & Bartlett, S. R. (2022). It is time for us all to embrace person-centred language for people in prison and people who were formerly in prison. *The International Journal of Drug Policy, 99*, 103455.
Haydon, D. (2020). Detained children: Vulnerability, violence and violation of rights. *International Journal for Crime, Justice and Social Democracy, 9*(4), 16–30.
Hodgson, J. (2024). Institutionalised violence and child imprisonment in England and Wales: A case for abolition. *Justice, Power and Resistance, 7*(1), 21–38.
Japaridze, M. (2023). The best interests of the child in the case law of the European courts: Experience for EU member states and candidate countries. *International Comparative Jurisprudence (Online), 9*(1), 24–38.
Kadilu, M. (2017). *Protecting the rights of detained juvenile delinquents: Tanzania's compliance with international standards* [Doctoral dissertation, Acharya Nagarjuna University].
Kaime, T. (2005). The convention on the rights of the child and the cultural legitimacy of children's rights in Africa: Some reflections. *African Human Rights Law Journal, 5*(2), 221–238.
Kaime, T. (2009). The foundations of rights in the African charter on the rights and welfare of the child: A historical and philosophical account. *African Journal of Legal Studies, 3*(1), 120–136.
Kamwendo, E. (2009). *The invisible prisoners: A case of children in Malawian prisons* [Master's dissertation, Lund University].
Kanyuka, M. (1989). Social control and punishment of young offenders in Malawi. *Acta Criminologica: African Journal of Criminology & Victimology, 2*(1), 66–76.
Khamari, A. (2023). Rehabilitation and social reintegration of children in need of care and protection: A comprehensive analysis. *Journal of Emerging Technologies and Innovative Research, 10*(9), 77–85.
Kilkelly, U., Forde, L., Lambert, S., & Swirak, K. (2023). *Children in conflict with the law: Rights, research and progressive youth justice*. Springer Nature.
Kilkelly, U., & Pleysier, S. (2023). Rights of the child in the child justice system. *Youth Justice, 23*(2), 135–139.
Kupchik, A. (2003). Prosecuting adolescents in criminal courts: Criminal or juvenile justice? *Social Problems, 50*(3), 439–460.
Lonardo, L. (2022). The best interests of the child in the case law of the court of justice of the European Union. *Maastricht Journal of European and Comparative Law, 29*(5), 596–614.
Lount, S. A., Hand, L., Purdy, S. C., & France, A. (2018). Tough talk: Youth offenders' perceptions of communicating in the youth justice system in New Zealand. *Australian & New Zealand Journal of Criminology, 51*(4), 593–618.
Marwandana, A. Z., Muchtar, S., & Azisa, N. (2022). Detention of children in conflict with the law in the child criminal justice system. *International Journal of Health Sciences, 6*, 1455–1467.
Matczak, M. (2018). Why judicial formalism is incompatible with the rule of law. *Canadian Journal of Law & Jurisprudence, 31*(1), 61–85.

McLernon, S. (2017). Why courts need to embrace plain language. *Georgetown Journal on Poverty Law & Policy, 24*(3), 381–399.

Moraa, T., & Gor, G. (2023). The nexus between the best interests of the child and detention of children in conflict with the law. *Kabarak Journal of Law and Ethics, 7*, 25–51.

Mphasha, L. E., & Mutele, T. C. (2014). Challenges facing the accused in the use of English only in criminal court proceedings: Experiences from the Vhembe District, Limpopo Province, South Africa. *Journal of Social Sciences (Delhi, India), 41*(3), 385–394.

Mwambene, L., & Mawondza, O. (2017). Children's rights standards and child marriage in Malawi. *African Studies Quarterly, 17*(3), 21–44.

Odala, V. (2012). Childhood under Malawian laws as the constitution becomes of age. *Malawi Law Journal, 6*(1), 97–120.

Peeler, K. R., Hampton, K., Lucero, J., & Ijadi-Maghsoodi, R. (2020). Sleep deprivation of detained children: Another reason to end child detention. *Health and Human Rights, 22*(1), 317–320.

Rap, S. (2016). A children's rights perspective on the participation of juvenile defendants in the youth court. *The International Journal of Children's Rights, 24*(1), 93–112.

Reid, L. (2022). The language of incarceration and of persons subject to incarceration. *Public Health Ethics, 15*(2), 191–193.

Ruggiero, J. A. (2018). Culture, change, and cultural lag: A commentary and a challenge. *Sociology Between the Gaps: Forgotten and Neglected Topics, 3*(1), 1–3.

Smith, T. F. (1985). Law talk: Juveniles' understanding of legal language. *Journal of Criminal Justice, 13*(4), 339–353.

Sormunen, M. (2020). Understanding the best interests of the child as a procedural obligation: The example of the European court of human rights. *Human Rights Law Review, 20*(4), 745–768.

Stalford, H., & Hollingsworth, K. (2020). "This case is about you and your future": Towards judgments for children. *Modern Law Review, 83*(5), 1030–1058.

Steytler, N. C. (1993). Implementing language rights in court: The role of the court interpreter. *South African Journal on Human Rights, 9*(2), 205–222.

Suri, T. (2019). "Do you understand these charges?": How procedural communication in youth criminal justice court violates the rights of young offenders in Canada. *Semiotica, 2019*(229), 173–191.

Thompson, A. (2018). "The ins cannot simply send them off into the night": The language of detention in US court cases on migrant child detention. *PlatForum, 16*, 79–97.

Tosouni, A. (2014). "We're not supposed to have nothing in here": Life in juvenile jail through the voices of incarcerated girls. *Criminology, Criminal Justice, Law & Society, 15*, 60.

Tran, N. T., Baggio, S., Dawson, A., O'Moore, É., Williams, B., Bedell, P., Simon, O., Scholten, W., Getaz, L., & Wolff, H (2018). Words matter: A call for humanizing and respectful language to describe people who experience incarceration. *BMC International Health and Human Rights, 18*(1), 41.

Van den Brink, Y. (2019). Young, accused and detained; awful, but lawful? Pre-trial detention and children's rights protection in contemporary western societies. *Youth Justice, 19*(3), 238–261.

van der Houwen, F., & Jol, G. (2017). Juvenile court: Creating (an atmosphere of) understanding. *Language and Law, 4*(1), 34–59.

Van Domselaar, I. (2022). 'Plain' legal language by courts: Mere clarity, an expression of civic friendship or a masquerade of violence? *The Theory and Practice of Legislation, 10*(1), 93–111.

Conventions

The African Charter on the Rights and Welfare of the Child (ACRWC), Adopted by the 26th Ordinary Session of the Assembly of Heads of State and Government of the OAU Addis Ababa, Ethiopia – July 1990. Entered into force on 29 November 1999.

The United Nations Convention on the Rights of the Child (CRC): 1989. Adopted by the UN General Assembly Resolution 44/25 of 20 November 1989 and entered into force on 2 September 1990.

The United Nations Standard Minimum Rules for the Administration of Juvenile Justice (The Beijing Rules') Adopted by General Assembly resolution 40/33 of 29 November 1985.

Statutes

The Child Care Protection and Justice Act, Chapter 26:03 of the Laws of Malawi (29 July 2010).

The Constitution Act 20 of 1994, Laws of Malawi (16 May 1994).

The Criminal Procedure and Evidence Code (CPEC), Act 36 of 1967 Laws of Malawi.

The Penal Code, Chapter 7:01 of the Laws of Malawi (1 April 1930).

Theme 2

Witnesses with disability

5 Whose access to justice? Civil procedure rules and the right of access to justice for persons with disability in the High Court of Malawi

Thokozani Soko and Wellman Kondowe

Introduction

The right to access justice has recently attracted attention in international human rights law (Fina et al., 2017). It is a key to realising the human rights of marginalised and vulnerable groups, including persons with disabilities (Fina et al., 2017). The right of access to justice is enshrined in Article 13 of the United Nations Convention on the Rights of Persons with Disabilities (UNCRPD) (United Nations, 2008). It states that

> state parties shall ensure adequate access to justice for persons with disabilities on an equal basis with others through the provision of procedure and age-appropriate accommodations to facilitate their influential roles as direct and indirect participants as witnesses in all legal proceedings, including at investigative and other preliminary stages.
>
> (United Nations, 2008)

The Protocol to the African Charter on Human and Peoples' Rights on the Rights of Persons with Disabilities in Africa provides the right of access to justice in Article 13. This article also recognises customary law processes as part of access to justice and legal assistance for persons with disabilities (African Union, 2018). Malawi ratified the UNCRPD in 2009 and signed the protocol in 2022. In Malawi, access to justice is provided under section 41 (2) of the Constitution of the Republic of Malawi, in which every person has the right of access to any court of law or any other tribunal for acts violating the rights and freedoms granted by him or her by the Constitution or any other law (Constitution of the Republic of Malawi, 1995). It further states that every person has the right to an effective remedy (Constitution of the Republic of Malawi, 1995, s. 41 (3)). The Constitution also recognises that every person is equal before the law, regardless of the status of that particular person (Constitution of the Republic of Malawi, 1995, s. 41 (1)). In addition, the Persons with Disability Act 2024 provides that persons with disabilities have the right of access to justice and includes the obligations of the Court, such as providing

DOI: 10.4324/9781003569435-8

various accommodations to PWDS. Previously, the 2012 Disability Act, which the 2024 Persons with Disability Act replaced, did not provide for the right of access to justice.

Malawi's court structure compromises of Subordinate Courts, the High Court, and the Supreme Court of Appeal (Constitution of the Republic of Malawi, 1995, ss. 106, 108, 110). Securing legal remedies before these Courts requires following the procedure rules – civil procedure rules and criminal procedure rules. This chapter focuses on the civil procedure rules provided under the Courts (High Court Civil Procedure) Rules (CRP). The Chief Justice makes these rules with the authority granted by the Courts Act (Courts Act, Chapter 3:02, Laws of Malawi, s. 67).

Despite efforts to construct an equitable legal system, the High Court of Malawi's civil procedure rules contain intrinsic barriers that impede people with disabilities from properly accessing justice. These rules exclude people with disabilities in a variety of ways, such as denying litigation capacity, requiring inaccessible document formats, failing to recognise and accommodate diverse linguistic needs, including Sign Language and alternative forms of communication, imposing disproportionate financial burdens, and privileging oral English communication over other modes of expression. These barriers not only create practical obstacles, but also reinforce linguistic discrimination, collectively contradicting the principles of equal access and linguistic rights outlined in international conventions, such as the UNCRPD and undermining the fundamental right of persons with disabilities to fully participate in legal proceedings.

Against this background, this chapter examines the civil procedure rules in the High Court of Malawi to determine if they provide for access to justice for PWDs. The first part of the chapter outlines the Human Rights Model of disability, which the chapter adopted as an analytical framework. It will also distinguish this Model from other models of disability. The second part outlines the concept of access to justice, the third part gives an overview of the High Court Civil Procedure Rules, and the fourth part discusses PWDs' challenges when applying the civil procedure rules. The final part proposes the way forward.

The Human Rights Model

The Human Rights Model (HRM) of disability regards human dignity as a central principle of human rights (Degener, 2016). In this model, every person is viewed as important and valued. The human rights paradigm emphasises the innate dignity of each person, with regard solely to their medical characteristics (Degener, 2016). The individual is given autonomy and choices; most importantly, the problem is in society (Degener, 2016). In other words, the HRM views PWDs as subjects of the law and not objects of charity (Hwang et al., 2024). There are three fundamental elements of human rights (Brosnan, 2017). Firstly, human rights are considered equal, which means every person has them by being human (Brosnan, 2017). Secondly, human rights are inalienable, which means they cannot be taken away. Finally, human rights are universal, entailing that every person has the same rights.

The UNCRPD was the first treaty for PWDs that follows the human rights approach, as manifested in Article 1, which states that the purpose of the Convention is to 'promote, protect and ensure the full equal enjoyment of all human rights and fundamental freedoms by all persons with disabilities and to promote respect for their inherent dignity' (United Nations, 2008, p. 3). Before the UNCRPD, human rights treaties, such as the Universal Declaration of Human Rights, the International Covenant on Civil and Political Rights, and the International Covenant on Economic Social and Cultural Rights did not specifically refer to PWDs, as they were regarded as another status, which would be seen as an indication that the International Community considered persons with disabilities to be of lesser worth than other people (Basser, 2011). As a result, PWDs would claim protection under the law based on another identity, such as race and gender, which left them without hope as the treaties did not address the specific needs and obstacles that PWDs faced (Van Weele, 2012).

The HRM is a departure from the Medical Model, which regards disability as an impairment that needs to be prevented and cured through medical or biological involvement (Roeher institute, 1996). The medical model of disability places the problem in the individual, and the reason for the exclusion is seen in the person's impairment (Degener, 2016). Oliver (1990) prefers to describe it as an Individual Model and treats medicalisation as one aspect of the Individual Model. He reasons that the Individual Model locates the problem in the individual and states that the problem results from the functional limitations of the body or mind arising from the disability (Oliver, 1990). The Medical/Individual Model has been condemned for its negative impact on the human rights of PWDs since they are seen as objects of charity who need shelter and care, justifying the creation of segregated surroundings for disabled persons, such as special schools, living institutions, or sheltered workshops (Degener, 2016).

Preceding the HRM was the Social Model, which found its genesis in the statement of the Union of Physically Impaired Against Segregation (UPIAS) and the Disability Alliance's activists, which states:

> In our view, it is a society that disables physically impaired people. Disability is imposed on top of our impairments by how we are unnecessarily isolated and excluded from full participation in society. Disabled people are, therefore, an oppressed group in society.
>
> (The Union of the Physically Impaired Against Segregation and The Disability Alliance, 1976)

Unlike the Medical Model, the Social Model suggests that disability is oppression by society, not an impairment (Shakespeare, 2002). The Social Model has been commended for its stratagem to break the barricades that PWDs encounter in society and promote their inclusion (Shakespeare, 2002). Additionally, it has been used to emancipate PWDs because they do not perceive themselves as the problem, but as the society (Shakespeare, 2002).

Much as both models recognise that society oppresses PWDs, the Human Rights Model acknowledges that every person is entitled to human rights and every person has dignity regardless of their body status, unlike the Social Model, which excludes impairment as the cause of disability (Degener, 2016). Degener (2016) articulates that 'human rights do not require the absence of impairment for one to be recognised as a right holder' (p. 3).

In addition, the HRM incorporates both civil and political rights and social, cultural, and economic rights, which are essential for every person. The Social Model focuses only on anti-discrimination law and civil rights, a partial solution to the challenge (Degener, 2016). Besides, the HRM recognises human variations, unlike the Social Model, which isolates itself from the issue of impairment (Degener, 2016).

Further, the HRM encompasses manifold human identities, unlike the Social Model, which does not recognise identities (Degener, 2016). For example, a disabled person might be visually impaired or one with mental impairment. Besides, PWDs might be women, men, or children (Degener, 2016). Different identities are included under the HRM, and all are accorded human rights. The preamble of the UNCRPD provides an example that recognises diversity even within persons with disabilities (United Nations, 2008).

Critics of the Human Rights Model argue that the human rights approach fails to recognise people's ability to pursue their freedoms, especially PWDs who need protection from harm or material deprivation (Brosnan, 2017). They also argue that the model sets out the rights of PWDs and the duties of the party states without giving practical guidance on how the same should be implemented and enforced (Barnes & Oliver, 2012). Consequently, they contend that it has had no impact on securing political rights for persons with disabilities within and across the states (Barnes & Oliver, 2012).

Access to justice and people with disabilities

The term 'access to justice' connects two concepts, access and justice. Full understanding of the concept of access to justice, therefore requires an understanding of both concepts (Nkhata, 2020). The term access to justice is challenging to define as it focuses on two objectives of the legal system; the system by which people may claim their rights or resolve their disputes under the general auspices of the state and the system that is equally accessible to all and leads to outcomes that are individually and socially just (Flynn, 2015). In applying it to disability, access to justice is a broad concept. It encompasses people's adequate access to the systems, procedures, information, and locations used to administer justice (Bekele et al., 2018). There are three components of access to justice. The first component is substantive access to justice, which is concerned with evaluating the claims to rights that individuals seeking redress may make (Bahdi, 2007). It zeroes in on the 'content of the legal rules and principles which shape the decisions about those who make a justice claim' (Flynn, 2015, p. 13). Flynn (2015) argues that it goes beyond the court rulings and hinges on the laws that promote substantive equality. Further, developing a law that promotes equality can only be achieved if disadvantaged people are involved. In the context of disability, involvement and participation are required (Flynn, 2015).

The second component is the procedural access to justice. According to Bahdi (2007), this means institutions where one might bring a claim, the rules governing the complaint and the parties' conduct once the complaint is brought within that particular institution, and the external factors that impact the nature and calibre of the encounter for individuals within that specific legal institution. Zietlow (1998) describes it as a means of administering justice. In the disability realm, it means removing barriers that hinder PWDs from bringing claims to court and participating in court proceedings (Flynn & Lawson, 2013). It goes beyond disputes or court proceedings and extends to structures, such as schools, residential claims, and working institutions that give rise to court claims (Flynn & Lawson, 2013). The third is symbolic justice, an 'approach which steps outside doctrinal law and asks whatever a particular legal regime promotes citizens' belonging and empowerment' (Flynn, 2015).

Access to justice in the UNCRPD

The United Nations Assembly adopted the United Nations Convention on the Rights of Persons with Disabilities in 2006 (Kayess & French, 2008). The objective of the UNCRPD is to 'promote, protect and ensure the full and equal enjoyment of all human rights and fundamental freedoms by all persons with disabilities, and to promote respect for their inherent dignity' (United Nations [UN], 2008, Art. 1). Persons with disabilities in the UNCRPD include those who have 'long-term physical, mental, intellectual or sensory impairments, which in interaction with various barriers may hinder their full and effective participation in society on an equal basis with others' (UN, 2006, Art. 1). The UNCRPD is a paradigm shift from the Medical Model of disability, which views PWDs as a problem, to the Human Rights Model, which views persons with disabilities as rights holders (Degener, 2016). Article 13 of the UNCRPD provides the right of access to justice. The drafters intended to give rights that were already existing, so they had no mandate to create new rights (Flynn, 2018). This means that the right of access to justice was familiar, although it was the first to be explicitly provided in the International Human Rights Convention (Flynn, 2018).

The right of access to justice under Article 13 has elements. The first is adequate access to justice. Flynn (2018) explains that in the context of disability, this is when the requirements for PWDs are fulfilled. An example is where reasonable accommodation is needed. Besides, legal representation and legal aid for persons with disabilities are prerequisites for adequate access to justice (Flynn, 2018).

Another element is equality with others. PWDs must be given the same opportunity to access justice as non-disabled persons (Flynn, 2018). In other words, persons with disabilities must not be discriminated against on the grounds of disability when accessing justice in various systems (Ortoleva, 2011). This also resonates with Article 5 of the UNCRPD, which prohibits discrimination based on disability and guarantees that PWDs have equal protection and benefits before the law (UN, 2006). The provision also discusses procedural accommodation as one element to achieving access to justice, defined as 'necessary and appropriate modifications and adjustments to ensure the participation of PWDs on an equal basis with others'. Unlike reasonable accommodations, procedural accommodations are not limited by the concept of disproportionate or undue burden (United Nations, 2020).

In Africa, the right of access to justice is provided under article 13 of the Protocol to the African Charter on Human and Peoples' Rights on the Rights of Persons with Disabilities (The African Disability Protocol), which calls for state parties to ensure equal access to justice for PWDS by providing procedural, age and gender accommodations and making customary law processes inclusive. Besides, it emphasises the need for training for all law enforcement and justice personnel, including legal aid. Unlike the UNCRPD, the Charter provides for a more detailed and expansive interpretation of access to justice, offering more guidance to the implementation. In Malawi, the right of access to justice is provided in section 32 of the Persons with Disability Act 2024, which ensures that persons with disabilities have the right to access justice tailored to their needs, requiring courts and tribunals to conduct proceedings in accessible locations, provide reasonable accommodations, including various communication formats, and make necessary adjustments to enable full participation of persons with disabilities in legal proceedings. While the Act addresses court accessibility and communication accommodations, it lacks comprehensive coverage of the justice system. Notable omissions include training for legal personnel, age-appropriate accommodations, legal aid, and customary law considerations. The provision also falls short in addressing awareness-raising and fails to explicitly state that accommodations should be provided at no cost. These gaps limit its effectiveness in ensuring full access to justice for persons with disabilities across all contexts and stages of legal proceedings. Besides, the 2024 Persons with Disability Act does not specifically recognise the legal capacity of persons with disabilities.

Access to justice for PWDs and Civil Procedure Rules

The Civil Procedure Rules for the High Court of Malawi are codified in the Courts (High Court Civil Procedure) Rules (CPR). The rules were enacted in June 2017. The regulations govern the procedure in the High Court Civil Division, Commercial Division, Revenue Division, and Financial Crimes Division, where civil claims are filed (Courts Act S 6A). The civil claim involves an allegation by one or more private-party claimants against one or more other party defendants engaged in, or perhaps failed to engage in, conduct that resulted in harm or injury to the claimant and for which that party seeks some redress (Croley, 2017). However, Ortoleva (2011) notes that the law can defend the rights of PWDs by allowing them to pursue their claims through courts. At the same time, the law also perpetuates the inequalities that PWDs face in the justice system, including the courts (Ortoleva, 2011). This chapter argues that the exclusion of PWDs in the Civil Procedure Rules highlights the challenges faced by PWDs in accessing justice in Malawi, requiring reform to promote a more inclusive and rights-based approach.

Commencing proceedings and legal capacity for persons with intellectual disabilities

The Civil Procedure Rules define a person with a disability as a child or a person who does not understand the nature and possible consequences of the proceeding, who is incapable of conducting the proceedings due to a physical disability or another form of disability, or who is incapable of giving instructions for the conduct of the proceeding (Courts (High Court) (Civil Procedure) Rules, 2017, Order 1, Rule 4). Under Order 6 Rule 19 of the CPR, a person with disabilities who falls under Order 1 Rule 4 can only commence an action through a litigation guardian whom the court appoints (Courts (High Court) (Civil Procedure) Rules, 2017). One group that is represented by *guardian ad litem* is persons with intellectual disabilities. The justification for excluding persons with intellectual disabilities from commencing the matter is found in the words of Lord Justice Chadwick in the *Masterman-Lister case (Masterman-Lister v Brutton & Co* (Nos 1 and 2)) [2002] EWCA Civ 1889 where he stated that:

> The pursuit and defense of legal proceedings are juristic acts only by persons with the necessary mental capacity. The court is concerned not only with protecting its process but also with protecting both parties to litigation. A defendant is entitled to expect that he will not be required to defend proceedings brought against him by a person of unsound mind acting without a next friend.
>
> (para. 65)

While the Masterman-Lister case established a precedent in English Law, the European Court of Human Rights also grappled with a similar issue of litigation capacity in *R.P. and Others v United Kingdom* (App no. 38245/08) [2012] ECHR 1796. In that case, the claimant challenged the decision of the Court that she lacked litigation capacity and, therefore, a solicitor was appointed on her behalf. In that case, it was held that the right of access to justice was not absolute and is subject to limitations, which are permitted by implication since the right of access to justice requires regulations that may vary from jurisdiction to jurisdiction due to the needs and resources of the particular jurisdiction. The Court continued to state that the State and Court, by coming up with such regulations, enjoy a certain margin of appreciation to enable them to make the relevant procedural arrangements to secure the excellent administration of Justice and protect the health of the person concerned.

The challenge that PWDs face is the lack of legal capacity to commence actions before a court because of their lack of cognitive abilities. Legal capacity is the ability to be a holder of rights (legal status) and an actor of rights (legal agent) (Flynn & Arstein-Kerslake, 2014). People with intellectual disabilities often face denial of legal capacity based on the notion that it should be evaluated according to one's ability to reason and understand, which is essentially mental capacity (Smith, 2022). This implies that cognitive capacity is crucial in determining whether an individual should be granted legal capacity.

Several approaches have been developed to assess mental capacity. The first is the status approach. According to Dhanda (2007), once a person is diagnosed with a disability or impairment, the law presumes a lack of capacity. This method infers incapacity from the medical impairment diagnosis (Flynn & Arstein-Kerslake, 2014). Dhanda (2007) notes that this approach has influenced legal formulations, resulting in laws that declare individuals with disabilities incapable of performing certain activities. The second is the outcome approach. In this method, an individual's legal capacity is rejected if they make what is perceived as a poor decision (Flynn & Arstein-Kerslake, 2014). For instance, if an individual undergoing psychiatric treatment decides to discontinue the treatment, their capacity may be questioned (Dhanda, 2007). The functional approach is the third and most widely adopted approach in many jurisdictions (Flynn & Arstein-Kerslake, 2014). This method assesses whether a person with an impairment or disturbance in the functioning of the mind or brain understands the decision and its reasonably foreseeable consequences (Flynn & Arstein-Kerslake, 2014). Many court jurisdictions, like in the preceding cases, adopt these discriminatory approaches, which leads to substituted decision-making. Likewise, the CPR adopted the status and functional approach to strip PWDs' litigation capacity, contrary to Article 12 of the UNCRPD, which provides them legal capacity (United Nations Convention on the Rights of Persons with Disabilities [CRPD], 2008). It is also contrary to Article 13 of the UNCRPD since the lack of litigation capacity excludes the PWDs from pursuing their claims or seeking remedies before the Court as someone with legal status and legal agency under Article 12 of the UNCRPD. Flynn (2018) notes that the *guardian ad litem*, a substitute decision-maker, may not present the party's interest in seeking remedies before the Court. Besides, the person's view is not considered since his mental capacity is questioned (Flynn, 2018). As a result, the *guardian ad litem* presents what he thinks is in the best interest of the PWDs rather than the PWD's will and preference.

This was emphasised in the UN principles and guidelines of access to justice when it was stated that:

> When legal capacity is removed from a person, substitute decision-makers (i.e., guardians, *guardians ad litem*, attorneys, or experts) are appointed by someone other than the persons concerned against their will, or decisions are made by substitute decision-makers based on the 'best interests' of the person's concerned, as opposed to being based on the will and preferences of such persons
>
> (United Nations, 2020)

Weller (2016) argues that Critical theory's reinterpretation of the UNCRPD challenges the idea of human identity solely based on abstract reasoning or rationality. Weller (2016) further argues that modern philosophy recognises humans' social, cultural, and emotional makeup, so accepting relational autonomy implies a different interpretation of Article 12 (2) of the CRPD, which challenges the notion that only individuals with reasonable and independent thinking have legal authority. Weller (2016) argues that the legal system must consider each individual's subjective reality.

Summons, documents and persons with visual impairment

The civil procedure requires the claimant or the legal practitioner to sign the summons (Order 5 Rule 1 of the CPR). However, the claimant with visual impairment will need the provision of a braille to sign the summons. The format of the summons is provided in the CPR in form one, and it is not favourable for persons with visual impairment since it does not exist in braille format. This entails that the CPR excludes persons with visual impairment from participating as direct parties to the proceedings since they would not sign the summons (Nkhata, 2020). In addition, Order 10 of the CPR states that the claimant or the legal practitioner shall sign any application filed to the Court by the claimant (Order 10 Rule 2 (1)(a) of the CPR). Like in summons, the application form provided under form 4 is not disability friendly. One might argue that persons with visual impairment are not excluded as direct participants since the rules allow the legal practitioner to sign the summons or the application on their behalf. However, Nkhata (2016) notes that for many lawyers, providing legal services to persons with disabilities can be an insult to their ignorance, and many lawyers regard it as inconvenient since they do not understand the needs of persons with disabilities unless the lawyer knows disability issues. Flynn (2018) notes that the key barrier to access to justice for people with disabilities is the lack of lawyers who have sufficient knowledge, training, and awareness to address the legal issues they are facing. As a result, people with disabilities are left hopeless without effective legal representation in court, resulting in a denial of access to justice in the court of law.

The Civil Procedure Rules (CPR) are clear that service of summons or any document must be personal on a defendant. This was emphasised in the case of *Malawi Communications Regulatory Authority v Jonathan Pinifolo* Civil Cause 330 of 2021 [2021] MWHC 167 (27 October 2021), where the Court held that the service of the summons should be provided to the defendant through personal service. The Court stated that the rationale behind this is to minimise the delays in the administration of Justice experienced in the old regime of the legal rules. However, for persons with disabilities, the service of the summons is not personal. It is through the litigation guardian. An example is Order 8 Rule 23 of the CPR, which states that the summons should be served on the litigation guardian where the person is a party. This defeats the rationale of personal service since the litigation guardian might take time to communicate to the PWD that he was served with the summons, which he needs to respond to within the time prescribed by law.

Communication and language problems for persons with speech, hearing, and intellectual disabilities

The trial process in the CPR does not accommodate persons with hearing and speech impairment who are both direct and indirect participants. For instance, Order 16 Rule 2 states that at the beginning of a trial, a claimant should make an opening address for ten minutes. The CPR also states that the court may hear the arguments from both parties as a preliminary process to determine if there are questions of law or issues that need to go to trial. In the common law system, the arguments in court and the opening address are mainly conducted orally in English. This can be a challenge on the person with speech impairment to address the court even in circumstances where the person has valid arguments. The authors acknowledge that Order 1 Rule 5 on active case management theoretically empowers judges to facilitate court proceedings. However, the authors argue that its application for persons with speech impairments remains problematic due to its lack of specific guidance on accommodations, reliance on judicial discretion, potential resource limitations in implementing technological solutions, and the tension between efficiency and the additional time often required for effective communication by individuals with speech challenges.

In addition, Order 17 Rule 2 of the CPR allows witnesses to prove facts by giving evidence, primarily recognising oral and written forms. While this provision doesn't explicitly exclude persons with speech-hearing impairments, it presents significant challenges for their direct participation in court proceedings. These individuals may struggle to articulate their thoughts or communicate their views effectively through conventional oral or written means, potentially impacting the clarity and completeness of their testimony. The court's allowance for cross-examination further complicates matters for witnesses with speech and hearing impairments, as responding clearly and promptly to questions can be particularly challenging.

Persons with intellectual disabilities also face challenges in communication. Voula Marinos et al. (2009) notes that persons with intellectual disabilities have problems following long sentences as well as multiple questions. In addition, persons with intellectual disabilities, as indirect participants, find it challenging to use pronouns either correctly or in a way that gives the listener a proper context. Further, they also have problems with abstract terms and leading questions. This brings a power imbalance in the Court between the party and witness who is non-disabled and a party or a witness who is disabled.

Besides, the CPR does not provide for the provisions of Sign Language or recognise Sign Language since the language used in Court is oral spoken English. In concluding observations for Malawi, the Committee on the Rights of Persons with Disabilities observed that there is a lack of Sign Language interpreters in the legal proceedings, which impedes access to justice for women with intellectual disabilities and 'deafblind women' (as used in the report) (Committee on the Rights of Persons with Disabilities, 2023). Research conducted in the Southern African Justice System (Dagut & Morgan, 2003) noted that Sign Language has different dialects, just like every language. To enable people with hearing and speech impairments to access justice effectively, a Sign Language interpreter must understand the Sign Language of the PWDs in the Court (Dagut & Morgan, 2003). However, most Sign Language interpreters only know the universal Sign Language, which poses a challenge when a person with disabilities does not understand the Sign Language. Unfortunately, there are no Sign Language interpreters employed as staff in the Judiciary (CRPD Committee, 2023), and the Civil Procedure Rules do not specifically recognise Sign Language as one of the languages that can be directly presented in Court by parties and witnesses with speech and hearing impairment. This is also contrary to the UNCRPD (2006), which recognises Sign Language and other non-spoken languages.

Sign languages are full-fledged natural languages capable of expressing the full range of human thought and experience since they contain complex grammatical structures and semantics, just like oral language (Sandler & Lillo-Martin, 2006). By only recognising oral language, the Malawian legal system denies the linguistic status of Sign Languages. Also, it promotes audism, which is the notion that presupposes that the spoken language is superior to the Sign Language (Bauman, 2004). The idea of linguistic human rights, as advocated by Skutnabb-Kangas (2000), asserts that every individual has the right to preserve, embrace, and fully develop their native language. For many deaf individuals, Sign Language is their primary communication form. By not recognising it in the CPR and not employing Sign Language interpreters, these individuals are effectively denied their linguistic human rights and, consequently, their right to fair participation in legal proceedings.

Cost of litigation

Lastly, Order 31 of the CPR states that the Court can order the litigation costs. Mainly, costs follow the event, meaning the person who loses the case pays the litigation costs. Ashrage (2020) observed that the expenses of legal proceedings could be exorbitant, including attorney fees, court fees, and evidence collection costs. A person with disabilities' financial burden may be limited by their income or additional costs, making it difficult to obtain legal assistance or file lawsuits. However, the UNCRPD recognises that PWDs, despite the instruments, continue to face barriers and violations of human rights, and Order 31 on the costs of the litigation is one of them.

Way forward: inclusive justice in the CPR

In their article, Nkhata et al. (2016) proposed that the first step in transforming the right to access justice in the criminal justice system is to audit the laws that hinder this right. This is the first step in achieving inclusive access to justice for PWDs. The same approach should be adopted in the civil justice system. The Chief Justice, who has the power to make the regulations and the rules under Section 67 of the Courts Act, can revise the regulations and ensure that the laws that discriminate against PWDs are revised. Under Article 4 of the CRPD (2006), the State must ensure that it abolishes the 'existing laws, regulations, customs and practices that constitute discrimination against persons with disabilities'. One of the provisions to modify or abolish is the provision that denies persons with intellectual disabilities the litigation capacity based on their disability. The UN International Principles on Access to Justice (United Nations, 2020) call for the

> repeal or amendment of all laws, regulations, policies, guidelines, and practices that directly or indirectly restrict the legal capacity of persons with disabilities, including those that allow for substituted decision-making and those that require that a person be 'of sound mind' to take any action, thereby excluding persons with disabilities from equal access to justice.
>
> (p. 12, para. h)

When revising the rules, the Chief Justice should consult persons with disabilities; the rules should consider the experiences and the views of persons with disabilities when reformed. This means that any committee constituted to review the procedural rules should include and involve persons with different disabilities, including children and women. As Ortoleva (2011) proposes, the State 'ensures that the reform of judicial, legal, and regulatory frameworks (codes, laws, constitutions, etc.) is done in consultation with DPOs and consistent with international standards on disability' (p. 316).

In addition, the Civil Procedure Rules should recognise Sign Language as a language and train judicial officers and interpreters of Sign Language (Ortoleva, 2011). Flynn and Lawson (2013) proposed Alternative and Augmented Communication (AAC) as an example of communication (p. 92). Under AAC, there are different methods of communication, such as signs, gestures, communication boards, voice output communication aids, and web-based applications. A person can communicate with or without assistance (Flynn & Lawson, 2013). The Civil Procedure Rules of Malawi should recognise AAC methods, particularly during the trial process when the witness is a person with speech and hearing impairment. In addition, the rules should recognise intermediaries or facilitators to 'enable clear communication among and between persons with disabilities and courts, tribunals and law enforcement agencies to ensure safe, fair and effective engagement and the opportunity to participate in legal processes fully' (United Nations, 2020, p. 15, para. 31).

Lastly, the rules, which include the forms that must be used when commencing a legal suit, such as summonses and notices, must be available by accessible means and in formats such as braille, easy-to-read, and plain language (United Nations, 2020). In addition, linguistic simplification would also promote inclusive justice for PWDs. This can be done by adapting the spoken and written information in a way that is accessible by PWDs using various means. Besides, the information (evidence) presented in the Court can be edited and made simple and clear to understand (White et al., 2021). It should be mandatory under the rules that the Court always provide procedural accommodations when dealing with PWDs in Court.

Conclusion

The CPR's exclusionary definition of disability, which prohibits individuals with intellectual disabilities from commencing an action on their own, is remarkably problematic. This clause undermines the legal capacity of persons with disabilities as stipulated in Article 12 of the Convention on the Rights of Persons with Disabilities (CRPD) (United Nations, 2008). Besides, the *guardian ad litem* makes decisions on behalf of the person with intellectual disabilities, which may lead to outcomes that do not fully reflect their needs and desires.

Access to Justice is further impeded by aspects of the Civil Procedure Rules (CPR) procedure, such as the need for personal service of documents and the lack of resources for those with speech or visual impairments. Due to a lack of braille and Sign Language facilities, people with disabilities are deprived of their meaningful participation in the judicial system.

The financial burden of legal proceedings, including attorney fees and court costs, is a significant obstacle that many people with disabilities face due to their limited financial resources. According to the UNCRPD, states must address these barriers as they are likely to impact persons with disabilities through such disproportionate expenses.

The reform of the CPR system is necessary to address these shortcomings and promote inclusive justice. The Chief Justice, whom the Courts Act empowers, must conduct a comprehensive review to eliminate discriminatory provisions and ensure all decisions align with international law, including the UNCRPD (Malawi Courts Act, 2010). This process must involve significant consultation with persons and their representative organisations to ensure that the reformed rules incorporate people's perspectives and experiences.

Furthermore, recognising and considering various communication necessities, such as Sign Language interpretation and alternative communication methods, is crucial in making it easier for people with disabilities to engage in legal proceedings. Judicial officers and interpreters must be trained in these areas to ensure effective communication and accessibility in the courtroom.

The Civil Procedure Rules of Malawi need reform to achieve inclusive access to Justice for persons with disabilities, which requires a comprehensive effort. Malawi can gain a legal system that truly honours the rights and dignity of all its inhabitants, including those with disabilities, by adopting the values of equality, autonomy, and accessibility in the UNCRPD.

References

Ashrage, A. (2020). Access to justice for PWDs in civil proceedings before federal courts of Ethiopia: Law and practice. *Mizan Law Review*, *14*(1), 28. https://www.ajol.info/index.php/mlr/article/view/201879

Bahdi, R. (2007). *Background paper on women's access to justice in the MENA Region*. International Development Research Centre (IDRC), Women's Rights and Citizenship Program (WRC) and the Middle East Regional Office (MERO), Middle East and North African (MENA) Regional Consultation. http://ssrn.com/abstract=1716864

Barnes, M., & Oliver, C. (2012). *The new politics of disablement*. Palgrave Macmillan.

Basser, L. A. (2011). Human dignity. In M. H. Rioux et al. (Eds.), *Critical perspectives on human rights and disability law* (p. 19). Martinus Nijhoff.

Bauman, H. L. (2004). Audism: Exploring the metaphysics of oppression. *Journal of Deaf Studies and Deaf Education*, *9*(2), 239–246.

Brosnan, L. (2017). The CRPD and human-rights based approaches: A magic wand for inclusion? In C. O'Mahony & G. Quinn (Eds.), *Disability law and policy: An analysis of the UN convention* (p. 204). Clarus.

Croley, S. (2017). *Civil justice reconsidered: Towards a less costly more accessible civil litigation system*. New York Press.

Dagut, H., & Morgan, R. (2003). Barriers to justice: Violations of the rights of deaf and hard-of-hearing people in the South African justice system. *South African Journal on Human Rights*, *19*(1), 27–56. https://doi.org/10.1080/19962126.2003.11865171

Degener, T. (2016). Disability in a human rights context. *Laws*, *5*(3), 35. https://doi.org/10.3390/laws5030035

Dhanda, A. (2007). Legal capacity in the disability rights convention: Stranglehold of the past or lodestar for the future. *Syracuse Journal of International Law and Comparative*, *34*, 429–462.

Fina, V. D., Cera, R., & Palmisano, G. (Eds.). (2017). *The United Nations convention on the rights of persons with disabilities: A commentary*. Springer.

Flynn, E. (2015). *Disabled justice? Access to justice and the UN convention on the rights of persons with disabilities*. Ashgate.

Flynn, E. (2018). Access to justice. In I. Bantekas, Michael Ashley Stein & Dimitris Anastasiou (Eds.), *The U.N. convention on the rights of persons with disabilities: A commentary* (p. 383). Oxford University Press.

Flynn, E., & Arstein-Kerslake, A. (2014). Legislating personhood: Realising the right to support in exercising legal capacity. *International Journal of Law Context*, *10*(1), 81–104.

Flynn, E., & Lawson, A. (2013). Disability and access to justice in the European Union: Implication of the United Nations convention on the rights of persons with disabilities. *European Yearbook of Disability Law*, *4*.

Hwang, Y. S., Chan, J., & Singh, N. N. (2024). Human rights, disability, and mindfulness. *Advances in Neurodevelopmental Disorders*, *8*, 7–16. https://doi.org/10.1007/s41252-023-00375-w

Kayess, R., & French, P. (2008). Out of the darkness into light? Introducing the convention on the rights of persons with disabilities. *Human Rights Law Review*, *8*(1), 1–34. https://doi.org/10.1093/hrlr/ngm044
Marinos, V., Griffiths, D., Gosse, L., Robinson, J., Olley, J. G., & Lindsay, W. (2009). Legal rights and persons with intellectual disabilities. In F. Owen & D. Griffiths (Eds.), *Challenges to the human rights of people with intellectual disabilities* (pp. 124–154). Jessica Kingsley Publishers.
Nkhata, C., Jason, J., & Raw, A. (2016). Beyond symbolism and rhetoric: The role of the legal community in advancing access to justice and development for persons with disabilities. In Southern Africa Litigation Centre (Eds.), *Goal 16 of the sustainable development goals: Perspectives from judges and lawyers in Southern Africa on promoting rule of law and equal access to justice* (p. 39). Southern Africa Litigation Centre. http://www.southernafricalitigationcentre.org
Nkhata, M. (2020). Access to justice for persons with disabilities: Exploring challenges and possibilities in the criminal justice system. *African Disability Rights Yearbook*, *8*.
Oliver, M. (1990, July). *The individual and social model of disability*. Paper presented at the Joint Workshop of the Living Options Group and Research Unit of the Royal College of Physicians, People with Established Locomotor Disabilities in Hospital.
Ortoleva, S. (2011). Inaccessible justice: Human rights, persons with disabilities, and the legal system. *ILSA Journal of International & Comparative Law*, *17*.
Roeher institute. (1996). *Disability, community and society: Exploring the links*. Roeher Institute, North York, Ont.
Sandler, W., & Lillo-Martin, D. (2006). *Sign language and linguistic universals*. Cambridge University Press.
Shakespeare, T. (2002). The social model of disability an outdated ideology? *Journal of Social Science and Disability*, *2*, 4.
Skutnabb-Kangas, T. (2000). *Linguistic genocide in education - or worldwide diversity and human rights?* Routledge.
Smith, J. (2022). Understanding legal capacity in mental health contexts. *Journal of Law and Society*, *45*(2), 1–15.
Union of the Physically Impaired Against Segregation and the Disability Alliance. (1976). *Fundamental principles of disability* (p. 13). UPIAS Commentary.
Van Weele, E. (2012). The UN convention on the rights of persons with disabilities in the context of human rights. In J. Anderson & J. Phillips (Eds.), *Disability and universal human rights: Legal, ethical and conceptual implications of the convention on the rights of persons with disabilities* (p. 10). SIM.
Weller, P. (2016). Legal capacity and access to justice: The right to participation in the CRPD. *Laws*, *5*(1), 13. https://doi.org/10.3390/laws5010013
White, R., Bornman, J., Johnson, E., & Msipa, D. (2021). Court accommodations for persons with severe communication disabilities: A legal scoping review. *Psychology, Public Policy, and Law*, *27*(3), 399–420.
Zietlow, R. (1998). Exploring a substantive approach to equal justice under law. *New Mexico Law Review*, *28*, 411.

International instruments

- Universal Declaration of Human Rights, G.A. Res. 217A (III), UN GAOR, 3d Sess., UN Doc. A/810 (10 Dec. 1948).
- United Nations. (2008). Convention on the Rights of Persons with Disabilities, 2515 UNTS 9 (CRPD) 3.
- United Nations. (2020). International principles and guidelines on access to justice for persons with disabilities. https://www.ohchr.org/en/special-

procedures/sr-disability/international-principles-and-guidelines-access-justice-persons-disabilities
- Committee on the Rights of Persons with Disabilities (CRPD). (2023). Concluding observations on the combined initial and second-period report to Malawi (CRPD/C/MWI/CO/1–2).
- Convention on the Rights of Persons with Disabilities, 13 Dec. 2006, 2515 UNT.S. 3.
- African Union. (2018). Protocol to the African Charter on Human and Peoples' Rights on the Rights of Persons with Disabilities in Africa. OAU/LEG/EXP/PI/1/2/18.

Legislation

- Constitution of the Republic of Malawi 1995.
- Courts Act, Chapter 3:02, Laws of Malawi.
- Courts (High Court) (Civil Procedure) Rules 2017.
- Persons with Disability Act No. 4 of 2024.

6 Intoxication, memory, and credibility

Intoxicated suspects and witnesses as a vulnerable group in Zimbabwe's justice system

Paul Svongoro and Stanley Madonsela

Introduction

Although research about intoxicated litigants is a relatively new topic in African contexts, available literature from other contexts generally confirms that intoxication can significantly impair an individual's memory and cognition, raising complex issues within the legal system, particularly concerning the credibility and reliability of crime accounts given by intoxicated suspects and witnesses (e.g., Compo et al., 2011; Hagsand, 2014; Monds et al., 2021). As observed elsewhere (e.g. Palmer et al., 2013; Evans et al., 2020), intoxicated individuals often represent a vulnerable group of suspects and witnesses in Zimbabwe's justice system. They are seen as a vulnerable group because they face unique challenges that can affect the fairness and outcome of legal proceedings.

This chapter, therefore, explores the impact of intoxication on witness and suspect participation in Zimbabwe's legal processes. The chapter uses document analysis, interviews, and court observations to understand the current legal framework, psychological effects of intoxication on memory and credibility, and societal biases. The study aims to identify gaps in research and practice, proposing recommendations for improving the treatment of intoxicated individuals in the justice system for a more equitable and just legal process.

Zimbabwe is facing health and safety issues due to an increase in alcohol and substance abuse. Studies show a high prevalence of intoxicated victims, witnesses, and suspects, especially in relation to violent crimes. This correlation between alcohol intake, impulse control deficit, and higher violence risk is evident in Zimbabwe, where alcohol/drug-related crimes are common.

Although research on the effects of alcohol on physical health, memory, and cognition has increased, forensic linguistics research is scarce. This chapter examines the perception of intoxicated confessions in Zimbabwe's justice system and their admissibility as evidence. It also examines police conduct of investigative interviews with intoxicated witnesses and suspects, focusing on the establishment of protocols for such interviews.

DOI: 10.4324/9781003569435-9

Research questions

To achieve the objective mentioned in the introduction section, the chapter sought to answer the following three questions:

- (i) What investigative interviewing techniques do the police employ when dealing with intoxicated suspects and witnesses?
- (ii) Are there any communication challenges faced by intoxicated suspects and witne.sses in Zimbabwe's justice system?
- (iii) What perceptions do the police and criminal courts have of the confessions given by intoxicated suspects and witnesses?

Zimbabwe's institutions of justice

Zimbabwe's judicial system comprises institutions that are essential in the administration and application of the law to settle disputes (Veritas, 2023). A few of these organisations are the Attorney-General's Office, the National Prosecuting Authority, the Ministry of Justice, Legal and Parliamentary Affairs and its various departments, courts and the Judicial Service Commission, the Police Service, the Prisons and Correctional Service, and last but not least, the legal practitioners, or lawyers, who make up the legal profession (Constitution of Zimbabwe Amendment (No. 20) Act of 2013).

However, this chapter examines the courts of law and the police service in Zimbabwe, which are established in Chapter 8 of the Constitution of Zimbabwe Amendment (No. 20) Act of 2013. Zimbabwe's main courts include local courts, magistrates' courts, administrative courts, labour courts, high courts, supreme courts, and constitutional courts. Local courts handle customary law cases, magistrates' courts handle appeals, administrative courts handle ministerial and public officials' decisions, labour courts handle employment and labour cases, high courts handle criminal and civil cases, supreme courts handle appeals, and specialised courts like Small Claims and Children's Courts (Veritas, 2023).

At this juncture, it is also important to make a distinction between criminal and civil courts. Under section 193 of the Constitution of Zimbabwe Amendment (No. 20) Act of 2013, criminal proceedings can only be handled by the Constitutional Court, the Supreme Court, the High Court, and Magistrates' Courts. However, members of the defence personnel, the Police, and other uniformed personnel who violate discipline may be disciplined by disciplinary tribunals.

According to Veritas (2023), criminal cases are those that attempt to punish persons who commit crimes, that is, violations of the law for which the State imposes penalty such as a fine, jail, etc. This is how criminal cases differ from other types of cases, sometimes referred to as civil cases. Cases classified as civil involve disagreements between individuals; under the law, an individual can also refer to a company or other corporate body.

The Zimbabwe Republic Police (ZRP) was established in 2013 under section 219 of the Constitution of Zimbabwe Amendment Act. Its primary duties include identifying, investigating, and preventing criminal activities, as well as safeguarding Zimbabwe's internal security, preserving law and order, and upholding the Constitution and the rule of law impartially. As the first point of entry in the justice system, the ZRP plays a crucial role in the country's security.

Cases involving intoxicated suspects and witnesses common in Zimbabwe's justice system

On a daily basis, the Zimbabwe Republic Police Stations, civil and criminal courts are inundated with reports and cases involving intoxicated witnesses and suspects. Some of these suspects and witnesses are involved in protection order cases in civil courts while others are involved in investigations of rape, robbery, and assault crimes.

However, when the police and courts deal with these persons, they are treated in the same way as sober persons as prescribed in Zimbabwe's Criminal Procedure and Evidence Act Chapter 9:07 (CPEA) and the Constitution of Zimbabwe Amendment (No. 20) Act of 2013. As regards suspects arrested for various crimes, they are presumed innocent until proven guilty as provided in the Constitution of Zimbabwe Amendment (No. 20) Act of 2013. The Constitution clearly stipulates that:

> A person accused or suspected of a crime has the right to be presumed innocent until proven guilty. Whether he committed that offence or not is a matter to be determined by a court, and until that happens the presumption of innocence operates in his favour.

In Zimbabwe, court officials and police officers frequently encounter intoxicated suspects and witnesses in their work lives. The number of intoxicated suspects would have been higher if they were taken to courts on the same day. Most suspects spend a day or two in police detention before being taken to court, resulting in higher frequency of inebriated suspects during police questioning.

An overview of intoxication, memory, and credibility

According to Monds et al. (2021), an interdisciplinary approach involving psychology, criminology, and legal studies is needed to understand the impact of intoxication on memory and credibility in the legal system. Memory models like the encoding-storage-retrieval framework suggest that intoxicated individuals face challenges in credibility assessment, often being scrutinised harshly due to perceived unreliability. Jurors in the US often base their decisions on personal experiences and opinions on intoxicating substances (Monds et al., 2021).

Literature review

Research on intoxicated witnesses and suspects has shown a complex relationship between alcohol consumption, memory accuracy, and credibility judgments (e.g., Yuille & Tollestrup, 1990; Monds et al., 2021). The study by Yuille and Tollestrup (1990) for example, demonstrates that while intoxication can impair memory recall, not all aspects of memory are equally affected. The three scholars just cited have also studied the diverse approaches and evidentiary standards across jurisdictions when it comes to the testimony of intoxicated individuals.

In Zimbabwe, the legal framework governing the admissibility of testimony from intoxicated witnesses is still evolving, reflecting broader debates on balancing the rights of individuals against the need for accurate and reliable evidence in criminal proceedings. Comparatively, jurisdictions such as Canada and the United Kingdom have implemented guidelines and judicial rulings aimed at more nuanced considerations of intoxicated testimony, emphasising the assessment of reliability over blanket disqualification (Monds et al., 2021).

Research on how alcohol affects witness recall is expanding (Evans et al., 2020; Janssen & Anne, 2019). However, there is still limited understanding about the impact of drunkenness on a suspect's behaviour and decision-making during questioning (e.g., Malloy et al., 2014; Evans et al., 2020) attempting to examine the behaviours of intoxicated suspects in interrogation situations. Stated differently, no research to date has looked at the relationship between intoxication and the chance of a suspect making a false or true confession, as stated by Evans et al. (2020). Numerous instances have been reported where defendants made false confessions while under the influence of alcohol, such as Eugene Vent, the first juvenile in the Fairbanks 4 case, who admitted to a confrontational and deceptive police interrogation (e.g., Malloy et al., 2014; Evans et al., 2020).

The Fairbanks 4 trial demonstrates the widespread assumption among experts that alcohol use might increase a suspect's susceptibility during questioning, so compromising the credibility of any confession made later. According to the self-reports of those in prison, there is a correlation between being intoxicated and feeling disoriented when speaking with police, which supports these hypotheses (Gudjonsson & Sigurdsson, 1994).

Gudjonsson and Sigurdsson (1994) argue that alcohol intoxication can impair a suspect's clear thought, potentially leading to false information. Another study suggests that higher intoxication during encoding increases the risk of surrendering to suggestion, despite no effect on misinformation vulnerability (Evans et al., 2019). Remarkably, even interrogator trainers are growing more cognisant of the issues surrounding questioning drunken suspects. For instance, Kozinski (2017) cautioned against coercion during drunken suspect interrogations because it can lead to false confessions. Nevertheless, they did not support a policy that forbids questioning drunken suspects.

Admissibility of confessions by intoxicated suspects and witnesses

One issue that dominates legal debates is that of admissibility of evidence in court. In the context of intoxicated suspects and witnesses, research has explored the admissibility of their evidence in courts of law (Palmer et al., 2013; Evans et al., 2020). Evans et al. (2020) verified that confessions made by suspects under the influence of alcohol are admissible in US courts based on their study on American courts. It is still unclear, though, how juries assess these kinds of confessions. For instance, Evans et al.'s (2020) study revealed that many jurors and respondents were unaware of the legality and the admissibility of questioning intoxicated suspects and their subsequent confessions in court.

Other jurors found intoxicated defendants more inappropriate and cognitively impaired than sober defendants, resulting in a lower likelihood of convicting them. Intoxicated confessions also influenced conviction decisions less than sober confessions. The study suggests investigators should avoid interrogating intoxicated suspects to avoid unconvincing confessions in court, indicating the need for caution.

In an earlier study, Compo et al. (2011) conducted an experimental study on the recall of intoxicated and sober witnesses during a crime scene. The study analysed participants who were intoxicated, placebo, or sober and overheard misinformation about a crime. Results showed that intoxicated witnesses provided more accurate or inaccurate information, while those intoxicated were not more prone to false information than those sober or placebo.

Unlike in the study by Evans et al. (2020), the study by Compo et al. (2011), sees no difference between confessions by intoxicated and sober suspects and witnesses. For Compo and others, this means confessions by both groups of people, both intoxicated and sober, should be admissible in court.

Gaps in research

Despite a growing body of literature on the intersection of intoxication, memory, and legal processes in the global south, particularly in Zimbabwe, there is a significant gap in research. The knowledge about the intersections of intoxication, memory, and credibility in Zimbabwe is mainly based on newspaper reports and court judgments, with no empirical studies conducted (e.g. ZW News, 2018; Manica Post, 2022; H-Metro, 2023). Existing studies often neglect socio-legal nuances, such as cultural perceptions of intoxication and the capacity of legal practitioners to assess the credibility of intoxicated testimony.

The preceding literature review on intoxication, memory, and credibility therefore provides a solid foundation for our analysis, connecting theoretical insights with the challenges faced in Zimbabwe's justice system. The methodology, data collection methods, and theoretical framework are discussed in the following section.

Research methodology

This qualitative study conducted in Zimbabwe collected data through document analysis of legal documents, interviews with police and court officials, and observation of suspect interviews and court trials. The researcher analysed primary documents like the Constitution of Zimbabwe Amendment (No. 20) Act of 2013 and the Criminal Procedure and Evidence Act Chapter 9:07 to understand provisions for handling intoxicated suspects and witnesses. Additionally, the researcher searched for case law documents where intoxicated suspects and witnesses participated in trials.

Finally, the researcher conducted a thorough search of Zimbabwean newspapers, including the *ZW News,* the *Manica Post,* and the *H-Metro,* to gather court news. The focus was on how trials proceeded after the court noticed intoxication in the accused or witness. The researcher also analysed the communicative behaviours of suspects and witnesses in court, examining how these behaviours influenced the court's decisions. The search aimed to provide a comprehensive understanding of court proceedings.

Apart from document analysis, the researchers also conducted semi-structured interviews with police officers and court officials to analyse their experiences with intoxicated suspects and witnesses, examining if police have specific protocols and procedures for interviewing suspects and witnesses. According to Gudjonsson and Pearse (2011), the Reid technique and PEACE model are the two influential methods of police interviewing practice, commonly used in the United States and the UK respectively.

A similar line of interviewing used with police officers was also followed with magistrates and public prosecutors. In total, four magistrates, three public prosecutors and seven police officers participated in the study. Each interview lasted for about 45 minutes.

The researchers conducted interviews, observed court proceedings, and conducted witness questioning at police stations. Observing court proceedings was challenging due to random observations. However, a court orderly encouraged the researchers to focus more on civil courts than criminal ones, as an inebriated complainant or accused would likely be present in most protection order hearings, especially those heard in the afternoon. The court orderly was correct, as more cases involving drunken parties were observed in civil court hearings than in criminal court proceedings. The researchers observed five cases from civil court and three from criminal court by the end of the one-month observation period.

This study used interviews and observation to understand the perspectives of intoxicated participants in Zimbabwe's justice system about access to justice. Researchers developed a coding process to analyse the data, moving from large amounts of responses to dominant themes. The researchers systematically searched and arranged interview transcripts and observation notes to understand the phenomena under study.

In examining the participants' views regarding intoxicated suspects and witnesses in Zimbabwe's justice system, thematic analysis was found to be highly appropriate. Using thematic analysis, the researchers were able to identify, analyse, and record patterns (themes) within the interview responses. This method organically emphasises pinpointing, examining, and recording recurrent themes that emerge from the data.

For this study, the analysis of participants' views followed the following steps to ensure a detailed analysis:

(i) Data preparation and organisation, including transcription of the participants' interview responses and the researchers' observation notes.
(ii) Data familiarisation where interview transcripts by different participants and observation notes were thoroughly reviewed to get a general sense of the information.
(iii) Identifying potential themes manually and then reviewing them to check whether some can be combined, refined, separated or discarded.
(iv) Reviewed themes to refine and validate these themes against the data set.
(v) Defined and named themes to clearly articulate what each theme represents and how it answers the research questions. The researchers articulated this information descriptively.
(vi) Produced the report which integrated these themes with the theoretical framework and research literature to present as findings or results of the study.

The study's reliability was enhanced by a comprehensive and credible analysis, identifying major themes. Researchers followed strict ethical guidelines to protect participants' rights and privacy, ensuring anonymity and secrecy. Participants were allowed to decline questions they felt uncomfortable with or leave at any time to minimise potential risks or discomfort.

Theoretical framework

The data collected from documents analysis, interviews and observations were analysed in the context of Hage's Social Justice Theory and Gudjonsson's Police Suspect Interviewing (Gudjonsson, 2003; Hage, 2005).

According to Hage (2005) and Hage and Kenny (2009), social justice is the equitable distribution of authority, resources, and responsibilities to all individuals, regardless of their background. It is the foundation of a democratic society, promoting equality of access, opportunity, collaboration, and inclusion. However, in certain social and economic situations, the absence of justice can lead to increased vulnerability and physical and mental pain.

In this context of the Social Justice Theory, the collected data were analysed to examine how the police and court perceived intoxicated suspects and witnesses as a vulnerable group in Zimbabwe's justice system. Furthermore, the study utilised social theory to examine the handling of intoxicated suspects and witnesses in Zimbabwe's justice system, and to assess the effectiveness of the system's laws and police interviewing procedures (Hage & Kenny, 2009). Preventive interventions in Social Justice Theory target risk factors and strengthen protective factors for vulnerable populations, occurring at both individual and societal levels (Hage & Kenny, 2009).

It is ideal to create preventive measures that advance social justice as systemic initiatives that lessen inequality in a range of contexts, including legal proceedings, and provide more favourable results. Consequently, effective interventions give teenagers, families, and communities the resources and inspiration required to bring about personal and structural transformation as well as advance social justice (Hage, 2005).

To understand police interviewing practice in Zimbabwe's police stations, the researchers also applied Gudjonsson and Pearse's Police Suspect Interviewing (Gudjonsson & Pearse, 2011). Gudjonsson and Pearse's theory focuses on two interrogation methods: the Reid technique and the PEACE model. Reid is a manipulative method used by US police forces, often associated with false confessions due to guilt-presumption and confrontation. According to Gudjonsson and Pearse (2011), the PEACE model, based on non-coerced suspects, aims to maximise true confessions while minimising false ones. Electronic recording of police interviews is frequently used in conjunction with the PEACE model to ensure accountability and openness while guarding against police-induced false admissions.

Using Gudjonsson and Pearse's Police Suspect Interviewing (Gudjonsson & Pearse, 2011), the researchers analysed police suspect interviewing during observation of police interrogation of suspects. Aspects of Gudjonsson and Pearse's Police Suspect Interviewing were also used to frame some of the interview questions which the researcher asked police officers. The questions revolved around how they question suspects, whether they have any prescribed protocol to follow when questioning aspects, any communication challenges they faced when communicating with intoxicated suspects etc.

In the next section of the chapter, we delve into the data analysis beginning with the current legal framework in Zimbabwe concerning intoxicated witnesses and suspects, outlining relevant laws, policies, and their implications for justice.

Data analysis and findings

As stated in the introduction section, this chapter sought to investigate police questioning of suspects and witnesses, communication difficulties faced by intoxicated suspects and witnesses, and confessions by intoxicated individuals were perceived by the police and the court. In order to investigate these issues, the researchers first looked at what Zimbabwe's statutes state regarding inebriated suspects and witnesses and the consequences for the administration of justice as shall be explained in the next section.

From the cases observed and from document analysis and as also corroborated by interviews with police and law officers, in most cases, intoxicated suspects and to some extent witnesses, admitted to the police and to the court that they had consumed alcohol and/or drugs, and they were usually arrested on the same day the crime was committed. Suspects were often sent straight to police stations for questioning after being apprehended by the authorities while intoxicated. In short, many suspects and witnesses were intoxicated either at the time of the crime, during police questioning, or when they appeared in court.

Others, particularly suspects who were out on bail, appeared in courts after they had taken alcohol or any other intoxicating substance(s) on their way to court, or on the day they were expected to appear in court. Other suspects claimed they appeared in court when they were still recovering from excessive consumption of alcohol on the previous day.

Current laws and policies and practices regarding intoxicated suspects and witnesses

Relevant legal documents such as the Constitution of Zimbabwe Amendment (No. 20) Act of 2013, the Criminal Procedure and Evidence Act [Chapter 9:07] and the Magistrates Court Act [Chapter 7:10], the Police Act [Chapter 11:10], the Civil Evidence Act [Chapter 8:01] and the Criminal Law (Codification and Reform) Act [Chapter 9:23], were examined to understand if they made any provisions for intoxicated suspects and witnesses in Zimbabwe's justice system. Right from the onset, the examination of these legal documents among others showed that only one provision is made in the Criminal Procedure and Evidence Act [Chapter 9: 07] concerning intoxication and court appearance. The provision relates to the state expected of an individual to stand trial. Other than that one provision, no other provisions specifically related to intoxicated suspects and witnesses are made in them.

From the analysis of the aforementioned documents, Zimbabwe's legal system, based on Roman-Dutch law and British common law, has its unique approach to handling cases involving intoxicated witnesses and suspects. The Criminal Law (Codification and Reform) Act and the Evidence Act for example, are pivotal in setting the foundation for how testimony and evidence are treated, including those from intoxicated individuals. Regarding what the law requires for one to be fit to stand trial, section 113B of the Criminal Procedure and Evidence Act states that:

113B Accused must be in his or her sound and sober senses

(1) Before commencing confirmation proceedings and at all times during the course thereof, the magistrate shall satisfy himself or herself that the accused is in his or her sound and sober senses, and if the magistrate

> *is, before commencing or any time during the course of the proceedings, satisfied that the accused is not in his or her sound and sober senses, the magistrate shall record that fact and order the accused to be kept in custody in such place for such period and under such conditions as to observation as the magistrate may think fit.*

From the researchers' scrutiny of relevant legal documents, it became apparent that it is section 113B (1) of the Criminal Law (Codification and Reform) Act which guides magistrates' discretion regarding the handling of intoxicated suspects and witnesses. Although provisions of this kind are sparse in Zimbabwe's laws, the inclusion of this provision for intoxicated persons means that Zimbabwe's laws attempt to safeguard the rights of intoxicated persons to a fair trial in line with the demands of social justice (Hage, 2005; Hage & Kenny, 2009). However, Zimbabwe's legal documents lack explicit provisions for intoxicated witnesses or suspects, allowing judicial and police discretion and interpretation. This results in courts relying on their own experiences and discretion to decide on how to proceed with cases involving intoxicated suspects and witnesses.

Intoxication can impact the credibility of testimony in court cases, requiring courts to balance it with the rights of the accused. Zimbabwean courts have historically treated intoxicated witnesses' testimony cautiously, requiring corroborating evidence to support claims made under alcohol or drugs. This practice is in line with safeguarding the integrity of the judicial process, ensuring decisions are based on reliable and accurate information (Hage, 2005).

Confirming this observation by magistrates and public prosecutors, is a case law example, *S v Mudzengerere and 3 Others (60 of 2024) [2024] ZWHHC 36*, in which Judge Munamato Mutevedzi of the Zimbabwean high court blasted the way the police handled the testimony of possible witnesses. The judge raised concerns about the falsification of vernacular court comments translated into English by the police, even if the witness is illiterate. The judge suggested that police should preserve original statements in vernacular and have qualified interpreters or translators translate them to prevent misrepresentations in court proceedings, especially when cases involve intoxicated suspects and witnesses.

Comparing Zimbabwe's approach to international standards reveals a varied landscape. In its Witnesses, cooperating witnesses and witness protection guidelines, the United Nations Office on Drugs and Crime (UNODC, 2023), provides guidelines on treating vulnerable witnesses, which can include those who are intoxicated, advocating for special measures to ensure their effective participation in the legal process. The UNODC (2023) highlights Australia and the UK's detailed protocols for assessing and managing intoxicated individuals' testimony, including expert psychological evaluations to determine the impact of substance use on memory and perception.

Zimbabwe's legal framework faces challenges for intoxicated witnesses and suspects due to unclear guidelines and protocols. The reliance on judicial discretion can lead to varying outcomes, potentially affecting the fairness and consistency of legal proceedings. The lack of explicit recognition of intoxicated individuals' vulnerability may result in marginalisation, impacting their right to a fair trial and the justice system's credibility.

The chapter examined Zimbabwe's legal framework for intoxicated witnesses and suspects, highlighting its complexities and challenges. It explores the psychological impact of intoxication on memory and credibility, and addresses communication challenges faced by intoxicated suspects and witnesses during police questioning and court appearances.

Communication challenges faced by intoxicated suspects and witnesses

As indicated in the methodology section, this study was qualitative, analysing legal documents, court newspaper articles, and police-suspect interviews. Due to time and resource constraints, experiments and quantitative analyses were not conducted. The findings were difficult to confirm, as it was unclear whether communication challenges experienced by suspects and witnesses were due to human error or linked to intoxication. From eight cases observed in civil and criminal courts, magistrates adjourned trials when they observed intoxication, but also asked questions to check sobriety before adjourning the trial. Some of the questions asked are as follows:

(a) *Did you hear and understand what has just been said?*
(b) *Do you know why you are here?*
(c) *Do you drink alcohol?*
(d) *Have you taken alcohol today?*

The suspect or witness's responses to some of these questions helped the magistrate decide on whether to proceed or adjourn the trial.

In a protection order case between siblings which I observed in the civil court of Mutare, after the details of the case were presented in court, the magistrate asked the accused person some questions. The way the accused person responded to the questions confirmed the magistrate's initial suspicions that he was drunk. The interaction, interpreted between English and Shona, was as follows:

Magistrate: Do you agree with or oppose your sister's application?
Accused: Which application? I am not aware of it.
Magistrate: Are you drunk?
Accused: I usually take black label but today I am not drunk.
Magistrate: You are not in a sober state and not respecting the court. There are prison officers at Mutare Remand Prison who will teach how to behave then you come back to court.

The magistrate adjourned the trial and remanded the accused in custody until further notice.

From the circumstances resulting in adjournments presented earlier, one can say that the impact of intoxication on memory is crucial in determining the reliability of testimonies from intoxicated individuals. Magistrates adjourned trials due to the likelihood of intoxicated suspects and witnesses providing unreliable testimonies. Interviews with magistrates and public prosecutors underscore the importance of individual discretion in intoxicated trials, as well as the significance of court and real-life experiences in decision-making. Judges judge cases based on the suspect's or witness's state and intoxication level. One magistrate said:

> *My friend, these days it is very easy to tell which type of alcohol has been taken. You can tell that this person has taken some beers and this one has taken* ***tumbwa****! You cannot proceed with a case in which you are dealing with* ***mboko*** *that has taken* ***msombo****!*

Despite being humorous, the magistrate's remark highlights a real problem with drug and substance abuse that affects Zimbabwe and other nations today. The three terms that are emboldened are associated with inexpensive alcoholic beverages that are frequently drunk in urban areas. All of these incredibly effective, inexpensive concoctions are referred to as *msombo* (an extremely potent substance) or *tumbwa* (literally, 'dogs'). *Mboko*, the final term, refers to a person who is completely inebriated. Nonetheless, the majority of magistrates' and judges' responses typically indicated that they had unfavourable opinions about drunken suspects, witnesses, and their testimony. According to the Social Justice Theory, these unfavourable opinions could lead to the unfair treatment of a certain group of individuals, such as drunken suspects (Hage & Kenny, 2009). For this group of persons, access to justice may be threatened by the degree of stigmatisation they experience as well as the possibility that their evidence would be discounted.

Communication challenges during police-suspect interviews

Interviews with police officers confirmed that, on occasion, they must retain inebriated detainees in holding cells because they are incapable of providing a coherent account of their past and present statements and are too inebriated to respond to questioning. According to some law enforcement officials, they arrest inebriated defendants when they exhibit obstructive behaviour (such as flatly declining to answer questions, which is legal) or when they start acting aggressively and violently. The views by police officers were also confirmed during observations of police-suspect questioning conducted by the researcher.

The researchers found that some suspects and witnesses became incoherent, incomprehensible, or stammering in their speech, while others had higher levels of forgetting past events, understanding questions, and entitlement to rights. Police used coercion to get cooperation, indicating a potential issue with the police's handling of these cases. The following statements were frequently used by police officers to coerce suspects to speak:

(i) Hey, do you think we are here to play?
(ii) Answer the question I have asked and stop playing with us.
(iii) You will get yourself in trouble if you don't cooperate with us. We want to assist you.
(iv) Throw him into the cells if he doesn't want to speak.
(v) Take him to CID if he continues to waste our time.

During interviews, police officers confirmed that they were trained in various interviewing techniques, including the non-confrontational approach, the PEACE model, cognitive interviewing, and the good cop/bad cop strategy. However, their decisions were influenced by individual suspects' circumstances. The techniques used depended on the cooperativeness of the suspects, and the circumstances with each suspect informed their decision-making process, leaving police officers to make their discretion in questioning.

From the preceding finding, it is clear that Zimbabwe's police is well informed about police suspect interviewing techniques including those proposed by Gudjonsson (2003) and by Gudjonsson and Pearse (2011). In addition, the police officers also showed a clear awareness of the weaknesses of each of the methods they identified. One police officer indicated that:

> *It is important to note that some techniques, such as the Reid technique, have been criticised for potentially leading to false confessions. For this reason, investigators must always ensure that the methods they use are ethical, legal and respect the rights of the accused.*

The instances of coercion utilised in cases (i) to (v) were purposefully used in accordance with the Reid police-suspect questioning model based on coercion, despite the fact that police officers stated they did not follow any set uniform or suspect questioning routine. Police personnel utilised all of the aforementioned statements to force criminals to speak. Regarding point (iv), it is well known that the holding cells at Zimbabwe's police stations are filthy, packed, and rife with bed bugs. If someone were not a devoted criminal, they would not want to spend even a single day in that facility. The Criminal Investigations Department (CID), a law enforcement agency notorious for its brutal techniques of extracting confessions from criminals, is mentioned in statement (v). The mere mention of that name can make someone rethink their actions. However, as mentioned by Gudjonsson (2003) and by Gudjonsson and Pearse (2011), such forms of coercion my result in false confessions. Finally, from the researcher's observations, it was also clear that sober suspects did not experience the same level of coercion as intoxicated suspects even if sober persons were accused of similar crimes.

Another communication challenged emerged during interviews with magistrates and prosecutors, most of them raised concerns about the police's handling of suspects and witnesses' statements, citing discrepancies between their vernacular languages and English recordings. Some suspects and witnesses viewed these statements as misrepresentations, and concerns were generally higher when the statements were taken from intoxicated individuals.

Challenges faced by intoxicated suspects from Zimbabwean case law

The challenges faced by intoxicated suspects and witnesses explained earlier were also confirmed by a few examples from Zimbabwean case law (*State v Tendai*; *State v Chenai*) and few others from South Africa (*Malebo v State*; *Masebeni and Another v State*).

In *State v Tendai*, an eyewitness to a robbery was under the influence of alcohol at the time of the incident. Despite providing a detailed account that matched evidence from the scene, the witness's testimony was questioned, emphasising their intoxication over the consistency and relevance of their account. This case underscores the dilemmas faced by the legal system in assessing the credibility of intoxicated witnesses and highlights the need for a more nuanced approach.

In *State v Chenai*, the suspect provided a confession while intoxicated. Later, the suspect claimed his confession was coerced and inaccurate due to their impaired state at the time the confession was made. The court struggled with evaluating the voluntariness and reliability of the confession, reflecting the broader challenge of handling statements made by intoxicated suspects.

What the preceding findings reveal about intoxicated suspects and witnesses

The preceding findings reveal that, in Zimbabwe, intoxicated witnesses and suspects often face societal and systemic biases, leading to scepticism about their testimony's reliability and dismissal. This stigmatisation undermines their credibility and contributes to a broader reluctance to engage with the justice system. Research has shown that alcohol and other substances can impair cognitive functions, affecting the encoding, storage, and retrieval of memories (Palmer et al., 2013; Evans et al., 2020). Acute intoxication typically leads to deficits in short-term memory, reduced ability to form new memories, and sometimes affects the reliability of long-term memories when recalled while intoxicated.

Palmer et al. (2013) comment on the degree of intoxication and substance consumed, stating that cognitive psychology research indicates that an individual's tolerance level and past substance use history, along with the level of intoxication and substance consumed, can all affect the degree of memory impairment (Palmer et al., 2013). Furthermore, a situation where memories generated while under the influence are more precisely recalled in the same state can arise due to the context in which memories are formed and recalled, a phenomenon known as state-dependent memory, which makes the evaluation of the reliability of testimony more difficult.

Implications of the communication challenges on the investigations and trial

The impact of intoxication on memory is a significant challenge for Zimbabwe's legal system. The credibility of witnesses and suspects relies on their accuracy, making understanding the effects of intoxication crucial for fair proceedings. Judicial and investigative processes must differentiate between normal human error and intoxication-induced memory inaccuracies. This is especially important when intoxicated witnesses or suspects' testimony is central to evidence. The risk of wrongful convictions or dismissal of credible testimonies is high, emphasising the need for informed legal practices that consider psychological insights.

Because of the interplay between alcohol, memory, and credibility, intoxicated witnesses and suspects in Zimbabwe's legal system confront several difficulties. People may become discredited or stigmatised, which makes it difficult for them to fully engage in the legal system. These difficulties are made worse by the fact that law enforcement and court personnel lack specific training on how to handle situations involving intoxicated people. Systemic issues plague Zimbabwe's legal system as well. For example, the lack of clear rules for assessing the credibility of intoxicated testimonies leads to inconsistent practices, exacerbated by the scarcity of forensic psychology-trained expert witnesses, causing decision-makers to rely on specialised knowledge.

Perceptions of magistrates, public prosecutors, and police officers towards intoxicated suspects and witnesses

Drunken conduct, alcoholism, and drug addiction are typically not acceptable in Zimbabwean society, especially in official contexts like courts and workplaces. Due to this cultural value, drunken suspects and witnesses are now viewed negatively in Zimbabwe's courtrooms. These negative perceptions result in such decisions like postponing sessions and keeping suspects in jail while their cases would have probably continued. To illustrate this, we will refer to one protection order case I heard at Mutare Civil Court and reported in the *Manica Post* newspaper of 22 July 2022.

The case involved two relatives who lived in the same family house but were in a dispute. The sister-in-law (the complainant) wanted a protection order against her brother-in law (the accused) citing various reasons which ranged from violent behaviour, physical assault and other forms of unheard-of behaviour like uprooting vegetables from the garden and defecating on the main door into the house. After the complainant presented her version of the case, the accused person who was believed to be intoxicated denied the allegations arguing that:

> *The allegations were fabricated by the complainant and her husband in a bid to evict me from the family house which they we are all sharing.*

Although the complainant's defence sounded very reasonable at law, the magistrate did not attempt to establish the veracity of his defence after noticing that the accused was drunk. Rather than asking the accused and complainant to provide the court with evidence to support their versions, the magistrate decided to focus on the state of the accused. He accused the accused person to be drunk and adjourned the matter. The questions one would ask is, *If the same line of defence were given by a sober person, would the court have ignored such defence?* This is particularly intriguing as there is no legislation in Zimbabwe that states a confession is acceptable just because the defendant was under the influence of alcohol when they made it. In reality, confessions made by intoxicated individuals are only suppressed in Zimbabwe and other contexts if it is determined that the information was provided against their will.

The preceding example and others clearly show that courts and law officials often discredit confessions from intoxicated suspects, despite their intention to provide a fair trial. Intoxicated suspects are more likely to receive higher guilt ratings and are more likely to be coerced into confessions at police stations, increasing their risk of incarceration compared to sober individuals who give their confessions freely.

Implications of the findings regarding the treatment of intoxicated persons

In Zimbabwe, intoxicated witnesses and suspects face significant stigmatisation, affecting their credibility and fairness in the justice system. Cultural attitudes often associate substance use with moral failing, impacting their testimony. This bias extends to the legal arena, where magistrates, prosecutors, judges, and law enforcement officials may have preconceived notions about the reliability of testimonies. According to Compo et al. (2011), the stigma associated with intoxication can hinder witnesses' willingness to engage with the justice system, leading to fear of disbelief or harsh judgment.

The issue of intoxicated witnesses and suspects in Zimbabwe's justice system is a significant concern, requiring a multifaceted approach involving legal reforms, training, and public awareness. The lack of standardised training for law enforcement and court officials on the impact of intoxication on memory and behaviour is a significant concern, potentially compromising the integrity of the justice process for intoxicated individuals. Addressing this gap is crucial for enhancing fairness and equity in legal proceedings.

Legal guidelines are needed to handle testimonies from intoxicated witnesses and suspects, assessing memory impact and credibility. Consistency and informed guidelines should be adapted from advanced protocols. Expert testimony on memory effects can enhance Zimbabwe's legal procedures. Legal reforms should strengthen protections for intoxicated individuals, including preventive interventions, safeguards against coercion, voluntary participation, and support services like legal aid and counselling.

At community level, public awareness campaigns on intoxication, memory, and credibility in the legal context are crucial to reduce societal stigma and encourage intoxicated individuals' participation in the justice system. Finally, interdisciplinary research collaboration between legal professionals, psychologists, and substance abuse experts can provide a more nuanced understanding

Conclusion

The intersection of intoxication, memory, and credibility presents significant challenges within Zimbabwe's justice system, affecting the treatment and perception of intoxicated witnesses and suspects as a vulnerable group. Through a detailed examination of the legal framework, examples from case law, and societal attitudes, this chapter has highlighted the complexities and implications of intoxication in legal contexts. Addressing these challenges requires a concerted effort to implement legal reforms, enhance training and awareness, and adopt a more informed and compassionate approach to handling cases involving intoxication. By adopting these recommendations, Zimbabwe can move towards a fairer and just legal system that respects the rights and dignities of all individuals, regardless of their intoxication status.

References

Compo, N. S., Evans, J. R., Carol, R., Villalba, D. K., Ham, L. S., Garcia, T., & Rose, S. (2011). Intoxicated eyewitnesses: Better than their reputation? *Law and Human Behaviour*. https://doi.org/10.1037/h0093951

Criminal Procedure and Evidence Act Chapter 9:07 (CPEA) and the Constitution of Zimbabwe Amendment (No. 20) Act.

Evans, A. M. J., Perez, G., Woestehoff, S. A., Olaguez, M. P., Klemfuss, J. Z., Vallano, J., Woody, W. D., Scherr, K. C., Carlucci, M. E., Carol, N. R., Hayes, T., Meissner, C. A., Michael, S. W., Russano, M. B., & Stocks, E. L. (2020). Juror perceptions of intoxicated suspects' interrogation-related behaviors. *Criminal Justice and Behavior, 47*(2), 222–246. https://doi.org/10.1177/0093854819888962

Evans, J. R., Schreiber Compo, N., Carol, R. N., Nichols-Lopz, K., Holness, H., & Furton, K. G. (2019). The impact of alcohol intoxication on witness suggestibility immediately and after a delay. *Applied Cognitive Psychology, 33*, 358–369. https://doi.org/10.1002/acp.3502

Gudjonsson, G. H. (2003). *The psychology of interrogations and confessions: A handbook*. John Wiley & Sons, Ltd.

Gudjonsson, G. H., & Pearse, J. (2011). Suspect interviews and false confessions. *Current Directions in Psychological Science, 20*(1), 33–37. https://doi.org/10.1177/0963721410396824

Gudjonsson, G. H., & Sigurdsson, J. F. (1994). How frequently do false confessions occur? An empirical study among prison inmates. *Psychology, Crime & Law, 1*(1), 21–26. https://doi.org/10.1080/10683169408411933

Hage, S. M. (2005). Future considerations for fostering multicultural competence in mental health and educational settings: Social justice implications. In M. G. Constantine & D. W. Sue (Eds.), *Strategies for building multicultural competence in mental health and educational settings.* Wiley.

Hage, S. M., & Kenny, M. (2009). Promoting a social justice approach to prevention: Future directions for training, practice, and research. *Journal of Primary Prevention, 30,* 75–87.

Hagsand, A. (2014). *Alcohol-intoxicated eyewitnesses' memory* [Unpublished PhD thesis, Department of Psychology, University of Gothenburg].

H-Metro. (2023, February 23). *Man appears in court drunk, remanded in custody.* https://www.newsdzezimbabwe.co.uk/2023/02/man-appears-in-court-drunk-remanded-in.html

Janssen, S. M. J., & Anne, M. (2019). And one more for the road: Commentary on the special issue on alcohol and eyewitness memory. *Applied Cognitive Psychology, 33*(3), 456–462.

Kozinski, W. (2017). The Reid interrogation technique and false confessions: A time for change. *Seattle Journal for Social Justice, 16*(2), 4–14. https://ssrn.com/abstract=3002338

Malebo v State (A235/2017) [2018] ZAFSHC 130 (2018, January 11). South Africa: Free State High Court, Bloemfontein.

Malloy, L. C., Shulman, E. P., & Cauffman, E. (2014). Interrogations, confessions, and guilty pleas among serious adolescent offenders. *Law and Human Behavior, 38*(2), 181–193. https://doi.org/10.1037/lhb0000065

Manica Post. (2022, July). *Man appears in court drunk, locked up.* https://www.newsdzezimbabwe.co.uk/2022/07/man-appears-in-court-drunk-locked-up.html

Masebeni and Another v S (A266/20) [2021] ZAWCHC 84 (2021, May 5). South Africa: Western Cape High Court, Cape Town.

Monds, L. A., Cullen, H. J., Kloft, L., Sumampouw, N., van Golde, C., Harrison, A. W., & Otgaar, H. (2021). Police perceptions of eyewitness impairment due to alcohol and other drug use: A cross-cultural comparison. *Police Practice and Research,* 1–16. https://doi.org/10.1080/15614263.2 021.1979397

Palmer, F. T., Flowe, H. D., Takarangi, M. K. T., & Humphries, J. E. (2013). Intoxicated witnesses and suspects: An archival analysis of their involvement in criminal case processing. *Law and Human Behavior, 37*(1), 54–59.

S v Mudzengerere and 3 Others (60 of 2024) [2024] ZWHHC 36 (2024, February 7).

United Nations Office on Drugs and Crime (UNODC). (2023). *Witnesses, cooperating witnesses and witness protection guidelines.* Retrieved June 9, 2023, from https://www.unodc.org/unodc/en/frontpage/protecting-witnesses.html

Veritas. (2023). *Anatomy of Zimbabwe's justice system.* Retrieved June 10, 2024, from https://zwnews.com/anatomy-of-zimbabwes-justice-system/

Yuille, J. C., & Tollestrup, P. A. (1990). Some effects of alcohol on eyewitness memory. *Journal of Applied Psychology, 75*(3), 268–273. https://doi.org/10.1037/0021-9010.75.3.268

ZWNews. (2018, July 24). Gutu doctor insults Magistrate, appears in court drunk. *ZWNews.* https://zwnews.com/gutu-doctor-insults-magistrate-appears-in-court-drunk/

7 Vulnerability of girls with communication disorders in the Malawian criminal justice system

Wellman Kondowe, Evans Lwara, and Hajira Blamu Mitumba

Introduction

The significance of effective communication in the criminal justice process cannot be overemphasised. Judicial decisions on a given criminal matter are arrived at solely based on the facts gathered and presented before a court by the prosecution and defence. Problems arise when a case involves a victim, an accused, or an independent witness who has communication disorders. As defined by Bilinguistics (2014), a communication disorder is any condition that affects an individual's ability to communicate. Persons with communication disorders often struggle with challenges, ranging from difficulties in producing a single sound or speech to the inability to express wants and needs using either verbal or non-verbal communication. Kallail (1988) conceptualises communicative disorders under three planes: receptive (impairments related to language comprehension), expressive (impairments related to language production), and pragmatic language use (impairments related to contextual use of language).

One of the main receptive communication disorders is hearing impairment. Gibbons (2003) defines it as the inability of an individual to hear sound adequately, regardless of the severity of the disability. Such disorders may arise from improper development, damage, or diseases to any part of the hearing system (AY JNISHD, 2015). People with hearing impairment, and indeed, any form of communication disorder, are highly susceptible to abuse, mostly because the perpetrators of such abuses are confident of hiding behind the shield of their victims' communication deficits. It is vital, therefore, for states to take keen interest in the affairs of such people to ensure that they too enjoy all human rights. This is in line with Aspiration 3 of the African Union's Agenda 2063, which declares that Africa should be a continent that fully adheres to the universal principles of human rights and justice, where all have access to timely and affordable justice (African Union, 2015).

One of the main ways states can show genuine regard for individuals with communication disorders is by capacitating the criminal justice system so that they have access to justice when they have been abused (Malunga et al., 2017). This entails putting in place mechanisms that will effectively compensate for

DOI: 10.4324/9781003569435-10

the communicative deficits that a given judicial client bears so that the right to be adequately heard before the court is upheld for every court user. Such deliberate efforts are, particularly, important because communication disorders have been found to uniquely impact different aspects of a person's life, including employment opportunities, psychosocial well-being, and school performance (Mulwafu et al., 2019). Worse still, the reality of people with communication disorders is often misunderstood and unrepresented because they often live a solitude life by disassociating themselves from the people in the larger community out of fear or not knowing how to properly interact with others (Jakaza & Nyakudya, 2018).

Considering how deleterious communication disorders are in the life of an individual, scholars who are enthusiastic about social justice and inclusion have conducted various studies to understand the problem and its contextual application. Despite the multiplicity of such studies in Malawi, most of them document the vulnerability of women, girls, and children and other disadvantaged groups when accessing justice, mostly in sexual assault cases (e.g., Malunga et al., 2017). In the field of language and law, there is very little research output on the nature of disadvantages that communication disorders occasion on individuals bearing such disabilities within the criminal justice system in Malawi. This is despite the amplified state and judicial commitments proclaiming assurances that individuals with communication disorders and other disabilities will be protected and properly assisted as they go through the criminal justice system. This chapter seeks to fill this gap. It does so by analysing the nature and extent of challenges that are faced by the justice system in handling cases involving victim girls with communication disorders (GCDs), whom the law generically defines as girls (or women) with mental disabilities in section 139 of the Malawi Penal Code (2023 amendment). The justice system has a duty to ensure that such girls are properly supported to ensure that their cases are concluded to satisfaction. As pointed out by Jakaza and Nyakudya (2018), GCDs are in 'minority', but this does justify their discrimination by not paying attention to their communicative and other needs.

The study addresses three objectives as follows:

(i) To examine Malawi's constitutional and statutory provisions that promote access to justice for girls with communication disorders;
(ii) To assess challenges faced by police and courts in dealing with girls with communication disorders; and
(iii) To examine strategies that are put in practice at police formations and in courts to safeguard the rights of girls with communication disorders.

Rationale of the study

A 2015/16 survey conducted by Malawi's Demographic and Health Survey reports that 21 percent of women and girls in Malawi had experienced some form of sexual violence in their life, and that this occurred to them before the age of 18. Similarly, recent media reports highlight the gravity of the problem of violence committed against GCDs in various parts of the country. For instance, Dzuwa (2014) reports of a 27-year-old man in Malawi who was arrested in Zomba for attempting to defile an epileptic. The Malawi News Agency (2020) further reports of a traditional authority who defiled a woman with mental disability in Dowa District. Nyasa Times (2013) also reported of a clinician who was found guilty of defiling a patient with mental disability at Mzuzu Central Hospital. Beyond FM (2020) also carried out a story of a man who defiled an 18-year-old with mental disability in Chikwawa District.

Girls and women with mental disabilities, the majority of whom have serious communication challenges, constitute the largest group of victims who face defilement atrocities. The perpetrators know that the victims will not be able to shout out for help or report the incident. Some retrogressive cultural beliefs fuel the violence against GCDs. For example, some believe that sleeping with a female with mental disability can make one get rich or that having unprotected sex with a girl with disabilities will cure HIV (Able Child Africa, n.d.). Finally, this group of girls meet serious challenges when their cases enter the justice system, either at the police station or in court due to language and communication barriers. All this points to the need to have in place effective mechanisms for handling such cases in the justice system.

Literature review

International and regional safeguards for people with disability

There are a number of global regulatory provisions aimed at safeguarding the rights of all people and those with disabilities before the law. The Universal Declarations on Human Rights (UDHR) lists a number of provisions that safeguard everyone and promote equality for all. Article 1 states that 'all human beings are born free and equal in dignity and rights'. Article 6 further states that 'everyone has the right to recognition everywhere as a person before the law'. Article 7 stipulates, 'Everyone is equal before the law and are entitled without any discrimination to equal protection of the law'. Similarly, Article 26 of the United Nations International Covenant on Civil and Political Rights (ICCPR), states that 'all persons are equal before the law and are entitled without any discrimination to the equal protection of the law'. Article 14 (F) of the same ICCPR highlights that 'every person has the right to have free assistance of an interpreter if he cannot understand trial procedures in the language or signs he/she used in court'.

Internationally, the right to access justice by specifically persons with disabilities is provided for in Article 13 of the UN's Convention on the Rights of Persons with Disabilities. This protocol highlights that;

> states parties shall ensure effective access to justice for persons with disabilities on an equal basis with others, including through the provision of procedural and age-appropriate accommodation, in order to facilitate

> their effective role as direct and indirect participants, including as witnesses, in legal proceedings, whether at investigative or preliminary stage.
> (African Union, 2018)

Article 7.2c of the Protocol to the African Charter to Human and People's Rights on the Rights of Persons with Disabilities in Africa intimates as follows: 'State parties shall take all appropriate and effective measures to ensure that persons with disabilities are provides with effective legal protection and support they may require in enjoying their legal capacity consistent with their rights, will and specific needs'. The 2017 Guidelines on the Conditions of Arrest, Police Custody and Pre-Trial Detention in Africa (simply known as 'Luanda Guidelines') also sets out States' obligations to provide all people with the rights to life, dignity, equality, security, a fair trial, and an independent judiciary.

From these instruments and provisions, it is clear that it is a global consensus that, before the law, persons with disabilities need not be discriminated against in any way because of the limiting condition that they bear. That is why the Convention on the Rights of Persons with Disabilities (CRPDs) emphasises among others that states must facilitate the learning of sign language and promote the linguistic identity of the deaf community. This is key in addressing communication deficits for persons with language disorders.

Challenges faced by girls with disabilities

Despite the international legal provisions outlined earlier, girls with disabilities continue to face many challenges. Women Enabled International (n.d.) notes that women and girls with disabilities make up almost one-fifth of the world's population of women. They experience unique forms of violence because of their disability. Women and girls with disabilities face greater social exclusion where some education systems, work training and some basic health services ignore and deny them their rights (Monederoa et al., 2014). They are also more vulnerable to dual-layered discriminations – being a woman and bearing a disability, making it easy to prey on them.

Statistics show that 80 percent of women with disabilities are at four times higher risk from suffering sexual violence than the rest of women, and such abuse is practised by people in their surroundings (healthcare professionals, caregivers, and relations). The vulnerability is even higher among girls with disabilities. Some of these girls are also exposed to forced sterilisation as well as to coercive abortions (Monederoa et al., 2014). Research has further shown that girls with intellectual impairment and communication difficulties are vulnerable to many forms of abuse, especially emotional and sexual abuse, which is perpetuated by cultural practices and norms (Sightsavers, 2018). Noticing the need for interventions on these malpractices, Able Child Africa (n.d.) developed Disability-inclusive Child Safeguarding

Guidelines to safeguard children with disabilities against sexual abuse. The Guidelines acknowledge that children with disabilities are 2.9 times more likely to experience 'sexual violence'. Children with intellectual disabilities are 4.6 times more likely to experience 'sexual violence' compared with other children.

Studies have also shown that girls face distinct barriers that prevent them from escaping sexual violence and seeking justice. Existing laws seldom address such specific concerns. The Justice system in some countries, like Zimbabwe, has been criticised for failing to adequately safeguard the rights of persons with disabilities, including girls. For example, Msipa (2015) argues that the justice system in Zimbabwe has for a long time been inaccessible for persons with disabilities because judicial procedures fail to adapt to meet their needs. The Law Society of Zimbabwe and other organisations acknowledge the inability to access preferential treatment from lawyers, although these experts have a privileged understanding of the law. Court cases for persons with hearing impairment in Zimbabwe are postponed several times due to the absence of a Sign Language interpreter. Some courts there are also found to lack interpreting services because they do not have employed court interpreters who have expertise in sign language meant to provide free representation for this vulnerable group of people (Svongoro & Ralarala, 2023). Similarly, perpetrators of injustice with hearing impairment also experience challenges in preparing and presenting their defence when they are not given adequate accommodations to support the trial process (Svongoro & Ralarala, 2023). Persons with communication disabilities thus face a variety of barriers in Zimbabwe, and this sometimes discourages them from reporting their victimisation.

Strategies put in practice at police stations and in courts to safeguard people with disabilities in other countries

Countries like the United States have a variety of resources that are made available to law enforcement agents, such as police during interactions with persons with communication disorders, such as those who are deaf. For example, auxiliary aids are widely used to ensure effective communication with persons with communication disorders (Farber, 2009). The lack of documentation of such strategies in Malawi implies that such services are not available to this group of people. In Zimbabwe for instance, the courts are guided on what to do in terms of procedural accommodations when administering justice to persons with language and communication difficulties. According to Svongoro et al. (2023), cases involving persons who are deaf, mute or hard-of-hearing witnesses or accused persons are mandated to utilise appointed intermediaries who are conversant with the language of the accused or witness. Likewise, the use of Sign Language and a competent Sign Language interpreter as well as other means of communication is supposed to be provided for (Svongoro et al., 2023). Much as the use of Sign Language is an important intervention, this chapter argues that we need to go beyond this by ensuring that persons with communication disorders are recognised as full human beings and that all their legal guarantees are fully practised.

Communication disorder in the laws of Malawi

The court, in *Rep. v Ishmael Mbidzi*, noted, 'the words idiots or imbeciles [defined as communication disorder in this chapter] are not defined in the Penal Code'. We further note that the court does not have a clear mechanism for proving a communication disorder even though for cases dealing with GCDs, one of the key requirements is that 'the complainant must be proved to be an idiot or imbecile' [*M'bwana v Rep* 8 MLR 159]. However, going through case law, we have noted that courts do not really consider medical reports, but rather testimonies from family members or guardians. In *Andy Victor v Rep.*, the judge argued, 'I do not understand positive proof of idiocy or imbecility to require medical evidence only. If there are persons who can positively testify as to the idiocy or imbecility of the victim [. . .] that should be sufficient proof'.

In *Rep. v Ishmael Mbidzi*, family members testified, 'The girl was epileptic and was not going to school. She could not cook, do any work or manage a house or relationships, or make independent decisions. Her relatives believed that she was an imbecile and the court was convinced'. Similarly, in *Rep. v Edwin Mtegha*, the court noted that upon looking at the victim, no reasonable person would have suggested that the victim did not have a disability. The magistrate found that the victim had a mental disability and that the accused person knew it. In *Rep. v Edwin Mtegha*, the prosecution brought a GCD for the court to observe the behaviour of the girl. It is clear, therefore, that in defining and proving communication disorder, the court does not have a prescribed criterion, but rather relies on precedents passed on through case law.

Theoretical framework

This study employed the analytical framework of Nancy Frazer's Social Justice Theory. Social justice is a multifaceted concept and is defined by Van den Bos (2003) as the fair and equitable distribution of power, resources, and obligations in society to all people, regardless of race or ethnicity, age, gender, ability status, sexual orientation, and religious or spiritual background. According to Fraser (1998), two key aspects of social justice are redistribution and recognition. Redistribution concerns a just distribution of resources in society so that everyone benefits from opportunities and process outcomes. Recognition, on the other hand, seeks to achieve a 'difference-friendly' world. It is inarguable that GCDs experience the world differently from those without communication difficulties. Therefore, the duty of states is to ensure that in any given case, systems that preserve status equality are put in place to allow every individual an opportunity to participate fully. Thus, the social justice approach calls for social arrangements that eliminate marginalisation of any kind while permitting all people to participate as peers in social life (Fraser, 2008). According to Frazer, to attain this, requires dismantling institutionalised obstacles that prevent some people from participating as equals in social interaction. In this theory, participation is an instrument for fulfilling the redistributive and recognition aspects of social justice.

The theory is particularly important in the context of communicatively challenged users of the criminal justice system. It provides conceptual frames for understanding the nature and extent of systemic barriers that inhibit GCDs from participating and benefiting fully from the criminal justice system. The chapter argues that the inability of the justice system to provide effective communication support systems denies these people a voice, which essentially places them on the receiving end of injustice. Having in place a working disability-responsive legal system as spelt out in the continental and global instruments can, therefore, not be overemphasised. It resonates with Enabler number 3 (Effective governance systems and institutions) of the Malawi 2063, which is the country's developmental blueprint that seeks to achieve an inclusively wealthy and self-reliant nation by 2063 (National Planning Commission [NPC], 2020).

Methodology

The study adopted a qualitative research approach with a sample size of 20 participants. In order to facilitate triangulation, a variety of techniques were employed for data collection – document analysis, key participants' interviews (KII), and Focus Group Discussions (FGDs). Purposive sampling technique was used to identify legal practitioners (judges, magistrates, state prosecutors and lawyers) as key participants. Data from police was collected using convenient sampling where we targeted only those police officers who have previously handled cases, involving GCDs.

Document analysis was used to address the first objective, which aimed at finding out the constitutional and statutory provisions that promote access to justice for GCDs. We analysed the Constitution of the Republic of Malawi, the Disability Act among other key documents. Data for the second and third objectives was collected from 12 police officers and eight judicial officers in Mzuzu City. The police sample included Assistant Commissioner of Police (Northern region); A Senior Superintendent and a General Duties Officer; an Assistant Superintendent and Head of Community Policing; a Detective Inspector (Criminal Investigative Division); a Station Prosecution Officer; two Inspectors, and three Detective Sub-inspectors. Seven of them were male and five were female. Their qualifications range from the

Malawi School Certificate of Education (MSCE) to master's degree. All the participants had been in service for a period of between 16 to 29 years. The sample for judicial officers comprised three high court Judges; five Senior Resident Magistrates. All the judicial officers have been in-service for over seven years.

This research obtained an ethical approval from the Inspector General of Police in Malawi on 12 May 2024 with a reference number C/75/1/55. The approval was on condition that all the materials collected are to be used for academic purposes only and that the researcher will maintain confidentiality. Another set of approvals were obtained from the Chief Justice and the Registrar of High Court and the Supreme Court of Appeal in Malawi.

Findings

Constitutional and statutory provisions that promote access to justice for GCDs in Malawi

The Malawi government's ratification of the Convention on the Rights of Persons with Disabilities in 2009 and the passing of the Disability Act in 2012 (and later on amended in 2024) remains the foundational framework for the promotion of the rights of people with disabilities in Malawi. According to Nkhata (2020), these developments remain vital in the realisation of the rights of people with disabilities. The Malawi Disability Act (2012) defines disability as 'a long-term physical, mental, intellectual or sensory impairment which, in interaction with various barriers, may hinder the full and effective participation in society of a person on equal basis with other persons'. Section 3 (a) of the Act amplifies the need for the Government of Malawi to adopt policies and legislation on the equalisation of opportunities for persons with disabilities in order to promote and protect this group's rights. However, the Act does not specifically refer to issues of access to justice for persons with disabilities, including those with communication disorders.

It is the Constitution of the Republic of Malawi that makes direct reference to issues of access to justice, particularly, in section 41 (2) and (3) where it guarantees every person the right to access justice and legal remedies. This provision is general; it does not advance any guarantees that uniquely apply to persons with specific disabilities. As Flynn and Lawson (2013) in Nkhata (2020) argue, people with different kinds of disabilities will experience different challenges in their access to justice.

The Malawi Penal Code makes specific provisions relating to girls and persons with disabilities. Section 138 of the Code provides for the offence of defilement of a girl in general, while defilement of a person with a mental disability is tried under section 139. Section 138 (1) stipulates, 'Any male person who has sexual intercourse with a female child shall be guilty of a felony and shall, upon conviction, be liable to imprisonment for life'. Section 139, The

Malawi Penal Code, makes specific provisions relating to girls and persons with disabilities. stipulates that

> any man who, knowing a woman or girl to be a person with a mental disability, has or attempts to have sexual intercourse with a woman or a girl, under circumstances not amounting to rape, but which prove that the offender knew at the time of the commission of the offence that the woman or girl has am mental disability, commits an offence and shall, upon conviction, be liable to imprisonment for life.

GCDs, who have been victimised, thus, find solace in these sections.

The Criminal Procedure and Evidence Code (CPEC) is another critical instrument that safeguards the rights of persons with disabilities before the law. On the examination of a witness with communicative disorders, section 211 of the CPEC states that a witness who is unable to speak may give his evidence in any manner in which he can make it intelligible, as by writing or by signs; but such writing must be written, and the signs made, in an open court. Evidence so given is deemed to be oral evidence.

Despite the goodwill towards persons with disabilities that is reflected in the fore-discussed legal instruments, there are a number of provisions that seemingly work against the safeguarding of the rights of persons with disabilities. For instance, Nkhata (2020) reports grey areas in different provisions relating to the conduct of criminal trials that raise red flags for persons with disabilities. Section 138 of the CPEC, for example, allows a court to proceed with a trial or committal proceedings even where the accused person does not understand the proceedings as long as he/she is considered not having a mental disability. Such provisions would essentially legitimise the court's decision to proceed hearing a case involving GCDs and other communicatively disadvantaged persons even if their communicative needs have not been fully met.

Challenges faced by police and courts when handling cases involving GCDs

There are a number of legal provisions, such as the Luanda Guidelines, which provide guidance on how the police and courts in Malawi should handle cases involving GCDs during investigations, when taking witness statements, and during prosecution. For examples, on the conditions of arrest, police custody and pre-trial detention, the Luanda Guidelines recommend that special measures be taken when handling children, women, disabled or non-national offenders or witnesses. With regard to those with disabilities, the Guidelines call upon law enforcers to ensure access to justice through 'the provision of interpreters [and] information in accessible formats and/or independent third parties who are not employed by the law enforcement authority and who are appropriately qualified' (African Commission on Human and Peoples' Rights [ACHPR], 2017, p. 19).

However, the study found that a myriad of challenges persists in the justice system. One of the major challenges that was reported in the police stations is lack of professional training in Sign Language for police officers. This is a very important intervention because it was acknowledged that cases involving girls and other people with communication disorders are reported at the stations. As such, the need for professional Sign Language support is high. Unfortunately, the curriculum for training police officers and legal practitioners in Malawi does not incorporate Sign Language orientation. The Malawian Justice system does not, therefore, have qualified interpreters to competently bridge communication gaps between GCDs and other parties in the justice system.

In the absence of formal Sign language training, short courses would significantly make a difference. However, it was reported that such courses are hard to come by. For instance, some police officers who have served in the justice system for as many as 20 years have never had the privilege of receiving in-service training on Sign Language. Only two of the police officers we interacted with reported to have received some short training in Sign Language. However, such training is facilitated by non-governmental and other organisations, hence are erratic. In addition to the irregularity of the training, the standard of the Sign Language in which officers are trained, in some cases, differs a lot from the Sign Language being used by the victim or witness. The problem with lack of formal training is that the justice system will gap-fill with inefficient alternatives, such as interpretation by family or other unprofessional Sign Language interpreters. Upholding critical interpreting ethical principles, which are critical for earning the respect and trust of all parties to a case, such as impartiality, having no opinion, and keeping out of the case is difficult with the use of interpreters chosen out of convenience (Edwards, 1995). To make things worse, there is no budgetary provision for the outsourcing of external Sign Language interpreters. Ineffective interpretation is, therefore, inevitable, making the potential for unjust case conclusions, such as wrongful convictions or acquittals a reality.

One of the major effects of the communication barrier is that some cases get unnecessarily prolonged. This is occasioned by several factors, including the search for an appropriate intermediary communicator and because investigations and examination of witnesses in court take more time. It was reported that sometimes it could take up to three hours of an examination session. The police also acknowledged that it is extremely difficult to investigate and prosecute such cases unless the suspect is caught red-handed. The prolonged examination sessions affect the duration and speeding of the cases. Since most of the cases involving GCDs attract a lot of attention from the general public and interested organisations, such delays make people perceive the delivery of justice negatively. Due to such delays, evidence can also be lost (Kondowe, 2022). Although cases of victimisation of GCDs are prevalent in our society, it was reported that very few are reported to the police.

Strategies put in place at police and courts to remedy communication deficits among GCDs

There are a number of strategies that the police and courts use to remedy for communication deficits in cases involving girls with communication disorders. Some are discussed next.

Soliciting intermediary communication services of parents/guardian or any close family member

It was reported that the assistance of a parent, a guardian or a close family member is usually sought to extract information from a girl with communication disorders. For instance, in *Rep. v Edwin Mtegha*, the grandmother of the victim testified on behalf of the victim. Parents and guardians are engaged because of their familiarity with the communication system of their ward. It was, however, quickly pointed out that using parents might compromise the credibility and believability of the victims' stories since they may twist the stories to suit their interests in the case.

Soliciting intermediary communication services of a known Sign Language specialist

It was also reported that in some cases, investigators and prosecutors engage known Sign Language specialists to assist with interpretation services. Much as an independent specialist might be a good alternative to parents or guardians, there are very few professionally trained Sign Language specialists in Malawi. There are also no official guidelines on the terms of engagement for such specialists at police stations, which is against the concerns and principles of the Luanda Guidelines.

Soliciting intermediary communication services of a police officer who is trained in Sign Language

This was also reported as an alternative that the police exploit to bridge communication gaps. However, as already mentioned, the curriculum for training police officers does not have provisions for Sign Language training. The few available short courses made available to officers are erratic and highly inadequate. This means that most stations do not have police officers with authoritative Sign Language proficiency.

Asking the person with a communication disorder to write the statement

It was also reported that sometimes, victims or witnesses are asked to write their statement instead of verbalising it through an intermediary. The drawback with this strategy is that most persons with communication disorders are illiterate, hence not able to read or write.

Discussion

The gap between theory and practice in the safeguarding of the rights of GCDs in Malawi

Although the study found that Malawi has a number of policy and legislative frameworks for safeguarding and promoting the rights of people with disabilities, the situation on the ground remains largely unsupportive. For instance, Malawi rectified a number of international and regional instruments, such as the *Universal Declarations on Human Rights*; *the United Nations on International Covenant on Civil* and *Political Rights*; *the UN's Convention on the Rights of Persons with Disabilities*; and *the African Charter to Human and People's Rights.* All these instruments convey the universal principle of equality, which suggests that all human beings, regardless of one's condition, should be treated with the same level of respect and recognition before the law. The Disability Act 2012, which was drafted to domesticate the disability provisions in these international instruments, remains a loose tool that is not sufficiently complemented in practice. However, Section 139 of the Malawi Penal Code criminalises the act of knowingly having unlawful canal knowledge of GCDs, and that anyone who contravenes this shall be guilty of a felony and shall be liable to imprisonment for 14 years. This chapter argues that this provision on its own is not enough to safeguard the rights of GCDs.

Another demonstration of goodwill is shown by the government's acknowledgement of the challenges facing people with disabilities in as far as access to justice is concerned. In the 2019–2024 Strategic Plan, The Malawi Judiciary (2019, p. 19) points out as follows:

> The Judiciary recognises that it does not have adequate capacity to effectively address the needs of people with disabilities. Although some facilities exist that are disability friendly, there is a lot more that needs to be done in terms of policies and guidelines, knowledge and skills of judicial officers and members of staff to handle people with disabilities, as well as improvements in the infrastructure.

The Judiciary constructed this Strategic Plan around a bold theme – expanded, inclusive, accessible justice for all. Unfortunately, what obtains on the ground remains far from providing meaningfully inclusive and accessible justice for all because systematic accommodations are not being made to meet the communicative needs of GCDs. As Malunga et al. (2017) point out, states are mandated to recognise persons with disabilities and assist them to exercise and enjoy their legal rights on an equal basis with others. With an insufficient language support system, you do not expect the GCDs to participate actively and meaningfully in the legal process. According to the Social Justice Theory when people are deprived of the opportunity to participate, it is difficult for them to be recognised and benefit equally from resources and opportunities in society. The GCDs are, therefore, bound to continue suffering systematic discrimination before the law.

A justice system that recognises people with disabilities must be able to provide a clear definition of different disabilities. Concise definition of disability and related terms is an important tool for improvement in the life of people with disabilities (Alman, 2014). Through proper definition, there is a clearly marked distinction between people with and people without disability as well as between people with different disabilities. This facilitates easy identification of a specific disability population to target with a programmatic intervention. In Malawi, the people with communicative and other disorders are largely excluded in the justice system. A good example is the case of persons with intellectual disabilities. There are no proper legal mechanisms in Malawi that succinctly identify and describe them, yet when it comes to cases involving them, it is a legal requirement that a complainant must be proved to be with that disability [*M'bwana v Rep* 8 MLR 159]. With lack of a proper legal definition, police and courts largely rely on family members or anyone who can positively testify to the intellectual disability of a victim. This is strong evidence that girls and other people with communication disorders are yet to earn full recognition before the Malawian justice system, essentially subjecting them to social subordination and disrespect (Fraser, 1998).

Definitional indeterminacy in the justice system lays fertile ground for the proliferation of inappropriate legal terminology. Taking, as a point of reference, in *Rep. v Ishmael Mbidzi* [Criminal Case No. 41 of 2019], the judge noted that 'the words idiot or imbeciles are not defined in the Penal Code and they should be taken to carry their ordinary meanings – that of someone being "foolish" or "stupid"'. Such ordinary meanings of disability-related terms perpetuate the dehumanisation of disability. They are offensive and, hence, discriminatory, yet they were used in official legal instruments of Malawi before being replaced just recently. To promote fairness and equality before the law, inclusive vocabulary and definitions need to be used all the time.

The status of language issues in the Malawian justice system

In Malawi, the issue of language remains peripheral in the justice system. There are no noticeable practical steps taken to bridge linguistic gaps faced by people with communication disorders. As a country that practises common law, cases are argued orally in court and evidence is put to test through examination. Such a complex process requires effective use of language because any lapses in communication may result in factual misrepresentation that leads to negative or incorrect judicial outcomes. As Gibbons (2003) points out, some players in the justice system choose to exploit some prevailing communication challenges to discredit vulnerable people. Consequently, stories told by those with communication disorders become unbelievable due to lack of clear communication measures. Vulnerable people can consequently be traumatised, and fairness can be endangered.

Girls with communication disorders are largely victims of sexual assault. As such, they encounter multiple layers of challenges once their cases enter the justice system. For instance, some evidence, like vaginal traces of semen can quickly get lost due to late reporting or lack of knowledge on what counts as evidence in sexual assault (Kondowe, 2022). In such a case, the justice system solely relies on the victim's narrative. However, with most of such victims also suffering serious memory degradation (Kondowe, 2022), their ability to handle cross-examination sessions and to provide crucial details about the time and dates of occurrence of the alleged offence becomes impaired. It is, therefore, sad that the Malawi police and courts are not living up to the moral imperative of investing significantly in the language support mechanisms for such groups of people. As highlighted in Fraser's Social Justice Theory, the recognition dimension requires that linguistic and other injustices that are rooted in social identities be dealt with so that a status of equality among all people ensues. To achieve this, the justice system must deliberately put in place practical steps to nurture Sign Language and other intermediary systems of communication within its ranks.

Both police and legal professionals raised genuine concerns regarding the poor system for handling the communication needs of GCDs. The need for greater and effective utilisation of Sign Language was overwhelmingly recommended. Unfortunately, Sign Language is not integrated within the police and legal professionals' formal training curricula with a lucky few receiving erratic short courses. This is happening at a time when some countries like South Africa and Zimbabwe have taken serious steps in promoting Sign language in the courts and made it one of the court's official languages. The police and courts, thus, resort in soliciting intermediary communication services of relatives or known Sign Language specialists outside the justice system. The unreliability of this alternative has been well documented. For instance, relatives may provide skewed information to advance their stakes in the case, and as Gibbons (2003) points out, they might face difficulties to sign some legal technical vocabulary. This practice also compromises the key ethical requirements of legal interpreting such as accuracy, impartiality, role boundary and conflict of interest. Using information sourced through such an unreliable alternative communication intermediaries can easily mislead the courts into making wrong convictions or acquittals. This underscores the need for Sign Language professionals who have dual specialisation in both Sign Language and the law.

Conclusion and policy recommendations

The study sought to understand the experiences of girls with communication disorders in the Malawian criminal justice system. Much as there are a lot of well-meaning statutory, policy, and regulatory instruments providing for the protection and promotion of the rights of people with various kinds of disabilities, the justice system continues to face many challenges in handling communication-related disabilities. This is worsened by the fact that most of the strategies that are put in place to deal with these challenges are unsystematic and strewn with many gaps. The impression that is created is that the interests of the communicatively disadvantaged are faintly recognised and that, as long as the justice system remains linguistically less inclusive, the legal status of GCDs seeking justice in the Malawian criminal justice system will never be at par with the rest of the people.

For this reason, the Malawi government needs to take a number of measures to address the disadvantages and inequalities faced by GCDs. Being a signatory to various international treaties and declarations, Malawi has the responsibility of showing commitment to the same in practice. There must also be a deliberate effort to include specific and detailed issues of people with disabilities in her various disability related national policies and laws. Furthermore, different professionals, such as the police, lawyers, magistrates, judges must receive specific training concerning persons with communication challenges. The University of Malawi (formerly known as Chancellor College) is already offering specialised disability rights law courses. Government can take advantage of this and other relevant institutions to advance Sign Language literacy among legal trainees through both long and short-term courses.

In relation to this, vital professions in the justice system such as the police, prosecutors, and interpreters should also go for refresher courses that would allow them to deal with cases of people with communication challenges and other disabilities positively. The Malawian courts should be given a mandate to hire Sign Language experts to ensure fair justice to GCDs.

Finally, in order to ensure proper communication, persons with communication challenges should be sent to school, so that they acquire skills for proper interaction with others in society. Parents should be made aware of children with disabilities' right to education and its many other benefits. Unless such policy measures are implemented, access to justice for GCDs will remain a concept on paper.

References

ACHPR. (2017). *Guidelines on the conditions of arrest, police custody and pre-trial detention in Africa.* https://apcof.org/wp-content/uploads/2017/03/conditions-of-arrestpolice-custody-and-pre-trial-detention-in-africa-luanda-guidelines-trainee-manual.pdf

African Union. (2015). *Agenda 2063: The Africa we want*. https://au.int/sites/default/files/documents/33126-doc-framework_document_book.pdf
African Union. (2018). *Protocol to the African charter on human and peoples' rights on the rights of persons with disabilities in Africa*. https://au.int/en/treaties/protocol-african-charter-human-and-peoples-rights-person-disabilities-africa
Ali Yavar Jung National Institute of Speech and Hearing Disabilities (AY JNISHD). (2015). *Hearing impairment*. http://www.ayjnihh.nic.in
Alman, B. M. (2014). Definitions, concepts, and measures of disability. *Annals of Epidemiology, 24*(1), 2–7.
Bilinguistics. (2014). *Communication disorders: A resource for students, parents and professionals*. https://bilinguistics.com/wp-content/uploads/2014/11/Resources-on-Communication-Disorders-for-Parents-and-Professionals.pdf
Edwards, A. B. (1995). *The practice of court interpreting*. John Benjamins.
Farber, B. J. (2009). Police interactions with deaf persons. *AELE Monthly Law Journal, 3*, 101–111.
Flynn, E. & Lawson, A. (2013). Disability and access to justice in the European Union: Disabilities. *European Yearbook of Disability Law, 4*.
Fraser, N. (1998). *Social justice in the age of identity politics: Redistribution, recognition, anticipation*. (Discussion Papers/Wissenschaftszentrum Berlin für Sozialforschung, Forschungsschwerpunkt Arbeitsmarkt und Beschäftigung, Abteilung Organisation und Beschäftigung, pp. 98–108). Wissenschaftszentrum Berlin für Sozialforschung gGmbH. https://nbn-esolving.org/urn:nbn:de:0168-ssoar-126247
Fraser, N. (2008). *Scales of justice: Reimagining political space in a globalizing world*. Polity Press.
Gibbons, J. P. (2003). *Forensic linguistics: An introduction to language in the justice system*. Wiley-Blackwell.
Jakaza, T. N. & Nyakudya, D. (2018). Living with hearing and speech impairment: Challenges and options. *Journal of Development Administration, 3*, 9–17.
Kallail, K. J. (1988). Assessing and treating communication disorders. *American Family Physician, 37*(2), 312–316.
Kondowe, W. (2022). Towards the principle of believability: A new socio-pragmatic model in forensic settings. In M. K. Ralarala, R. H. Kaschula & G. Heydon (Eds.), *Language and the law: Global perspectives in forensic linguistics from Africa and beyond* (pp. 261–278). Sun Press.
Malawi Government. (2012). *Disability act no. 8 of 2012*. Malawi Government.
Malawi Judiciary. (2019). *Strategic plan (2019–2024)*. Malawi Judiciary.
Malunga, B., Kanyongolo, N. R. & Mbano-Mweso, N. (2017). Access to justice of children with disabilities in defilement cases in Malawi. *African Disability Rights Yearbook*, 25–39. http://doi.org/10.29053/2413-7138/2017/v5n1a2
Monederoa, J. A. G., Cuestab, C. U. & Anguloa, B. N. (2014). Social image of disability: Vulnerability of the dignity of women with disability and social exclusion contexts. *Social and Behavioral Sciences, 161*, 115–120.
Msipa, D. (2015). How assessments of testimonial competence perpetuate inequality and discrimination for persons with intellectual disabilities: An analysis of the approach taken in South Africa and Zimbabwe. *African Disability Rights Yearbook, 3*, 63–90. https://www.adry.up.ac.za/articles-2015/msipa-d
Mulwafu, W., Tataryn, M., Polack, S., Viste, A., Kragerud, F. & Kuper, H. (2019). Children with hearing impairment in Malawi: A cohort study. *Bulletin of the World Health Organization, 97*(10), 654–662. http://doi.org/10.2471/BLT.18.226241
National Planning Commission (NPC). (2020). *Malawi vision 2063*. https://npc.mw/wp-content/uploads/2021/02/MW2063-VISION-FINAL.pdf
Nkhata, M. J. (2020). Access to justice for persons with disabilities in Malawi: Exploring challenges and possibilities in the criminal justice system: *African Disability Rights Yearbook*, 124–149. http://doi.org/10.29053/2413-7138/2020/v8a6

Sightsavers. (2018). *Safeguarding policy*. https://www.sightsavers.org/wp-content/uploads/2019/09/Sightsavers-Safeguarding-Policy-ENGLISH.pdf

Svongoro, P. & Ralarala, M. K. (2023). Zimbabwe's constitutional safeguards for persons with communication disabilities. In R. S. Kaschula, M. H. Ralarara, & G. Heydon (Eds.), *Language, crime and courts in contemporary Africa and beyond: Studies in forensic and legal linguistic in Africa and beyond* (pp. 51–71). Sun Press.

Van den Bos, K. (2003). On the subjective quality of social justice: The role of affect as information in the psychology of justice judgments. *Journal of Personality and Social Psychology*, *85*, 482–498.

8 Communication barriers faced by deaf citizens when accessing police services in Zimbabwe

Tawanda Matende, Patson Kufakunesu, and Victor Mugari

Introduction

This chapter discusses the communication system used by deaf citizens when accessing police services in Epworth Suburb, Harare, Zimbabwe. Epworth is a high-density suburb with a population of approximately 200,000 people. It is labelled as a high-crime-rate community where all sorts of activities are carried out, populated by mainly poor residents in Harare and where Zimbabwe's cultural diversity is well represented (Msindo et al., 2013). This chapter examines police officers' knowledge and attitudes towards serving deaf citizens, the communication methods used, the barriers to reporting crimes, and how these practices impact the legal rights of deaf citizens in the Epworth Community. The chapter aims to understand the challenges faced by deaf citizens during critical stages of police interaction, including crime reporting, statement recording, and seeking assistance. The term 'deaf' is used to describe all kinds of deaf people, including those who are hard of hearing.

Sign Language (henceforth SL) is an officially recognised language under the current Constitution of Zimbabwe (Amendment Number 20) Act, Section 6 (4) 2013. It is clearly stated within the constitution that *the state must promote and advance the use of SL and must create conditions for its development.* This means that SL can be used in whatever sphere where communication is needed. Such official recognition calls for research on SL that would guide language planning activities meant to develop and promote SL. However, not much research has been done in terms of research in SL as a follow-up to the constitutional provisions of 2013. Thus, the current research which assesses the nature of communication in the legal domain addresses this gap.

SL issues within the global context

De Meulder (2023) published a study examining the impact of the legal recognition of SLs on the linguistic human rights of Deaf communities. Her study highlighted the importance of comprehensive legal frameworks and the involvement of deaf leaders in the recognition process. Motivated by the need to interrogate the controversy surrounding language rights for Deaf

DOI: 10.4324/9781003569435-11

communities, Trovato (2013) raises the question that; is the right to SL, the same as the right to a minority language? A minority language is a language that is spoken in a country by a small portion of the population and typically does not have an official status; for example, is not enforced by the law, but can aspire to have one (Trovato, 2013). According to Krausneker (2003), SLs are 'minoritised minority languages', they are minority languages in numerical terms and are unequal in terms of power; consequently, they are then minorised by institutions, policies and research which either ignore them or even explicitly exclude them. Trovato (2013) argues that the right to SL is not only as strong as the right to a minority language, but is indeed even stronger, because it is the right to have normal, social and cognitive developments. These observations inform the researchers about how language policies contribute to the violation of linguistic rights of the Deaf with specific focus on the use of SL in the legal domain.

Bauman and Murray (2013), helped to shift the narrative around deafness, positioning it as a source of diversity and cultural wealth rather than a deficit/disability. Their work has influenced educational policies and curriculum development leading to the increased inclusion of Deaf culture and SL in classrooms and learning materials. Cameron et al. (2020) work on indigenous SLs in Canada has raised awareness about the unique linguistic and cultural needs of these communities leading to the development of language documentation and revitalisation initiatives. Sall's (2022) research on Senegalese sign language (SSL) has provided valuable insights into the linguistic structure, usage, patterns, and sociolinguistic status. Salls work highlighted the need for the Senegalese government to officially recognise SSL and develop policies to support its use in various domains, such as education, health care and public services. These scholars, along with many others, have continued to build upon the foundational work of earlier SL advocates, expanding the scope and depth of research, advocacy, and policy initiatives in support of SL rights globally.

In most countries, there is a serious shortage of SL interpreters (Wit, 2011). Russell (2013) observes that in Canada, some jurisdictions, police services and courts rely on staff members who may only have minimal signed language proficiency to interpret for interactions involving citizens who are deaf. This almost leads to miscommunications and the very real potential for grave errors that have an impact on the Deaf and the services that they are trying to access (Russell, 2013). Russell's study resonates well with Miller (2001) who notes that the provision of SL interpreters to deaf suspects, defendants and offenders has been a problematic issue in the criminal justice system. Inconsistency in the provision of interpreter services results largely from the ignorance of criminal justice professionals regarding deaf people's communication needs and accommodation. However, Tallroth (2012) argues that while the use of interpreters can bridge language gaps and facilitate communication, it does not really promote the use of the language; it merely relies on a norm and accommodation approach (Kymlicka & Patten, 2003) for people lacking proficiency in the majority language, while neglecting to recognise the distinct cultural and linguistic identity for signers. These observations are very insightful to this discussion for they inform the researcher about the communication challenges faced by deaf people in the legal settings and possible solutions that can be offered.

The police in the UK rely on Sign Language Interpretation Services (SLIS) in their interactions with a citizen who is deaf and uses British Sign Language (BSL) across most areas of policing – for example, either at the station or in other public and private locations, and face-to-face or via video-conferencing (Skinner & Napier, 2023). De Meulder and Haualand (2021) have challenged the unquestioned acceptance that SLIS have become the institutionally normative solution to grant deaf signers access to public services, and thus SLIS could be considered as a social institution within the broader public institution context. De Meulder and Haualand (2021) go on to criticise this institutional position as one that replaces or conceals the need for language-concordant provisions to be made available. The dependency on interpreters to enable the police to engage with BSL users is linked to the lack of opportunities for deaf signers to play an active role in policing, masked by the assumption that the provision of SLIS is adequate.

In the United States, Brunson (2007) examined the experiences of 12 deaf signers in negotiating access when interacting with legal authorities. The preference was to be provided with an ASL-English interpreter, but Brunson identified that there were often problems with this request. Brunson summarised these problems across three themes: (i) difficulties in obtaining desired accommodation (2007, p. 80), where deaf signers discussed the various problems they faced when they requested or attempted to negotiate for an interpreter; (ii) dealing with a problematic accommodation (2007, p. 80), where deaf signers discussed how they negotiated situations in which an interpreter behaved in a way that negatively impacted the outcome of the situation; and (iii) enduring a partial accommodation (2007, p. 86), where deaf signers highlighted that even when an interpreter was present, the interpreter was unable to provide access due to their lack of skill in the given situation. Brunson concluded that '[d]eaf people have very little control over the accommodation they receive and yet are held fully responsible for ensuring its efficacy' (2007, p. 77), therefore the burden of access to the police was unfairly distributed.

According to Miller (2001), a review of federal criminal cases in New York involving violence, sex offenses, and drug offenses allegedly committed by persons with hearing loss revealed that the most commonly attempted method of communication used by law enforcement agents was spoken English (i.e., no accommodation at all) which was used in 40.9 percent of the arrests. Court records indicate that 22.7 percent of suspects in these cases had to communicate through signing family members, friends, or law enforcement employees, 13.6 percent were interrogated by law enforcement agents using note writing (Miller, 2001). Only 13.6 percent of the suspects were provided with professional interpreters at the time of arrest or during subsequent legal proceedings and approximately 9.1 percent of suspects in this group were unable to be accommodated and were later deemed incompetent by the court (Miller, 2001). Miller's study helps this current study with a foretaste on the challenges faced by deaf people in the legal system. The current study focuses on the linguistic practices involving the Deaf in Zimbabwe within the legal domain.

Lack of deaf awareness and barriers to communication have been highlighted in studies investigating crime reporting by victims. Glasser et al. (2021) investigated these barriers in the US. They found that not only are victims with disability and deaf victims reluctant to report to the police because of the communication barrier, they may also fear being judged as vulnerable and in need of protection. Powers and Hayes (2024) note that misconceptions and stereotypes in law enforcement responses to disabled or deaf victims of interpersonal violence are a major challenge, police officers often do not understand their disabilities and are unresponsive to the victim's needs. Police officers are not aware that deaf people might need an interpreter to communicate, and not all can lip-read or write notes.

Sociolinguistic status of Sign Language in Zimbabwe

Senator David Coltart, the then Minister of Education and Culture in the foreword of the *Zimbabwean Sign Language Dictionary,* notes that deaf people and educators have long recognised a need to document Zimbabwean signs and develop Zimbabwean Sign Language. The first such effort saw the publication of *Volumes 1 and 2 of the Zimbabwe National Sign Language Dictionary.* Miti (2011) states that, 'the existence of several varieties can impede effective communication between deaf people who use different varieties'. This exposes any education system because it is difficult to decide or determine the dialect that should be used for formal communication and as a medium of instruction at school. To ease such anomalies, Miti (2011) further opines that there is need to develop a unified standard variety for use in formal and informal communication across Zimbabwe.

According to Mugari et al. (2019), ZSL has several variations that inhibit communication among deaf people. For this reason, the harmonisation of SL variations is required to bridge the differences and culminate into a standard and formal ZSL which facilitates better communication among the Deaf. Mugari et al. (2019) argue that if the different varieties of SL across the country remain unrecognised and uncategorised, communication barriers among the Deaf and those who work with them will continue. This seriously hinders the development of SL and the socialisation capabilities of the Deaf. The foregoing study informs the researchers about SL variations in Zimbabwe and is of paramount significance to the present study, which focuses on examining the acceptability of the assumed standard forms by the Deaf.

Mugari and Matende (2022) observe that, the majority of urban/rural deaf dwellers and their children, were not involved in the compilation of most dictionaries. The assumed standard forms are not acceptable because SL variation has not been thoroughly researched due to varied reasons. According to ADAM (2015), a standardisation exercise which excludes the language community is unacceptable. SL in Zimbabwe is still in the lower levels of standardisation and it is riddled with intrinsic regional varieties and there are still incongruences between the said standard forms and the actual language usage (Mugari & Matende, 2022).

Additionally, the research, conducted by Mugari et al. (2019) in the ten provinces of the country confirmed anecdotal evidence among the Deaf community that there are SL variations. According to the study, variations in SL are largely attributed to the influence of SLs from other countries such as Germany, United Kingdom and United States. In addition, the variations are attributed to the lack of popularisation of the dictionaries that have been produced by the Ministry of Primary and Secondary Education, possibly exacerbated by the fact that the language is not taught as a curriculum subject.

As a special minority language worldwide, SL has not been spared from the dearth of notable development in Zimbabwe, a quality which it shares with a host of other minority languages (Mugari & Matende, 2020). Worse still, there has been a worrying development in various domains where these minority languages are not similarly treated. According to Mugari and Matende (2020), there is a caste of major minority languages which has been catapulted by the current discoursing and focus on minority languages that others have gotten more impoverished than others.

An assessment of the Zimbabwe School Examination Council results for Grade seven and Ordinary level shows that the educational outcomes of deaf children are poor and lower than their hearing counterparts (Deaf Zimbabwe Trust, 2013). In 2014, only 10 percent of the deaf candidates who sat for Grade seven examinations passed (Deaf Zimbabwe Trust, 2013). The failure is mainly attributed to lack of SL in the classroom. According to Musengi et al. (2013), the use of spoken languages as an approach to teach deaf pupils may be indicative of what Bauman (2004) calls audism. Audism, which parallels racism and sexism, involves Saussure's historical privileging of sound over sign in what philosopher Jacques Derrida identifies as 'phono-centrism' (Musengi et al., 2013). This means that spoken languages such as Shona and English have historically had status over SLs such as SL in Zimbabwe because of audism (Musengi et al., 2013). Such studies are critical in portraying the extent of marginalisation that the Deaf are exposed to in other domains.

The current study investigates whether similar challenges repeat themselves in the legal domain. Choruma (2006) points out that; accessibility is a problem particularly for those with reduced mobility or in wheelchairs and those with visual and hearing impairments. Matende et al. (2023) observed that SL is not prioritised in hospitals and clinics. In fact, the language provisions relating to the use of SL in Zimbabwe are not being implemented. The Deaf community in Zimbabwe is excluded from accessing health information due to a plethora of challenges in the health system which include communication barriers, lack of SL interpreters in the health domain, stigmatisation and negative attitudes from the medical practitioners (Matende et al., 2023). These studies are significant to this study because they show that despite designing a language policy to enhance the use and development of SL, challenges are still being faced on implementation, which highlights the need for the assessment of language policies before, during and after implementation.

Theoretical framework

This study employed a conceptual framework that considers both the disability model and the cultural model of deafness. The disability model views deafness from a medical perspective, as a physical impairment in the ability to hear, classifying individuals as 'deaf' or 'hard of hearing' (Scharp & Barker, 2021). In contrast, the cultural model takes a social constructivist view, considering deafness not as a disability, but as a difference. Those referred to within the cultural model use the uppercase 'Deaf' convention and are often part of the Deaf community, which has its own norms, language, and shared features with the broader surrounding cultures (Glickman & Carey, 2023). By incorporating both the disability and cultural perspectives, the study aimed to establish a comprehensive conceptual framework for understanding the experiences of the Deaf community.

Methodology

This chapter investigated the communication system, barriers, and challenges faced by the Deaf community in accessing police services in the Epworth suburb of Harare, Zimbabwe. The researchers employed a qualitative approach, using questionnaires, structured interviews conducted by a signing researcher, and documentary analysis of relevant legal frameworks. Purposive sampling targeted police officers, SL interpreters, and deaf individuals from the Epworth area. The sample of 30 participants was deemed representative, and the data was analysed thematically to identify key themes and subthemes related to deaf-police communication. The findings shed light on the limitations of current practices, such as the reliance on limited interpretation resources and lack of awareness among police, which pose significant barriers for the Deaf community in reporting crimes and accessing essential police services.

Communication challenges

In-depth interviews with 15 deaf residents of Epworth revealed deep frustration and distrust towards the local police force. Many participants recounted trying to report crimes or seek assistance, only to be turned away or dismissed due to the officers' inability to communicate effectively. One of the interviewed deaf women said, '*When I went to the police station to report the theft of my phone, the police just shook their heads and motioned me to leave. They made no effort to find an interpreter or write things down – I felt completely ignored*'. Another interviewee, a 49-year-old man, stated, '*I've stopped even trying to contact the police because they handcuffed me when my boss alleged that I stole his money. What is the point when they will not listen or understand me?*' The interviews highlighted a pervasive sense that the Deaf community in Epworth is effectively excluded from the protection and services of law enforcement. Brennan and Brown (1997) cited in Skinner and Napier (2023, p. 4), described the use of handcuffing as 'gagging', where the detained deaf person is incapacitated linguistically and found a general lack of trust and confidence in the police because of the low level of deaf awareness and the prevalence of police stereotyping deaf signers as 'being disabled' and less educated.

Participants unanimously called for mandatory SL training for all police personnel in the area, as well as the provision of qualified interpreters at each police station. Without such accommodations, the Deaf citizens of Epworth will continue to face significant barriers in accessing critical public safety resources. The findings of this study confirm Kusters (2024) observation that marginalised groups may face biases, stereotypes, and a lack of understanding from police officers which can result in insensitive or discriminatory treatment. The absence of specialised training and awareness about the unique experiences and needs of the Deaf community contributes to violation of linguistic human rights.

Interviewed police officers stationed in Epworth, acknowledged the significant communication barriers they face when interacting with Deaf community members. One police officer respondent explained, '*We want to help, but without any sign language training or access to interpreters, it is incredibly difficult to understand what someone who is deaf is trying to tell us*'. Another police officer noted, '*I have had situations where a deaf person has come in to report a crime, and we ended up just staring at each other, unable to communicate. It is frustrating for both of us*'. The officers unanimously cited lack of resources and inadequate personnel training as the root causes of these issues. As one sergeant stated, '*Our station simply does not have the budget to provide sign language classes for the staff. We are doing the best we can with the limited skills and tools we have*'. These candid admissions from law enforcement agents highlight the need for systemic change, including mandatory SL instruction and the employment of qualified interpreters, in order to improve access to police services for Epworth's deaf residents. Similar findings were noted by Dziva et al. (2018), who pointed out that the criminal justice system lacks clear policies, guidelines and standardised protocols for the provision of SL interpretation services. This leads to inconsistent and ad hoc approaches, with no clear accountability or quality assurance measures.

The qualitative data presented in the preceding two paragraphs paints a concerning picture of the communication barriers that the Deaf in Epworth, Zimbabwe, face when trying to access police services. The perspectives from both the police officers and the Deaf community members highlight the systemic nature of the problem. On one side, the officers openly acknowledge their inability to effectively communicate with deaf individuals, citing a lack of training and resources as the root cause. This admission of the existence of a problem is important, as it demonstrates a willingness to address the issue, even if the solutions are not yet in place. On the other hand, the experiences recounted by the deaf residents underscore the consequences of these communication gaps. Feelings of frustration, dismissal, and isolation have led many to simply disengage from seeking police assistance altogether. This breakdown in the provision of public safety services for the Deaf community is unacceptable and represents a significant violation of their rights.

The use of basic signs and rudimentary signs

Responses from the interviews showed that the police at times use basic signs and rudimentary signs to communicate with the Deaf when carrying out investigations since they are not proficient in SL. Police officers who handle crimes of a sexual nature committed against deaf women and deaf children in a manner sensitive to the victim are referred to Victim Friendly Coordinators and they are found at each and every police station in Zimbabwe. These Victim Friendly Coordinators use some basic signs and finger spelling and when they find themselves stuck, they also rely on Leonard Cheshire Disability Zimbabwe, Deaf Zimbabwe Trust, and Sunrise Sign Language Academy Trust for the services of SL interpreters. This practice, however, infringes on the rights of the Deaf in accessing fair trial and justice because police officers are not able to deal directly with sensitive cases like rape and the rights of the Deaf. The following examples illustrate this. *Police officer interviewee:*

> *I cannot hear what the Deaf people say, as a result I use a mixture of mimes and gestures to establish rapport and by doing so I can understand them.*

Information gathered through interviews with police officers revealed that police officers are not proficient in any one of the variant forms of SL used in Zimbabwe but only know some basic signs and this makes it difficult for them to investigate cases involving the Deaf whether as witnesses, defendants or complainants and to interrogate them. Consequently, the cases involving the deaf are ill-received and ill-investigated by the police because of communication barriers. Practice at the police station is violating the rights of the Deaf to use a language of their choice as provided for in Section 6:3 (a) of the Constitution of Zimbabwe, which states that 'the state and all institutions and agencies of government at every level must ensure that all officially recognised languages are treated equitably'. Practice at the police station also violates the provisions of section 22 (3)(c) of the Constitution Government of Zimbabwe Amendment (No 20) 2013 Act, which mandates institutions of government to encourage the use of forms of communication suitable for People With Disabilities (PWDs).

The interviewed police officer pointed out that some workshops about SL training for police officers are being done but the profit is minimal since police officers are only trained in the basics of SL by some organisations serving Deaf and Hard of Hearing communities. The basic SL training that police officers are undergoing is, therefore, inadequate because SL proficiency demands that one continues to use it with the Deaf. Findings of the research also reveal that these basic SL training workshops will not equip the police officers to investigate cases involving the Deaf when they go to report at the police station because the workshops are not consistently and systematically done. In addition, another interviewed police officer revealed that very few police officers are able to attend SL workshops due to financial constraints since tuition is paid to Deaf-focused organisations offering training in SL. He also pointed out that the time of training in SL for police officers is very limited to learn the language because of its complex grammar.

Furthermore, lack of a codified and standardised SL in Zimbabwe hinders the free flow of communication between SL interpreters who use 'standard' signs while people who are deaf use home signs which they call natural signs of the Deaf culture. From a linguistic perspective, every language and every user community has their norms and this also holds for SL communities. However, these norms are often ignored, overlooked, or only implicitly/informally executed (ADAM, 2015). One of the interviewed SL interpreters noted that SL must be properly standardised and popularised to avoid communication challenges between SL interpreters and the Deaf whenever they are hired by the police or court to offer interpretation services. In another instance one of the interviewed police officers who had completed SL training at King George VI school of the Deaf, revealed that most of the people who are deaf do not use the so-called assumed 'standard signs' enshrined in the dictionaries. This shows that there is a loose connection between the standard forms and those in actual language usage which obviously causes communication problems between SL interpreters and the people who are deaf during the process of administering justice in the legal settings be it at the police station or in the courtroom. Mugari and Matende (2020) rightly note that, the compatibility challenges that the Deaf meet when they interact with their speaking counterparts exacerbate their communication plight and as long as their language is not developed, their concerns and contributions will never be heard. Home signs are also common, and they also differ from family to family. Thus, SL interpreters end up finger spelling or compromising some signs in a bid to convey meaning to people who are deaf in the courtroom.

The underdevelopment of SL or delay in coming up with a proper standardised SL by the government and different key stakeholders which can be used in different domains, the legal fraternity included, is indeed contrary to what the Constitution says. It is clearly noted within the Constitution Chapter 1 Section 6 (4). The major limitations of Section 6 of the Constitution are that it falls in the realm of what Bamgbose (2000) calls 'Declaration without implementation'. SL in Zimbabwe being a minority language worldwide, Zimbabwe included, warrants promotion. In fact, section 6 of the Constitution determines the language rights of citizens who are deaf in Zimbabwe which must be honoured. It 'embraces language as a basic human right and multilingualism as a national resource' (Hornberger, 2002, p. 30), which then allows people who are deaf to use SL in public life.

The unanimous calls from both groups for mandatory SL training and the employment of qualified interpreters point to clear, actionable steps that could help bridge this divide. Implementing such systemic changes would go a long way towards ensuring that deaf citizens in Epworth are able to fully access and benefit from law enforcement protections. Overall, the data highlights an urgent need for police departments to better accommodate the communication needs of marginalised populations in order to uphold principles of equity and justice.

The use of written and spoken English

Interviews also revealed that police officers use written or spoken English to communicate with the Deaf people reporting at the police station. This practice serves well for those who are literate but does not work well with the illiterate. Literature is replete with researchers recording how most deaf high school leavers barely manage to achieve a 4th grade reading level (Wauters et al., 2006). Thus, the majority of people who are deaf have limited access to legal information due to communication barriers caused by some linguistic practices that do not accommodate them as revealed by one of the Police officers who said, *'People who are deaf miss out on vital information about the law enshrined in the constitution and without proper access to information the country's Laws are not understood and the Deaf cannot be responsible or abiding law citizens'.*

The police officers use written English instead of SL, which is the only language of the deaf. This practice of writing statements or carrying out investigations by writing statements on paper in English instead of using a SL interpreter during statement recording is not appropriate; for the deaf who are illiterate the problems are even more serious. They cannot communicate without the services of an interpreter when reporting to the police. Majority of the deaf are illiterate. It is only the partially deaf who are able to lip read and write in English. This means that those who are profoundly deaf cannot communicate and express themselves in any other way besides SL or a SL interpreter (Kusters, 2024). Furthermore, the high costs associated with hiring qualified SL interpreters poses a significant barrier for the cash-strapped criminal justice system. This results in the unavailability of interpretation services particularly in lower-level courts and police stations (Dziva et al., 2018). The police officers who are responsible for compiling the initial reports of the cases, docket compilation and the subsequent evidence gathering, which is the bases of the court stage, are not equipped to deal with cases involving people who are deaf as a result of the unavailability of SL interpreters and a special unit that deals with cases that involve the deaf at police stations in Zimbabwe.

However, according to Skinner and Napier (2023), the police accounts reinforce the argument made by De Meulder and Haualand (2021, p. 12) that the

> presence of an interpreter should not imply that communication in bilingual settings is 'taken care of,' and should be considered a signal to professionals that they need to be cautious about the linguistic and communicative challenges and loopholes in that specific situation; and that the attempted provision of SLIS can actually be exclusive rather than inclusive.

The practice at the police station in Epworth shows that the Deaf in Zimbabwe have limited access to legal information. Chapter 63 (a) of the Constitution of Zimbabwe states that 'every person has the right to use the language of their choice' and Chapter 62 (i) provides that 'every citizen or permanent resident . . . has the right of access to any information held by the State or by any institution or agency of government at every level, in so far as the information is required in the interests of public accountability'. However, despite these constitutional provisions, SL is not prioritised and its use in the legal processes in general remains largely on paper. This contributes evidence to Lane et al.'s (1996, p. 422) argument that 'internationally recognised languages rights are universally violated when it comes to signed language minorities'.

Dependency on Deaf guardians and friends

Legal personnel and law enforcement agents interviewed for this research revealed that they rather depend on Deaf guardians and friends of the Deaf in investigating or handling legal cases that involve the Deaf to bridge the communication gap than to learn SL. This is the commonly adopted method of communication used by police officers, lawyers, and prosecutors to communicate through friends, signing family members, and deaf guardians. However, the use of deaf guardians and friends has some implications. Firstly, it implies that police officers cannot interrogate an accused deaf person involved in a civil or a criminal case directly. Thus, they cannot get first-hand information. Secondly, the SL proficiency level of these friends, relatives and guardians of the deaf is not known and this can have grave consequences during police interrogations or investigations. As with interpreting for any language, using family or friends to interpret is suboptimal, with confidentiality concerns and the risk of information being translated incorrectly by accident or on purpose (Abou-Abdallah & Lamyman, 2021).

Access to qualified SL interpreters is a longstanding challenge for law enforcement agencies when interacting with deaf individuals. Relying on 'deaf guardians' (Deaf community members) as ad hoc interpreters, raises concerns about impartiality, accuracy and confidentiality. The 'deaf literature' likely refers to deaf culture, history, norms and communication protocols that are not well understood by hearing police officers. Having Deaf community members provide context and interpretation of this cultural information could be helpful. However, utilising untrained deaf individuals as interpreters may not provide the same level of linguistic and legal expertise as professional, certified SL interpreters. Therefore, the use of Deaf community members as interpreters is likely to lead to miscommunication or incomplete information being conveyed. Data that was gathered for this study also revealed negative attitudes by the police as contributing immensely towards the denial of linguistic and legal rights of the Deaf in the legal settings in Zimbabwe. This is clearly illustrated by the following examples:

Deaf interviewee:

> *When I used signs to communicate with police officers at the public enquiry counter they started laughing with amazement and when some of them quickly noticed that I am Deaf, they went out one by one. Those police officers who remained told me to sit on the bench whilst they offer their services to the hearing people without any hindrances and delays. My case was postponed more than eight times.*

Police Officer:

> *Deaf people are arrogant, bullies and are always emotionally charged when communicating using SL,* nechimumu hausundi *(with a deaf person you cannot make progress) unless you talk to his/her friends or relatives.*

Negative attitudes by police officers hinder effective communication with the Deaf in the legal settings in Zimbabwe. Responses from Deaf people during interviews and focus group discussions, as illustrated, revealed limited interest by police officers and the legal personnel to take up cases involving the Deaf unless they are accompanied by their relatives or friends when reporting at police stations.

The Deaf fear and shun police officers because they are not accommodative and, instead, stigmatise and discriminate them giving preferential treatment to the hearing people at police stations. This exclusion of the Deaf from access to justice makes them feel shunned and ill-treated. These negative attitudes clearly explain the reason why the majority of the people who are deaf do not appreciate the importance of reporting crime cases to the police. One of the interviewed police officers who has undergone training in SL clearly revealed that enforcement of the law by the police in the Deaf community requires proficiency in the language used by the Deaf and most members of the police develop negative attitudes whenever a deaf person comes to report a case at a police station. The primary reason why the police exhibit negative attitudes towards the Deaf is that it is a colossal task for them to engage in investigations of matters that involve the Deaf without proficiency in SL. The National Disability Policy (NDP) section 3:22.10 is yet to be implemented. NDP section 3:22.10 states that 'All those working in the justice system must be provided with awareness-raising and training programs in relation to addressing the rights of persons with disabilities in particular in the context of access to justice'. Without providing the relevant training aimed at equipping members of the justice delivery system such as the police with SL skills, linguistic rights for the Deaf will continue to be violated at police stations.

Attitudes of legal professionals and police officers towards the Deaf and the use of SL may actually require SL and Deaf awareness programmes. Responses from interviewed police officers revealed that lack of proper understanding of Deaf culture and perceived complexity of the linguistic structure of SL is one of the major influences of the negative attitude displayed by police officers to the Deaf.

Responses from the interviewed police officers also revealed that it is ineffective for police officers to solely depend upon SL interpreters during investigations because police officers must create an open environment to extract information from a person who is deaf. SL interpreters lack the terminological exactitudes which help police officers during investigations or during interrogations when dealing with sensitive cases like theft, rape and murder involving people who are deaf, be it the complainant or the accused persons. The only bastion panacea is for police officers to have some SL skills and an understanding of Deaf culture, which is the bedrock of the Deaf community for them to be able to enforce the law effectively in matters involving people who are deaf at police stations. Thus, interviewees suggested the establishment of the police Deaf network unit which would provide valuable solutions to the aforementioned challenges of communication barriers.

The formation of police departments at local, regional, and national levels that specialise in cases involving deaf individuals is proposed as a possible solution to the communication challenges faced by deaf people in their interactions with police officers in Zimbabwe. Interviewed police officers suggested that the establishment of a dedicated police unit to deal specifically with people who have hearing impairments and other forms of disabilities at police stations could help curb the difficulties faced by the Deaf community in legal settings. This recommendation stems from the fact that the Zimbabwe Republic Police have successfully implemented specialised units, such as the Victim Friendly Unit, to handle sensitive crimes against vulnerable populations in a more appropriate manner. Similarly, a specialised police department focused on assisting and communicating effectively with deaf citizens could help improve the overall experience and outcomes for the Deaf community when engaging with law enforcement in Zimbabwe.

These recommendations resonate well with the Police Link Officer for the Deaf (PLOD) scheme in the UK. One positive example where the UK police have considered deaf signers is through the (PLOD) scheme. PLOD is a voluntary network of officers who are conscious of the access issues faced by deaf signers, and in their available time work towards promoting better community relations and equal access (Lumseden & Black, 2020; Race & Hogue, 2017). PLOD officers come from various ranks and departments and will have completed, at minimum, deaf awareness training, while many will have gone on to obtain varying levels of qualification in BSL.

The establishment of a Police Deaf Network Unit, henceforth (PDNU), can also provide solutions to the challenge of limited access to legal information by the Deaf. One of the interviewed police officers revealed that a (PDNU) will go a long way to curb the challenges that people who are deaf face in accessing justice. He said, '*let us have a special unit because the basis is faulty, issues involving people who are deaf reported at police stations are ill-received and ill-investigated by the police because of communication barriers*'. This PDNU will be a linking network between the Deaf and the police. Platforms of communications between the citizens of Zimbabwe and police officers such as websites, televisions, radios, complainer's desk, suggestion boxes and WhatsApp platforms were observed in the study as excluding the Deaf community since they are designed in formats that suit the hearing people. The establishment of a PDNU is very crucial because within this unit police officers will be able to carry out some campaigns, educate the Deaf about the law, and offer counselling services to them in formats they understand for example in SL and legal information in videos of SL.

Conclusion

The study found out that the legal system in Zimbabwe relies on limited resources like SL interpreters from Deaf-focused organisations, basic signs, and written/spoken English, which pose communication barriers for the Deaf community when reporting crimes, giving statements, and accessing police services. There is also a lack of awareness and understanding among police officers regarding the importance of SL interpretation and the rights of people with disabilities. This implies that SL remains marginalised in the legal system, denying Deaf Zimbabweans their legal and linguistic rights. Proposed solutions include establishing a specialised Police Deaf Network Unit, developing enabling legal policies and a Deaf Bill of Rights, training SL court interpreters, capacity building for police, and standardising SL with the ultimate goal of ensuring that linguistic rights for the Deaf are respected in the justice delivery system in general and in attempts to access police services by members of the Deaf community.

References

Abou-Abdallah, M., & Lamyman, A. (2021). Exploring communication difficulties with deaf patients. *Clinical Medicine*, *21*(4), 380–383.

ADAM, R. (2015). Standardization of Sign Languages. *Sign Language Studies*, *15*(4), 432–445. http://www.jstor.org/stable/26190997

Bauman, D. H. (2004). Audism the metaphysics of oppression. *Journal of Deaf Studies and Deaf Education*, *9*, 239–246. https://doi.org/10.1093/deafened/enh025

Bauman, D. H., & Murray, J. (2013). Deaf studies in the 21st century 'deaf gain and the future of human diversity'. *The Disability Studies Reader*, *4*, 246–262.

Bamgbose, A. (2000). *Language and exclusion: The consequences of language policies in Africa*. Transaction Publishers.

Brennan, M., & Brown, D. (1997). *Equality before the law: Deaf people's access to justice*. Deaf Studies Research Unit.

Brunson, J. L. (2007). Your case will now be heard: Sign language interpreters as problematic accommodation in legal interactions. *The Journal of Deaf Studies and Deaf Education*, *13*(1), 77–91.

Cameron, D., Eliud, P., & Ahmad, I. (2020). *Improving sign language recognition by combining hardware and software techniques* (pp. 87–92). 3rd International Conference on Data Intelligence and Security, South Padre Island, TX. https://doi.org/10.1109/ICDIS50059.2020.00018

Choruma, T. (2006). *The forgotten tribe: People with disabilities in Zimbabwe*. Progression Report. www.progressio.org.uk

Deaf Zimbabwe Trust. (2013). The precarious future of deaf children and the futility of life for deaf adults. *The Deaf Bulletin*, *2*. www.deafzimbabwetrustorg

De Meulder, M. (2023). Understanding deafhood: In search of its meaning. *American Annals of the Deaf*, *157*(5), 428–438.

De Meulder, M., & Haualand, H. (2021). Sign language interpreting services: A quick fix for inclusion. *Translation and Interpreting Studies*, *16*(1), 19–40.

Dziva, C., Munatsi, S., & Zvobgo, E. F. (2018). Implementation of the 2006 convention on the rights of persons with disabilities in Zimbabwe: A review'. *African Journal of Disability*, *7*(0), a389. https://doi.org/10.4102/ajod.v7i0.389.

Glasser, A., Mande., V., & Huenerfauth, M. (2021). Understanding deaf and hard of hearing users' interest in sign language interaction with personal assistant devices. *Proceedings of the 18th International Web for all Conference*. http://dx.doi.org/10.1145/3430263.3452428

Glickman, N. S., & Carey, J. C. (2023). Measuring deaf cultural identities: A preliminary investigation. *Rehabilitation Psychology*, *38*(4), 275–283.

Government of Zimbabwe. (2013). *Constitution of Zimbabwe amendment (no. 20) act*. Government Printers.

Hornberger, N. (2002). Multilingual language policies and the continua of biliteracy: An ecological approach. *Language Policy*, *1*(1), 27–51.

Krausneker, V. (2003). Has something changed? Sign languages in Europe: The case of minorised minority languages. *Deaf Worlds*, *19*(2), 31–46.

Kusters, A. (2024). More Than Signs: International Sign As Distributed Practice. *Signs and Society*, *12*(1), 37–57.

Kymlicka, W., & Patten, A. (2003). Language rights and political theory. *Annual Review of Applied Linguistics*, *23*, 3–21.

Lane, H., Hoffmeister, R., & Bahan, B. (1996). *A journey into the deaf-world*. Dawn Sign Press.

Lumseden, K., & Black, A. (2020). 'Sorry, I'm Dead, it's Too Late Now': Barriers faced by d/deaf citizens when accessing police services. *Disability and Society*, *37*, 476–495.

Matende, T., Svongoro., & Phiri, B. (2023). Language mediation during consultations between deaf patients and health care providers at Chivhu Hospital, Zimbabwe. *NAWA Journal of Language and Communication*, *17*(1), 81–96.

Miller, K. R. (2001). Access to sign language interpreters in the criminal justice system. *American Annals of the Deaf*, *146*(4), 328–330.

Miti, L. (2011). Preface. In *Zimbabwean sign language dictionary*. King George VI Centre.

Msindo, P., Gatsi, P., & Choguya, N. (2013). Squatter settlements an urban menace in Zimbabwe? Examining factors behind the continued resurfacing of squatter

settlements in Epworth Suburb, Harare. *Journal of Settlements and Spatial Planning*, *4*(2), 171–182.
Mugari, V., Mabugu, P. R., & Nyangairi, B. (2019). Variation of sign language in Zimbabwe. In P. Mpofu & E. Chabata (Eds.), *Language revitalisation: A matter of survival for marginalized communities and cultures* (pp. 131–172). UZ Press.
Mugari, V., & Matende, T. (2020). Sign language policies, practices and challenges in Zimbabwe's universities. *Journal of Linguistics and Language in Education*, *14*(2), 19–37.
Mugari, V., & Matende, T. (2022). The acceptability of Zimbabwe sign language standard forms: A case study of deaf vendors in Harare City centre. In L. Mukaro, G. Ncube, H. Mushangwe, Y. Chikwangura, & M. Chipara (Eds.), *Unlocking an untapped potential: Multilingual perspectives of language and development in Zimbabwe* (pp. 294–309). UZ Press.
Musengi, M., Ndofirepi, A., & Shumba, A. (2013). Rethinking education of deaf children in Zimbabwe: Challenges and opportunities for teacher education. *Journal of Deaf Studies and Deaf Education*, *18*(1), 62–74.
Powers, R. A., & Hayes, B. E. (2024). Victim and third-party reporting of violent victimization to the police in incidents involving victims with disabilities. *Journal of Research in Crime and Delinquency*, *61*(2), 268–302. https://doi.org/10.1177/00224278221131493
Race, L., & Hogue, T. E. (2017). 'You have the right to remain silent': Current provisions for d/deaf people within regional police forces in England and Wales. *The Police Journal: Theory, Practice and Principles*, *91*(1), 64–88.
Russell, D. (2013). *Synopsis prepared for ASL translation*. Association of Visual Language Interpreters of Canada.
Sall, A. (2022). Multilingualism, linguistic policies and endangered languages in Senegal. University of Dakar, Senegal. *Journal of Multicultural Discourses*, *2*(5), 55–70.
Scharp, K. M., & Barker, B. A. (2021). I have to social norm this: Making meaning of hearing loss from the perspective of adults who use hearing aids. *Health Communication*, *36*(6), 774–781.
Skinner, R., & Napier, J. (2023). 'Help is on the way' (in) accessible policing in the UK through sign language interpreting. *Translation and Interpreting Studies*, *13*(3), 85–104.
Tallroth, P. (2012). Multilingualism in Finland: A legal perspective. *Language and Law*, *1*. https://www.languageandlaw.de/volume-1/3339
Trovato, S. (2013). A stronger reason for the right to sign languages. *Sign Language Studies*, *13*(3), 401–422.
Wauters, L. N., van Bon, W. H. J., & Tellings, A. E. J. M. (2006). Reading comprehension of Dutch deaf children. *Reading and Writing: An Interdisciplinary Journal*, *19*, 49–76. https://doi.org/10.1007/s11145-004-5894-0
Wit, M. de. (2011). *A sign language interpreter in inclusive education: The view of deaf persons on their quality of life* [MA thesis, Heriot-Watt University]. Retrieved from https://www.mayadewit.nl/s/Maya-de-Wit-MA-Thesis-February-11-2025-for-web-j6n9.pdf

Theme 3

Language as a barrier in access to justice

9 Sign Language and the law in Zambia

Promoting equal access to justice for a linguistic and cultural minority

Gabriel Simungala and Humphrey M. Kapau

Introduction

Drawing on document analysis and systematic literature review, this chapter discusses the intersection of Sign Language and the law in Zambia, highlighting how linguistic diversity is recognised and acknowledged in policy documents but fails to translate into adequate representation for the Deaf community in legal contexts. Using two stages of the justice system, during arrests by law enforcement agencies and appearances before the courts of law, the chapter points to limitations in the Zambian Constitution, which recognises linguistic diversity in Article 258, mandating English as the national official language while other (indigenous) languages may be used in various domains including the justice system (Government of Zambia, 2016). Even though this clause appears to respect, promote, and protect the diversity of all the languages spoken in Zambia, there is no specific mention of Sign Language. Therefore, the chapter considers the Deaf community as a linguistic and cultural minority that requires special consideration in their pursuit of equal access to justice. It has been said that the Deaf community often faces significant barriers in legal systems around the world (Elder & Schwartz, 2018; Kermit et al., 2011), primarily due to the shortage of specialised legal Sign Language interpreters and the inherent variability in Sign Language itself (Brunson, 2008).

Although Zambia is a signatory to the United Nations Convention on the Rights of Persons with Disabilities (Kalaluka, 2013), which emphasises, among other things, the importance of linguistic rights for Deaf persons, the chapter gleans potential ongoing challenges the Deaf community faces within the courts and before law enforcement agencies. Arising from the aforesaid, the chapter seeks to address three interrelated objectives, namely: to discuss how the lack of specialised Sign Language training can act as a barrier to equal access to justice; to explore how Sign Language variation between a deaf individual and a Sign Language interpreter can compromise equal access to justice; and to spotlight Sign Language as both a linguistic and human right for the Deaf community. To adequately address the objectives of this chapter, the following section provides a historical context of Sign Language in Zambia, followed by a section that locates and places Sign

DOI: 10.4324/9781003569435-13

Language within the broader sociolinguistic contexts of Zambia. This is followed by a section that attempts to frame Sign Language as an indispensable (multimodal) approach to meaning making. The findings are then discussed, followed by a summary and conclusion drawn from archival data and a systematic literature review.

Historicising Sign Language in Zambia

The history of Sign Language in Zambia can be traced to the first school for Deaf persons, founded in 1955 at Magwero Mission in the Eastern Province of Zambia near Chipata district by Dutch missionaries. Since then, Chanda (1997) reports that several Deaf schools, Deaf school units, Deaf clubs, and Deaf centres have been established nationwide. The second school for Deaf persons in Zambia, Valley View Government School, was opened in 1968 in the Copperbelt Province, specifically in Kitwe district, near Kalulushi. This school was established to cater to local parents who could not afford to send their Deaf children to Magwero. Valley View provided a more accessible option for families in the region, thereby expanding access to education for Deaf children in the Copperbelt area. In 1971, education for children with special needs (Deaf children included) became the responsibility of the Ministry of Education after the establishment of the Special Education Inspectorate.

Initially, there was no specialised teacher training, and teachers for Deaf learners were trained either in Zimbabwe or South Africa. For this reason, Malunga (2007) records that the government of Zambia took a step further by bringing all schools previously started by the missionary agencies under control and turning them into government-aided institutions. Since most of the teachers in the field were untrained, the government also established the Zambia Institute on Special Education (ZAMISE) to train teachers for special needs education (cf. Kalabula, 1998; Katwishi, 1995). Today, the University of Zambia trains teachers of special education needs, including Sign Language. However, as it will become apparent, Wakumelo (2009) has questioned the curriculum for this training, particularly its potential to train Sign Language interpreters and translators adequately. Only two academic institutions in Zambia offer Sign Language training as part of special education, with a few other non-academic institutions championing the plight of Deaf persons and occasionally offering short courses in Sign Language.

Unlike Zambia, in South Africa, Kenya, and Zimbabwe, Sign Language is one of the officially recognised languages as stipulated in the Constitution (cf. Jiseve, 2023; Matende et al., 2023; Mnyandu, 2016). This entails that in public life in general and in the legal settings, Sign Language is at par with any other language referred to in the Constitution (Matende et al., 2022). To specifically respond to the unique needs of Deaf persons and those with hearing impairments, the Zambia National Association of the Deaf (ZNAD) was formed. This formation was motivated to safeguard the interests of persons with hearing impairments (Chanda, 1997). In 1997, Professor V. M. Chanda, working with ZNAD and the Ministry of Education, embarked on a lexicographic project to produce the first-ever Zambian Sign Language Dictionary Project. The dictionary would serve as a foundation for the formal development of Zambian Sign Language (ZAMSL), ensuring the preservation and promotion of indigenous signs in Deaf education. The genesis and implementation of this dictionary project for Sign Language was regarded as a first step towards developing a Zambian National Sign Language (Chanda, 1997).

According to the African Sign Languages Resource Centre (n.d.), the development of what can be considered Zambian Sign Language (ZAMSL) gained prominence as Deaf learners began combining home signs created by local Deaf children and the Sign Language brought back by children who had been transferred from Magwero, the first Deaf school, to Valley View, the second Deaf school. This phenomenon, referred to as local Sign Language, highlights the variation between the Sign Language used in schools and the one used in communities. This dynamic becomes particularly evident when discussing Sign Language within a multimodal framework. Sign Language, like any natural language, evolves organically within formal education settings or through daily social interactions. Due to the viability of local Sign Language, Chanda (1997) noted the growing importance of Deaf education in Zambia and the realisation that Deaf individuals use indigenous signs, many of which are shared across the different provinces of Zambia. This recognition led to the decision to compile a Zambian Sign Language Dictionary, with its core composed of standardised local signs, while other signs were borrowed from American Sign Language (ASL).

Locating Sign Language in the sociolinguistic spcctrum of Zambia

Regarding how many languages exist in Zambia, Kashoki (1978, p. 9) argues that 'one of the frequently asked questions about the language situation in Zambia is how many languages are there in this country'. Tambulukani (2015) generalises this assertion when he argues that the question of how many languages exist in Africa often does not find a definite answer. It is the case that dialect and language have been a source of so much contention among the people of Zambia as everyone contends theirs is a language and not a dialect. To this end, Muyebaa (1998) argues that there are statistically 73 tribes and about 16 languages and dialects spoken in Zambia. The use of the term 'tribe' other than 'language' by Muyebaa (1998) is explained by Kashoki (1990) as the root cause for different figures given to the number of languages spoken in Africa and Zambia in particular.

While many assume that 72 languages are spoken in Zambia, others have stated that there are between 20 to 25 languages. Tambulukani (2015) refers to Kashoki (1990, p. 109), who he argues claims that Zambia has 'approximately 80 Bantu dialects' grouped into 'slightly over 20 more or less mutually unintelligible clusters of languages'. As a result of these seeming contradictions,

Mambwe (2014, p. 2) adds that 'it is not rare to find school textbooks record 73 languages, a number that equates to the 73 ethnic groupings found in Zambia'. Nevertheless, he says that studies have shown that fewer than 73 languages (estimated between 20 and 26 languages) are spoken in Zambia. Of the indigenous languages described previously, seven language clusters have been identified per province except the North-western Province, which has three. The said seven regional languages are used besides English, the national official language, for purposes such as broadcasting (both on radio and television), literacy campaigns, and the official dissemination of information.

Ethnologue categorises Zambian Sign Language as 'developing' (Eberhard et al., 2024). With the appearance of a Sign Language interpreter on the national broadcaster, the Zambia National Broadcasting Corporation, during the news bulletins or presidential address, it can be said that Sign Language has made a footprint on the sociolinguistics of Zambia. Unfortunately, records of how many people use Sign Language are hard to find. Two main institutions provide formal training in Sign Language in Zambia: the University of Zambia (UNZA) and the Zambia Institute of Special Education (ZAMISE). Unfortunately, both institutions focus on training individuals to work in educational settings, primarily as Sign Language teachers at the primary and secondary school levels. This implicates our discussion on the need for sign language interpreters with specialised skills in legal contexts.

Sign language as a multimodal approach to meaning making

In an attempt to frame Sign Language as an indispensable approach to meaning making given the linguistic diversity we witness, we draw on the notion of multimodality which is an interdisciplinary approach that understands communication and representation to be more than about language as we know it (Kress, 2010). Multimodality refers to the phenomenon of human communication, where meaning is derived from multiple semiotic modes, not just spoken language. This approach is central to a growing field of research that looks beyond linguistic resources to explore how meaning is constructed through a variety of modes (Adami, 2016). The notion that spoken or written language is the sole element in meaning making during communication has been increasingly questioned due to the complexities of contemporary communicative and representational practices (Kress, 2010). Mambwe (2014) highlights this shift by observing that a new generation of scholars advocates for a paradigm shift, wherein language is no longer theorised as the only tool for meaning making. Instead, it is seen as one part of a broader set of semiotic resources used for communication.

Within the broader understanding of multimodality, we find a combination of multiple sensory and communicative modes, such as sight, gaze, gestures, sound, print, images, video, music, and so on, in any given communicative event (Kress & van Leeuwen, 2006; Iedema, 2003). This is where Sign

Language is located. This is because Sign Language is a visual means of communicating using gestures, facial expressions, and body language. According to the National Children's Deaf Society of the United Kingdom, Sign Language is a visual language that uses hand shapes, facial expressions, gestures, and body language. Sign Languages have their own vocabulary, construction, and grammar. The Encyclopaedia Britannica (2024) broadens this definition by stating that Sign Language is any means of communication through bodily movements, especially of the hands and arms, used when spoken communication is impossible or undesirable. The encyclopaedia's definition is broadened because it does not consider Sign Language as exclusive to Deaf individuals, but to all actors in communicative events.

From the various conceptualisations of Sign Language, it can be understood as a multimodal meaning-making approach, for it incorporates a combination of visual, spatial, and gestural modes to communicate meaning. Unlike spoken languages, which rely solely on auditory and verbal elements, Sign Language engages multiple semiotic resources simultaneously, such as hand movements (manual signs), facial expressions, body posture, and spatial orientation. This makes it inherently multimodal, as it uses more than one mode of communication to convey meaning. The practice of Sign Language is older than speech. It is for this reason that we argue that Sign Language is multimodal. Dressman (2019) historicises that communication has always been multimodal since time immemorial. In conversations, for example, we resort to several modes beyond language – gestures, gaze, posture and proxemics – to make meaning. In this regard, Sign Language may be as coarsely expressed as mere grimaces, shrugs, or pointings; or it may employ a delicately nuanced combination of coded manual signals reinforced by facial expression and perhaps augmented by words spelled out in a manual alphabet (Encyclopaedia Britannica, 2024).

In the quest for inclusivity, there has been a call for the role of multimodal learning in the recognition of Sign Language. In this connection, Ferreira et al. (2019) exploits multimodal learning techniques in Sign Language recognition (SLR) in human-computer interaction using systems meant to automatically translate Sign Language into text or speech to reduce the communicational gap between Deaf and hearing people. Since Sign Languages use manual and facial means of expression, Vonagris et al. (2008) have proposed a recognition system that aims for signer-independent operation and utilises a single video camera for data acquisition to ensure user-friendliness. Ferreira et al. (2019) noted that research in Sign Language recognition has significantly advanced in recent years. According to Vonagris et al. (2008), the present achievements provide the basis for future applications to support the integration of Deaf people into the hearing society. However, while all this is still in development, the Deaf community continues to appear before the courts of law and law enforcement agencies with the many challenges and setbacks that will become apparent in the following sections.

Methodology

The present undertaking drew on document analysis and a systematic literature review for data. Document analysis is a systematic procedure for reviewing or evaluating documents, which can be used to provide context, generate questions, supplement other types of research data, track change over time, and corroborate other sources. In other words, Cardno (2018) observes that document analysis is a method for investigating the nature of documents to look at both what lies behind it and within it. This means that this method involves examining and interpreting data to uncover meaning, gain understanding, and come to a conclusion (Dalglish et al., 2020). As a research method, documentary analysis recommends itself to many qualitative researchers as straightforward, efficient, cost-effective, and manageable. Its major advantage is the availability of documents, usually at little or no cost to the researcher (Cardno, 2018). For this undertaking, the documents subjected to analysis include the Constitution of Zambia, 2010/2021 Census Reports, the Disability Act, the Mental Disorders Act, the National Policy on Disability the, the United Nations Convention on the Rights of Persons with Disabilities, and the 2013 Ministry of Education Curriculum Framework.

Document analysis was supplemented by a systematic literature review, a type of review that collects multiple research studies and summarises them to answer a research question using rigorous methods (Oliver & Tripney, 2017). A systematic literature review identifies, selects, and critically appraises research to answer a clearly formulated question (Bowman-Perrott et al., 2016). Systematic reviews follow a clearly defined protocol or plan where the criteria are clearly stated before the review is conducted. In this regard, we used research gate and google scholar and specifically drew on studies produced in the last 20 years on sign language and the law. The initial search was global, but we refined it to include studies done in Africa. In what follows, we discuss the findings under three thematic strands.

Findings and discussion

Lack of specialised Sign Language training: a barrier to equal access to justice

This section shows that the absence of full-fledged specialised training in Sign Language interpretation and translation represents a significant obstacle to inclusivity, particularly in accessing justice for the Deaf community in Zambia. In this regard, the section opens with clauses from the Zambian Constitution which relate to the two stages of the justice system which the chapter discusses. For the stage of arrest, we draw from Article 13 on the protection of right to personal liberty Clause 2, which states that 'Any person who is arrested or detained shall be informed as soon as reasonably practicable, in a language that he understands, of the reasons for his arrest or detention'. When an individual is before the courts of law, we draw on Article 18 on the provisions to secure protection of law which states that 'Every person who is charged with a criminal offence shall be permitted to have without payment the assistance of an interpreter if he cannot understand the language used at the trial of the charge'. Armed with this reality of the constitutional provisions, we are quick to note that though Sign Language is not explicitly mentioned in any of these provisions, it is factored in at the two stages mentioned just like the indigenous languages are not named in the Constitution but are used. It would seem that the constitutional provisions cited earlier do not seem to sufficiently motivate practice. With only two institutions (UNZA and ZAMISE) offering Sign Language training, it is clear that more needs to be done to ensure that the Deaf community has access to a free and fair trial. Wakumelo (2009) pointed out this issue over a decade ago, and unfortunately, little has changed since then. The fact that only two institutions offer Sign Language training highlights the urgent need for greater efforts to address the communication barriers that the Deaf community faces. The United Nations Convention on the Rights of Persons with Disabilities, to which Zambia is a signatory, mandates that providers of goods and services, including the justice system and law enforcement agencies, must ensure effective communication access for Deaf individuals on an equal basis with non-disabled people (Elder & Schwartz, 2018). This obligation forms the basis of our argument that the current gaps in Sign Language training, particularly in critical sectors like law enforcement and the Judiciary, must be addressed urgently.

The challenges faced by the Deaf community in the courts of law can be traced back to the education system. Deaf learners are among the most disadvantaged in terms of educational outcomes, as Kelly et al. (2022) emphasise. These disadvantages stem from gaps in teacher training. In his situational analysis of the use of Sign Language in the education of Deaf persons in Zambia, Mulonda (2013) observed that UNZA and ZAMISE are the primary institutions offering training programmes for teachers of Deaf learners. However, these institutions are insufficient to meet the needs of the many special schools for Deaf persons across the country. Furthermore, as noted by Wakumelo (2009), the curriculum at these institutions does not give Sign Language the prominence it requires (Mulonda, 2013). While Sign Language should be taught as a full-fledged language, it is instead treated as a component of special education, reinforcing a medical view of deafness as a form of language handicap rather than acknowledging it as a linguistic and cultural experience (Mulonda, 2013). This approach has far-reaching consequences for educational achievement and the effectiveness of Sign Language interpretation in other critical sectors, including the justice system.

In addition to lapses in the nature of educational outcomes as the major contributor to injustices towards Deaf persons as discussed earlier, the political will to drive Sign Language as equal to spoken languages has contributed to the marginalisation of the Deaf community in law-related spaces and discourses. The developmental outcomes scored in the development of the Zambian Sign Language and curriculum development of Sign Language at UNZA and ZAMISE are efforts mostly championed by enthusiasts and technocrats of language with little or no financial backing from politicians. The same can be said about the extent to which Sign Language is incorporated in the judicial system. Although every Zambian has the right to be heard in a language they are most conversant with (including Sign Language by extension), there exists little political will to train and provide quality services for Deaf people.

Wakumelo (2009) further notes that training at ZAMISE initially focused on specialisations in various disabilities, but this has since shifted to hybrid specialisation. This shift has important implications for how Deaf individuals are supported across different domains, particularly in legal contexts where precise and specialised Sign Language interpretation is essential.

> Previously when it was a certificate course the students specialised in one disability and those that specialised in the Deaf did Sign language as a core course. But with the change to the diploma program the students have to do courses in all types of disabilities. The Sign language course was dropped as a core course and some students did not see the need for it.
>
> (Wakumelo, 2009)

The Sign Language teacher training just described provides a glimpse into the availability of Sign Language interpreters in the courts of law and law enforcement agencies. Since only UNZA and ZAMISE offer such training, it must be noted from the onset that the training primarily focuses on educational contexts with less or no consideration of multidisciplinary relevance in the scope of the training. Essentially, this entails that the purpose of the training is to teach in special schools (cf. Mulonda, 2013). However, graduates of these institutions have successfully applied their skills in other areas, such as religion and media. In other words, even though these two institutions orient their training towards education, all the Sign Language specialists thriving in Zambia in various domains such as religion and the media and most notably in the Judiciary are products of the said institutions. In a sense, this reflects the versatility of the Sign Language training, but also raises issues of quality Sign Language interpretation in all other domains as the said graduates are primarily teachers trained for primary and secondary schools. This also raises issues with the needed sign language interpreters' ratio as these are divided between those pursuing a teaching career and those pursuing different careers such as media and broadcasting.

Furthermore, considering the nature of legal discourse which is inherently technical and demand precision at various levels of linguistic engagements, the current curricula affordances that UNZA and ZAMISE provides its graduates entail a compromised interpretation of legal discourse in the judiciary when such graduates are co-opted in the legal fraternity. While it is admirable that the judiciary in Zambia endeavours to provide Sign Language interpreters for cases that need the same, the absence of specialised legal training for

Sign Language interpreters means that Deaf individuals may still face significant barriers in accessing a fair trial. The fact that graduates from UNZA and ZAMISE are primarily trained to teach at primary and secondary school levels entails that their skills may not be sufficient for specialised fields such as legal interpretation. In legal contexts, precise and accurate communication is crucial for justice and fairness. Lee (2009) emphasises that (Sign Language) interpreting in legal settings has been seen as an area that requires specialised skills and training. Without specialised training in legal Sign Language interpretation (Roberson et al., 2012), the Deaf community as a minority group may face significant barriers to accessing a free and fair trial. Despite advocacy and awareness efforts, Byrne et al. (2021) report that little progress has been made to address this gap, even though real-life examples of injustices involving Deaf individuals in the criminal justice system continue to surface. This reality may not be far from the Zambian realities.

Building on the argument of lack of specialised Sign Language services in the legal system in Zambia, Haualand (2009) reveals that Sign Language interpreting is crucial for securing the human rights of Deaf individuals. Consequently, the lack of well-trained Sign Language interpreters infringes these rights. This issue is particularly pressing in Zambia, as the current training programmes at ZAMISE and UNZA are focused on preparing teachers rather than interpreters, with Sign Language being only a component of special education and a limited curriculum. Even though the graduates have applied themselves exceptionally well, this approach lacks the depth and specialisation needed to address the broader needs of the deaf community, particularly in legal contexts. Haualand and Allen (2009) point to an international survey of 93 countries, predominantly in the developing world, revealing that few countries had established Sign Language interpreter services or formal education and training opportunities for interpreters. Zambia is no exception to this finding. According to Roberson et al. (2012), in many Western countries, interpreting in legal contexts is a specialised field requiring advanced skills and targeted training. This highlights the urgent need for Zambia to develop dedicated Sign Language interpreter training programmes to safeguard the rights of the Deaf community.

Sign Language variation as a potential barrier to equal access to justice

In their discussion of Sign Language variation, Lucas et al. (2003) provide practical examples that are highly relevant to the current discourse on Sign Language use in legal contexts, such as courts of law or law enforcement agencies. Variations in Sign Language are evident particularly in the varieties employed by interpreters and Deaf individuals in courts. Lucas et al. (2003) argue that linguistic variation means people have different ways of expressing the same concept. For example, in spoken English, some might say 'soda', while others prefer 'soft drink', or some may say 'sofa' instead of 'couch' or 'davenport'. The linguistic relativism of concepts in different types of Sign Language connotes variance of signifiers (langue) and signified (parole) on the cline of signification. Drawing on this understanding, we consider that variation in Sign Language poses significant challenges in courts of law. These variations can lead to misunderstandings, misinterpretations, or breakdowns in communication for Deaf individuals, potentially compromising their access to justice. Ensuring that the specific Sign Language variety used by Deaf individuals is accurately interpreted becomes critical to safeguarding fair legal proceedings.

Sign languages, like spoken languages, exhibit both regional and social variation. There is, therefore, sociolinguistic variation and change in Sign Languages. This entails that variations must of essence to factored in for a fair trial. The insights provided by Lucas et al. (2013) highlights the importance of considering the specific Sign Language varieties used by interpreters and deaf individuals involved. This is crucial because variation in spoken or signed languages can significantly impact communication. For instance, in a study of Sign Language variations in selected Copperbelt and Lusaka primary special schools in Zambia, Chibwe (2015) considered how variation in Sign Language between teachers and pupils impacts academic performance. Therefore, for purposes of adhering to human rights as will be discussed further in the next section, Sign Language variation calls for careful attention to ensure that the interpreter's variety matches the one used by a Deaf individual, thus avoiding miscommunication that could compromise the fairness of legal proceedings or interactions with law enforcement.

It is important to recognise that Deaf communities are typically minority communities embedded within larger majority populations, whose languages operate in a different modality such as spoken and often written, unlike Sign Languages, which lack the same level of written systems or extensive literatures (Schembri & Johnston, 2013), but draw on multimodal affordances. In the Zambian context, nearly all Sign Language interpreters come from the majority community that communicates through spoken language, which functions under dynamics very different from those of Sign Language. Without delving into the ongoing debates about whether deafness constitutes a linguistic minority or a disability, we concede to Sabatello's (2004) perspective which suggests that contemporary human rights discourse increasingly views the Deaf community as an ethnic or linguistic minority group entitled to rights of recognition and preservation. This understanding is crucial in legal contexts because variations in Sign Language, especially in courtrooms can further marginalise Deaf individuals, potentially compromising their right to a fair trial.

In courts of law, variation in Sign Language becomes a critical factor to consider, as it manifests at different levels and can potentially hinder a free and fair trial. Lucas and Bayley (2011) note that Sign Language variation is primarily observed at the phonological and lexical levels, with less attention given to variations in morphology and syntax. Without delving deeply into these specific variations, Schembri and Johnston (2013) highlight that sociolinguistic factors driving variation in signed-language communities include a signer's age, region of origin, gender, ethnicity, and socio-economic status.

Given these complexities, variation in Sign Language can present significant challenges in legal contexts. For example, suppose a court interpreter is familiar with one variation, but not the specific version used by a Deaf individual before the court. In that case, it is a given that this mismatch may lead to inaccurate interpretations, resulting in the miscommunication of key testimony or legal concepts.

Sign Language as a linguistic and human right for the Deaf community

So far, we have established that for the Deaf community, Sign Language is not just a multimodal communication tool, but a fully developed language with its own unique structure and deep cultural significance. For this reason, we should restate the fact that Sign Language interpretation requires specialised training. However, as noted in the section on the sociolinguistics of Zambia, Sign Language is not fully recognised as a language in its own right. The Zambian Constitution is silent on the matter of Sign Language, which means that the 72 languages acknowledged in the country do not include it. In Zambia's language policy and planning, only English is designated as the national official language, alongside seven indigenous languages (Tonga, Bemba, Lozi, Nyanja, Kaonde, Lunda, and Luvale) classified as regional languages, while other languages spoken in various localities are overlooked.

Additionally, while Zambia has signed the African Charter on the Rights and Welfare of the Child, it has yet to ratify it (Kalaluka, 2013). The country has implemented the Disability Act, which aims to eliminate all forms of discrimination against individuals with disabilities and regulate programmes targeting them (Zimba, 2016). The Convention on the Rights of Persons with Disabilities (CRPD), adopted in December 2006, marked a significant milestone in recognising disability rights. However, Zimba (2016) notes that despite some progress in domestication – such as the enactment of the Persons with Disabilities Act and the launch of a national disability policy – there has been insufficient implementation of the CRPD. This lack of recognition and effective policy implementation highlights the ongoing challenges faced by the Deaf community in achieving equitable rights and access to services.

According to Wilcox et al. (2012), the CRPD is the first international human rights treaty to explicitly recognise Sign Languages in their own right, mentioning them in Articles 2, 9, 21, 24, and 30. Furthermore, the Convention acknowledges the importance of Deaf culture, as seen in Article 30 (4). This is particularly notable as 'no other disability group and their needs are mentioned overtly as precisely and often in the Convention as the Deaf/Deafblind group' (Wilcox et al., 2012, p. 14). The frequent and precise mention of Deaf persons in the CRPD underscores the critical role of Sign Language and Deaf culture in international human rights discussions. Zambia, being a signatory to the CRPD, as highlighted by Kalaluka (2013), provides an avenue for the Deaf community in the country to benefit from the potential protections and opportunities set out in the Convention (Demeulder, 2014). As a linguistic and cultural minority, the Deaf community and other persons with disabilities the world over consider the CRPD to be a milestone in the struggle to officially recognise disability as a human rights issue. Writing with insights from the legal system, Kalaluka (2013) observes that in Zambia, as in most African countries, persons with disabilities often suffer social exclusion and marginalisation arising from cultural prejudices and stigma that attach to their disabilities. Drawing on lived experiences, we can confirm that the marginalisation and exclusion of the Deaf community is evident in our society today.

The Deaf community has a right to use Sign Language in different domains. To this end, it is important to underscore that linguistic rights that accrue to every individual, the deaf included, refer to the rights that combine language rights and human rights, focusing on the protection of languages within minority groups to prevent assimilation and linguistic genocide. In other words, linguistic right refers to the entitlement of individuals or communities to use and preserve their language in both private and public life. For Deaf persons, this includes their access to justice, although Kalaluka (2013) seems to suggest that individuals with disabilities are often denied the basic human rights that are available to non-disabled persons. In the case of language, disability rights are crucial for maintaining linguistic diversity, protecting minority languages such as Sign Language, and ensuring that all people have the ability to communicate in their preferred language without facing discrimination. The starting point to ensuring the language rights of Deaf individuals are protected and adhered to is by beginning to actively view Deaf persons as not linguistically disabled, but linguistically differently abled.

Having Sign Language accepted as a mother tongue from birth is the most important human right for Deaf children because Sign Language is the only language they can acquire spontaneously and naturally without teaching, provided they have exposure to it (Jokinen, 2000). Therefore, in legal contexts such as courts of law and law enforcement agencies, the provision of Sign Language interpretation becomes a crucial tool for securing the human rights of the Deaf community, as emphasised by Haualand (2009). Though more needs to be done, it is clear that the Zambian government through ministries of Justice and Education respects this provision as the courts always have Sign Language interpreters for fair trials and selected schools are dubbed special schools to provide for the education of Deaf. As noted earlier, these realities align with human rights discourse, which frames the use of Sign Language as a linguistic right, affirming the community's right to recognition, preservation, and use of their language in all aspects of life.

Summary and conclusion

This chapter has drawn on document analysis and a systematic review of literature to argue that Sign Language variation, inadequate Sign Language interpreter/translator training, and a lack of awareness of Sign Language as a linguistic and human right can potentially contribute to unequal access to justice for a linguistic and cultural minority such as the deaf community in Zambia. In particular, the chapter has argued that the issue of language variations is not exclusive to spoken languages. This understanding is crucial in legal contexts because variations in Sign Language, especially in courtrooms and before law enforcement agencies can rob the Deaf community of an opportunity to be heard. Crasborn et al. (2009) opines that linguistic variation is challenging for Sign Language interpreters and education. As Zulu (2019) noted in Zambian schools, which Crasborn et al. (2009) had already pointed out, it would be appear that these variations are evident. The variations are normative practice that starts in the community and can potentially be found in the confines of a courtroom. If say a court interpreter is familiar with one variation, but not the specific Sign Language variety used by a Deaf individual, it is a given that this mismatch may lead to inaccurate interpretations.

In the observance of the Convention on the Rights of Persons with Disabilities (Kalaluka, 2013), which highlights, among others, the importance of linguistic rights for Deaf persons, legal practitioners and law enforcement officers have praised the Judiciary which abides by the constitution provision and ensures that any individual brought before the court should use a language they know well. In this connection, the chapter has noted that the judiciary in Zambia endeavours to provide Sign Language interpreters for cases that need the same. However, the absence of specialised legal training for Sign Language interpreters means that deaf individuals may still face significant barriers in accessing a fair trial. Without specialised training in legal Sign Language interpretation (Roberson et al., 2012), the Deaf community as a minority group may face significant barriers to accessing a free and fair trial. The Sign Language teachers who are co-opted to as Sign Language interpreters beyond the confines of the class do not possess sufficient skills for specialised fields like Sign Language legal interpretation. Notwithstanding, the work the said Sign Language interpreters do is still commendable, because they strive for precise and accurate communication which is crucial for justice and fairness to prevail.

Finally, the chapter has argued for the intersection of linguistic rights and human rights for the deaf community as a cultural and linguistic minority. This is because linguistic rights are central to maintaining cultural heritage and identity. Even though persons with disabilities such as Deaf persons often suffer social exclusion and marginalisation arising from cultural prejudices and stigma that attach to their disabilities (Kalaluka, 2013), the chapter has argued that Zambia is making strides in the right direction. The chapter has shown that the Judiciary always ensures that courtrooms have Sign Language interpreters for fair trials needing one. For Haualand (2009), the provision of Sign Language interpretation is a critical tool for securing the human and linguistic rights of the Deaf community. Additionally, the chapter has pointed to the Ministry of Education which runs selected schools dubbed 'special schools' to provide for the education of Deaf persons. By protecting linguistic rights and viewing Deaf individuals and communities can maintain and express their linguistic identity and they can access opportunities, services, and justice in their preferred language.

References

Adami, E. (2016). Multimodality. In O. Garcia, N. Flores, & M. Spotti (Eds.), *Oxford handbook of language and society* (pp. 451–472). Oxford University Press.

African Sign Languages Resource Centre. (n.d.). Home. Retrieved November 22, 2024 from https://africansignlanguagesresourcecenter.com/

Bowman-Perrott, L., de Marín, S., Mahadevan, L., & Etchells, M. (2016). Assessing the academic, social, and language production outcomes of English language learners engaged in peer tutoring: A systematic review. *Education and Treatment of Children*, 359–388.

Brunson, J. L. (2008). Your case will now be heard: Sign language interpreters as problematic accommodations in legal interactions. *Journal of Deaf Studies and Deaf Education*, *13*(1), 77–91.

Byrne, B., Elder, B., & Schwartz, M. (2021). Enhancing deaf people's access to justice in Northern Ireland: Implementing Article 13 of the UN convention on the rights of persons with disabilities. *Scandinavian Journal of Disability Research*, *23*(1), 74–84.

Cardno, C. (2018). Policy document analysis: A practical educational leadership tool and a qualitative research method. *Educational Administration: Theory and Practice*, *24*(4), 623–640.

Chanda, V. M. (1997). Lexicography and sign language engineering: The Zambian experience. *Lexikos*, *7*, 192–206.

Chibwe, J. (2015). *Contribution of sign language variations to academic performance of learners with hearing impairments in selected Copperbelt and Lusaka primary special schools in Zambia* [Doctoral dissertation, The University of Zambia].

Crasborn, O. N. N. O., & Bloem, T. O. N. Y. (2009). Linguistic variation as a challenge for sign language interpreters and sign language interpreter education in the Netherlands. *International Perspectives on Sign Language Interpreter Education*, *4*, 77–95.

Dalglish, S. L., Khalid, H., & McMahon, S. A. (2020). Document analysis in health policy research: The READ approach. *Health Policy and Planning*, *35*(10), 1424–1431.

Demeulder, M. (2014). The UNCRPD and sign language peoples. In A. Pabsch (Ed.), *UNCRPD implementation in Europe – a deaf perspective. Article 29: Participation in political and public life* (pp. 12–28). European Union of the Deaf.

Dressman, M. (2019). Multimodality and language learning. In M. Dressman & R. W. Sadler (Eds.), *The handbook of informal language learning* (pp. 39–55). Wiley-Blackwell.

Eberhard, D. M., Simons, G. F., & Fennig, C. D. (2024). *Ethnologue: Languages of the world (Edition)*. SIL International. Retrieved November 4, 2024, from https://www.ethnologue.com

Elder, B. C., & Schwartz, M. A. (2018). Effective deaf access to justice. *The Journal of Deaf Studies and Deaf Education*, *23*(4), 331–340.

Encyclopaedia Britannica. (2024). *Encyclopaedia Britannica*. Retrieved November 2, 2024, from https://www.britannica.com

Ferreira, P. M., Cardoso, J. S., & Rebelo, A. (2019). On the role of multimodal learning in the recognition of sign language. *Multimedia Tools and Applications*, *78*(8), 10035–10056.

Government of Zambia. (2016). *The Constitution of Zambia (Amendment) act no. 2 of 2016*. Government Printer.

Haualand, H. (2009). Sign language interpreting: A human rights issue. *International Journal of Interpreter Education*, *1*(1), 7.

Haualand, H., & Allen, C. (2009). *Deaf people and human rights*. The World Federation of the Deaf and the Swedish National Association of the Deaf.

Iedema, R. (2003). Multimodality, resemiotization: Extending the analysis of discourse as multi-semiotic practice. *Visual Communication*, *2*(1), 29–57.

Jiseve, K. K. (2023). *From the hands to the eye; the role of Kenya sign language in realization of the right to access to justice for the deaf community in Kenya* [Doctoral dissertation, University of Nairobi].

Jokinen, M. (2000). The linguistic human rights of sign language users. In *Rights to language* (pp. 207–217). Routledge.
Kalabula, D. M. (1998). *Special education in Zambia: A historical review and education for the visually handicapped children* [Unpublished master's dissertation, University of Birmingham].
Kalaluka, L. (2013). Towards an effective litigation strategy of disability rights: The Zambia experience. *African Disability Rights Yearbook, 1*, 165.
Kashoki, M. E. (1978). The language situation in Zambia. In M. E. Kashoki & S. Ohannesian (Eds.), *Language in Zambia* (pp. 9–46). International Africa Institute.
Kashoki, M. E. (1990). *The Factor of language in Zambia*. Lusaka: Kenneth Kaunda Foundation.
Katwishi, S. (1995). *Viability of developing early identification and intervention services for young children with impairments in Zambia* [Unpublished PhD thesis, University of Birmingham].
Kelly, J. F., McKinney, E. L., & Swift, O. (2022). Strengthening teacher education to support deaf learners. *International Journal of Inclusive Education, 26*(13), 1289–1307.
Kermit, P., Olsen, M. J., & Olsen, T. (2011). Safe in the hands of the interpreter? A qualitative study investigating the legal protection of deaf people facing the criminal justice system in Norway. *Disability Studies Quarterly, 31*(4).
Kress, G. R. (2010). *Multimodality: A social semiotic approach to contemporary communication*. Routledge.
Kress, G. R., & Van Leeuwen, T. (2006). *Reading images: The grammar of visual design*. Routledge.
Lee, J. (2009). Conflicting views on court interpreting examined through surveys of legal professionals and court interpreters. *Interpreting, 11*(1), 35–56.
Lucas, C., & Bayley, R. (2011). Variation in sign languages: Recent research on ASL and beyond. *Language and Linguistics Compass, 5*(9), 677–690.
Lucas, C., Bayley, R., & Valli, C. (2003). *What's your sign for pizza? An introduction to variation in American sign language*. Gallaudet University Press.
Lucas, C., Mirus, G., Palmer, J. L., Roessler, N. J., & Frost, A. (2013). The effect of new technologies on sign language research. *Sign Language Studies, 13*(4), 541–564.
Malunga, T. (2007). *An investigation on the use of sign language and oral language by regular teachers teaching hearing impaired children* [Unpublished PhD thesis, University of Oslo].
Mambwe, K. (2014). *Mobility, identity and localization of language in multilingual contexts of urban Lusaka* [PhD thesis, University of the Western Cape].
Matende, T., Mugari, V., & Gotosa, K. (2022). Language and the legal process in Deaf communities: An analysis of sign language court interpretation and linguistic rights of the Deaf in selected courtrooms in Harare Urban, Zimbabwe. *London Journal of Research in Humanities and Social Sciences, 22*(9), 23–35.
Matende, T., Svongoro, P., & Phiri, B. (2023). Language mediation during consultations between deaf patients and health care providers at Chivhu Hospital, Zimbabwe. *Namibian Journal of Linguistics, Literature and Communication Studies, 17*(1), 81–96.
Mnyandu, N. L. (2016). *The provision of interpreting services in isiZulu and South African sign language in selected courts in KwaZulu-Natal* [Doctoral dissertation].
Mulonda, M. (2013). *A situational analysis in the use of sign language in the education of the deaf in Zambia: A case of Magwero and St Joseph Schools for the Deaf*. University of Zambia.
Muyebaa, K. C. (1998). *The mismatch in the Zambian language policy*. Conference abstracts. WCCES 10th World Congress, 12–17 July. University of Cape Town, Cape Town.

Oliver, S., & Tripney, J. (2017). Systematic review and meta-analysis. In *The BERA/Sage handbook of educational research* (pp. 452–475). Sage.
Roberson, L., Russell, D., & Shaw, R. (2012). A case for training signed language interpreters for legal specialization. *International Journal of Interpreter Education, 4*(2), 6.
Sabatello, M. (2004). Disability, cultural minorities, and international law: Reconsidering the case of the deaf community. *Whittier Law Review, 26*, 1025.
Schembri, A., & Johnston, T. (2013). Sociolinguistic variation and change in sign languages. In R. Bayley, R. Cameron, & C. Lucas (Eds.), *The Oxford handbook of sociolinguistics*. https://doi.org/10.1093/oxfordhb/9780199744084.013.0025
Tambulukani, G. (2015). *First language teaching of initial reading: Blessing or curse for the Zambian children under primary reading program?* [Unpublished PhD thesis, The University of Zambia].
Vonagris, U., Zieren, J., Canzler, U., Bauer, B., & Kraiss, K. F. (2008). Recent developments in visual sign language recognition. *Universal Access in the Information Society, 6*, 323–362.
Wakumelo, N. M. (2009, August). *Provision of education for the deaf in Zambia: The situation and challenges*. Paper presented at the University of Zambia School of Education and the Directorate of Research and Graduate Studies Conference.
Wakumelo, N. M., & Miti, L. (2010, June). *A journey into the deaf world: Issues of language and culture*. Paper presented at the African Languages Association for Southern Africa (ALASA) Conference, University of Botswana.
Wilcox, S., Krausneker, V., & Armstrong, D. (2012). Language policies and the deaf community. In B. Spolsky (Ed.), *Cambridge handbook of language policy*. Cambridge University Press.
Zimba, Y. (2016). *United Nations convention on the rights of persons with disabilities: Current state in Zambia: Perspective from PWDs*. [Master's thesis, Diaconia University of Applied Sciences].

10 Challenges of foreign language and migrant workers in South African courts

A critical examination of linguistic justice

Josephat Mutangadura and Tebogo J. Rakgogo

Introduction

The judicial system is a fundamental pillar of a fair and just society. Nevertheless, foreign-language migrant workers in South Africa sometimes encounter numerous difficulties when trying to navigate this system. Language obstacles hinder their comprehension of legal procedures and also undermine their capacity to advocate effectively for themselves. This chapter analyses the linguistic challenges these migrant workers encounter, highlighting the urgent requirement for adjustments to maintain linguistic fairness. South Africa has a diverse and lively society that includes a substantial population of migrant workers from different parts of the world (Mabilo, 2023). These persons frequently face a legal system that, despite its dedication to impartiality, can be challenging to traverse because of language barriers. This study begins with a summary of the language situation in South African courts and moves on to the specific challenges faced by non-native speakers of any of the languages used in South Africa. Docrat and Kaschula (2019) claim that a large body of South African law clearly recognises people's right to communicate and receive communication in a language they understand, notably in court. The right to a fair trial is explicitly protected under section 35(3)(k) of the Constitution.[1] Courts are required to offer a skilled translator during criminal proceedings if the accused does not comprehend the language used in court.

The study was largely qualitative, making use of semi-structured interviews. Semi-structured interviews were held with foreign language migrant workers who have experienced the trial court system, as well as lawyers, interpreters, and judges who have worked with them. the purpose of these interviews was to explore personal experiences with the court system, perceptions of fairness, and specific challenges faced due to language barriers

1 Section 35(3)(k) provides that every accused person has a right to a fair trial, which includes the right to be tried in a language that the accused person understands or, if that is not practicable, to have the proceedings interpreted into that language.

DOI: 10.4324/9781003569435-14

and cultural differences. The study also had to identify and examine detailed case studies of trial proceedings involving foreign language migrant workers, focusing on the role of language and cultural barriers in the legal process and outcomes. These case studies were then used to illustrate specific challenges, identify gaps in the current system, and highlight best practices or successful interventions. Content analysis was used to identify themes, patterns, and narratives that provide deeper insights into the experiences of participants and the systemic issues within the trial court system. Informed consent was obtained after explaining the purpose of the study and how the data would be used. The research also considered the cultural sensitivity and emotional impact of discussing legal challenges and ensured participants had access to support if needed.

Background

South African courts are civil and criminal courts that oversee the dispensing of justice in the country. These courts are established by the South African Constitution and the South African Act of Parliament (South African Government Information, 2009/2010). The Department of Justice and Correctional Development (DoJ & CD), finance these courts, which were formed under Section 165 of the Constitution of the Republic of South Africa, Act No. 108 of 1996. They are divided into regional, district, and magistrates' courts, as well as the high court's interim division, the Supreme Court of Appeal, and the Constitutional Court. A crucial element of South African legislation, particularly in court proceedings, guarantees individuals the right to communicate and be communicated with in a language that they completely understand. Section 35(3)(k) of the Constitution ensures the entitlement to a just and impartial legal proceeding. If the defendant lacks an understanding of the language used during the legal procedures, the court is obligated to engage the services of a qualified translator. The Constitution has only a limited number of articles that require and regulate government institutions to ensure the equitable use of indigenous languages across all levels of society, ranging from the national to the local level. The National Language Policy Framework (Act No. 108 of 1996) ensures that all languages are given equal status and can be utilised in all contexts. The Official Languages Statutes, such as Act No. 12 of 2012, are specific instances of these acts.

Elsewhere in nations such as Malaysia, where migrant labourers constitute a considerable portion of the labour force, the inability to communicate effectively due to language differences has been recognised as a major hindrance to obtaining legal assistance and achieving justice (Wahab & Khairi, 2020). Migrant workers who do not possess sufficient language skills may encounter difficulties in comprehending their rights, navigating legal procedures, and obtaining remedies in instances of exploitation, abuse, or unjust treatment (Wahab & Khairi, 2020). Migrant workers in Africa face various obstacles, including language hurdles, lack of proper documents, fear of deportation, financial limitations, xenophobia, and prejudice. These factors together make them hesitant to seek legal support and justice (Jaiswal, 2024). The presence of these hurdles establishes a recurring pattern of susceptibility for migrant workers, resulting in their exclusion and lack of sufficient assistance or safeguarding within the established legal structure (Jaiswal, 2024; Wahab & Khairi, 2020). The lack of translators or language support services in legal settings worsens the impact of language obstacles on migrant workers' ability to access justice (Balekang, 2023). The lack of linguistic support obstructs efficient communication between migrant workers and legal experts, hindering workers' capacity to comprehend legal proceedings, demand their rights, and get justice (Balekang, 2023).

Language barriers and other socio-economic challenges like inadequate financial resources, restricted mobility, and unstable living conditions make justice for migrant workers difficult (Ng, 2022). The overlapping obstacles hinder the ability to obtain legal services and perpetuate disparities and injustices experienced by migrant workers in Africa (Ng, 2022). To overcome language barriers in accessing justice for migrant workers, a comprehensive strategy is needed. Such a strategy should include the provision of language support services, the promotion of cultural competence among legal professionals, and the implementation of policies that guarantee linguistic inclusivity in legal processes (Čebron, 2021). Stakeholders can improve access to justice for migrant workers, protect their rights, and create a fair legal environment for everyone, regardless of their language skills, by acknowledging and addressing language barriers (Čebron, 2021; Balekang, 2023).

The South African linguistic diversity and the legal system

South Africa is known for its extensive linguistic diversity, as its constitution recognises 11 official languages: isiZulu, isiXhosa, Afrikaans, Sepedi (Northern Sotho), Setswana, English, Sesotho (Southern Sotho), Xitsonga, siSwati, Tshivenda, and isiNdebele. The presence of multiple languages in this country reflects its complex social structure and emphasises a dedication to cultural and linguistic inclusivity. The legal system in South Africa is moulded by its colonial past, primarily influenced by Roman-Dutch law and British common law. English and Afrikaans have historically been the primary languages used in the legal field, particularly in higher courts and legal documents. Nevertheless, the post-apartheid constitution of 1996 represented a notable change in attitude towards accepting and celebrating the linguistic variety inside the country. This initiative aimed to address past inequities stemming from language bias and enhance the inclusivity of the judicial system for all citizens of South Africa.

Linguistic problems pose a substantial hindrance to migrant workers in Africa, impeding their access to justice by obstructing their capacity to obtain legal aid, comprehend their rights, and navigate legal institutions proficiently. The usage of various languages in court proceedings can complicate legal processes and heighten the probability of misunderstandings, particularly when intricate legal terminology and sophisticated language structures are involved. There is a shortage of proficient interpreters and translators who can effectively work within the legal field, especially for languages that are not widely spoken (Kaschula, 2021). The limited availability of resources can postpone legal processes and perhaps affect the impartiality and precision of trials. Ensuring the uniform and precise translation of legal documents and procedures into many languages presents a substantial obstacle. Translation errors might result in law misunderstandings and unfair legal consequences.

The South African legal framework related to the rights of non-English speakers in the judicial system

South Africa, being a country with many languages and 11 official languages, has distinctive difficulties in guaranteeing equitable access to justice for persons who are not proficient in English. The post-apartheid era ushered in substantial modifications to the legal structure, aiming to redress historical inequities and foster inclusiveness (Eck, 2021). The South African legal system experienced a significant transition with the adoption of the democratic Constitution in 1996. This development aimed to align with societal shifts and acknowledge the diverse legal cultures within South Africa (Eck, 2021). This transition was essential in recognising the varied language backgrounds of the people and the necessity to accommodate individuals who do not speak English within the judicial system. Nevertheless, notwithstanding the progress made in the legal sphere, there are still obstacles to overcome when it comes to putting language policy into practice, particularly in the realm of higher education (Cele, 2021). The language policy is crucial for guaranteeing equal access and social integration in higher education in South Africa (Cele, 2021). The implementation of a national language policy framework is crucial in establishing an inclusive environment that enables persons to actively engage in legal proceedings irrespective of their linguistic heritage. Nevertheless, the execution of these policies frequently suffers from insufficient oversight and resources, so impeding the successful achievement of language rights for individuals who do not speak English.

Within the framework of the legal system, it is imperative to protect the rights of individuals who do not speak English to guarantee equitable and impartial treatment in accordance with the law. This encompasses the provision of language support services, such as interpretation and translation, to assist efficient communication during judicial procedures. The absence of linguistic assistance might erect obstacles for individuals who do not speak English, so constraining their capacity to comprehend and engage in legal proceedings (Wijk, 2024). The attitudes towards other language variations, particularly accents, can influence the perception of non-English speakers in legal environments. Research has indicated that individuals can experience bias or unfair treatment due to their specific accent in English, emphasising the importance of recognising and respecting linguistic diversity within the legal system (Goatley-Soan, 2018). It is essential to confront these prejudices in order to protect the rights of those who do not speak English and to foster a legal climate that is more inclusive.

Efforts to decolonise the curriculum and foster linguistic diversity are crucial in legal education to ensure that future legal professionals are prepared to serve a wide range of linguistic populations (Eck, 2021). By initiating a reset of legal education, South Africa can strive towards a legal system that is more inclusive and representative, ensuring the protection of the rights of all individuals, irrespective of their linguistic origin. The legal framework in South Africa has made significant progress in acknowledging the rights of those who do not speak English inside the judicial system. Nevertheless, there are still obstacles to overcome in successfully executing language policy and guaranteeing equitable access to justice for individuals with varying linguistic backgrounds.

The legal framework pertaining to linguistic rights

The South African Constitution ensures the right to a just trial and the right to receive information in a language that is comprehensible to the individual. Nevertheless, this entitlement is often compromised due to insufficient interpretation services and limited finances (Mabilo, 2023). This chapter examines the current legal rules and their execution, assessing their effectiveness in safeguarding the language rights of migrant workers.

According to section 35(3)(k) of the South African Constitution, every accused individual is entitled to a trial conducted in a language they comprehend. If this is not feasible, they have the right to have the proceedings interpreted. Notwithstanding this clause, there have been countless cases when migrant workers have undergone trials without adequate interpretation. The legal framework provides an analysis of the legal framework, specifically highlighting its deficiencies in safeguarding the linguistic rights of individuals who are not native speakers.

Interpreters have a vital function in facilitating communication across different languages in court settings. Nevertheless, the consistency of interpretation services' quality and availability is lacking. The training, accreditation, and obstacles encountered by court interpreters in South Africa are another challenge to this whole process (Mabilo, 2023). The consequences of inadequate interpretation of legal results emphasise instances where misinterpretations have resulted in wrongful convictions. Furthermore, the absence of standardised training and accreditation procedures results in considerable variation in the proficiency of interpreters (Mabilo, 2023). This legal framework examines these difficulties, offering a comprehensive critique of how the current system inadequately caters to the requirements of non-native speakers.

Impacts of language and interpreting on fairness and justice

Linguistic barriers can severely impact the fairness of legal proceedings. This section delves into the broader implications of these challenges, discussing how they affect the perception of the justice system among migrant workers and the potential for systemic biases. It also explores the psychological and emotional toll on individuals who struggle to understand and be understood in court. This confirms the notion that if someone is able to communicate in English, the trial will be conducted in English. The significance lies in the right to communicate in one's native language and the right to be comprehended by the court in that language. Leung (2019) emphasises that bilingual or multilingual defendants may have a higher level of comfort and proficiency in their native language than the language used in the courtroom. The court will evaluate linguistic competency based on the defendant's ability to communicate in the language that the court uses.

Mpasha and Mutele (2014) argue that the use of court interpreters is necessary to safeguard the rights of all parties involved in legal proceedings. Hence, court interpreters/translators must possess knowledge of the cultural context of the populations they are assisting, particularly with regard to their use of figurative language. Consequently, the accused must be subjected to trials conducted in their respective African languages[2] in order to ensure their full participation in the legal proceedings. However, the South African context gives the right to linguistic justice in one of their official languages.

This study explores these issues in depth, highlighting the need for systemic changes to ensure that all individuals, regardless of language proficiency, can receive a fair trial. While comprehensive in theory, South Africa's legal framework faces challenges in its implementation, particularly regarding the rights of non-English speakers. The Constitution of South Africa guarantees the right to a fair trial, which implicitly includes the right to interpretation. However, legislation and policy often fall short in practice, as detailed by the South African Human Rights Commission's report (2019), which calls for a more robust enforcement of these rights. South Africa's adherence to international agreements like the International Covenant on Civil and Political Rights mandates the provision of these rights to all individuals, irrespective of language (United Nations, 2021).

Legal aid and representation

Assistance with legal aid and representation for migrant workers faces numerous hurdles, primarily due to language and cultural barriers. A study by Solechan (2023) underscores that these workers often refrain from

2 African Languages in the South African sense refers to other languages other than English and Africans, which are official in the country.

seeking legal help because they are unaware of their rights and are apprehensive about the repercussions of engaging with legal systems, which may include deportation. Additionally, the existing legal aid services often do not cater to the linguistic needs of migrants, further limiting their access to justice (Truong, 2022). This underscores the need for legal aid programmes to incorporate multilingual support and outreach initiatives targeting migrant communities. South Africa can tackle these problems and advocate for linguistic variety to ensure the rights of all its inhabitants and to foster inclusivity in legal settings. Legal assistance for migrant workers is crucial in guaranteeing and safeguarding their rights in different nations. Multiple studies have emphasised the significance of legal aid for migrant workers. Boucher (2018) highlights the significance of legal representation through government entities such as the Fair Work Ombudsman in attaining favourable results for foreign workers. This highlights the importance of legal assistance in tackling matters of employment conditions and guaranteeing equitable treatment for migratory workers. Furthermore, the efforts of Burmese support organisations like The Yaung Chi Oo Workers' Association in Mae Sot, as referenced by Pangsapa (2015), highlight the crucial role that civil society and NGO activism play in offering legal guidance and assistance to migrant workers concerning their working conditions (Pangsapa, 2015).

Several studies have examined the legal protection structures and frameworks that exist for Indonesian migrant workers. The difficulties encountered by legal aid organisations in providing assistance to migrant workers have been recorded. Bada and Gleeson (2023) highlight that although there has been a significant increase in worker centres and legal advocates assisting immigrant workers, certain organisations are limited in handling issues involving illegal workers (Bada & Gleeson, 2023). The aforementioned constraint, as emphasised by Guild and Figueroa (2018), in addition to the unavailability of these establishments in suburban and rural regions, emphasises the obstacles that migratory workers encounter in obtaining legal aid. Widyawati (2018) examines a legal protection framework that prioritises the fulfilment of rights for Indonesian migrant workers overseas. This includes provisions for legal aid, guidance, compensation, and insurance claims (Widyawati, 2018). In the same vein, Nugroho et al. (2023) stress the significance of creating protection centres for Indonesian migrant workers in the host nation. They provide detailed guidelines for safeguarding their rights and welfare (Nugroho et al., 2023).

Scholars have extensively studied the international legal framework on the rights of migratory workers. Ruhs (2012) emphasises the importance of international legal instruments, such as the UN's International Convention on the Protection of the Rights of All Migrant Workers and Members of Their Families, in safeguarding the rights of migrant workers worldwide (Ruhs, 2012). Furthermore, the significance of organisations such as the International

Labour Organisation in establishing guidelines for safeguarding the rights and welfare of migrant workers highlights the crucial function of legal frameworks. When analysing the difficulties encountered by migrant workers in obtaining legal safeguards, it is essential to take into account the influence of elements such as instability and susceptibility to social risks. Zhao (2023) examines the correlation between precarity among transient migrants and their limited social and legal safeguards. With a focus on migrant workers from China in Brunei, the study emphasises the necessity of strong legal structures to address the vulnerabilities experienced by migrant workers (Zhao, 2023). Similarly, Schoultz et al. (2023) examine the legal frameworks surrounding vulnerability in court proceedings concerning migrant workers, highlighting the significance of acknowledging and tackling the distinct obstacles this marginalised population encounters within legal contexts (Schoultz et al., 2023). The study explores the challenges of protecting migrant workers from exploitation under Sweden's criminal law system, focusing on how precarious migration status and labour conditions contribute to exploitation and the difficulty of securing legal justice for these workers.

To guarantee that migrant workers receive essential support and protection while contributing to their host society, countries should focus on removing obstacles to accessing legal aid, implementing comprehensive legal protection models, and adhering to international legal frameworks. It is crucial to make efforts to improve legal aid services and reinforce legal frameworks for migrant workers in order to advance social justice and protect the rights of all individuals, regardless of their migration status. The right to a fair trial is foundational to the justice system; however, for foreign-language migrant workers, this right is often compromised. Case studies by the National Institute of Justice (2018) and Blood (2020) illustrate instances where inadequate interpretation led to misunderstandings and wrongful convictions. The European Court of Human Rights has repeatedly emphasised the importance of competent interpretation as part of the right to a fair trial, setting a precedent for international standards that South Africa could aspire to (Human Rights Watch, 2020).

Presentation of findings from interviews

The role of the interpreter and language challenges in migrant trials

Interpreters have had a significant impact on South African courtrooms for an extended period, as demonstrated by the 1944 Magistrates' Courts Act, which mandates magistrates to get capable interpreters for defendants who cannot comprehend the court's language. Nevertheless, researchers and judicial officers have scrutinised and criticised this particular position. The interpreter frequently assumes the role of a mediator between two opposing parties, obligated to serve both impartially. However, their position within the court hierarchy, their role as a cultural intermediary between speakers of

African indigenous languages, and a system that often seems inaccessible can compromise their impartiality.

The role of interpreters in migrant worker legal proceedings

This study drew responses from migrant workers, interpreters, magistrates and human rights lawyers. Interpreters are relied on to safeguard the interests of the accused in cases where the language of the court is different from that of the accused. Language interpreters play a vital role in ensuring justice is accessible to all, regardless of linguistic background. All interview respondents agreed that interpreters bridge communication gaps for non-native speakers in South African courts, where diversity is the norm. However, they also noted that the profession continues to face numerous challenges (established by this study) that compromise the quality of interpreting and, consequently, the fairness of judicial proceedings.

The study presents key challenges faced by language interpreters in cases of migrant workers in South African courts. The majority of migrant workers come from Zimbabwe, Malawi, Mozambique, Nigeria, and Bangladesh, among other foreign nationals. Finding someone who is fluent in these languages is not easy due to the multiplicity of these nationals. Fellow Zimbabweans, Mozambicans or Malawians can be enlisted as interpreters. However, the South African system is not able to keep a live register of these interpreters for each court sitting across all provinces.

Inadequate training and accreditation

According to human rights lawyers interviewed, one of the primary challenges is the lack of standardised training and accreditation for court interpreters in foreign language cases and Indigenous South African languages. Many interpreters enter the profession without formal training, significantly varying their skills and competence (Mabilo, 2023). In this case, interpreters who responded acknowledged that such privileges are not readily available to foreign language interpreters. Such a situation results in mere native speakers being enlisted as interpreters without any professional background.

Interpreter 1.

> *Unlike in some countries where interpreters must undergo rigorous training and certification, South Africa does not have a uniform standard space for foreign nationals. This results in disparities in the quality of interpretation provided in different courts.*

Another seasoned interpreter confirmed that

> *In most cases, migrant workers either go without an interpreter as they are forced to go through the trial in English, or they have to do with mere fellow language speakers who are not professional interpreters.*

A human rights lawyer complained,

> *Court interpreting requires knowledge of legal terminology and procedures, which many interpreters lack due to insufficient training programs.*

Without a standardised accreditation process for these foreign national interpreters, courts often employ interpreters with varying levels of proficiency, impacting the consistency and reliability of interpretation services.

Resource constraints

A study by Mabilo (2023) in Polokwane revealed that courts often face budgetary constraints that limit the availability and quality of interpretation services. The magistrate interviews also confirmed that courts in Limpopo province host many foreign language cases due to their proximity to Zimbabwe and Mozambique. In the end, more budgetary resources would need to be allocated to these foreign language cases than local language interpreting. The magistrate also said,

> *'Resource limitations can lead to overburdened interpreters who have to handle multiple cases simultaneously, reducing the quality of their work'. Limited financial resources mean that courts cannot always afford to hire highly qualified interpreters or provide ongoing training and development in most of the common foreign languages like Shona, Chewa, Igbo, Hausa and other languages spoken across the South African borders.*
>
> *Due to the high demand for their services, foreign language interpreters are frequently overworked, which can lead to fatigue and potential errors in interpretation.*

Ethical and professional challenges

Interpreters must navigate various ethical and professional challenges that can affect their performance and the integrity of the judicial process. One Chewa interpreter retorted,

> *The South African situation is normally fraught with xenophobic impressions and expressions, which plays into the neutrality of court proceedings and interpreting. Maintaining neutrality is critical yet challenging, especially in emotionally charged cases.*

Interpreters must avoid influencing proceedings while ensuring accurate communication. It was revealed that *'at times, interpreters end up not expressing certain things for fear of outrage and fightback from the host communities'*.

Upholding confidentiality is a fundamental ethical requirement in court interpreting and legal proceedings. However, the majority of participant interpreters revealed they sometimes struggle with maintaining this confidentiality, particularly in smaller communities where they may have personal connections. Foreign nationals are found in every province of South Africa, including small rural communities.

Technical and logistical issues

The law is evolving with technology. Most nations have language-specific court-interpreting equipment. Installing enough software and equipment in non-funded foreign languages is tough. The 2022 South African census showed that Shona and Chewa are spoken daily, thus Limpopo participants supported adding them in schools. This would also help build translation tools for this commonly spoken language in the province. Court interpreting is complicated technically and logistically. The interpreters acknowledged that poor quality or lack of appropriate interpreting equipment can hinder the delivery of accurate and clear interpretation. Interpreters seem to work within the constraints of courtroom procedures and dynamics, which can be unpredictable and demanding.

Psychological stress and burnout

Considering the large numbers of foreign nationals in South Africa across all the provinces, especially Limpopo, Gauteng, Western Cape, and KZN, there are likely to be so many cases going on every court day.

A magistrate in Gauteng said,

> *The nature of the work can lead to significant psychological stress and burnout among interpreters, especially when few language specialists have to service so many court sittings.*

In Mpumalanga, one magistrate said,

> *Some of the cases involving foreign nationals are so daunting and nerve-wracking at times. Imagine a case of ritual murder and the mythical explanations that go with it.*

Interpreting traumatic testimonies and being immersed in distressing cases can have a profound emotional impact on interpreters.

A lady interpreter retorted,

> *The high-pressure environment, combined with heavy workloads, often leads to burnout, affecting our mental health and our ability to perform effectively.*

Language and cultural complexities

The current study uncovered many cases of language and culture disparities in legal interpreting. Africa's linguistic diversity includes numerous dialects and regional language variations, complicating the task of accurate interpretation. Interpreters must translate words and convey cultural meaning, which is often challenging. The major outcry from the magistrates was that finding an interpreter with specific competence for all the various foreign languages was not easy.

One of the magistrates said,

> *A simple case is the Shona Language from Zimbabwe, where more than 5 varieties are spoken. An interpreter from a Zezuru dialect may not properly represent another Shona speaker of the Karanga, Manyika or Ndau dialect in a legal case.*

Understanding and accurately conveying cultural contexts is crucial yet difficult, especially when interpreters are not fully versed in the cultural backgrounds of the parties involved. The study revealed that certain terms from one variety do not carry the same meaning in another, culturally and linguistically, as the accused argued when contesting the interpreting results. Usadolo and Kotze (2015) state that good interpreting requires cultural and forensic knowledge as well as language skills. Their reasoning considers Mikkelson's (1999) discovery that term substitution is not simply dependent on interlingual requirements. In addition, a concept in one culture may not be equal in another. An interpreter must be able to use descriptive language to convey the notion. Usadolo and Kotze (2015) analyse dialect and its daily obstacles for African court interpreters from other nations.

Impact of language barriers on justice and equity in migrant worker cases

In the absence of a professional interpreter, the migrant worker encounters difficulties comprehending the accusations and articulating his defence.

An interpreter retorted,

> *As a result, there was a conviction, but it was later overturned due to a more accurate understanding that uncovered many mistakes throughout the trial.*

The other interpreter agreed that linguistic issues have led to some unnecessary convictions. Such cases are common. Numerous migrant workers interviewed reported similar experiences when linguistic hurdles prevented them from fully participating in their legal representation, resulting in unfair trials and convictions. This happens in judicial courts and workplace disciplinary hearings nationwide. After his employer failed to get an interpreter, one foreign worker was fired. He felt innocent of the charge, but his English was not sufficient enough to defend himself.

Language limitations can weaken legal procedures in several ways. Migrant labourers in Limpopo and Mpumalanga reported many miscommunications. The interviews showed that such occurrences are worse in remote regions like the Northern Cape and Eastern Cape, where first-language interpreters are scarce. Miscommunications between the court and the defendant might affect evidence and verdicts. Migrant workers with limited language skills rarely understand their legal rights or support systems, resulting in bad decisions and inadequate legal representation. Legal documents show that the accused can request an interpreter even if the case is adjourned until one is found. The accused cannot receive such benefits in remote provinces. Language barriers exacerbate judicial biases.

One accused stated that

> *Non-native speakers may be seen as less trustworthy or dependable, which might impact the opinions of judges and prosecutors.*

Equity and systemic disparities

Language barriers exacerbate systemic imbalances in the legal system, disproportionately impacting migrant workers. These inequalities typically lead to disproportionate convictions. A human rights lawyer said,

> *Migrant workers may face more severe penalties as a result of misunderstandings or an inability to effectively explain mitigating factors. Migrant workers encounter challenges when attempting to avail themselves of appeal chances.*

One bold interpreter agreed that

> *Migrant workers who lack comprehension of the legal process are less inclined to contest unfair rulings, resulting in unopposed instances of wrongful convictions.*

In general, individuals who are unable to navigate the legal system owing to linguistic barriers face significant limitations in accessing justice, which in turn perpetuates cycles of disadvantage and injustice. Another interpreter further acknowledged that they also give up when it comes to this since court interpreting is exhausting and emotional at times. Magistrates acknowledged this crisis but defended their position in that if cases must proceed, sometimes they have to make a judgment based on what is available in these migrant worker trials.

The psychological and emotional toll

Migrant workers experience substantial psychological and emotional distress due to their incapacity to adequately communicate in legal situations.

According to the human rights lawyers interviewed,

> *The combination of not comprehending the proceedings and the apprehension of unfair results can result in worry, sadness, and a feeling of powerlessness.*

The burden of confronting legal proceedings without a comprehensive comprehension can induce significant tension and worry. Legal experts confirmed that language limitations can also prevent migrant workers from exerting influence on the outcome of their cases, resulting in feelings of powerlessness and dissatisfaction.

Another migrant worker acknowledged that

> *If the interpreter and the magistrate failed to put across your case, the results always disadvantage me as the accused.*

Discussion

This research on the impact of language barriers in South African courts uncovers several crucial factors that hinder the administration of justice and fairness for migrant workers. The results emphasise the significant impact of language difficulties on legal results, interpreting effectiveness, and the general welfare of individuals who are not native speakers. This study examined each significant discovery, emphasising its consequences and the necessity for extensive policy overhauls. Based on the researcher's observations, it is evident that some of the accused foreign nationals claim to have a grasp of the English language, and some even have a basic understanding of local languages. However, it is apparent that they encounter difficulties at certain points, necessitating the postponement of the case in order to secure competent interpreters for that particular language. Furthermore, the court now relies on a few foreign interpreters to provide interpretation services for the majority of the cases.

Mpasha and Mutele (2014) claim that many African languages struggle to create legal vocabulary. This happens mostly when English terms are translated into African languages. English words may be foreign in African languages. When the interpreter doesn't understand the foreign language's perspective, like Zimbabwe's IsiNdebele, the process gets more difficult. In South Africa, this phrase is interpreted differently, which could cause confusion.

The study found significant differences in interpretation service quality and accessibility among South African courts. There are no interpreters in the accused person's native tongue, or a large percentage of foreign national interpreters lack professional training, resulting in many misinterpretations and communication breakdowns. This mismatch affects trial fairness since precise and effective communication is vital for justice (Svongoro, 2017; Hlophe, 2004). Interpreter shortages lengthen judicial sessions and delays. Long periods of ambiguity can harm migrant workers' legal status and well-being. The results suggest that interpreters need standardised training and certification to ensure they have the skills and knowledge to do their jobs well.

Language barriers have a substantial impact on the legal results experienced by migration workers. The study revealed elevated levels of misunderstanding in instances involving individuals who are not native speakers, resulting in erroneous convictions and more severe sentencing. This disparity underscores the structural injustices inherent in the legal system, as those who are not native speakers face a disadvantage solely as a result of language distinctions (Choshi, 2009; Hlophe, 2004). Migrant workers sometimes have obstacles in comprehending the allegations brought against them or successfully advocating for their defence due to insufficient interpretation services. Their limited understanding hinders their ability to fully engage in legal processes, leading to unfair outcomes. Enhanced interpretation services and more knowledge among legal practitioners are necessary in order to address the difficulties encountered by those who are not native speakers.

Migrant workers experience significant psychological and emotional strain as a result of language limitations. The study demonstrates that a lack of comprehension of judicial procedures and ineffective communication results in increased tension, anxiety, and powerlessness on the part of migrant workers. The emotional turmoil experienced by these individuals might have enduring consequences on their psychological well-being, impairing their capacity to navigate the legal system and maintain personal welfare (Svongoro, 2017; Hlophe, 2004). These findings highlight the necessity of establishing support mechanisms to assist migrant workers in managing the stress associated with legal processes. Offering psychological assistance and assuring access to dependable interpretation services might alleviate these negative consequences and aid in preserving their mental well-being.

Interpreters encounter training, accreditation, and ethical issues (Svongoro, 2017). Lack of training and accreditation causes major issues for interpreters. Many interpreters lack accreditation and struggle to understand complex legal terminology, according to the poll. The lack of standardised training hurts their performance and court interpreting services. In addition, translators have ethical challenges, such as the need to uphold impartiality and confidentiality, which are further complicated by the intense atmosphere of courtrooms. These issues highlight the need for formal language training and accreditation programmes that include ethical and professional standards. The study reveals inherent inequalities in the way migrant workers are treated inside the court system. Language hurdles exacerbate prejudices and result in uneven access to justice since those who are not native speakers are subjected to more severe penalties and encounter more difficulties in appealing unfair rulings. In order to rectify these discrepancies, the study proposes a number of recommendations, as summarised next.

Standardised training and certification

The study highlights the necessity for uniform court interpreter training and accreditation. Many interpreters enter the field without training, resulting in variances in their skills with complex legal terminology and procedures. This inconsistency affects interpretation and trial fairness. Standardisation ensures that all court interpreters are proficient, delivering consistent and accurate interpretation services. It also helps professionalise the sector, recognising interpreters' skills and knowledge. To provide consistent and high-quality court interpretation, requiring organised training and certification. Courtroom interpreters must be trained and certified uniformly to ensure quality and consistency. Court interpreters in South Africa vary in skill and efficacy due to inconsistent standards. Implementing thorough training programmes and a certification process can solve the problems, increasing the fairness and equity of the court system for non-native speakers.

Enhanced funding

Directing additional resources into interpretation services to tackle deficiencies and enhance the accessibility and proficiency of interpreters. Increased financing for interpretation services in South African courts is crucial for guaranteeing fairness and equality for individuals who are not native speakers, especially migrant workers. Sufficient financial resources are essential to ensure the provision of top-notch interpretation services, tackle shortages, and provide thorough training and certification programmes for interpreters.

Improved legal aid

Offering customised legal assistance to those who are not native speakers, which includes the provision of legal advisors proficient in several languages and access to instructional materials. Enhancing the provision of legal assistance for migrant workers in South African courts is vital for guaranteeing fairness and equality. judicial assistance that is easily available, thorough, and customised to the requirements of individuals who are not native speakers can help reduce the negative consequences of language obstacles and guarantee equitable judicial proceedings.

Cultural competency training

Implementing compulsory training for legal professionals to enhance their comprehension of cultural disparities and the difficulties encountered by migrant workers. Providing effective legal aid to migrant workers in South African courts requires cultural competency. Cultural competency involves understanding, respecting, and responding to cultural differences and needs. Cultural competency among legal practitioners can improve service and ensure fairness for non-native speakers. Understanding cultural and linguistic differences helps legal aid professionals communicate clearly with migrant workers. Legal professionals and clients gain confidence from cultural awareness. Migrant workers are more likely to get legal help if they feel understood and respected. Culturally competent lawyers can better represent their clients by addressing cultural factors that may affect their legal decisions.

Support networks

Creating support networks for migrant workers, encompassing psychological assistance and access to resources for navigating the legal system. Establishing resilient support networks for migrant workers navigating the South African judicial system is essential for guaranteeing justice and fairness. These networks can offer crucial resources, emotional assistance, and direction, aiding migrant workers in overcoming the multitude of problems they encounter. In order to be efficient, support networks for migratory workers should encompass the subsequent components. Providing legal support in the languages spoken by migrant workers is essential for effective help. This encompasses the provision of interpreters, legal consultants proficient in multiple languages, and translated legal papers. Support networks can also have centres as dedicated facilities where migrant workers may conveniently access a range of services, seek guidance, and interact with fellow individuals encountering similar difficulties. Professional Counselling Services also provides mental health assistance and counselling services specifically designed to assist migrant workers in managing the stress and anxiety that may arise from legal proceedings.

Lastly, support such as offering informative sessions and workshops on legal entitlements, navigating the legal framework, and accessing accessible resources are also important.

Engaging in collaboration with NGOs and government agencies to offer extensive assistance and resources.

Conclusion

This study underscores the serious difficulties encountered by foreign language migrant workers in the South African trial court system. Language obstacles, insufficient interpretation services, and restricted access to legal assistance disproportionately hinder their capacity to engage fully and equitably in judicial procedures. Migrant workers often struggle to understand their charges, communicate with legal counsel, and follow courtroom rules, which violates their right to a fair trial. Cultural differences might lead to miscommunication and bias in adjudication.

These systemic concerns require targeted changes. The trial court system must be accessible and equitable for all, regardless of language or culture, by improving interpretation services, legal aid awareness, and legal professional cultural competency training. These recommendations can help South Africa improve its judicial system and meet its constitutional and international obligations to protect the rights of all people, including foreign language migrant workers, without linguistic or cultural barriers.

References

Bada, X., & Gleeson, S. (2023). *Scaling migrant worker rights.* Retrieved June 24, 2024, from https://doi.org/10.1525/luminos.138

Balekang, G. (2023). *"If the person dies, the picture remains in my mind": Experiences of healthcare workers in the provision of healthcare services to migrants in Botswana.* Springer. Retrieved June 20, 2024, from https://doi.org/10.21203/rs.3.rs-3351488/v1

Blood, K. (2020). Case studies of three wrongful convictions. *Merrimack College Criminology Student Publications.* Retrieved from https://scholarworks.merrimack.edu/cgi/viewcontent.cgi?article=1013&context=crm_studentpub

Boucher, A. (2018). Measuring migrant worker rights violations in practice: The example of temporary skilled visas in Australia. *Journal of Industrial Relations, 61*(2), 277–301.

Čebron, U. (2021). Language as a trigger for racism: language barriers at healthcare institutions in Slovenia. *Social Sciences, 10*(4), 125. Retrieved June 20, 2024, from https://doi.org/10.3390/socsci10040125

Cele, N. (2021). Understanding language policy as a tool for access and social inclusion in South African higher education: A critical policy analysis perspective. *South African Journal of Higher Education, 35*(6). Retrieved June 15, 2024, from https://doi.org/10.20853/35-6-3730

Choshi, M. K. (2009). Law and language: Solution for multilingual societies. *Direito, Língua e Cidadania Global*, 149–164.

Docrat, Z., & Kaschula, R. (2019). Monolingual language of record: A critique of South Africa's policy directive. In M. K. Ralala, R. H. Kaschula, & G. Heydon (Eds.), *New frontiers in forensic linguistics: Themes and perspectives in language and law in Africa and beyond.* Sun Press.

Eck, M. (2021). Decolonising legal education in South Africa: Is it time to press the reset button? *Journal of Decolonising Disciplines, 2*(2). Retrieved June 18, 2024, from https://doi.org/10.35293/jdd.v2i1.45

Goatley-Soan, S. (2018). Worlds apart: A study of attitudes toward varieties of South African English accents in a United States employment scenario. *Journal of Language and Social Psychology, 37*(6), 692–705.

Guild, A., & Figueroa, I. (2018). The neighbors who feed us: Farmworkers and goverment policy – Challenges and solutions. *Harvard Law & Policy Review, 13*, 157–186.

Hlophe, J. (2004). Receiving justice in your own language the need for effective court interpreting in our multilingual society. *Advocate, 17*(1), 42–47.

Human Rights Watch. (2020). Retrieved June 28, 2024, from https://www.hrw.org/world-report/2020

Jaiswal, A. (2024). Do black women's lives matter? A study of the hidden impact of the barriers to access maternal healthcare for migrant women in South Africa. *Frontiers in Sociology, 9.* Retrieved June 20, 2024, from https://doi.org/10.3389/fsoc.2024.983148

Kaschula, R. H. (2021). *Languages, identities and intercultural communication in South Africa and beyond.* Routledge.

Leung, J. H. C. (2019). *Shallow equality and symbolic jurisprudence in multilingual legal orders.* Oxford University Press.

Mabilo, T. J. (2023). *Transforming courtroom interpreting through multilingualism: A study of courtroom interpreting in the Limpopo province* [Unpublished master's thesis, Tshwane University of Technology].

Mikkelson, H. (1999). *Interpreting is interpreting or is it?* Retrieved June 21, 2024, from file:///D:/CHAPTERS%20FOR%20PUBLICATION/InterpretingisInterpreting.pdf

Mpasha, L. E., & Mutele, T. C. (2014). Challenges facing the accused in the use of English only in criminal court proceedings: Experiences from the Vhembe District, Limpopo Province, South Africa. *Journal of Social Sciences*, *41*(3), 385–394.

National Institute of Justice. (2018). Wrongful convictions: The issues and the unheard voices (NIJ Report No. 251446). *U.S. Department of Justice*. Retrieved from https://www.ojp.gov/pdffiles1/nij/251446.pdf

Ng, S. (2022). Health inequalities amongst refugees and migrant workers in the midst of the covid-19 pandemic: A report of two cases. *Asian Bioethics Review*, *14*(2), 107–114.

Nugroho, A., Firmansyah, D., Ashilah, F., & Permatasari, E. (2023). The urgency of providing Indonesian migrant workers protection centres in the country of placement. *International Joint Conference on Arts and Humanities*, 83–90.

Pangsapa, P. (2015). When battlefields become marketplaces: Migrant workers and the role of civil society and NGO activism in Thailand. *International Migration*, *53*(3), 124–149.

Ruhs, M. (2012). The human rights of migrant workers. *American Behavioral Scientist*, *56*(9), 1277–1293.

Schoultz, I., Spanger, M., Jokinen, A., Jahnsen, S., Muhire, H., & Pekkarinen, A. (2023). Constructions of migrant victims of labour exploitation in Nordic court cases. *International Review of Victimology*, *30*(2), 261–281.

Solechan, S. (2023). Access To Information For Migrant Workers. *Russian Law Journal*, https://doi.org/10.52783/rlj.v11i3.1536

South African Human Rights Commission Report. (2019). Retrieved June 21, 2024, from https://www.sahrc.org.za/home/21/files/Annual%20Report%202019.pdf

Svongoro, P. R. (2017). *Court interpreting in Zimbabwe: A descriptive study of consecutively-interpreted rape trials in regional magistrates' courts*. Government Printers.

Truong, A. (2022). Linguistic legal deserts: Addressing language access in the United States legal system for limited English proficient Asian Americans and Pacific Islanders. *Boston University Law Review*, *102*(3), 1125–1158. https://www.bu.edu/bulawreview/files/2022/05/TRUONG.pdf

United Nations. (2021). United Nations Human Rights Report 2021: South Africa. *United Nations South Africa*. Retrieved from https://southafrica.un.org/sites/default/files/2022-06/OHCHR_Report_2021.pdf

Usadolo, S. E., & Kotze, E. 2015. Communicative challenges of interpreting in cross-border languages in South African courtrooms. *South African Journal of African Languages*, *35*(1), 57–65.

Wahab, A., & Khairi, A. (2020). Right to justice and legal aid barriers to the vulnerable non-citizens in Malaysia. *Malaysian Journal of Society and Space*, *16*(1). Retrieved June 15, 2024, from https://doi.org/10.17576/geo-2020-1601-02

Widyawati, A. (2018). Legal protection model for Indonesian migrant workers. *Journal of Indonesian Legal Studies*, *3*(2), 291–304.

Wijk, C. (2024). Montreal cognitive assessment test: Psychometric analysis of a South African workplace sample. *African Journal of Psychological Assessment*, *6*. Retrieved June 18, 2024, from https://doi.org/10.4102/ajopa.v6i0.151

Zhao, K. (2023). Precarity among transient migrants: Mainland Chinese workers in Brunei Darussalam during the Covid-19 pandemic. *Asian and Pacific Migration Journal*, *32*(3), 498–520.

11 Foreign language speakers, migrants, and refugees in Kenyan courts

Joyce Kasili and Lydia Anyonje

Introduction

Various scholars in the field of language and law have lamented that legal language is a form of communication that is difficult to be understood by non-legal individuals (Gibbons, 2003; Tiersma, 1999; Melinkoff, 1963). It is a language which is characterised by linguistic complexity and archaism (Tiersma, 2008). According to Haworth (2015), the nature of this language hampers comprehension rather than aiding it in a court set-up, a factor that leads to possible misunderstandings between legal and non-legal experts. Haworth (2015) asserts that this complex language is obscure and often leads to accusations and obfuscation, a situation that calls for the use of services of a legal counsel. The language therefore only serves the interests of legal professionals when it was also expected to serve interests of lay persons. This often leads to communication problems among which 'miscommunication', viewed as 'disadvantages before the law' (Eades, 2008). This is corroborated by Haworth (2015) who indicates that members of the lay public face communication challenges whenever they need to communicate with the law institution which operates on its own practices and norms.

Vulnerability

The term vulnerability has changed over time to not only address the potential to endure physical harm but also to address psychological, moral, and spiritual suffering (Merriam Webster, 2019). Anchored in social and behavioural sciences, 'vulnerability' has been used in many disciplines such as psychology, sociology, medical and health sciences, disaster and humanitarian studies, as well as economic and political studies (Wisner, 2016). On the other hand, Pariotti (2023) and Darity (2008) suggest that vulnerability implies threats to human rights. Nguyen-Trung et al. (2019) regard vulnerability as the lack of access to power, resources, and assets that prevents a person from properly and effectively forecasting, coping with, and recovering from the effects and impacts of risks and disasters.

DOI: 10.4324/9781003569435-15

While the term is viewed differently by Merriam Webster (2019), Pariotti (2023), and Nguyen-Trung et al. (2019), vulnerable individuals find themselves in situations where they are deprived of important aspects of life that make them humans.

In Africa, vulnerability applies to foreign language speakers, refugees, migrants, marginalised groups, minority tribes, women and children, people living with HIV and Aids, people living with disabilities, people with albinism, LGBTI persons, certain ethnic groups, and occupational groups (Das & Espinoza, 2020). In the current study, foreign language speakers, migrants and refugees are persons who find themselves in foreign spaces and are forced to speak languages little known to them in set ups such as the courtroom. This is a factor that renders them vulnerable. Such groups may eventually acquire only limited proficiency in the languages of their host countries.

Martin (2023) attributes vulnerability to 'situations'. He suggests that groups such as refugees, minorities, and patients find themselves vulnerable due to specific contexts and that such groups should be afforded special protection, attention, or assistance. Foreign language speakers, migrants, and refugees are part of the groups that experience vulnerability.

In Kenya, for instance, English and Kiswahili, the official languages, are also the languages of the courts. Some foreign language speakers may possess some competence in these languages, and some may not. English may attract more speaker-ship due to its international status as opposed to Kiswahili. Nevertheless, some foreign language speakers residing in the country speak some level of Kiswahili. However, the fact that they cannot speak English and Kiswahili fluently does not guarantee effective communication. This is a situation that makes them more vulnerable especially when they appear in the courts. These groups therefore experience twofold vulnerability: vulnerability due to displacement from their original abodes and linguistic vulnerability.

Foreign language speakers

A foreign language is a non-native language spoken outside the environment where it is commonly used (Moeller & Catalano, 2015). In this regard, foreign language speakers are individuals who communicate in a language different from that which is spoken in a given environment. In Kenya, foreign language speakers include nationals and expatriates from other countries who do not speak English or Kiswahili. Although English is a foreign language elsewhere, in Kenya, it is an official language. Therefore, the two languages are not foreign for Kenyans.

Migrants

There is no universal definition of a migrant. The International Organization for Migration (IOM, 2024) defines the term 'migrant' as a person who moves away from his or her place of usual residence, whether within a country or across an international border, temporarily or permanently, and for a variety of reasons. In this chapter, the term is used to refer to persons who have moved away from their countries of origin for varied reasons and now reside in Kenya. These individuals do not speak Kenyan languages, including English and Kiswahili which are the languages of the courts. They are foreign language speakers.

Refugees

A refugee is a person who resides outside their country of origin for reasons of feared persecution, conflict, violence, or other circumstances that have seriously disturbed public order and, as a result, requires international protection (UNGA, 2018). Some of the refugees may be speakers of the national and/ or official languages of the host countries whereas some may speak completely different languages. Numerous refugees from a wide range of backgrounds reside in Kenya; depending on their ancestry, they may or may not be regarded as foreign language speakers.

Legal framework and vulnerability

The Constitution of Kenya, 2010 provides for an accessible and fair justice system geared to dispense justice within stipulated timelines to all citizens without any form of discrimination, fear, or favour (Government of Kenya, 2010, Article 48–51). Further, Article 159 of the Constitution of Kenya lays down principles to guide the administration of justice, including equality before the law, efficiency in the delivery of justice, mainstreaming of alternative justice systems, and the importance of substantive justice regardless of legal procedures and technicalities. According to Helbling et al. (2015), citizens seek justice through both formal and non-formal mechanisms. Cases are therefore either taken to court through lawyers or arbitration is done by traditional courts or other groups such as the police, religious elders, or family members.

Research, however, indicates that many Kenyans are not able to access legal services in the formal justice system as stipulated in the constitution due to many factors including financial constraints, long delays or other reasons (Logan, 2017). For this reason, some citizens opt for cheaper services provided by non-governmental institutions which are largely funded by donors. Such institutions include FIDA (Federation of Women Lawyers), Kituo cha Sheria, Public Law Institute (PLI), KELIN Kenya (KELIN), International Commission of Jurists in Kenya (ICJ- Kenya), The CRADLE (Children's Foundation), Transparency International (TI), and Law Society of Kenya (Kenya National Report on Global Access to Justice, 2018).

Kituo cha Sheria has over the years focused on empowering marginalised and poor people to access justice though legal aid education, advocating for equitable access to justice, establishing community partnerships, and undertaking public interest litigation. The organisation provides legal advice regarding family law, land disputes, employment and labour disputes, landlord and tenant issues, criminal offenses, accident claims, rape cases, women's rights issues, and refugee issues. Other organisations that advocate for vulnerable groups in Kenya and specifically foreign language speakers, refugees and migrants include HIAS Kenya, Refugee Consortium of Kenya, International Rescue Committee, International Organization of Migration, Department of Refugees Services, and United Nations Commission for Refugees.

Objectives of the study

The study aimed at examining the current court practices regarding foreign language speakers, migrants, and refugees. It also explored possibilities of available means of ensuring fair hearing and treatment for such vulnerable groups in courtroom deliberations and proposing practical solutions to address the challenges foreign language speakers face.

Theoretical underpinnings of vulnerability

The study was anchored on three theories, namely: the vulnerability theory, the Framing theory and the Critical Discourse Analysis theory (CDA). The three theories are complementary to one another, especially where foreign language speakers like migrants and refugees arraigned in court are concerned.

Vulnerability theory

The vulnerability theory, which was put forth by Martha Fineman in 2008, acknowledges that people are vulnerable at some point during their lives. The situation is dire for foreign language speakers, migrants, and refugees given that they are away from their homes and that they speak non-native languages. These groups do not normally have a guarantee of living as comfortably as they would have wished under normal circumstances. In Kenya for instance, they are housed in far off settlements away from centres where they can obtain services, including legal aid (Muindi & Mberu, 2019). According to Fineman (2008), it is the responsibility of the state to find ways to reduce or alleviate the vulnerability.

Framing theory

The framing theory was posited by Gregory Bateson in 1972. Bateson asserts that the way information is presented to the audience (the frame) influences the choices people make about how to process and interpret that information. Entman (1993) defines Framing as 'the process of culling a few elements of perceived reality and assembling a narrative that highlights connections among them to promote a particular interpretation'. In this regard, the court system processes the information regarding the cases of foreign language speakers, migrants, and refugees based on the frames or how the information is presented. Therefore, in cases where the language used in court is not understood by these groups, there is likelihood that their voices will not be entirely incorporated when building and finally determining their cases. Additionally, the manner in which the language interpreter presents information to the accused determines their response, and by extension, the judges' interpretation of that response and the subsequent ruling thereof.

Critical Discourse Analysis

The Critical Discourse Analysis theory (CDA), proposed in the early 1990s by a group of scholars namely, Theo Van Leeuwen, Gunther Kress, Teun Van Dijk, and Norman Fairclough (Wodak & Meyer, 2001), is premised on social problems, particularly on the role of discourse in the production and reproduction of power abuse or domination (Van Dijk, 2001). CDA, then, sets up a relationship between language and power. In that sense, Wodak (2001) regards it as fundamentally concerned with analysing opaque as well as transparent structural relationships of dominance, discrimination, power, and control as manifested in language.

The language used in court is contextual. According to Song (2010), context can be linguistic, situational or cultural. Linguistic context refers to the relationship between the words, phrases, sentences, and even paragraphs. Situational context, refers to the environment, time, and place in which the discourse occurs, and also the relationship between the participants while cultural context refers to the culture, customs, and background of epoch in language communities in which the speakers participate.

Certain aspects of the utterances and their meanings in court are likely to contribute to dominance and discrimination, a relationship that Van Dijk (2001) draws between language and power. Van Dijk (2015) attaches more attention on the reproduction of social inequalities and the abuse of power and explores the importance of context on discourse production and discourse understanding.

In this chapter, the discourses produced in court regarding foreign language speakers, refugees, and migrants may have a bearing on the outcome of the cases depending on the utterances, how they are made and the interpretation by those with power to decide the outcome. These theories underpin this study and give insights into the phenomenon under study.

Courtroom discourse and vulnerability

Communication takes the centre stage during courtroom interactions. On one hand, the plaintiff and the respondents together with their witnesses put in their cases and on the other, the court listens and consequently responds. According to Lininger (2021), the court has the responsibility of testing the veracity of the presented facts and ensuring that justice is served, and that there is fair treatment to the two opposing sides.

Whilst these are normal court processes, courtroom language is different from day to day discourses, making it difficult for ordinary people to follow proceedings (Tkacukova et al., 2022). Ranosa-Madrunio (2013) confirms that the courtroom discourse deviates from the ordinary conversations where the lawyer takes charge of the proceedings, including turn taking in the discussions. Some plaintiffs, respondents, and witnesses are vulnerable, their vulnerability being as a result of either personal or situational circumstances (Gulati et al., 2022).

Foreign language speakers, migrants, and refugees are among these vulnerable groups. They live away from their initial homes and are thus vulnerable due to ethnicity, language, and cultural issues. Makanje (2020) asserts that the court has the duty of identifying the vulnerable and treating them as such, using special measures when they make their presentations in court. This is reinforced by what Madrunio and Villanueva (2016) attest to pointing out that testifying in court can be a stressful experience for vulnerable witnesses, due to the manner of questioning by some lawyers. In their study, it was found out that leading and forceful questions commonly used in cross-examinations might deter the vulnerable witnesses from telling the real truth. This is a factor that is likely to interfere with the trial. Madrunio and Villanueva (2016) propose that there is need to examine the use of language in the cross-examination of vulnerable witnesses.

For this reason, every justice system must take into consideration the adoption of a given language in the courtroom deliberations and there is a particular need for the court to accord the vulnerable groups such as foreign language speakers, migrants, and refugees, special consideration with regard to language use. This gives room for fair treatment and therefore access to justice.

Giladi and Petherbridge (2021) view vulnerability as part of daily experiences and as such it cannot be wished away. The authors stress the fact that it is exigent that vulnerability is taken into consideration during courtroom deliberations. This is echoed by Lorana and Kelly (2012) who affirm that the law enforcers have to take vulnerable populations into consideration, guarding their rights and catering for their vulnerability within the justice system.

According to Docrat et al. (2021), the language of record policy for courts determines and regulates the use of language in courtroom discourse. The language of the court is therefore the language in which proceedings take place and in which court records are kept. This language can be the official or national language of a particular institution. Malan (2009) alludes to the fact that unofficial languages can also be used in such situations by the accused, accusers, and witnesses if and when given a chance to choose. This situation may arise in a case where the accused persons are linguistically vulnerable and cannot express themselves in the official language of the land in question.

The non-speakers of the official language (the accused and their witnesses in this case) rely on interpretation. However, interpreters can be linguistically limited since they are not necessarily legal practitioners and this therefore renders the non-speakers' languages used in courts vulnerable. A study by Berk-Seligson

(2009) has shown that using police officers to carry out interpreting functions in court is counterproductive. In the case of Juan López where a Mexican man was accused of engaging in sodomy with a minor, a police officer was assigned to interpret for the detainee. Having minimal proficiency in speaking and understanding Spanish, the language of the court, he was limited in interpreting from and to L1 and L2. Consequently, the detainee, who could not completely comprehend the questions of the interrogating officer, had to try to communicate using his very limited ability to speak English characterised by code-mixing and thus rendering the interaction incomprehensible. This is likely to affect the outcomes in cases of this nature. Foreign language speakers, migrants, and refugees may go through a similar experience when arraigned in court in Kenya where English and Kiswahili are used.

Linguistic justice

Access to language, a component of linguistic justice, is in itself representative of fair treatment of people of all linguistic backgrounds and respect for everyone's fundamental language rights (Lee et al., 2019). In courtroom situations, plaintiffs, respondents, and their witnesses who do not speak the language of the court need to be catered for. In terms of language use in pursuit of justice. It is therefore important to ensure that justice is attained in terms of language use in courts. This resonates with Quadri et al. (2023) who asserts that language justice uplifts the fundamental rights of people to communicate in their primary language, centring the autonomy of all individuals to speak in their preferred language. Providing for people who speak various languages is one approach to guarantee that they have access to linguistic justice.

According to Lee et al. (2019), language justice approach also recognises that language rights are human rights and seeks to promote these rights by providing people with opportunities to choose and participate in their preferred languages in order to prevent linguistic discrimination. This then means that allowing individuals to speak languages that they are comfortable with in courtroom situations is a move that is likely to curb linguistic discrimination and thus promote justice. However, it may not be practical to have interpreters in all languages. Satia and Maritim (2022) find that one of the challenges faced by the judiciary in Kenya is the backlog of cases. So, whereas the choice of a language of preference in court may alleviate linguistic discrimination, it may also lead to delayed justice.

Methodology

The study adopted a qualitative approach which made use of in-depth interviews and Focus Group Discussions (FGDs) to have a deeper understanding of the effect of the language(s) used in courtroom proceedings when vulnerable groups are arraigned.

These techniques (interviews and FGDs) were preferred for data collection because they were deemed more likely to give more in-depth information on the experiences of foreign language speakers, migrants, and refugees in courts. According to Gill and Baille (2018), such techniques can provide significant and meaningful insight into participants' experiences which was the point of focus for this study. Additionally, the techniques were the most appropriate given the fact that in Kenya, access to court recordings is restricted. Further, foreign language speakers, migrants, and refugees being disadvantaged persons are rare in our communities and seldom appear in court, and when this happens, it is selective, making any other method of data collection inadequate.

Twelve participants, identified with the help of prison officers, took part in the in-depth interviews. They comprised of four foreign language speakers (three males, one female), four refugees (three males, one female), and four migrants (one male, three females) who had had experiences with Kenyan courts, giving a total of seven male and five female key informants.

They were drawn from Nairobi, Kakamega, and Busia regions. These regions were purposively selected due to surging numbers of the vulnerable groups. The small sample was deemed appropriate since it allowed the researchers to focus on the experiences of the foreign language speakers, migrants, and refugees in the courtroom deliberations where these vulnerable persons were involved. This is corroborated by Subedi (2021) who observes that a small sample allows the researcher to be focused on the in-depth understanding in a particular social and cultural context, which generally is not possible in studying the larger samples. The researchers also conducted three FGDs, one in each of the selected regions and each group comprising of eight refugees, four males and four females. These refugees were approached in refugee camps after obtaining clearance.

Due to the state of insecurity in the country including Nairobi, Kakamega, and Bungoma regions, during the time of research, and the need to make the participants feel as safe as possible, respondents were recruited using purposive sampling. The respondents were contacted by research assistants, who were themselves residents of the selected regions, and asked whether they would like to participate in the research project. In total, four research assistants (two males and two females) were hired due to their familiarity with the geographical areas in the study. These individuals had knowledge of research methods, having completed university studies. They conducted the interviews at different times and in different regions. Data was recorded by use of recorders and later transcribed for interpretation by the researchers.

Informed written consent was obtained from the participants who were also reassured of data confidentiality. The researchers also obtained clearance from the prison's directorate of legal affairs and research department at the prison's headquarters and from refugee centres to carry out the research.

Demographic information of the participants

Table 11.1 indicates the demographic information of the participants.

Table 11.1 Foreign Language Speakers, Migrants, and Refugees in Court

Sex	*Age*	*Highest level of education*	*Country of origin*	*Length of time in Kenya*	*Status*	*Language(s) spoken*	*Period in court*
Male (7)	21–30 (4)	Primary (5)	Congo (5)	3–7 years (5)	Foreign language speakers (5)	Lingala (5)	2017 (2)
	31–40 (2)	Secondary school (1)	Nigeria (2)	Above 7 years (2)	Refugees (5)	French (5)	2019 (2)
	41–50 (1)	College (0)			Migrants (2)	Kiswahili (5)	2023 (2)
	Above 51 (0)	None (1)				English (2)	2024 (1)
Female (5)	21–30 (3)	Primary (2)	Congo (3)	3–7 years (3)	Foreign language speakers (3)	Lingala (3)	2017 (1)
	31–40 (1)	Secondary school (0)	Nigeria (2)	Above 7 years (2)	Refugees (3)	French (3)	2019 (1)
	41–50 (1)	College (0)			Migrants (2)	Kiswahili (3)	2022 (2)
	Above 51 (0)	None (3)				English (2)	2023 (1)

The table indicates that seven men and five women had had an experience with the courts in Kenya.

Most of our participants were aged between 21 and 40 years (seven). The ages between 41 and 50 had few individuals who had been in court, while the age bracket of 51 and above had none. This could be attributed to the fact that by that age, they had either been acquitted or had served their terms.

Three participants were arraigned in court in 2017, three in 2019, two in 2022, three in 2023, and one in 2024. Most of the participants of the FGDs were arraigned in court between 2018 and 2021. Therefore, foreign language speakers, migrants, and refugees who participated in this study were arraigned in court between 2017 and 2024.

Regarding the level of education, most had only primary school level (seven) whilst only one had attained secondary level. Notably, none of the participants had a college education and one participant did not have any formal education. This is a situation that renders them more vulnerable as a result of ignorance of the laws that govern countries where they find themselves.

The participants comprised of eight foreign language speakers, who also had the refugee status and (four) migrants. Eight of these individuals had stayed in Kenya for a period of between three and seven years, while four had stayed for more than seven years. Regarding language(s) spoken, all the foreign language speakers, who were also refugees, spoke French, Lingala and Kingwana, a version of Kiswahili. The rest (four) spoke English. This means that more refugees and migrants (eight) spoke French compared to English which was spoken by only four. Focus group participants spoke French, English, Kiswahili, and Lingala. This is indicative of the variance that exists between the languages spoken by individual foreign language speakers, migrants, and refugees versus that of those spoken by the courts. This is consistent with the language of the court in Kenya Constitution 2010 (Satia in print). Satia further argues that it is a requirement for courts specify on record the language used in the proceedings.

The participants appeared in court for various crimes: five appeared for stealing, four for sexual abuse, and three for violence.

Findings and discussion

Current practices in court regarding foreign language speakers, migrants, and refugees

It was evident from the responses of the participants that they did not understand the language used in court. Three of them responded as follows:

P6: I couldn't understand some terms and phrases.[1]
P3: The language used was foreign to me.
P4: It was not clear at all.

1 The letters P and G have been used to stand for Participants and Group in Focus Group Discussions.

The preceding responses show that the court uses terms and phrases that the participants found difficult to understand and which are unfamiliar to foreign language speakers, migrants, and refugees. These groups are not only lay persons, who generally do not understand the language used by professionals in court, but are also vulnerable. Some of the difficult terms cited by the participants include, *Locus standi*, *Judicata*, and *Nolle Prosecui*. This is contrary to Blake's (2019) assertion that a lay person must be able to understand the court processes and the language and questioning of the legal professionals working within it. Additionally, this contravenes the Kenya Constitution, 2010 (see Article 21(3), which provides that all state organs and all public officers have the duty to address the needs of vulnerable groups within the society. The language needs for this particular group were not met, a factor that points to discrimination. Power and domination are meted on the plaintiff/respondent, who is linguistically challenged, since the outcome is dependent on the interpretation of the court officers. Here, the court professionals exercise power and dominance over the plaintiffs/respondents through the language that is not well grasped by the refugees and migrants. While carrying out their duties, the legal professionals do not take into consideration the inefficiencies due to language deficiencies of the plaintiffs and respondents. This goes against the rights of individuals who cannot understand the language of the proceedings.

The participants expressed that the language used posed serious problems for them when they are arraigned in the courts of law. Besides the normal challenges facing ordinary people in court, refugees and migrants experience even bigger challenges which are mainly compounded by language complexity. They indicated that this exposed them to difficulties and frustrations in comprehending the proceedings as two of them said:

P1: I couldn't hear, and this disturbed me.
P2: I did not speak the same language with fluency, so it was very difficult.

The participants in the study can erroneously conclude that they were ignored and thus discriminated against on grounds of origin, and this goes against the provisions of the Kenya Constitution, 2010 (Article 27(2) which states that the state shall not discriminate directly or indirectly against any person on any ground.

The participants further expressed their frustration emanating from the manner in which the discourses were carried out. Some of them said:

P7: The people spoke with low tones so I couldn't hear everything.
P3 (G1): I did not fully understand the language that was being used.
P4 (G1): I couldn't hear much.

The preceding responses indicate that language-related challenges are some of the outstanding problems that foreign language speakers, migrants, and refugees experience in Kenyan courts. The problem is aggravated when foreign language speakers, migrants, and refugees are arraigned.

Research participants further stated that the challenges they experienced contributed to the final determination of their cases. As much as there is a provision in the Kenyan law of seeking redress when one does not understand the language of the court (see Article 165 of the Constitution of Kenya, 2010), it is difficult for foreign language speakers, migrants, and refugees to enjoy these rights. They often passively accept verdicts as they are. Their status as vulnerable persons deprive them of the will to stand up for their rights. They are too conscious of being in a foreign country and having committed a crime, they are unable to stand up for their rights.

This means that justice was not seen to have been served in the cases of the foreign language speakers, migrants, and refugees due to the language-related challenges that they experienced. This is a real area of concern given that courts are the institutions charged with the responsibility of upholding justice in every state across the world. According to Blake (2019), if the people using courts cannot effectively participate through lack of understanding, there is a risk of denying access to justice. This is a situation that may prompt the affected to raise appeals against negative outcomes of their cases. The current study resonates with the vulnerability theory, which states that human beings are all vulnerable at some point in their lives. In this case, foreign language speakers, migrants, and refugees are linguistically vulnerable.

Extent to which current discourses in court avail justice for foreign language speakers, refugees, and migrants

The language used in court was different from that spoken by the participants and FGD participants. Some were provided with interpreters, and some were asked to speak Kiswahili as expressed here:

P3 (G3): The court provided an interpreter.
P6 (G1): The court asked me to speak Kiswahili.
PI8: The court did not do anything.

The preceding responses reveal that courts in Kenya only conduct court proceedings in English or Kiswahili and not any other language. The fact that some of the foreign language speakers, migrants, and refugees did not fully understand the language used during proceedings and failed to get help from the court demonstrates that the court did not carry out their full mandate regarding such groups. This could be attributed to the mistaken assumption by the courts that because the Congolese spoke some Kiswahili while the Nigerians spoke English, they could therefore not only effectively express themselves but also comprehend court proceedings. This assumes that someone who cannot speak English should be able to communicate in some Kiswahili, which highlights an ingrained assumption that attributes linguistic proficiency in this case, Kiswahili. Notably, the level of language competence required of speakers in a court of law is the bare minimum that enables them to understand a few words. This was not achieved by the participants in this study.

While there exist provisions for appealing in circumstances where verdicts are arrived at without considering the language proficiency of litigants (KECA, 2021:363-KLR), the Nigerians and Congolese victims in this study did not make any attempt. This could be due to their ignorance of their rights in a foreign country. The fact that these particular groups are legally hosted in a foreign country (in this case, Kenya) accords them the right to enjoy their rights and freedoms. This may also be due to the sense of guilt they have with regard to the nature of the crimes for which they find themselves arraigned in courts.

Most of the participants felt that the language used in court did not avail the justice they sought. They generally did not have a lawyer to represent them. This shows that the language used in court was not sufficient to avail justice to most foreign language speakers, migrants, and refugees who were arraigned in court. Notably, none of these individuals was provided with a lawyer. Whereas the Kenya Constitution, 2010 provides for representation by an advocate in court, it is only a preserve of capital offenses or in cases where 'substantial injustice would otherwise result' (see Article 50(2)(h)). In this study, the participants expected to be represented by legal counsels despite the nature of their crimes, an indication that they were ignorant of the provisions of the constitution. This may be a widespread feeling even among the natives of the land, a fact that reveals that many have not internalised the provisions of the Kenya Constitution, 2010. Nonetheless, on the right to a fair trial, Chapter 6 of the Manual on Human Rights for Judges, Prosecutors and Lawyers stipulates that accused persons have a right to legal counsel of one's own choosing (see section 211(1) of the Criminal Procedure Code of Kenya). This may call for civic education for enlightenment on rights and entitlements of individuals.

Only two participants were provided with a court interpreter while the rest of the FGD discussions did not have any. However, the two participants who were lucky to have interpreters did not fully benefit from the services of the interpreters since there were words used during the court deliberations that they did not understand. They further indicated that the interpreters did not capture the cultural aspects of their discourse. This could be an addition to the inability to understand what is said because of the interpreters' failure to express cultural nuances thereby making it difficult to understand what was being communicated. This means that some aspects of language were left out or misconstrued and that certain key linguistic elements and cultural components were lost during the interpretation. Some of these cultural aspects included Euphemisms, idioms, and proverbs which make complete meaning only in the first language of the foreign language speakers. Thus, there was distortion and modification of meaning.

An earlier study by González et al. (2012) asserts that faithful reproduction of the linguistic features by court interpreters during court proceedings is elusive since critical details are often left out. This is in line with the framing theory that underpins this study which postulates that the manner in which information is presented to the audience influences the interpretation of the same. In this case, the interpreter's conceptualisation of the proceedings of the court room can inadvertently influence the litigants and consequently have a bearing on the final verdict of the court.

All the 12 participants indicated that inclusion and fair treatment was missing in the court deliberations. Most of them cited 'language barriers/difficulties' as the main problems that they faced. Based on this, the participants felt that they did not exhaustively state their cases. This finding agrees with Docrat et al. (2021) who point out that a second language speaker does not receive the same treatment as a native speaker even when provided with interpreting services. This calls for intervention as far as language justice is concerned.

Most of the participants and participants of the FGDs alleged that justice was not served as a result of the discourse in court regarding their cases. This means that some foreign language speakers, migrants and refugees do not access justice in the Kenyan courts of law.

Practical solutions for ensuring fair hearings and treatment of vulnerable groups during courtroom deliberations

From the responses of the participants and FGD participants, it is evident that there is need for the courts to do more to ensure that justice is served to foreign language speakers, migrants, and refugees. The participants had the following to say regarding what the courts should do during the court discourses to ensure that justice is served:

P1: The courts should provide an interpreter and a lawyer.
P6 (G1): The courts should use a language easily understood by foreign language speakers.

The preceding example shows that the foreign language speakers, refugees, and migrants feel that the courts have the potential to serve them better if they play their role effectively.

Most of the participants were not aware of any existing policy regarding their rights during hearing when they have been arraigned in court. Equally, the focus group discussion participants had no knowledge of such a policy. While the Kenyan Law provides for choice of language, the accused persons are comfortable with during court hearings, the participants in the study had no knowledge of such a policy.

This points to the fact that individuals who are arraigned in court including foreign language speakers, migrants, and refugees are ignorant of any policies regarding their rights during court proceedings and that if they are in existence, they are not being followed.

The participants proposed that some components should be included in such a guideline to ensure justice is upheld for foreign language speakers, migrants, and refugees. Some of their responses were as follows:

P3: Creating awareness among foreign language speakers of the existence of such a policy where these foreign language speakers can access their services.
P4: Provision of legal aid.
P3: Use of simpler language.
P10: Provision of court interpreters.

FGD participants had similar suggestions, including the need for proper treatment and a friendly tone while addressing foreign language speakers, migrants, and refugees. These findings reveal that there is need for policies that address the needs of vulnerable people such as foreign language speakers, migrants, and refugees in court contexts. Such legal framework must be inclusive as far as language is concerned. The critical discourse analysis theory sheds light on the language needs of foreign language speakers, migrants, and refugees. The justice of these groups is largely dependent on the discourses produced in court, some of which may contribute to dominance and discrimination. This dominance and discrimination is a product of the interplay between language and power.

Conclusion and recommendations

The findings of this study point to the plight of vulnerable individuals and particularly foreign language speakers, migrants, and refugees who find themselves arraigned in court. Language use is not entirely inclusive in court proceedings where foreign language speakers, migrants, and refugees are concerned. Having only some level of proficiency in a language does not guarantee full participation in court. Ensuring that individuals, including the vulnerable, make a conscious choice of the language to be used in court can go a long way towards ensuring that justice is not only done but seen to have been done.

There is need for development of policies tailored to the needs of vulnerable groups and individuals and where they already exist, they need to be improved in order to serve all court users in the pursuit of justice.

All states across the world including Kenya stand to gain if they implement legal frameworks that take into consideration the conduct and treatment of foreign language speakers, refugees, and migrants. Such a framework should stipulate the environment under which court discourses should take place including issues such as provision of lawyers and interpreters.

Policies that are enacted in Kenya and elsewhere should also address the issue of the use of first or indigenous languages during court proceedings, which are currently conducted using English or Kiswahili. Interpreters should be able to capture all the requisite content of court deliberations including the linguistic and cultural aspects of the discourse. All court interpreters must be trained.

References

Berk-Seligson, S. (2009). *Coerced confessions: The discourse of bilingual police interrogations.* Mouton de Gruyter.

Blake, N. (2019). *Understanding courts: A report by justice chair of the committee.* www.justice.org.uk https://files.justice.org.uk/wp-content/uploads/2019/01/06170235/Understanding-Courts

Chapter 6 the right to a fair trial: Part I – from investigation to trial in human rights in the administration of justice: A manual on human rights for judges, prosecutors and lawyers. Retrieved August 18, 2024, from https://www.ohchr.org/sites/default/files/Documents/Publications/training9chapter6en

Darity, W. A., Jr. (Ed.). (2008). *The international encyclopedia of the social sciences.* Course Technology.

Das, M. B., & Espinoza, S. A. (2020). *Inclusion matters in Africa.* World Bank Group.

Docrat, Z., Kaschula, R. H., & Ralarala, M. K. (2021). *A handbook on legal languages and the quest for linguistic equality in South Africa and beyond.* Sun Press.

Eades, D. (2008). Language and disadvantages before the law. In J. Gibbons & M. T. Turell (Eds.), *Dimensions of forensic linguistics.* John Benjamins Publishing Company.

Entman, R. M. (1993). Framing: Toward clarification of a fractured paradigm. *Journal of Communication, 43*(4), 51–58.

Fineman, M. A. (2008). The vulnerable subject: Anchoring equality in the human condition. *Yale Journal of Law and & Feminism, 20*(1), 9–15.

Gibbons, J. (2003). *Forensic linguistics: An introduction to language in the justice system.* Wiley.

Giladi, P., & Petherbridge, D. (2021). The vulnerable dynamics of discourse. *Royal Institute of Philosophy Supplement*, 195–225. https://doi.org/10.1017/S1358246121000151; https://www.cambridge.org/core/journals/royal-institute-of-philosophy-supplements/article/abs/vulnerable-dynamics-of-discourse block

Gill, P., & Baillie, J. (2018). Interviews and focus groups in qualitative research: An update for the digital age. *British Dental Journal, 225*(7), 668–672.

González, R. D., Vásquez, V. F., & Mikkelson, H. (2012). *Fundamentals of court interpretation: Theory, policy and practice* (2nd ed.). Carolina Academic Press.

Government of Kenya (GoK). (2010). *The constitution of Kenya, 2010.* Government Printer.

Gulati, G., Cusack, A., Kelly, B. D., Dunne, C. P., & Kilcommins, S. (2022). Recognizing and responding to vulnerability: Securing access to justice for vulnerable accused persons in Ireland in. *Irish Judicial Studies Journal, 6*(2).

Haworth, K. (2015). Linguistics and the law. In K. Allan (Ed.), *The Routledge handbook of linguistics.* Routledge.

Helbling, J., Kälin, W., & Nobirabo, P. (2015). Access to justice, impunity and legal pluralism in Kenya. *The Journal of Legal Pluralism and Unofficial Law, 47*(2), 347–367. https://doi.org/10.1080/07329113.2015.1080430

International Organization for Migration. (2024). *UN migration.* IOM.

Kenya National Report on Global Access to Justice. (2018). https://globalaccesstojustice.com/

Lee, J., Lundin, M. C., Mercado, A. P. N., & Uliasz, A. (2019). Language justice. *Legal Services in the Management Information Exchange Journal*, 1–8.

Lininger, T. (2021). Judges' ethical duties to ensure fair treatment of indigent parties. *Fordham Law Review, 89*, 1237. https://ir.lawnet.fordham.edu/flr/vol89/iss4/8

Logan, C. (2017). *Ambitious SDG goal confronts challenging realities: Access to justice is still elusive for many Africans.* https://africaportal.org/publication/ambitious-sdg-goal-confronts-challengingrealities-access-to-justice-is-still-elusive-for-many-africans/

Lorana, B., & Kelly, R. (2012). Vulnerabilities in the courtroom. In N. Asquith & I. Bartkowiak-Theron (Eds.), *Policing vulnerability* (pp. 233–246). Federation Press.

Madrunio, M., & Villanueva, V. (2016). *Examining the language in courtroom interrogation of vulnerable and non-vulnerable witnesses.* https://www.researchgate.net/publication/343318926_Examining_the_Language_in_Courtroom_Interrogation_of_Vulnerable_and_Non-Vulnerable_Witnesses

Makanje, G. D. (2020). The protection of vulnerable witnesses during criminal trials in Malawi: Addressing resource challenges. *African Human Rights Law Journal*, 206–232. http://dx.doi.org/10.17159/1996-2096/2020/v20n1a8

Malan, K. (2009). Observations on the use of official languages for the recording of court proceedings. *Tydskrif Vir Die Suid- Afrikaanse Reg*, 141–155.

Martin, A. K. (2023). Why vulnerability matters. In *The moral implications of human and animal vulnerability.* Palgrave Macmillan. https://doi.org/10.1007/978-3-031-25078-1_2

Melinkoff, D. (1963). *The language of the law.* Little Brown.

Merriam Webster. (2019). *Vulnerable.* https://www.merriamwebster.com/dictionary/vulnerability

Moeller, A. J., & Catalano, T. (2015). Foreign language teaching and learning. In *International encyclopedia of the social and behavioral sciences* (2nd ed., pp. 327–333). Elsievier. https://doi.org/10.1016/B978-0-08-097086-8.92082-8

Muindi, K., & Mberu, B. (2019). *Urban refugees in Nairobi: Tackling barriers to accessing housing, services and infrastructure* (IIED Working Paper). IIED. ISBN: 978-1-78431-753-9. http://pubs.iied.org/10882IIED

Nguyen-Trung, K., & Forbes-Mewett, H. (2019). *Defining vulnerability.* https://doi.org/10.1108/978-1-78756-911-920191004

Pariotti, E. (2023). Vulnerability and human rights: Which compatibility? *Internal Journal of Semiotic Law*, *36*, 1401–1413. https://doi.org/10.1007/s11196-023-09977-y

Quadri, N. S., Wilkins, S., Krohn, K., Mann, E. M., Stauffer, W. M., & Walker, P. F. (2023). Language justice: Addressing linguistic disparities begins with language data collection. *The American Journal of Tropical Medicine and Hygiene*, *109*(1), 1–3. Retrieved July 18, 2024, from https://doi.org/10.4269/ajtmh.23-0237

Satia, E., & Maritim, R. (2022). Power and meaning in the *Kaaburwo*: A traditional court among the Arror of Kenya. In M. K. Ralarala, R. H. Kaschula, & G. Heydon (Eds.), *Language and the law: Global perspectives in forensic linguistics from Africa and beyond* (pp. 375–394). African Sun Media.

Song, L. (2010). The role of context in discourse analysis. *Journal of Language Teaching and Research*, *1*(6), 876–879. https://doi.org/10.4304/jltr.1.6.876-879

Subedi, K. R. (2021, December). Determining the sample in qualitative research. *Khim Raj Subedi Scholars' Journal*, *4*, 1–13. Scholars' Journal. ISSN: 2645-8381. Published by Scholars' Association of Nepal A Multidisciplinary Peer Reviewed, Open Access Journal. https://www.nepjol.info/index.php/scholars

Tiersma, P. (1999). *Legal language.* Chicago University Press.

Tiersma, P. (2008). The nature of legal language. In Gibbons & Turell (Eds.), *Dimensions of forensic linguistics.* John Benjamins Publishing Company.

Tkacukova, G. N., Gee, T. M., & Morton, R. (2022). The journey to comprehensibility: Court forms as the first barrier to accessing justice. *International Journal for the Semiotics of Law = Revue internationale de semiotique juridique*, *35*(5), 1733–1759. https://doi.org/10.1007/s11196-021-09870-6

United Nations General Assembly (UNGA). (2018). *Refugees and migrants.* UNGA.

Van Dijk, T. A. (2001). Multidisciplinary critical discourse analysis: A plea for diversity. In Wodak & M. Meyer (Eds.), *Methods of critical discourse analysis* (pp. 95–120). Sage.

Van Dijk, T. A. (2015). Critical discourse analysis. In D. Tannen, H. E. Hamilton, & D. Chiffrin (Eds.), *The handbook of discourse analysis* (pp. 466–485). John Wiley & Sons, Inc.

Wisner, B. (2016). Vulnerability as concept, model, metrics and tool. In *Natural hazard sciences Oxford research encyclopedias*. Oxford University Press.
Wodak, R. (2001). What is CDA about: A summary of its history important concepts and its developments. In W. R. M. Meyer (Ed.), *Methods of CDA* (pp. 1–13). Sage Publications.
Wodak, R., & Meyer, M. (2001). *Critical discourse analysis: History, agenda, theory, methodology*. Retrieved August 18, 2024, from https://miguelangelmartinez.net/IMG/pdf/2008_Wodak_Critical_Discourse_Analysis_Ch_01.pdf

12 Legal status of Malawi Sign Language

Implications on language rights and access to justice for the hearing impaired

Martin Zoloni and Deborah Ndalama-Mtawali

Introduction

This chapter examines the level of recognition status the Malawi Sign Language (MSL) has as a way of protecting the d/Deaf's language rights and their access to justice. The Deaf community in Malawi is a minority group of people that cannot use the spoken language as a channel of communication. According to Mweri (2014), they are a minority group because their language is only used by a small population. Being a minority linguistic community, there is need to protect their linguistic and cultural identity (Mweri, 2014). Lack of legal protection through legislation may lead to marginalisation, which can result in linguistic disadvantages before the law. The linguistic disadvantages create barriers to communication between the Deaf litigants and the courts. Thus, MSL becomes an alternative channel of communication to the spoken language for approximately 400,000 deaf and hard-of-hearing individuals in Malawi.

Reagan (2019) loosely defines deafness as the absence of the ability to hear. Woodward (1972 cited in Batterbury et al., 2007) has stated that the term 'Deaf' refers to people that share a national language, culture, and identity. Because of their deafness, deaf people have been sidelined by hearing societies (Senghas & Monaghan, 2002). The main distinction between the use of deaf and Deaf is that the former refers to audiological issues, while the latter is a sociological and cultural reference; such that those who lose their hearing later in life would be termed by the latter and not former (Senghas & Monaghan, 2002, p. 71). However, due to the interconnectedness and multidimensional nature of the situation, scholars prefer to use d/Deaf terminology. Therefore d/Deaf is a mixed situation that points to audiological and sociocultural conditions. In this study the term 'd/Deaf' is used both as a generic term and a group of people who use SL as their mother tongue and identify themselves as culturally deaf.

In 2011, the World Federation of the Deaf (WFD) declared sign language as the mother tongue for the deaf, a language that deaf children can acquire, hence a fundamental human right for these deaf children. Matende et al. (2022) noted that for Deaf people to effectively participate fully in society,

DOI: 10.4324/9781003569435-16

they require access to sign language for them to interact with the outside world. Thus, the use of MSL is critical to ensuring access to the rights and freedoms provided in the Constitution of Malawi. Nevertheless, this is affected when the language and its users lack legal protection and recognition. De Meulder (2015) posits that the necessity to pass a law to recognise SLs as languages is a clear demonstration [. . .] of the inferior status of SLs. This status renders the deaf community vulnerable. Unless action is taken to legally protect their language, the Deaf community will continue to be vulnerable. This results in the marginalisation of SLs, which have historically not been regarded as independent languages. For example, Reagan (2019) argues that through human history, SLs were not recognised as real languages, even though it is quickly pointed out that that is not the case now. Batterbury and Ladd (2007, p. 2904) also posits that for over 300 years of human history, people that use SL have been seen as retarded, primitive, savage, and feebleminded, among others. Sign languages are not simply a series of gestures, but independent languages in their own right (Sutton-Spence, 2005). The Convention on the Rights of People with Disabilities (United Nations, 2006) recognises SL as being equal to spoken languages and promotes the use of SL. There is therefore a need to legally recognise SLs.

Legal acknowledgment of SL is a requirement for deaf LHRs (Krausneker, 2008). This is because all persons have rights to a language globally, including deaf people, which makes SL a human right matter (Sibanda & Chimbenga, 2016 in Matende et al., 2022). However, SLs have been sidelined on language policy and planning issues. For example, in Ghana, Adjei et al. (2024) argue that the failure of the government to include SL in educational curriculum makes it impossible to facilitate communication with Deaf people. Further, they argue that the lack of standardisation and mainstreaming of SL leads to linguistic exclusion of the Deaf from mainstream life. Plaza-Pust (2016) asserts that sign languages have a status of minority languages; as such, they are subject to the same antagonistic language planning measures affecting the other minor languages. De Meulder et al. (2019) observe that among the minority languages globally, SLs are the least recognised compared to spoken languages. Subsequently, policymakers end up categorising deaf and SLs issues in disability legislation. As one of the minor languages in Malawi, MSL does not explicitly enjoy the recognition of the status of a minor language, and therefore it is not even a surprise that it is not explicitly recognised in the legal system. Demessie (2021) asserts that the term 'language' is commonly associated with spoken language, and it is rare to interpret it in connection with SL. This might be the situation in Malawi and could be one of the contributions to the sidelining of MSL in 'language-related discourse' (Demessie, 2021, p. 35).

In the case of this chapter, the assessment of legal documents is crucial in assessing the legal status of MSL and its users to understand the disadvantages they have when accessing justice. In this study, 'recognition' means the officially granting legal status and legal protection to SLs through language rights legislation (De Meulder, 2015). Explicit recognition refers to legislation that officially recognise and protect sign language while implicit recognition refers to legislation that obliquely recognises the use of SL through disability access measures (De Meulder et al., 2019). These two terms will be widely used in this study to understand how the legal documents include or exclude MSL in their frameworks.

Sign Language and vulnerability before the law

Language is critical in the criminal justice system. For deaf individuals, Sign Language (SL) is crucial as it is the sole language that the deaf can effectively use to articulate themselves before the police during time of arrest and the courts. When SL is not effectively used, the deaf witnesses and accused person(s) become vulnerable before the law. Vulnerability has received a number of definitions, but in the context of this chapter, the term 'vulnerable' is based on Ngure and Nganga's (2023, p. 364) summary of Luchjenbroers and Aldridge's (2008) definition, who define vulnerable people as 'those that are unable to make favourable presentation of themselves in the court system as a result of fear or distress that can also result from social, political, and economic factors'. For the deaf individuals, vulnerability comes from the communication barriers that exist between them as witnesses or accused person(s) and the criminal justice system. With the complexity of the legal language, it becomes difficult for the deaf complainants or accused persons to comprehend the court proceedings or police interrogation without sign language interpreters. Even when sign language interpreters are used, the requirement for precision in the courts renders deaf individuals vulnerable before the law.

Studies have reported communication challenges deaf people have encountered in the criminal justice system (Docrat et al., 2017; Svongoro & Ralarala, 2023). According to Eades (2008), the first challenge the Deaf community faces is lack of access to competent interpreters. The second major problem is absence of laws that recognise SLs as independent and complex languages. To the Deaf community in Malawi, the use of MSL in the criminal justice system is critical when accessing justice; hence, 'language rights become a question about social justice' (Haualand & Holmström, 2019, p. 4). In this regard, lack of explicit recognition of MSL in legal documents is detrimental to the Deaf community, which relies primarily on MSL to communicate with the criminal justice system.

In line with this chapter, the lack of legal protection of MSL promotes inequality before the criminal justice system. Article 12 (1) (e) of the Constitution of Malawi states that all persons have equal status before the law. This is also echoed in Article 26 of the International Convention on Civil and Political Rights (ICCR, 1966), that 'All persons are equal before the law and entitled without any discrimination to the equal protection of the law'. These two provisions express the centrality of equality before the law. However, equality cannot be achieved if other members of the society are treated differently due to lack of access to their language. Eades (2008) posits that language is one of the core factors because successful participation in the legal system depends, to the larger extent, on language manipulation. Legal recognition of the MSL is a major step that can help promote the language and enhance access to justice for the deaf. As a signatory to international legal instruments, which guarantee the right to SL, it is anticipated that Malawi should recognise the MSL in its legal documents.

Language and access to justice

Language is arguably a vital tool that facilitates access to justice. Participants in the court proceedings understand each other when all the parties are proficient in the language of the courts. In Malawi, English remains the only language of the courts. The Deaf community is not proficient in English; hence, it is difficult for them to comprehend the proceedings without assistance of court interpreters (Egwelu, 2022). To ease communication barriers between the deaf suspects and witnesses and the English-speaking courts, the courts should provide interpreters. Professional interpretation is the only channel of communication available to facilitate appropriate comprehension and meaningful engagement in the trial proceedings (Egwelu, 2022). Interpreters therefore help facilitate access to court proceedings (Lwara et al., 2024). Yet, the Deaf community's access to justice is hindered due to unavailability of professional court interpreters (Svongoro & Ralarala, 2023; Bacik, 2007).

This chapter is cast within the language rights, which is one of the subfields of forensic linguistics. Language rights (LRs), and human rights (HRs), form LHRs. However, not all LR's that are essential to accomplish one's basic needs and live a dignified life are considered LHR's (Skutnabb-Kangas, 2000). This study is motivated by the communication challenges that the Deaf face in the criminal justice system. The study critically analyses how legal documents in Malawi recognise MSL and promote the LHRs of the deaf. The chapter answers the following research questions: (i) How do Malawi's policy and legislation documents recognise or ignore MSL? (ii) How does legal recognition of MSL violate or promote access to justice? (iii) What are the implications of the legal status of MSL on the LHRs and access to justice for the deaf in Malawi? The findings of the study will provide the path for future language planning and policies to avoid violating the Deaf community linguistic rights in the criminal justice of Malawi.

Literature review

Several studies have been conducted to understand the level of marginalisation of SL globally. Bryne et al. (2021) studied the implementation of Article 13 of the UN Convention on the Rights of Persons with Disabilities in Northern Ireland. They wanted to understand how access to justice in the d/Deaf community is enhanced. The study found that d/Deaf have limited access to the justice system and that present provisions for d/Deaf's legal needs are not in line with UNCRPD.

New Zealand passed the New Zealand Sign Language Act of 2006 to legally recognise and protect New Zealand Sign Language. However, some sections that have deafness argue that it is a predicament and not a disability as people like to name it (Park et al., 2015). Here, predicament is meant to be understood in the words of Shakespeare who states that a predicament is a challenge, or expresses difficulty which can be minimised but not entirely avoided (Shakespeare, 2008, p. 243 cited in Park et al., 2015). But we would like to argue that Park et al. (2015) was dealing with a segment of Deaf people who had lost their hearing later in life and hence that would explain why they wanted to call it a predicament and not a disability. However, despite whatever terminology is used, whether it is a disability or a predicament, the point is that these people need to be treated as the rest of the population and hence should not be discriminated or sidelined.

In South Africa, Docrat et al. (2017, p. 261) argue that access to justice for the deaf in remains critically limited due to among other things 'badly trained interpreters' and 'the inability of the south African police to deal with Deaf complaints during the investigative stages'. They argue that no clear directions are provided in the constitution to ensure the inclusion of South African Sign Languages (SASL). Adjei et al. (2024) argue that in Ghana about 3 percent of the population are People With Disabilities (PWD), d/Deaf inclusive and despite legal provisions protecting such, the countries commitment remains low. These, and more, show the numerous challenges that the d/Deaf go through. Emond et al. (2015) and Kuenburg (2016) state that Deaf people face barriers in accessing information.

Despite these rich studies in Africa and beyond, little research has been conducted on Malawi to investigate the legal status of MSL and its implication on the rights and access to justice for the deaf. Through this study, insights can be drawn on how Malawi can formulate an inclusive approach to explicitly recognise and protect (MSL) that guarantees, respects, upholds linguistic rights and cultural identity, and provides access to justice for the Deaf community

Theoretical framework

The present study is thrust within the Critical Theory to evaluate the legal status of MSL to understand how legislation establishes, perpetuates, and hinders or promotes access to justice among the deaf people. The proponent of the Critical Theory, Tollefson (1991), observed that language policies typically serve the interests of the powerful and privileged groups and it is a mechanism by which dominant groups use to marginalise the minority groups in society. Additionally, Tollefson (1991) observes that the interests of these dominant groups are often hidden and embedded in powerful ideologies, which have broadly been normalised. Ndhlovu and Makwavarara (2023) posit that the critical theorist's objective is to expose and challenge associated ideologies and policies, thereby bringing about transformation and social justice.

The major concern of the Critical Theorists is how language policies generate social inequalities among the minority, in this case, the Deaf community, by marginalising them while the dominant groups continue to enjoy the privileges. They analyse how language policies are used to serve the needs of the dominant groups in a country or society and how the deaf, as a minority linguistic group, can advance their interests by attempting to change the policies

Researchers in Critical Theory understand that language policies create and tolerate different systems of social inequalities. The researchers, as social advocates, do not only understand how these dominant groups establish and sustain these social inequalities through language use, but also find ways of resolving these inequalities. Critical scholars posit that policy planning processes for selected languages have the potential to either include or exclude certain groups in functional domains such as the criminal justice system and education. One such mechanism is allocating language in the criminal justice system to determine who has access to justice. Official languages are instruments used to manifest authority, hence making the peripherised groups helpless (Tollefson, 1991, 2006). Despite SLs being given the legal status in some countries to protect their rights, dominant language groups continue to dominate and perpetuate using the law as a weapon to perpetuate the dominance of the hearing group (Bryan & Emery, 2014 in De Meulder, 2016). Using the key principles of this theory, this chapter examines the Constitution of Malawi and related Acts of parliament which regulate the use of language in Malawi criminal justice system to understand the level to which these legal documents violate or promote the LHRs and access to justice for the deaf.

Methodology

In order to understand the legal recognition of the MSL, the current study adopted document analysis as a primary data collection method and analysis. The study is qualitative in nature seeking to unearth in detail the status of MSL. Qualitative research emphases the comprehension of the context and attempts to explain the intentionality of the behaviours (Ary et al., 2019). The primary legal documents analysed include the Constitution of Malawi, Disability Act 2012, Legal Aid Act and Criminal Procedure and Evidence Code. The study was analysed in line with CRPD because of its bearing on access to justice for the Deaf community. These legal documents were selected based on their relevance in offering a foundational understanding of the legal recognition of MSL and are touching on access to justice for the deaf. They were also selected for their relevance to the research problem which seeks to examine the language rights that the d/Deaf are accorded according to the legal documents. Complementary secondary data was collected from diverse online sources, enriching the analysis. These documents were retrieved from the internet and were acknowledged accordingly. After eliciting information from these documents, different themes were developed. The data was then analysed descriptively using the Critical Language Policy Framework. This comprehensive analysis aimed to unveil how legal documents, particularly those used in the criminal justice and education systems violate or promote the linguistic human rights and access to justice for the Deaf community.

Findings and discussion

Status of MSL in legal documents

This section assesses whether the legal documents, specifically those that provide access to justice, acknowledge MSL as a unique language. These documents include the Constitution, the Disability Act of 2012, and the Legal Aid Act 2010. While these legal documents have various articles that provide access to justice for the deaf people, this study is mainly concerned with articles that focus on Sign Language, which has positive effects on access to justice for the Deaf community.

The Constitution of Malawi is the foundation for human rights including that of the deaf. The Constitution of Malawi contains human rights (HRs) and language rights related issues. Section 5 of the 1994 (amended 2017) Constitution of Malawi establishes the supremacy of the Constitution as the supreme law of Malawi. In this case, the Constitution of Malawi gives direction on all crucial issues in Malawi. Language related issues are among those that the Constitution is expected to give direction about the status of each language in Malawi.

Chapter 4 of the Constitution of Malawi contains the Bill of Rights, which generally highlight some language issues related to discrimination, personal expression when using one's language, and access to one's language in the criminal justice system. The study found the following language rights related issues from the Constitution of Malawi. These excerpts apply to language preferences in the criminal justice system. Frist, Article 20 (1) of the Constitution of Malawi forbids any form of discrimination based on language. On language and culture, Article 26 states that, 'Every person shall have the right to use the language and to participate in the cultural life of his or her choice'.

Article 20 of the Constitution mentions discrimination of one's language and Article 26 reinforces this by stating that one should reflect their culture through their language. The study revealed that these two pieces of legislation implicitly recognise the deaf as a separate culture with their own language, which they can use in their everyday interactions. The study revealed that implicit acknowledgment of the linguistic identity of the Deaf community in the Constitution of Malawi excludes MSL as a distinctive language. The Constitution further lacks a section dedicated to the promotion, development, and the use of MSL, and other forms of communication and technologies available to Deaf communities and other people with disabilities.

On the fair trial of the accused persons, Article 42 (1)(a) and (e) states that a detained person, including persons who have been sentenced to serve a jail term have the right to be informed of the reasons for their detention in a language they comprehend and challenge the legality of their detention or sentence through a direct challenge in a court or through legal representation in a court of law. Additionally, Articles 42 (2)(a) and 42 (f)(ix) state that every arrested individual or every person accused of a crime has the right to be notified of their right to remain silent and the consequences of speaking during police reading of Miranda rights and recording of statements. It further states that the accused persons have the right to have their trial conducted in a language they understand. In an event where the accused cannot understand the language used in the trial, the state must provide interpreters at the expense of the state.

The preceding articles reveal that the Constitution of Malawi protects the freedom to access justice in any language. It provides language rights for the accused before the law by being told the reason of their arrest and being tried through the language they can understand or through interpreters where the accused person(s) fails to understand the language of the law. For the deaf, SL is the only language they can effectively use and understand. Therefore, MSL is supposed to be clearly stated in Article 42 of the Constitution of Malawi. However, the study established that the Constitution of Malawi does not explicitly mention MSL as one of the languages the courts and the police should use.

Furthermore, the study analysed whether the Malawi Disability Act of 2012 recognises MSL. The Malawi Disability Act was enacted as a mechanism for promoting and protecting the rights of people with disabilities in Malawi. The study found that the Malawi Disability Act of 2012 recognises and gives status to MSL as a national and official language of the country. Article 8 of the Act is dedicated to accessibility of people with disabilities for both physical environment and provision of accommodation. Article 8 (f) the government shall take appropriate measures towards 'developing a MSL as a national language for persons with hearing impairments and recognising it as an official language'. The Act explicitly recognises MSL as a medium of communication of the Deaf community. It is elevated to status of English and Chichewa, which are official and national languages respectively in Malawi despite the latter lacking a language policy statement promulgated by parliament. However, we notice the lack of communication that the Constitution of Malawi and this Act have. While the former leaves it to implicit recognition, the latter accords it high status, leaving one wondering what the guide should then be.

The elevation of MSL to the rank of national and official language is an attempt to recognise its users as a distinct community with an independent natural language. The Act is not clear on how the objectives of developing MSL will be achieved. Nevertheless, the Act reflects a positive step towards an acknowledgement of the language and cultural diversity of the Deaf community and their right to use their language in the criminal justice system.

Additionally, the Legal Act of 2010 was enacted to provide access to justice and was analysed to see if it recognises MSL. Article 8 of the Act is about the eligibility for legal aid in criminal matters. The Act does not explicitly recognise MSL as a language for legal aid services. Likewise, the Criminal Procedure and Evidence Code (CP&EC) of Malawi does not explicitly recognise the usage of MSL when the courts encounter communication challenges when deaf individuals appear as witnesses or accused persons before the courts.

It is crucial to note that explicit recognition of MSL is not a solution that will reduce all the problems the Deaf community encounters in the criminal justice system in one day. However, the legal recognition of SL helps empower the users (the deaf) to claim their space in society, freeing them from burden of the need for perpetual justification about themselves (Krausneker, 2003). It is therefore imperative for the government to take more actions to promote and protect MSL. The major reason being that the official recognition of SL is an essential pre-condition for LHRs for the deaf (Krausneker, 2008). Nevertheless, legal recognition of MSL will help the deaf individuals access justice. Therefore, it is essential for the government to recognise the MSL as a language in all legal documents that deal with access to justice as it represents justice for the deaf.

Legal status of MSL and access to justice

The study further looked at whether the explicit or implicit legal recognition of MSL violates or promotes access to justice for deaf people. The rights of the accused persons are critical in accessing justice. In the reading of the Constitution of Malawi, Article 42 provides three rights for the accused under the law. These are: firstly, that any person accused of a crime has the right to be informed in a language that they understand. Secondly, the accused persons also have the right to an advocate. For the deaf accused persons, SL is the channel of communication. Finally, the article further states that where the accused fails to understand the language used in the courts or police, interpreters must be provided. Provision of interpreters is crucial as it facilitates communication between the court and the accused person(s). In this case, Malawi government has the responsibility to provide sign language interpreters free of charge to guarantee that the deaf accused person(s) has equal access to justice like members of the speaking community.

Contrary to these provisions, the study found that the deaf people have implicit rights to use their language due to lack of explicit recognition of MSL in the Constitution of Malawi, the Legal Aid Act, and the Criminal Procedure and Evidence Code (CP&EC). This is inconsistent with the Disability Act of 2012, which recognises MSL as an official language. As an official language that was accorded an institutional status, it would have been reflected in these two Acts to promote language of the deaf. However, it relegates the Deaf community to the peripheral. This confirms the low status and promotion of MSL in Malawi. Lack of explicit recognition of MSL violates the rights of the

Deaf community when accessing justice, as the procedural accommodation when the courts are confronted with communication barriers is not assured in the Criminal Procedure and Evidence Code.

This has negative effects on the Deaf community in their access to justice. Firstly, this lack of explicit recognition of MSL as official languages has the potential of limiting the usage of MSL in court trials, recording of statements and reading of Miranda rights by police and communication with the legal advocates; hence, making the deaf vulnerable before the criminal justice system. Secondly, lack of mandatory sign language interpretation recognition in the Legal Aid Act and CP&EC to assist the deaf individuals in the criminal justice system creates a barrier for them to access justice. Thirdly, it can create inadequate access to legal information in MSL, hence limiting the comprehensions of their legal rights and legal procedures. Lastly, it can lead to a lack of resources and support for its development and promotion, hence, violation of linguistic rights of the Deaf community.

Explicit recognition of languages in the Constitution is crucial as it is 'regarded as a symbol of institutional support' (Kufakunesu & Svongoro, 2022, p. 94). Therefore, implicit recognition of MSL may lead to lack of support in the criminal justice system of Malawi. This can promote discrimination before the law through lack of access to interpreters to facilitate access to justice. The study revealed that Article 42 does not explicitly recognise MSL professional interpretation services in the legal domain. It further confirms the reality about lack of professional sign language interpreters in the courts. Wazakili (2016) reports that cases of deaf litigants were postponed in some parts of Lilongwe due to lack of sign language interpreters. This agrees with Svongoro and Ralarala's (2023) findings in Zimbabwe, where the accessibility to sign language interpreters is not guaranteed, leading to abandonment of the cases involving the deaf accused persons. Failure to grant the deaf access to MSL is denying them justice.

The Disability Act focuses on physical accessibility and access to information and technology for the people with disabilities, but the deaf also have the right to be heard in MSL in the court of law. The study established that Article 8(f) of the Act explicitly recognises MSL as an official channel of communication for the Deaf community. The Act obligates public institutions offering services such as the courts, police stations, and prisons to make reasonable measures to make available professional sign language interpretation in the criminal justice system. Likewise, the explicit recognition of MSL is crucial as it raises awareness about the role of MSL in accessing justice and promotion of a more inclusive criminal justice system. Lastly, the explicit recognition of MSL empowers the Deaf community to campaign for their rights and access to justice in Malawi. Enacting this law was the first step towards the recognition of LHRs of the Deaf community in Malawi. Linguistic Human Rights, according to CRPD, includes the right to a fair trial. Skutnabb-Kangas and Phillipson (1995, p. 2) assert that when people are denied their LHRs, they are also hindered from accessing other fundamental human rights, including their right to . . . fair trial . . . and preservation of their cultural identity. The recognition of MSL in the Disability Act is one way of promoting LHRs for the Deaf community in accessing justice.

Despite this mandate to develop MSL and use it in the official domain, actual implementation of access to MSL remains a great challenge. The provisions remain unrealistic as 12 years down the line, MSL is yet to be adopted by criminal justice institutions to develop forms of communication in SL. This continued lack of development, promotion, and protection of MSL is a clear demonstration of the violation of the language rights of the deaf individuals in the criminal justice in Malawi. It will further exacerbate the absence of MSL interpreters in the courts, hence denying the Deaf community access to justice. This agrees with Tollefson's (2006) observation about the concerns of critical theorists as he posits that a critical approach sees language policies as potential instruments for perpetuating social inequalities and serving the interests of the dominant groups.

Implications of legal recognition status of MSL on the LHRs and access to justice

Our analysis also looked at the implications of explicit recognition of MSL in the legal documents on the LHRs and access to justice. The first implication is that legal status of MSL confers deaf people right to their linguistic and cultural identity as stipulated in Article 20 and 26 of the Constitution of Malawi. Unfortunately, the findings reveal that the Disability Act of 2012 identifies the Deaf community based on disability rights and not explicitly as an independent linguistic community with its own language in the Constitution. This is gross violation of LHRs and a breach of deaf individuals collective rights to live as a distinct group (Demessie, 2021). Implicit recognition of MSL violates their right to access to information in their language, which is the bedrock for accessing justice. For the deaf, the right to SL is the right to one's first language and not just any language (Trovato, 2013). Therefore, most LRs ought to be viewed as human rights or LHRs in the context of the Deaf community. Trovato (2013) further argues that appropriate protection for the deaf as a distinctive language community can be realised when their right to SL is enacted and implemented as LHRs.

This lack of recognition and protection is dangerous and violates LHRs for the Deaf community as it may result in a 'forced linguistic assimilation' (Skutnabb-Kangas, 2000 cited in Demessie, 2021, p. 46), This forced linguistic assimilation can make the deaf people vulnerable before the courts. It is postulated that the language rights for the deaf are not only based on disability rights, but also on human rights, minority rights, and cultural rights (De Meulder, 2015; Skutnabb-Kangas, 2000). These scholars claim that SLs as natural languages have a linguistic minority status, and they have their own culture, history, and identity. Therefore, it is imperative for explicit recognition of the Deaf community as a distinctive cultural and linguistic group that deserves legal protection and promotion of their SL using a LHRs approach. For this reason, there is a need to enact MSL Act using the LHRs approach to ensure their equal access to justice as their spoken language counterparts.

Explicit recognition of MSL promotes equal access to legal materials and communication for the Deaf community. This implies that for the deaf to have equal access to justice, there is need for them to have access to legal information. However, the lack of explicit recognition of MSL in the Constitution of Malawi, Legal Aid Act, and CP&EC is a clear demonstration that the deaf individuals are not assured of access to legal information and services in MSL. This is a testament that LHRs are violated, if the deaf are not provided with professional interpreters who can help them access information. It is, therefore, imperative that the Constitution of Malawi, Legal Act, and CP&EC should be amended to explicitly recognise MSL.

Conferring explicit legal acknowledgement to MSL is not only about language rights, but also about the right to be distinct and to be valued for their difference (De Meulder, 2015). Therefore, the Constitution of Malawi should reflect the rights of the deaf individuals as a distinctive minority linguistic community and uphold their right to be different and so be respected for the difference. As a state, Malawi has the obligation to explicitly recognise MSL as an independent language, recognise its existence, and promote its use for official function as CRPD (2006) Article 21 (b and e) state. The implementation of the legislation will eventually promote the LHRs for the deaf and improve access to justice.

From these observations, it is worth noting that there is a gross violation of LHRs of the Deaf community in Malawi. The legal documents that are key to providing access to justice for the deaf do not recognise MSL as a language. For the deaf and hard of hearing to be integrated in the criminal justice system, there is need to have MSL recognised in the Constitution, Legal Aid Act, and CP&EC. The linguistic exclusion of the deaf in these legal documents denies the deaf the opportunity for equal involvement in the trial and ensuring access to justice, hence, justice is denied. It also violates their access to LHRs.

The clear legal status of MSL in the Constitution would not only support the language rights of the deaf, but also gesture an obligation to promote access to justice for the speakers that MSL represents. The government of Malawi and various stakeholders should, therefore, be committed to the Constitution to promote linguistic diversity and make sure that the Deaf community has access to arrangements that accommodate their linguistic needs in the criminal justice system. This will be in concordance with Article 21(e) of the CRPD, which compels member states to recognise the importance of SLs, hence should promote their use. The CRPD further gives the Deaf community equal status with other members of the society to the acknowledgement and sustenance of their explicit linguistic distinctiveness, including SL and deaf culture. This implies that in implementing CRPD, the government must address the issue of access to justice for the Deaf community to achieve equality before the law. The Constitution of Malawi, the Legal Aid Act, and

CP&EC should explicitly recognise MSL, since these documents are key to access to justice.

Conclusion

The findings clearly demonstrate that MSL is not explicitly recognised in the Constitution of Malawi, Legal Aid Act, and CP&EC except the Disability Act of 2012. This implies that the Deaf community is implicitly excluded from the country's criminal justice system. The implicit recognition of MSL in the legal documents is the genesis for linguistic marginalisation and inequality for the deaf individuals in the criminal justice in Malawi. This exclusion constitutes a barrier to effective communication in the courts, rendering the deaf vulnerable when accessing justice. This gap can be reduced with proper legislation that prioritises the Deaf community as a distinct culture with a distinct language and promotes their MSL. This study shares the view that the decision to protect and promote MSL through legislation should be on the basis that it is a LHR for the Deaf community. There is, therefore, a need for consolidating all the legal documents – the Constitution of Malawi, Legal Aid Act, CP&EC, and the Disability Act – to speak with one accord on explicit recognition of MSL and protect the LHRs and access to justice for the Deaf community.

References

Adjei, S. B., Sam, S. T., Sekyere, F. O., & Boateng, P. (2024). Ubuntu philosophy and the experiences of deaf people in Ghana. In O. Mutanga (Ed.), *Ubuntu philosophy and disabilities in Sub-Saharan Africa* (pp. 163–183). Routledge.

Ary, D., Jacobs, L. C., Irvine, C. K. S., & Walker, D. A. (2019). *Introduction to research in education* (10th Edn.). Cengage.

Bacik, I. (2007). Breaking the language barrier: Access to justice in the new Ireland. *Judicial Studies Institute Journal*, *2*(110), 109–123.

Batterbury, S. C., Ladd, P., & Gulliver, M. (2007). Sign language peoples as indigenous minorities: Implications for research and policy. *Environment and Planning A*, *39*(12), 2899–2915.

Bryan, A., & Emery, S. (2014). The case for deaf legal theory through the lens of deaf gain. In H.-D. L. Bauman & J. Murray (Eds.), *Deaf gain: Raising the stakes for human diversity* (pp. 37–62). University of Minnesota Press.

Byrne, B., Elder, B., & Schwartz, M. (2021). Enhancing deaf people's access to justice in Northern Ireland: Implementing article 13 of the UN convention on the rights of persons with disabilities. *Scandinavian Journal of Disability Research*, *23*(1), 74–84. https://doi.org/10.16993/sjdr.744

Demessie, E. (2021). Recognition status of Ethiopian sign language and the deaf in key legislations: A critical review from linguistic human rights perspective. *Ethiopian Journal of Human Rights*, *6*(1).

De Meulder, M. (2015). The legal recognition of sign languages. *Sign Language Studies*, *15*(4), 498–506. https://doi.org/10.1353/sls.2015.0018

De Meulder, M. (2016). *The power of language policy: The legal recognition of sign languages and the aspirations of deaf countries*. Jyväskylä University Printing House.

De Meulder, M., Murray, J. J., & McKee, R. L. (2019). Introduction: The legal recognition of sign languages: Advocacy and outcomes around the world. In *The Legal recognition of sign languages* (pp. 1–16). Multilingual Matters.

Docrat, Z., Kaschula, R. H., & Ralarala, M. K. (2017). The exclusion of South African sign language speakers in the criminal justice system: A case-based approach. In M. K. Ralarala., K. Barris, E. Ivala, & S. Siyepu (Eds.), *African languages and language practice research in the 21st century: Interdisciplinary themes and perspectives* (pp. 261–277). Casas.

Eades, D. (2008). Language and disadvantage before the law. In J. Gibbons & M. T. Turrel (Eds.), *Dimensions of forensic linguistics* (Vol. 5, pp. 179–195). John Benjamins.

Egwelu, T. (2022). *Legal recognition of East African sign languages key towards inclusion.* Retrieved July 5, 2024, from https://www.globalissues.org/news/2022/11/30/32544

Emond, A., Ridd, M., Sutherland, H., Allsop, L., Alexander, A., & Kyle, J. (2015). Access to primary care affects the health of deaf people. *British Journal of General Practice*, *65*(631), 95–96.

Haualand, H., & Holmström, I. (2019). When language recognition and language shaming go hand in hand–sign language ideologies in Sweden and Norway. *Deafness & Education International*, *21*(2–3), 99–115.

International Covenant on Civil and Political Rights (ICCPR). (1966), art. 14, S. Exec. Doc. E. 95-2, 999 UNTS.

Krausneker, V. (2003). Has something changed? Sign languages in Europe: The case of minorised minority languages. *Deaf Worlds: International Journal of Deaf Studies*, *19*(2).

Krausneker, V. (2008). *The protection and promotion of sign language and the rights of their users in Council of Europe member states needs analysis.* Council of Europe.

Kuenburg, A., Fellinger, P., & Fellinger, J. (2016). Health care access among deaf people. *Journal of Deaf Studies and Deaf Education*, *21*(1), 1–10.

Kufakunesu, P., & Svongoro, P. (2022). Linguistic minority and courtroom discourse in Zimbabwe. In M. K. Ralarala, R. H. Kaschula, & G. Heydon (Eds.), *Language and the law: Global perspective in forensic linguistics from Africa and beyond* (pp. 79–99). Sun Press.

Luchjenbroers, J., & Aldridge, M. (2008). Language and vulnerable witnesses across legal contexts. *Journal of English Linguistics*, *36*(3), 191–194. https://doi.org/10.1177%2F0075424208321209.

Lwara, E., Kondowe, W., & Ndalama-Mtawali, D. (2024). Entrenching effective multilingualism in Malawian courtrooms through interpreting services: What do we learn from the 2019 presidential elections case? In W. Kondowe, P. Madula, & C. M. M. Kamanga (Eds.), *Multilingualism in Southern Africa* (Vol. 1, pp. 122–142). Routledge.

Malawi Constitution. (1994). *Amended (2017).* Malawi Constitution.

Malawi Government Criminal Procedure and Evidence Code Act of 1967.

Malawi Government Disability Act of 2013.

Malawi Government Legal Aid Act of 2010.

Matende, T., Mugari, V., & Gotosa, K. (2022). Languages and the legal processes in deaf community: An analysis of sign language court interpretation and linguistic rights of the deaf in selected courtrooms in Harare Urban, Zimbabwe. *London Journal of Research in Humanities and Social Sciences*, *22*(9), 23–36.

Mweri, J. G. (2014). Diversity in education: Kenyan sign language as a medium of instruction in schools for the deaf in Kenya. *Multilingual Education*, *4*, 1–14.

Ndhlovu, E., & Makwavarara, Z. (2023). The teaching and learning of sign language at the University of Zimbabwe. *East African Journal of Education and Social Sciences*, *4*(2), 10–24. https://doi.org/10.46606/eajess2023v04i02.0271

Ngure, E. W. M., & Nganga, S. (2023). Men as vulnerable disputants in the Kikuyu traditional elders' courts. In R. H. Kaschula, M. K. Ralarala, & G. Heydon (Eds.), *Language, crime and courts in contemporary Africa and beyond* (Vol. 4, pp. 51–70). Sun Press.

Park, J., Fitzgerald, R., & Legge, M. (2015). The predicament of d/deaf: Towards an anthropology of not-disability. *Human Organization, 74*(2), 154–163.
Plaza-Pust, C. (2016). *Bilingualism and deafness: On language contact in the bilingual acquisition of sign language and written language* (Vol. 7). Walter de Gruyter GmbH & Co KG.
Reagan, T. (2019). The politics of L2/Ln sign language pedagogy. In *The Routledge handbook of sign language pedagogy* (pp. 262–275). Routledge.
Senghas, R. J., & Monaghan, L. (2002). Signs of their times: Deaf communities and the culture of language. *Annual Review of Anthropology, 31*(1), 69–97.
Shakespeare, T. (2008). Disability: Suffering, social oppression, or complex predicament? In *The contingent nature of life: Bioethics and limits of human existence* (pp. 235–246). Springer Netherlands.
Sibanda, P., & Chimhenga, S. (2016). Accessibility of curriculum by learners with hearing impairment in schools: A case study of Bulawayo secondary schools in Zimbabwe. *Global Journal of Advanced Research, 3*(10), 947–952.
Skutnabb-Kangas, T. (2000). 2 linguistic human rights and teachers of English. In J. Hall & W. Eggington (Ed.), *The sociopolitics of English language teaching* (pp. 22–44). Blue Ridge Summit, Multilingual Matters. https://doi.org/10.21832/9781800417984-005
Skutnabb-Kangas, T., & Phillipson, R. (1995). *Linguistic human rights. Overcoming linguistic discrimination.* Mouton de Gruyter.
Sutton-Spence, R. (2005). *Analysing sign language poetry.* Palgrave.
Svongoro, P., & Ralarala, M. K. (2023). Zimbabwe constitutional safeguards for persons with communication disabilities: Implications for access to justice. In R. H. Kaschula, M. K. Ralarala, & G. Heydon (Eds.), *Language, crime and courts in contemporary Africa and beyond* (Vol. 4, pp. 51–70). Sun Press.
Tollefson, J. W. (1991). *Planning language, planning inequality: Language policy in the community.* Longman.
Tollefson, J. W. (2006). Critical theory in language policy. In T. Ricento (Ed.), *An introduction to language policy theory and method.* Blackwell Publishing.
Trovato, S. (2013). A stronger reason for the right to sign language. *Sign Language Studies, 13*(3), 401–422.
United Nations. (2006). *United Nations convention on the rights of persons with disabilities.* United Nations.
Wazakili, M. (2016). Report on access of courts in Lilongwe: Justice for persons with disabilities. *Disabled Women Africa.* Retrieved January 10, 2024, from http://www.makingitwork-crpd.org/sites/default/files/2019
Woodward, J. C. (1972). Implications for sociolinguistic research among the deaf. *Sign Language Studies,* (1), 1–7.

Theme 4

The poor and the illiterate before the courts of law

13 Courtroom interpretation and the dilemma of the poor and illiterate as accused and witnesses in court

Jones Hamburu Mawerenga and Godwins Lwinga

Introduction

The chapter analyses the intersectionality of legal interpretation and the dilemma of the poor-illiterate as accused and witnesses in Malawi's courtrooms. There is an ongoing debate on language policies which suggests that irrelevant language policies employed in Africa have disenfranchised many citizens to the extent that they fail to meaningfully participate in the socio-economic fabric of their respective countries. Malawi's recent English-only policy in some domains such as the education sector is a major example of this. The policy has re-ignited the question of what languages are suitable for use within the various sectors in Malawi. Kishindo (2001) argues that due to high illiteracy levels, English's employment as the courts' language of record hampers access to justice and heightens vulnerability, especially for the poor-illiterate masses. The provision of courtroom interpreters has potential to solve the problem. However, it is not. The communication gap widens between the accused, the witnesses, the interpreters, the judges/magistrates, thus, which potentially may distort the accused and witnesses' accounts.

Language challenges associated with the use of foreign languages in various sectors has been observed. This is confirmed by Dingfelder Stone (2018, p. 1) who asserts that

> in the past few decades, the increased rates of international trade, travel and migration have led to a rising number of civil, criminal defendants and courtroom participants who do not speak the language of the court in which they find themselves.

Thus, questions arise regarding the courts' capacity to ensure the protection of the rights of vulnerable groups vis-à-vis legal interpretation has inadequately been discussed. The issue of the vulnerability of the poor-illiterate people has also been noted. Albright and Soto (2008, p. ii) mention that: 'When democratic rules are ignored and there is no law capable of providing shelter, the people who suffer most are those who can least afford to lose'. Kanyongolo (2006, p. 26) indicates that the judiciary has the ability to facilitate easy access

DOI: 10.4324/9781003569435-18

to justice for the poor-illiterate by 'expanding the availability of *pro bono* legal services; and introducing flexibility in the language policy of the courts to allow more use of vernacular languages in official court proceedings'.

Despite these noticeable concerns, the status quo in Malawi's courtrooms on English's employment as the courts' official language or language of record has not changed. Although a number of initiatives and relatively recent legal provisions to accommodate democratic principles are being launched to modernise access to quality justice, the legal (courtroom) interpretation/translation practice aimed at safeguarding fairness and justice is still in its infantile stages notwithstanding some progressive legal provisions on the same (Steytler, 1993).

Research questions and organisation of the chapter

The chapter employed qualitative research methods, namely: participant observation, in-depth interviews, Focus Group discussion (FGDs), and content analysis. The chapter sought to engage with the following four research questions:

(i) How is court interpretation practiced in Malawi's courtrooms?
(ii) What are some of the challenges inherent in courtroom interpretation in Malawi?
(iii) What are the attitudes of the Malawian public towards the use of court interpreters?
(iv) How best can courts use legal translators to ensure that access to justice for the accused and witnesses is achieved?

In pursuit of the aim of the study, the chapter is divided into four sections. First, it engages with Malawi's language policies in various political eras. Second, it conceptualises vulnerability. Third, it presents a discussion on the concept of legal interpretation. Fourth, it presents a discussion on English and court interpretation in Malawi.

Language policy in Malawi during different historical periods

Gandara and Gomez (2009, p. 581) acknowledge that defining 'language policy is problematic because the field of language policy and planning (LPP) is relatively new'. The elusiveness is also largely due to Africa's long desire not to detach herself from the language of the colonisers (Djité, 2008).

Matiki (2001) observes that Malawi's language policies have enabled the dominance of English as the language of record in the administrative and legislative spheres. Malawi has seen three major historical periods each with its language policy and preferred objectives. The historical periods are the colonial (1891–1964), the one-party (1964–1994), and the multiparty democratic (1994 to date).

Colonial period before 1891–1964

The language policy of this period was aimed at using language that would promote reading, writing, and doing simple arithmetic. Both mission and colonial schools were instrumental in providing this kind of education (Issa & Yamada, 2013). Kayambazinthu (1998) argues that the central and southern regions of Malawi were dominated by the Chichewa vernacular language and its variations such as the Chimang'anja and Chisena vernacular language popularly spoken in the Lower Shire and the Chinyanja vernacular language popularly spoken in the southern end of Lake Malawi. The Chiyao vernacular language is dominant in the Eastern region districts of Mangochi, Machinga, Balaka, and Zomba. Moreover, the following four vernacular languages are dominant in the Northern region of Malawi: Chitumbuka, Chitonga, Chingonde/Chinyakyusa, and Chisukwa/Chilambya/Chinyiha (Phiri et al., 1992).

One-Party Period (1964–1994)

During Kamuzu Banda's era (1964–1994), language policy favoured English and Chichewa. President Banda declared both languages as official at the 1968 Malawi Congress Party (MCP) convention. Particularly, Chichewa was declared as a national language and English as the official language (Issa & Yamada, 2013). Matiki (2001) argues that through a presidential decree, it was expected that the two languages would play official roles in Malawi's public sphere. However, that did not happen. Instead, Banda himself placed more emphasis on English as he himself rarely addressed Malawians using Chichewa but preferred to use English which was interpreted into Chichewa. Kishindo (2001, p. 4) argues that

> English and Chichewa are the prescribed languages for education in Malawi. Chichewa is used as a medium of instruction for the lower classes and taught as a subject throughout the system up to university level. English is the language for higher education, government, administration, legislature and judiciary.

Multiparty democratic period (1994 to the present)

In 1994, the multiparty democratic dispensation started in Malawi and the government changed the language policy by accommodating many ethnic (indigenous) languages. Some of the indigenous languages are available on the public media such as MBC Radio and MBC TV, particularly employed for news broadcasting and advertising (Issa & Yamada, 2013). In 1998, the government of Malawi advocated for other indigenous languages to be given prominence rather than just English and Chichewa.

Kretzer and Kumwenda (2016, p. 31) argue that the English language is considered to be

> an economically relevant language for upward social mobility; consequently, the mother tongue has a very low reputation in Malawi. This is heightened by the fact that Malawi's language policy is influenced by many international organizations like the World Bank and many other agencies since the country is aid-dependent and cannot decide on issues independently.

Consequently, English is offered as a compulsory subject at the Malawi School Certificate of Education (MSCE) level and during the first year at many universities regardless of the degree programme being pursued by the student. In addition, English is the medium of instruction for tertiary level of education in Malawi (Kishindo, 2001).

Kretzer and Kumwenda (2016, p. 20) describe language policy as 'a deliberate effort to change or influence a community's use of a particular language, a variety of a language or languages. It is concerned with official efforts to influence the relative status and use of one or more languages'. Malawi's language policy stipulates English and Chichewa as the official languages of the country (Kretzer & Kumwenda, 2016). Citizens, however, are free to use other indigenous languages in their day-to-day activities.

Matiki (2002) argues that some parents resist the use of vernacular languages in Malawi's education system because they consider them to have no apparent economic value. Kretzer and Kumwenda (2016, p. 35) have indicated that

> the language policies which the country has pursued have seen Chichewa, which had 50.2% speakers nationally in 1966, increase its number of speakers substantially to almost 80% in 2015, while speakers of other indigenous languages have diminished significantly.

The Malawian society has a huge positive attitude towards English. The English language is considered by many as a proper academic language in comparison to the prevailing negativity towards vernacular languages such as Chichewa, ChiYawo, Chitumbuka, Chilomwe, Chisena, etc. (Kretzer & Kumwenda, 2016). Some Malawians despise indigenous languages such as Chichewa. Unsavoury remarks are often directed at those that have decided to major in indigenous languages. For instance, Kamwendo (2010, p. 278) explains that in the university campuses, some people make distasteful remarks towards students who are studying indigenous languages like 'za Chichewa zomwe zija mpaka kukhala nazo professor?' (You mean that Chichewa has made him rise to full professorship?) or 'Inu kubwera ku university kudzaphunzira ndakatulo basi?' (You came all the way to the university simply to study Chichewa poetry?)

A study by Issa and Yamada (2013) on language instruction in schools in Mangochi discovered that some teachers and learners had a negative attitude towards chi-Yao. The impression that the research participants showed was that using English as a language of instruction signified 'real schooling' (Issa & Yamada, 2013, p. 161). It is not surprising, therefore, that Kretzer and Kumwenda (2016, p. 35) argue that 'the status of English has also risen significantly as it has remained the main language of education, trade and industry, governance, the judiciary, legislature and media in Malawi'.

Conceptualising vulnerability

According to Berzins McCoy (2013),

> the etymological formation of the term 'vulnerability' is derived from the Latin word *vulnus* ('wound') and refers to the inherent capacity for human beings to suffer from various causes. Thus, vulnerability is associated with victimhood, deprivation, dependency, pathology, fragility, weakness, defenseless, helplessness, susceptibility to wounding and to suffering.
>
> (p. 246)

However, this susceptibility is 'a universal, inevitable, enduring aspect of the human condition"' (Fineman, 2010, p. 178).

Fineman (2010, p. 180) conjectures that all people are

> vulnerable and prone to dependency (both chronic and episodic), and the state therefore has a corresponding obligation to reduce, ameliorate, and compensate for that vulnerability. . . . Therefore, the state must provide equal access to the various societal institutions that are responsible for ensuring service delivery such as education, healthcare, security, judiciary etc.

Fineman's (2017, p. 135) vulnerability theory provides a pattern which helps to raise questions that challenge established assumptions concerning the state and citizens' responsibility. The state's responsibility includes considering which laws serve the citizens better. Such being the case, vulnerability theory goes beyond the normative claim for equality.

Thus, it can be argued that

> a vulnerability approach calls for the to be responsive to the realities of human vulnerability and its corollary, social dependency, as well as to situations reflecting inherent or necessary inequality, when it initially establishes or sets up mechanisms to monitor these relationships and institutions.
>
> (Fineman, 2017, p. 135)

The issue of vulnerability and the law has been adequately discussed in the literature (Kanyongolo, 2006; Chikopa, 2015; Nyirenda, 2015; Otchere et al., 2020). However, what has not received adequate attention is how court interpretation exacerbates vulnerability for the poor-illiterate as accused and witnesses in accessing formal justice.

Nyirenda (2015, p. 2) argues that vulnerability or what vulnerable groups or persons are is too complex to be defined in 'clear and succinct terms'. Generally, vulnerability concerns groups of 'people who are easily susceptible to discrimination, marginalization, or criticism' (Southern African Litigation Centre, Judiciary of Malawi & National Association of Women Judges and Magistrates of Botswana, 2015, p. iii). Nyirenda (2015, p. 2) adds that vulnerability affects 'people who encounter discriminatory treatment or is in need of special attention and protection by the state, in order to avoid exploitation'. The Integrated Household Survey (2005, p. 7) gives the following categories of vulnerable groups:

> women, children, persons with disabilities, the elderly, refugees, internally displaced persons, national minorities, migrant workers, persons living with HIV, sexual minority groups, and persons with serious illnesses or health conditions. The list of such is endless. The poor people are poor when they lack capacity to live better, long, healthy, and creative lives. In addition, the poor are poor when self-respect and the respect of others is deprived of them.

Others have conceptualised vulnerability in relation to specified outcomes such as chronic poverty and malnutrition. This vulnerability is mediated by both household responses, that is, coping strategies and policy interventions such as risk reduction, risk mitigation, risk coping, etc. (Devereux et al., 2006).

The Malawi National Social Support Programme (Republic of Malawi, 2018) is more specific when categorising vulnerabilities as follows: (i) the ultra-poor households; (ii) elderly household heads with special needs or a chronic health condition; and (iii) children under five years. In this chapter, our interest is in the poor-illiterate as the accused and witnesses in Malawi's courtrooms. One of the characteristics of vulnerable persons is their apparent lack of education in general and legal illiteracy in particular. The vulnerable groups are also marginalised by sociocultural, political, economic challenges, and experience socio-economic and opinionated factors which potentially limit them in claiming and using their rights in order to access formal justice. It is further observed that one of the common challenges of vulnerable people is that 'they will not be able to surmount the practical hurdles of state institutions, including tribunals, and they will not be able to bribe their way through' (Nyirenda, 2015, p. 2). In addition, the vulnerable persons face a big challenge for payment of their legal fees. This is further compounded by the limited availability of legal aid services in Malawi which ultimately affects their legal representation in court (Nyirenda, 2015).

Gloppen and Kanyongolo (2007) observe that Malawi is a signatory to most major international human rights instruments. These include the 'International Covenant on Civil and Political Rights' (ICCPR); the 'International Covenant on Economic, Social and Cultural Rights' (ICESCR); the 'Convention on the Elimination of All Forms of Discrimination against Women' (CEDAW); the 'Convention on the Rights of the Child' (CRC); and the 'Convention on the Rights of Persons with Disabilities' (CRPD). Malawi being a signatory to these instruments, has a legal obligation to safeguard the rights of vulnerable groups or persons. Nyirenda (2015, p. 3) mentions that 'the Fundamental Principles of the Constitution (section 12) is key for the provision for gender equality, support for the disabled, full development of children, and support for the elderly'.

In addition, the Malawi Constitution (section 20) deals with the issue of inequality. It says:

> (1) Discrimination of persons in any form is prohibited and all persons are, under any law, guaranteed equal and effective protection against discrimination on grounds of race, colour, sex, language, religion, political or other opinion, national, ethnic or social origin, disability, property, birth or other status or condition. (2) Legislation may be passed addressing inequalities in society and prohibiting discriminatory practices and the propagation of such practices and may render such practices criminally punishable by the courts.

Further to this, Malawi's Constitution (section 41) vis-à-vis access to justice and remedies for all, provides that:

> (1) Every person shall have a right to recognition as a person before the law (2) Every person shall have the right of access to any court of law or any other tribunal with jurisdiction for final settlement of legal issues (3) Every person shall have the right to an effective remedy by a court of law or tribunal for acts violating the rights and freedoms granted to him or her by this Constitution or any other law.

From the preceding sections, it is clear that Malawi's Constitution takes the safeguarding of human rights and access to justice seriously. With these important provisions, 'can Malawi achieve the vindication, protection, and enforcement of the rights of vulnerable groups?' (Nyirenda, 2015, p. 3). The answer to the question is problematic for two reasons. First, looking at the issue of legal interpretation, which is not seriously accounted for achieving the vindication of the vulnerable people is problematic. Second, the failure by the courts in Malawi to allow the use of vernacular languages as the language of record in official proceedings is a serious impediment to the access of justice for the poor-illiterate (Kanyongolo, 2006). On the other hand, the Malawi judiciary has made strides towards making courts being friendly to every Malawian.

However, Nyirenda (2015) makes an important observation concerning the intersectionality of the vulnerable people and the courts. He says: 'Vulnerable persons are already disadvantaged. The first thing for them is to find the court, then how to approach the court, and finally there is the difficulty of explaining why they have come to court' (Nyirenda, 2015, p. 4).

In order to serve the needs of the vulnerable people, courts must do an assessment and adapt to such needs. Important to such adaption requires ensuring that the courts proximity to vulnerable groups is within reach as far as distance in concerned. Several factors jeopardise the vulnerable persons' access to justice such as the location (village, town, city) and proximity (far from their home) of the courts can be intimidating to the vulnerable persons; the physical structure and set-up of the courts themselves can have a major impact to the vulnerable; the manner in which clients are welcomed at the courts; the procedures for lodging a formal complaint; and the trial procedures, especially the use of English exacerbates the vulnerability. Nyirenda (2015) intimates that the prevailing opinion in Malawi's public sphere is that the predicament of vulnerable groups is generally neglected by the courts. For instance, issues of strict adherence to courtroom procedures and high standards of the burden of proof placed on the accused persons and witnesses, give the impression that decisions by courts fall short of recognising with adequacy the circumstances of the vulnerable groups or persons.

Writing in the context of India, Sathe (2002) argues that the courts are mandated to ensure that the rule of law is observed by all citizens in the country and that their rights are protected, especially the rights of the vulnerable groups. We conjecture that public interest litigation and proactive court systems involve the interests of the accused and witnesses. In this regard, the courts' aim is to satisfy the needs of its clients. This calls for a serious reflection on how best courts can serve the interests of the clients rather than their own. In terms of how the needs of the poor and illiterate are served, the Malawi courts fall short significantly because of the use of English as the language of the courts which disenfranchises most of its clients.

According to the National Adult Literacy and Education Strategic Plan (2022–2027) released by the Ministry of Gender, Community Development and Social Welfare (Republic of Malawi, 2022), the adult literacy rate in Malawi is at 72.2 percent. What it means is that almost 27 out of 100 adult men and women cannot read and write (Wali, 2024). Irrespective of the illiteracy of clients, the court should provide a conducive environment for public interest litigation, that is, a deliberate approach of ensuring that vulnerable groups have access to justice. In so doing, the courts would be helping the masses of the poor, who are characterised by socio-economic marginalisation, illiteracy in both law and the English language, and are afraid to approach the courts. In addition, regardless of who or what they are, the courts are obliged to uphold the human dignity, equality and rights of all people (Nyirenda, 2015).

Discrimination and vulnerability are inseparable for the vulnerable groups or persons common in many sectors of society. The vulnerable groups or persons are many times likely to be discriminated than any other group. With the emergency of human rights, discrimination is a serious offense. The United Nations Human Rights Committee (UNHRC, 1989/90) defines discrimination as:

> Any distinction, exclusion or preference which is based on any ground such as race, colour, sex, language, religion, political or other opinion, national or social origin, property, birth or other status, and which has the purpose or effect of nullifying or impairing the recognition, enjoyment or exercise by all persons, on an equal footing, of all rights and freedoms.
>
> (General Comment No. 18: Non-Discrimination)

Otchere et al. (2020) argue that the government of Malawi has in its efforts recognised vulnerabilities in the country. For instance, the Malawi National Social Support Programme (Republic of Malawi, 2018) recognises social, demographic, and life-cycle vulnerabilities in the population. Consequently, these categories of vulnerabilities have been used to develop a framework for remedial action.

The concept of court interpretation

Courtroom interpretation entails rendering oral messages from the source language (SL) to the target language (Ngarambe & Ruvebana, 2023). Some scholars refer to courtroom interpretation as legal interpretation or forensic interpreting (Russell & Hale, 2008). The objective of courtroom interpretation is to make 'communication possible despite language barriers that exist between litigants and court personnel' (Mikkelson, 2017, p. 1). Laster and Taylor (1994, p. 5) indicate that 'the public has expectation that the interpreter will play an active and discretionary role, considering the cultural dimensions of communication between members of different ethnic, cultural and linguistic communities'. The term 'court interpreting' is widely used to refer to any kind of legal interpreting, but the courtroom is in fact only one of several contexts in which legal interpreting may take place.

One of the challenges created within the law and judiciary is courtroom interpretation. It is observed that the legal interpretation fails to serve the interests of the vulnerable people. The situation has the potential to hamper the provision of justice to vulnerable groups (Kanyongolo, 2006). In order to deal with the problem, Kanyongolo (2006, p. 26) suggests that 'introducing flexibility in the language policy of the courts to allow more use of local languages in official proceedings is helpful in minimizing vulnerability'.

English and courtroom interpretation in Malawi

Malawi's legal system is largely modelled on English common law with some influence of customary law (Mvula, 2010; Ntaba, 2016), yet it is observed that:

> The poor Malawians may be unable to access the justice system simply because they do not understand it, or lack knowledge about it. They may be illiterate, which severely hampers their ability to interact with the justice system. In Malawi, the law is drafted and administered in the official language, English, which many poor people are unable to speak and/or read thereby excluding the majority of the population that speak only local languages.
>
> (Nkonkomalimba, 2017, p. 6)

According to one magistrate's experience of 20 years in the judiciary, that courtroom interpretation plays a critical role in the administration of justice in Malawi. He notes that the words 'interpretation' and 'translation' are used interchangeably; however, the most familiar and commonly used term is 'interpretation' (Interview with magistrates, 2024). He continues to say that though the term 'interpretation' is more familiar than translation in the courtrooms and during hearing, interpretation is more of a technical term than translation. What he means by that is drawn from Section 9 of the Malawi Constitution which provides that

> The judiciary shall have the responsibility of interpreting, protecting and enforcing this Constitution and all laws and in accordance with this Constitution in an independent and impartial manner with regard only to legally relevant facts and the prescriptions of law.
>
> (Republic of Malawi (Constitution) Act, 1994)

The way the judicial system works, composed of the judges, magistrates, and support staff, what it means is that collectively they all have the responsibility to interpret the constitution and the laws of Malawi. In this sense, interpretation means adding meaning to certain words and concepts. However, this responsibility is technically limited to judges. Therefore, the question becomes: Are there courtroom interpreters in the judiciary? According to a magistrate who participated in the study, the Malawi judiciary does have courtroom interpreters which are commonly referred to as courtroom translators. The court clerks are the ones that do the interpretation.

On the training of courtroom interpreters, one magistrate mentioned that there is no such training. Here, formal training is referred to a training offered by a college or university. Another magistrate who was interviewed for the study said that she has never heard of any courtroom interpreters training that can qualify one to be a courtroom interpreter. Court interpreters are initially recruited by the Judiciary Service Commission (JSC) as court clerks or court marshals. Their core function is to register court cases and process them while court marshals provide internal security and maintain discipline during court sessions and also serve court summons and documents to clients. When need arises, these court clerks and court marshals are informally or internally trained to work as court interpreters (Interview with magistrates, 2024).

Two magistrates who participated in the study indicated that they have not heard of any trainings for the courtroom interpreters, however, reports indicate that the judiciary offers a nine-month basic course in selected legal subjects to some of its staff such as new recruits and serving court clerks in order to equip them with essential skills concerning court procedures. Upon successful completion of the training, the attendees are appointed as lay magistrates. Lay magistrates are holders of a Malawi School Certificate of Education from the Malawi Institute of Development or Chancellor College with a diploma in law. Of course, it is not clear if these selected legal subjects include courtroom interpretation (Ntaba, 2016).

The training offered by the judiciary supposedly to courtroom interpreters is formal and it used to take place at Staff Development Institute (SDI) Malawi, formerly, Mpemba Staff Development Institute; however, it has been many years since it was suspended. Staff Development Institute (SDI) – Mpemba, established in 1962, is a government-based training and research institute located at Mpemba in Blantyre. Its initial objective was to offer civil service training. As of today, it forms the training arm of the Malawi Civil Service under the Department of Human Resource Management and Development in the Office of the President and Cabinet. It offers local training and consulting services to both private and public sectors. However, a magistrate at Nkhata Bay District Magistrate Court mentioned that training interpreters at Mpemba had become difficult (Nyondo, 2015). It is not elaborated why it had become difficult. However, this training was found inadequate to prepare junior judicial officers to effectively discharge their duties. Edge Kanyongolo, professor of law at Chancellor College quoted in Ntaba (2016, p. 99), has indicated that "At least one stakeholder interviewed for this report expressed reservations about the adequacy of the course to prepare those who undergo it to handle the demands of judicial office".

Institutions of higher learning have recognised the need for training the courtroom interpreters to sharpen their skills in interpretation. One lecturer in the Department of Languages and Literature at Mzuzu University recommends equipping the courtroom interpreters with knowledge of language and communication, crime, and law including sociolinguistics (Nyondo, 2015).

Selection procedures of a court interpreter for a case

The Mzuzu High Court has about ten court interpreters. Each presiding judge and magistrate is assigned a special interpreter. The judges and magistrates, however, are free to use any courtroom interpreter who is available or who is competent for a particular case. Normally, a court clerk who registered a case becomes an automatic interpreter. Alternatively, the presiding magistrate or judge may assign any of the available clerks or court marshals to interpret any case before him or her. The presiding magistrate or judge is involved in the selection process since he or she has absolute discretion (Interview with magistrates, 2024).

Due to the limited number of court interpreters and their lack of knowledge and skills of interpretation, a case can fail to commence hearing. For instance, there was case involving immigrants from Ethiopia and none of the suspects knew English. The presiding magistrate adjourned to source a competent interpreter. The interpreter outsourced. When an interpreter is outsourced interpreter, he or she takes an oath of interpreting correctly without misleading the court intentionally and should he or she be discovered to have misled the court intentionally, he or she would be prosecuted. This makes it difficult for outsiders to come and work as courtroom interpreters (Interview with magistrates, 2024).

From the preceding, two scenarios lead to outsourcing courtroom interpreters. First, the judiciary is understaffed with courtroom interpreters. Second, sometimes the judiciary lacks competent courtroom interpreters. Both scenarios have potential to delay or deny access to justice for the poor-illiterate as the accused or witnesses. On the other hand, outsourcing courtroom interpreters can have advantages.

English as the language of the courts

One magistrate who participated in the study observed that English is a challenge for many Malawians. Some prosecutors and courtroom interpreters struggle to speak English too. Similarly, in South Africa, scholars have been discontented with the promotion and use of English in the courts. They fear the African languages will soon become extinct because they are rarely promoted to be used in the courts:

> It is for this reason and many others that the promotion of English as the language of record in court raised the discontent amongst academics, researchers and the public about lack of equal status that has been accorded to languages in South Africa by the South African Constitution. A common discontent is that African languages will soon become extinct.
>
> (Choshi, 2019, p. 149)

Gloppen and Kanyongolo (2007) observe that poor rural people, many of them poor and illiterate, have limited recourse to justice. The poor-illiterate as the accused and witness face a dilemma when English is being used during court hearings. There is a great deal of self-doubt and embarrassment. A magistrate once received complaints about the prevalence of exaggeration in the interpretation. Such interpretations give a picture about convicts as worst sinners who deserve the worst punishment. For instance, where the magistrate said: 'This is a very serious offence'. The court interpreter said: 'Khothi lasanga kuti imwe muli munthu muheni chomene, chigawenga' (the court has found you to be a very bad person; the worst of criminals). When such interpretations are commonplace, there is potential of miscarriage of justice due to the language barrier of English being used during hearings. One magistrate mentioned another incident in which an interpreter could interpret to make him harsh or lenient with the client. The magistrate did not understand the language of the accused. He discovered he had made a wrong ruling due to the courtroom interpreter's erroneous interpretation.

In another incident a magistrate presided over a case in which a defendant struggled to speak English. The accused was told to speak in Tumbuka but insisted on speaking English. Later on, the accused revealed to the magistrate that he insisted on speaking English because he had observed that people who spoke English were favoured and won their cases. Whether it is, indeed, true that English speakers are favoured is beyond the scope of this study; however, with the way English is revered, one would be tempted to argue that the allegation is correct. It is a temptation for magistrates to have great respect for lawyers, professionals, and whites who speak good English in court. It is easy to be taken away and misled (Interview with magistrates, 2024).

The attitudes of the Malawian public towards the use of court interpreters

For the elite, English is advantageous; however, for local masses just the thought of standing before an English-speaking judge is intimidating. A magistrate presided over a divorce case of young primary school dropouts. The clients were visibly fearful. The magistrate broke the rule and switched to Chichewa. After that, the clients looked relaxed. Later on, the woman, one of the primary school drops, found an opportunity to talk to the magistrate. She confessed that all along she believed magistrates did not know Chichewa since they always used English. She was surprised when the magistrate spoke Chichewa in court.

Another respondent, Plaintiff Female X, explained that in 2018 she requested Mzuzu High Court to annul her marriage with her husband of 2 years. At the time of the study, she possessed a bachelor of arts degree (English language) and was a teacher at a government secondary school. The case was heard in the private chambers of a female magistrate. Before the hearing started, the presiding magistrate asked the appellant to state the language she was comfortable to express herself. She chose Chichewa. The accused (her husband) and the witnesses chose Tumbuka. A court interpreter was present to interpret in English what the magistrate said. Plaintiff Female X mentioned that she chose Chichewa because she was afraid she would not understand technical terms that the magistrate might use. She thought Chichewa would serve her better. On whether or not she felt the interpreter misinterpreted the statements of the magistrate, she said she did not detect any. One of the reasons was that the plaintiff paid less attention to what the interpreter was saying since she could hear the magistrate's English quite well.

How best can courts use courtroom interpreters to achieve access to justice for the accused and witnesses?

In many instances, it has been observed that the magistrates and judges insist on court interpreters giving the proper and correct interpretation before they proceed with the case (Nyondo, 2015). The interpreters should be used only for the benefit of the audience not for clients. We also believe that interpreters should be those who are competent in both languages, English and the particular language of a particular client. We are of the opinion that there should be a qualification for court interpreters which would make them to be professional and licensed interpreters.

Looking at the preceding observations, the lack of properly trained court interpreters is a serious issue that has potential to affect access to justice by the poor-illiterate as the accused and witnesses. The Legal Language Services (2024) argues that a minor discrepancy in interpretation can lead to serious errors in the trial. In 2003, in a Georgia court, in the United States, the lawyers representing in the *Holliday v State* case questioned the competence of the court interpreter. They argued that the interpreter left certain important words uninterpreted and this eventually led the judge to deliver a judgment that was deemed as not fair.

The significance of having well-trained court interpreters cannot be overemphasised. One of the important aspects of interpreters is the competence to accomplish proper and correct interpretation. 'Eight competencies have been highlighted: Language competency, intercultural competency, research competency, technological competency, thematic competency, transfer competency, service provision competency, and ethical competency' (Ngarambe & Ruvebana, 2023, p. 110).

Speaking on the disadvantages of wrong court interpretation, the Legal Languages Services (2024) reports that in 2011, an Australian court threw out a case due to an interpreter's mistake involving several Indonesian words. The words 'did you stop anyone moving?' were mistakenly translated into 'did you push anyone?' Fortunately, a juror who was well-acquainted with the Indonesian language noticed the translation error and he subsequently notified the judge. Throwing out a case costed Australian taxpayers a lot money. The Australian scenario emphasises the need to use professional interpreters and translators.

What is observed here can happen anywhere. In Malawi, the challenge of using incompetent court interpreters has been noticed and suggestions have been put forward to deal with it. In 2015, as part of their curriculum, Forensic Linguistics students at Mzuzu University (Mzuni) visited Nkhata Bay District Magistrate Court and made their observations. They indicated that it was important to accord proper training to Malawi's court interpreters who worked in magistrate courts. Doing so would ensure that impartial judgment is promoted (Nyondo, 2015). The students noted high levels of incompetence among interpreters. A class representative, argued that courtroom interpreters sometimes would interpret into local languages what was totally different from what the prosecutors said (Nyondo, 2015). Recommendations were that stakeholders including Mzuzu University need to 'take the task of training interpreters' (Nyondo, 2015). When this story was published in the *Nyasa Times* in 2015, it received reactions that supported the need to strengthen standards with regard to courtroom interpretation. It is noted that wrong interpretations have potential to take someone to jail.

The court interpreters need various skills to interpret accurately. For instance,

> the skill of using slang and colloquial language; maintain same tone; inflections and emotions of each speaker to ensure the message is understood correctly. In addition, cultural expressions and actions are of paramount importance to be taken in to account.
>
> (Legal Language Services, 2024, p. 1)

Conclusion

The chapter has presented a discussion on the intersectionality of legal interpretation and the dilemma of the poor and illiterate as accused and witnesses in Malawi's courtrooms. The chapter argues for the significance of courtroom interpretation because it enables the poor-illiterate as accused and witnesses to understand and follow the court proceedings. However, a more progressive step in ensuring that the poor-illiterate have access to justice is to substitute the language of the law, which in Malawi is currently English, with vernacular languages such as Chichewa, Chiyawo, Chitumbuka, Chitonga, Chinkhonde, Chilambya, Chisena, Chilomwe, etc.

The chapter has proffered a threefold justification for the employment of vernacular languages in the courts in Malawi. First, it would save the vulnerable persons from being poorly defended in the court because they can advise their legal counsel on how best to represent them. Second, it would help the vulnerable persons from being wrongly accused, misjudged, and unjustly condemned. Third, it would project a progressive step in transforming Malawi's legal system by demonstrating the willingness to accept public interest litigation that is cognisant of social rights as being relevant in the courts' jurisdiction.

References

Albright, M. K., & Soto, H. D. (2008). *Making the law work for everyone*. Commission on Legal Empowerment of the Poor.

Berzins McCoy, M. (2013). *Wounded heroes: Vulnerability as a virtue in ancient Greek literature and philosophy*. Oxford University Press.

Chikopa, L. P. (2015). Judicial activism and the protection of the rights of vulnerable groups in Malawi. In *Using the courts to protect vulnerable people: Perspectives from the judiciary and legal profession in Botswana, Malawi, and Zambia* (pp. 10–24). Southern Africa Litigation Centre.
Choshi, M. K. (2019). *Law and language: Solution for multilingual societies*. University of Venda.
Devereux, S., Baulch, B., Macauslan, I., Phiri, A., & Sabates-Wheeler, R. (2006). *Vulnerability and social protection in Malawi* (UK IDS Discussion Paper 387). Institute of Development Studies at the University of Sussex.
Dingfelder Stone, J. H. (2018). *Court interpreting and fair trial*. Palgrave Macmillan, European Commission, Legal Interpreting-Definition and Context. https://ec.europa.eu/education/knowledge-centre-interpretation/legal-interpreting-0/legal-interpreting_en
Djité, P. G. (2008). *The sociolinguistics of development in Africa*. Multilingual Matters.
Fineman, M. A. (2010). The vulnerable subject: Anchoring equality in the human condition. In *Transcending the boundaries of law* (pp. 177–191). Routledge-Cavendish.
Fineman, M. A. (2017). Vulnerability and inevitable inequality. *Oslo Law Review*, *4*(3), 133–149.
Gandara, P., & Gomez, C. M. (2009). Language policy in education. In G. Sykes, B. Schneider, & D. N. Plank (Eds.), *Handbook of education policy research*. Routledge.
Gloppen, S., & Kanyongolo, F. E. (2007). Courts and the poor in Malawi: Economic marginalization, vulnerability, and the law. *CON*, *5*(2), 258–293.
Issa, D. M., & Yamada, S. (2013). *Stakeholders' perception of the language of instruction policy in Malawian primary schools and its implications for the quality of education*. Nagoya University.
Judiciary of Malawi and National Association of Women Judges and Magistrates of Botswana (NAWABO). (2015). *Using the courts to protect vulnerable people: Perspectives from the judiciary and legal profession in Botswana, Malawi, and Zambia*. Southern Africa Litigation Centre.
Kamwendo, G. H. (2010). Denigrating the local, glorifying the foreign: Malawian language policies in the era of African renaissance. *International Journal of African Renaissance Studies – Multi-, Inter- and Transdisciplinarity*, *5*(2), 270–282.
Kanyongolo, F. E. (2006). *Malawi: Justice sector and rule of law* (Discussion Paper 26). AfriMAP and Open Society Initiative for Southern Africa.
Kayambazinthu, E. (1998). The language planning situation in Malawi. *Journal of Multilingual and Multicultural Development*, *19*(5–6), 369–469.
Kishindo, P. (2001). Language and the law in Malawi: A case for the use of indigenous languages in the legal system. *Language Matters*, *32*(1), 1–27.
Kretzer, M., & Kumwenda, J. (2016). Language policy in Malawi: A study of its contexts, factors for its development and consequences. *Marang Journal of Language and Literature*, *27*, 20–38.
Laster, K., & Taylor, V. L. (1994). *Interpreters and the legal system*. Federation Press.
Legal Language Services. (2024). *Court interpreting mistakes can lead to mistrials*. www.legallanguage.com
Matiki, A. J. (2001). The social significance of English in Malawi. *World Englishes*, *20*(2), 201–218.
Matiki, A. J. (2002). Language planning and linguistic exclusion in the legislative process in Malawi. *d'abril de*, *16–20*, 1–16.
Mikkelson, H. (2017). *Introduction to court interpreting*. Routledge.
Mvula, L. D. (2010). *Refugee status determination and rights in Malawi*. A paper presented at the Refugee Studies Centre Workshop Discussion on RSD and Rights in Southern and East Africa.

Ngarambe, T., & Ruvebana, E. (2023). Court interpreting practice in Rwanda: Challenges and strategies for fair justice. *Translation & Interpreting*, *15*(2), 108–124.
Nkonkomalimba, M. (2017). *Improved access to justice for unrepresented accused persons in the criminal justice system in Malawi.* Irish Rule of Law International (IRLI).
Ntaba, Z. (2016). *Sustainable development goal 16 and access to justice: The case of lay magistrates in Malawi.* In *Goal 16 of the sustainable development goals: Perspectives from judges and lawyers in Southern Africa on promoting rule of law and equal access to justice* (pp. 96–102). Southern African Litigation Centre.
Nyirenda, A. C. (2015). The role of the judiciary in protecting the rights of vulnerable groups in Malawi. In *Using the courts to protect vulnerable people: Perspectives from the judiciary and legal profession in Botswana, Malawi, and Zambia* (pp. 1–9). Southern Africa Litigation Centre.
Nyondo, P. (2015, October 16). Mzuzu University for training of Malawi court interpreters. *Nyasa Times.* www.nyasatimes.com
Otchere, F., Damoah, K. A., Handa, S., Barrington, C., & Tsoka, M. (2020). *Addressing lifecycle vulnerabilities of beneficiaries in the Malawi social cash transfer programme.* Centre of Social Research at the University of Malawi.
Phiri, K. M., Kalinga, O. J., & Bhila, H. H. K. (1992). The Northern Zambezia – Lake Malawi region. *General History of Africa. V: Africa from the Sixteenth to the Eighteenth Century*, 608–620.
Republic of Malawi. (2005). *Integrated household survey.* http://www.nso.malawi.net/data_on_line/economics/ihs/IHS2/IHS2_Report.pdf
Republic of Malawi. (2018). Malawi national social support programme II (MNSSP II). *Malawi Government Profile.* https://www.fao.org/faolex/results/details/en/c/LEX-FAOC190531/.
Republic of Malawi. (2022). National adult literacy and education strategic plan (2022–2027). *Ministry of Gender, Community Development and Social Welfare.*
Republic of Malawi (Constitution) Act of 1994. https://www.dvv-international.mw/fileadmin/files/southern-africa/National_Adult_Literacy_and_Education_Strategy_Signed_Copy.pdf.
Russell, D., & Hale, S. (Eds.). (2008). *Interpreting in legal settings.* Gallaudet University Press.
Sathe, S. P. (2003). *Judicial activism in India: Transgressing borders and enforcing limits.* Oxford University Press. (Original work published 2002)
Steytler, N. C. (1993). Implementing language rights in court: The role of the court interpreter. *South African Journal on Human Rights*, *9*(2), 205–222.
United Nations Human Rights Committee. (1989/90). Official records of the human rights committee, 1989/90. Volume 2, documents of the 37th to 39th sessions, 23 October 1989–27 July 1990 including the report of the committee to the general assembly. *United Nations Human Rights Council.* https://digitallibrary.un.org/record/213911?ln=en.
Wali, I. (2024, March 16). The painful, hefty price of illiteracy. *The Times Group.* https://times.mw/the-painful-hefty-price-for-illiteracy/

14 Access to justice by unrepresented litigants in Zimbabwe's courtrooms

Paul Svongoro and Eventhough Ndlovu

Introduction

Access to justice remains a pivotal yet challenging aspect for most legal systems worldwide, particularly for unrepresented litigants. This chapter explores the challenges faced by unrepresented litigants in Zimbabwe's courtrooms, focusing on the lack of legal representation. Zimbabwe's legal system, based on Roman-Dutch law and English common law, aims to uphold justice, equality, and fairness. However, unrepresented litigants face significant challenges due to lack of legal knowledge, procedural complexities, and financial constraints resulting from high legal fees. This high cost of legal representation impacts the effectiveness of the justice system and the protection of fundamental human rights, undermining the rule of law and basic human rights. Yet, in SA and other democratic countries, accused persons are guaranteed representation where they cannot afford it. This right is also underpinned by the UN declaration of human rights.

Driven by the desire to contribute to current debates on access to justice for disadvantaged members of the society, this chapter investigated how unrepresented litigants in Zimbabwean courts access the justice system. Due to the extremely high costs of legal representation in Zimbabwe, the majority of clients in the legal system are unrepresented litigants, also known as self-representing litigants or litigants-in-person, because they are unable to pay for legal fees.

Although the first is paragraph (e) of subsection (1) of section 70 of the Constitution of Zimbabwe, which states that any person accused of an offence has the right 'to be represented by a legal practitioner assigned by the State and at State expense, if substantial injustice would otherwise result', this right has historically not been guaranteed as most courts lack the financial means to provide such legal aid. As a result, a few privileged members of the public have resorted to hiring their own paid lawyers in the majority of cases.

However, the Zimbabwean court system is often inaccessible to ordinary people, causing concerns about the ability of marginalised, unrepresented litigants to access justice. The rigid rules and procedures make the courts strange for many, and it is crucial for the legal system to include accommodations to

DOI: 10.4324/9781003569435-19

help these litigants get the most out of their legal representation. This study aims to examine access to justice for unrepresented litigants in Zimbabwean courtrooms.

Definition of the term 'unrepresented litigants'

In this chapter, we used Williams' (2011) definition of unrepresented litigants. Williams (2011) contends that the terms unrepresented litigants, litigators in person, and self-representing litigants typically refer to the lack of a lawyer, such as a solicitor or barrister, managing the case and offering representation. On the other hand, unrepresented litigants can range from those who have gone entirely unaided to those who have received some assistance or advice from a legal adviser.

Williams (2011), further suggests that unrepresented litigants may be coerced into defending claims or actively participate in litigation. This could include a significant percentage of defendants who do not participate in the legal process. Therefore, unless otherwise indicated, the term unrepresented litigants refers to both in-person and self-representing litigants in a broader sense, as it is not always easy to distinguish between these groups based on facts (Williams, 2011).

While agreeing with William's definition of unrepresented litigants, Matsikidze (2014) contextualises unrepresented litigants as self-actors/self-actresses in Zimbabwe's courtrooms.

Legal aid in Zimbabwe

The Lilongwe Declaration on Accessing Legal Aid in the Criminal Justice System in Africa passed by the United Nations Office of Drugs and Crime (UNODC, 2011), defines legal aid as:

> legal advice, assistance, representation, education, and mechanisms for alternative dispute resolution; and to include a wide range of stakeholders, such as non-governmental organizations, community-based organizations, religious and non-religious charitable organizations, professional bodies and associations and academic institutions.

The most crucial issue is that legal aid refers to any form of legal advice, assistance, or representation received from other parties involved in a dispute, including law firms, government-hired lawyers, individuals on behalf of a litigant, and civic society organisations (CSOs), among others. However, Zimbabwe's law and justice institutions reveal a concerning disparity in access to legal aid and justice for poor citizens, despite the promising motto of the Judicial Service Commission, which includes all civil and criminal courts, on its website. The motto says, 'A Zimbabwe in which world-class justice prevails!' From this motto, Zimbabwe's justice system is deemed to meet international standards, particularly those in the developed world, and ensures fair and equitable treatment for all citizens, regardless of their social class or status.

In addition to the motto by Zimbabwe's Judicial Service Commission, the Constitution of Zimbabwe also makes a promise to provide legal aid to disadvantaged Zimbabweans when the need arises. Specifically, section 31 of Zimbabwe's Constitution states the following regarding legal aid:

> The State must take all practical measures, within the limits of the resources available to it, to provide legal representation in civil and criminal cases for people who need it and are unable to afford legal practitioners of their choice.

This clause in Zimbabwe's Constitution provides legal representation for poor citizens in civil and criminal cases. However, the government's inability to provide legal aid and the lack of legal aid offices in all districts make it impractical to enforce this constitutional right. Most Zimbabweans are unaware of their right to legal aid, and the lack of these offices makes the justice system less secure.

Apart from the preceding, section 31 of Zimbabwe's Constitution prioritises legal representation in court, neglecting other stages of the criminal justice process, leading to limited legal aid in police stations, prisons, and lower courts. Section 70(1)(j) grants accused persons the right to have trial proceedings interpreted into their language, which is universally applicable and not exclusive to minority language speakers. However, minority language speakers can access their minority language rights through general language rights in criminal proceedings.

Secondly, the state is obligated to provide an interpreter at its expense in criminal proceedings where a person cannot understand the court's language, even for economic reasons. This right is essential to facilitate an accused person's participation in Zimbabwe's adversarial legal system, as without it, justice will be denied. The state cannot refuse to provide it for any reason (Maja, n.d.).

Fourth, section 70(1)(j) of the Constitution does not grant a right to be tried in a language of choice, the accused's first language, or their own language. Instead, it requires the accused to be tried in a language they understand. This differs from the language spoken. For example, a person who speaks Sena and English would have proceedings conducted in English. However, courts' failure to provide language interpreters and lack of resident interpreters complicates communication between litigants and legal representatives, especially in cases involving deaf and hard of hearing litigants (See Ndlovu, 2017, 2023a).

The Legal Resources Foundation (LRF, 2018) reports that 65 percent of people in urban and 85 percent in rural magistrates' courts lack legal representation, despite the complex and technical procedures. This situation is worse in rural areas, as most legal aid providers offer assistance in urban areas, making it difficult for rural populations to access services unless they travel to urban centres (LRF, 2018).

The Legal Aid Directorate (LRF) in Zimbabwe claims that the country's informa pauperis (IP) intervention is not being fully utilised due to public ignorance of the resource. IP allows poor individuals to proceed in court without paying usual legal expenses. The LRF also found that lawyers are unwilling to defend clients in intellectual property disputes, leading the JSC to send most in need to Civic Society Organisations and the Legal Aid Directorate (LRF, 2018).

Legal aid in other parts of Africa

The Lilongwe Declaration on Accessing Legal Aid in the Criminal Justice System in Africa defines legal aid as 'legal advice, assistance, representation, education, and mechanisms for alternative dispute resolution; and to include a wide range of stakeholders, such as non-governmental organizations, community-based organizations, religious and non-religious charitable organizations, professional bodies and associations and academic institutions' (UNODC, 2011, p. vii). A UNODC survey found that legal aid laws in African countries like Botswana, Malawi, and Mozambique focus on a lawyer-centred model. However, these countries have a low number of lawyers, with most people in rural or peri-urban areas and lawyers in urban areas. Despite these laws, many African nations have low state budgetary allotments for legal aid, making access to legal aid challenging (UNODC, 2011).

The UNODC (2011) survey further reveals that the absence of a national policy for primary judicial services in African nations leads to court backlogs, delays, and high remand inmates, resulting in prison overpopulation and social marginalisation, especially in rural areas. The lack of affordable legal aid services further exacerbates this issue, leaving impoverished individuals with limited options (UNODC, 2011).

Objectives of the study

In the context of the brief introduction and situation analysis as regards the provision of legal aid in Zimbabwe and the rest of Africa presented earlier, this chapter sought to:

(i) Identify and analyse the barriers to justice for unrepresented litigants in Zimbabwe's courtrooms;
(ii) Compare the challenges faced in Zimbabwe with those in similar jurisdictions to draw lessons and insights; and
(iii) Propose actionable recommendations for policymakers, the legal community, and other stakeholders to improve access to justice for all, especially the unrepresented.

Literature review

Global perspectives on access to legal aid and justice

Access to justice is a fundamental aspect of the global legal system, ensuring everyone has access to justice, regardless of their financial situation or legal representation. This section explores previous research on this topic, focusing on unrepresented litigants, contrasting international perspectives with Zimbabwe's unique legal system.

Research from a variety of jurisdictions has brought attention to the major obstacles that people without legal counsel must overcome (Sande& Buhai, 2009; Williams, 2011; Hurter, 2016; Knowlton et al., 2016; Rice, 2022; Solo & Nsengaali, 2022). For instance, Sande and Buhai (2009) make observations about the United States and argue that having access to legal representation has a major influence on the results of civil litigation and frequently determines whether justice is done. This worldwide review creates a foundational understanding of the difficulties faced by unrepresented litigants, including as institutional biases, procedural complexity, and a lack of legal knowledge.

Sande and Buhai's (2009) study is the first that was determined to be pertinent to the current investigation. Sande's research in the US reveals that the justice system often disadvantages ordinary Americans who cannot afford legal assistance, are not eligible for free aid, or must represent themselves in court. This disequilibrium leads to unfair access to justice, as unrepresented litigants often have little chance against represented ones, exacerbated by the lack of representation (Sande & Buhai, 2009).

The US has not adequately addressed the issues faced by unrepresented litigants, despite the creation of self-help centres, alternative dispute resolution procedures, and unbundling of legal services. Despite strict judicial activism restrictions, judges may still assist unrepresented plaintiffs under the American adversarial system of justice (Sande & Buhai, 2009). On the other hand, the legal system and the role of the judge are interpreted differently in many civil law nations, giving common people easier access to the court system. In an attempt to increase everyone's access to justice, the American legal system may take some cues from the civil law system (Sande & Buhai, 2009).

Knowlton et al. (2016) conducted a study in the US, focusing on the significant number of family court conflicts, with hundreds of thousands of Americans seeking divorce, separation, or resolution of child-related issues each year (Knowlton et al., 2016). The study reveals that most Americans interact with US courts in family matters, with some hiring lawyers for representation. However, an increasing number of Americans do not have legal counsel for all or part of their cases, as previously noted by Sande and Buhai (2009).

Knowlton et al. (2016) also found that family matters with at least one self-represented party can reach 80–90 percent in certain courts, highlighting the importance of self-representation in legal situations. Courts often overlook litigants' perspectives, highlighting the challenges faced by unrepresented parties in legal situations (e.g., Williams, 2011; Hurter, 2016; Rice, 2022; Solo & Nsengaali, 2022). This information will aid family courts, attorneys, and communities in assisting litigants who do not fit the stereotypical model of two represented parties (Knowlton et al., 2016).

In addition to Sande and Buhai's research, Rice (2022) looked into the obstacles self-represented litigants encountered in their pursuit of justice. Rice's study examines the challenges faced by self-representing litigants in court, utilising John Rawls' theory of justice, despite the increasing prevalence of self-representation in the legal system, based on the Judiciary Act of 1789, which allows parties to handle their cases through a defence attorney or on their own.

Rice (2022) confirmed previous research (Sande& Buhai, 2009; Knowlton et al., 2016) by analysing participant perspectives obtained through in-depth interviews and showing that structural, economic, political, and doctrinal impediments affected self-represented litigation. These obstacles included the inability to obtain legal information and resources, the high expense of legal proceedings, political meddling, emotional problems on a personal level, unequal access to guns, and a lack of familiarity with the legal system (Rice, 2022).

Rice (2022) suggests improving the availability of legal information, promoting cooperation among parties, and simplifying training initiatives to support self-represented litigants. This could lead to a more accessible legal system for low-income self-represented litigants who cannot afford professional counsel, resulting in positive social change as self-representation litigation becomes more prevalent in the justice system (Rice, 2022).

Still in the global north, Williams (2011) conducted a UK literature review study to analyse the family justice system, focusing on family and civil courts. The study examined the number and nature of in-person litigants, distinguishing them from those with legal representation, the reasons behind in-person filing of lawsuits, the results of in-person litigation compared to those with legal representation, and effective steps for helping litigants face-to-face.

Williams' study, which analysed 1,334 family and 1,098 civil cases, found that unrepresented litigants are common in family matters. The family justice system, often involving violence, abuse, drugs, and alcohol, has long-term ramifications for children, parents, and society. Williams emphasised the need to ensure children and young people's views are heard and understood in decisions made by local authorities and courts, despite the consensus on the strength of the legal framework in the UK (Williams, 2011).

Hurter (2016) studied unrepresented litigants from the global south, specifically focusing on the unrepresented litigant phenomenon's expansion in South Africa. The phenomenon of litigants in person, also known as self-represented litigants or pro se litigants, has gained significant attention in common law countries like the United States, Canada, Britain, and Australia (Hurter, 2016). Professional counsel has been the standard in civil procedures for centuries, despite the right of self-represented litigants in common law. Despite extensive research, unanswered questions remain about self-represented litigants' spread (e.g., Knowlton et al., 2016; Rice, 2022; Solo & Nsengaali, 2022).

All that is certain, though, is that this phenomenon is putting extreme strain on every facet of the various justice systems, including the adversarial system itself (Hurter, 2016). South Africa's judicial administration has not adequately addressed the presence of litigants in person, despite significant advancements in understanding these phenomena in other common law nations. In the report, Hurter (2016) offers valuable suggestions based on the experiences of other common law nations to first mitigate and then manage the effects of such anticipated pressure.

Closer to home, Solo and Nsengaali (2022) studied how unrepresented litigants in Botswana may be impacted by impediments to justice in general and by these barriers in particular. Solo and Nsengaali (2022) highlight the challenges faced by those without literacy in accessing justice, particularly due to the intricate procedures of official courts. The legal system's challenges can lead to disengagement and disorientation, especially among the poor who often lack knowledge about their rights and resources (Solo & Nsengaali, 2022).

Communication between unrepresented litigants and court interpreters

In general, litigants in Zimbabwe face difficulties with interpreters who may not be fluent in their language due to hiring requirements based on bilingual status rather than qualifications, especially during the pre-trial stage where they are not guaranteed the right to an interpreter, and must go through the process without one. Ndlovu (2017, 2023a, 2023b) argues that section 50 of the Constitution's failure to guarantee interpreter rights poses significant challenges to unrepresented litigants, particularly ethnic minority language speakers and those who are deaf or hard of hearing, violating their right to justice.

During the pre-trial stage, unrepresented litigates have to deal with unqualified transpreters and cannot challenge or ascertain the correctness of the statements they are made to sign such that they end up incriminating themselves. Ndlovu (2017, 2023a) observes that the failure to guarantee arrested and detained persons the right to an interpreter means that their sections 50, 69, and 70 rights are also compromised.

Economic barriers to justice for unrepresented litigants

Economic barriers are another type of barrier that Solo and Nsengaali (2022) have identified. The goal of Legal Aid Botswana is to provide legal aid to litigants, particularly the poor, which is a good idea given how expensive litigation may be. A party with more resources can hire better attorneys and employ more effective strategies to win cases, despite the government providing justice, paying for court salaries, and providing necessary facilities for trial (Lasnet, 2015 cited in Solo & Nsengaali, 2022).

According to Solo and Nsengaali (2022), financial resources often impact access to justice, as some litigants choose not to have legal representation. The adversarial legal system can lead to prejudice and unfairness, affecting less privileged individuals and the wealthy. Longer cases result in more expensive litigation, while the wealthy benefit, causing impoverished individuals to settle for less (Solo & Nsengaali, 2022).

Procedural barriers to justice faced by unrepresented litigants

Researchers concur that access to justice is crucial for democratic societies. However, complex procedures in Zimbabwe's courts are often cited as a barrier by unrepresented litigants (Matsikidze, 2014; Ndlovu, 2017). According to Matsikidze (2014), Zimbabwe's initiatives on access to justice primarily focus on substantive law. Matsikidze argues that recent reforms to civil procedure rules were merely a gap-filling exercise, lacking a specific goal and not being inclusive of self-actor litigants. Matsikidze therefore, proposes simplification of civil procedure rules as a key approach to enhance court access and improve justice delivery (Matsikidze, 2014).

The aforementioned studies reveal the challenges unrepresented litigants face in court, including procedural, structural, linguistic, and financial issues. However, there is a significant gap in empirical research on Zimbabwe's experiences of unrepresented litigants, highlighting the need for regional research to guide practices and policies.

Methodology

This qualitative study analysed Zimbabwe's legislative instruments to assess the adequacy of provisions for unrepresented litigants' access to justice. Key documents included the Constitution of Zimbabwe, Court Acts, Magistrates' Department Standard Operating Procedures, and the Law Society of Zimbabwe regarding Tariffs or Fees for Legal Practitioners, which were accessed through document analysis.

Related to these legal documents, the study also analysed case law documents involving unrepresented litigants to understand if they faced challenges that could have been avoided with legal representation. Two cases were selected: *S v Bethe*, a chamber application for late noting of an appeal, and *Mbatha v Ncube and Another*, a chamber application for condonation and extension of time for direct access application due to non-compliance with r 9(7) of the Constitutional Court Rules. Both cases involved unrepresented individuals as appellants.

Apart from case law, the researchers also conducted interviews with stakeholders in the justice system and observed public court proceedings. They identified self-represented cases and compared their handling with trials involving represented litigants. This provided insights into procedural dynamics and interactions between unrepresented litigants and the judiciary. Observation also allowed for demographic data on case types, outcomes, and perceived barriers to justice.

By the end of the data collection period, which lasted four months, the researchers observed 12 cases in Zimbabwe's legal system, including four from civil and eight in criminal cases. The researchers conducted seven in-depth interviews with magistrates, public prosecutors, and six unrepresented participants to understand their experiences of self-representation, perceived efficacy of the legal system, and suggestions for improvements. The data were analysed thematically based on insights from interviews and observations.

In conducting interviews and observations, the study adhered to strict ethical guidelines to protect participants' rights and privacy, ensuring anonymity and secrecy. Participants for in-depth interviews were allowed to exercise their right to refuse answering any questions or leave at any time to minimise potential risks or discomfort.

Theoretical framework

The study analysed data using John Rawl's Theory of Justice and Nancy Fraser's Transformative Equality (Rawl, 1999; Fraser, 1997). The collected data were analysed thematically to allow for the identification of common themes and patterns related to access to justice. Rawl's Theory of Justice advocates for fairness, equal basic rights, and cooperation in an egalitarian economic system. It promotes political liberalism in a democracy, fostering civic unity despite diverse worldviews. Rawl's writings on the law of peoples advocate for liberal policy for a peaceful world order (Rawl, 1999, 2001). John Rawl's theory suggests that political and economic inequalities often lead to social status inequalities, causing lower-status individuals to be perceived as inferior (Rawl, 2001).

To complement John Rawl's Theory of Justice, the researchers also applied Nancy Fraser's Transformative Equality theory (Fraser, 1995, 1999). In her theory, Nancy Fraser presents a range of concepts she uses to explain the crises of injustice in contemporary capitalist societies (including in courts of law), as well as available responses to deal with these crises. These include needs interpretation; dependency and gender justice; participatory parity (e.g., in courts of law) and the economic, political and cultural dimensions of justice; abnormal justice and transformative practices.

The researchers, therefore, used John Rawl's Theory of Justice and Nancy Fraser's Transformative Equality Theory to examine Zimbabwe's law for unrepresented litigants. The researchers observed court accommodations during civil and criminal trials and explored barriers to full participation. They also explored the types of accommodations and reforms the Zimbabwean justice system can make to protect the rights of unrepresented litigants, aligning with Fraser's Transformative Equality theory.

Findings

The chapter examines Zimbabwe's criminal and civil courts to identify challenges faced by unrepresented litigants, revealing significant justice barriers and systemic issues within the judiciary and legal frameworks. The chapter also discusses accommodations made to protect the rights of unrepresented litigants highlighting successes and shortcomings.

Prevalence of unrepresented litigants

Although the study was not quantitative, the analysis of data collected through observation of court proceedings, document analysis, interviews with research participants and according to the figures produced by the Legal Resources Foundation (LRF, 2018) already cited earlier in the chapter, revealed a high incidence of self-representation, particularly in civil cases. Unrepresented litigants were especially prevalent in family law matters confirming a prior study by (Hunter, 1998; Knowlton et al., 2016). Common cases include domestic violence, child maintenance, and small claims, with unrepresented litigants requiring more court time. This inefficiency affects litigants, strains the judicial system, and violates the right to justice. Delays in justice administration violate section 69 of the Constitution, reducing the country's prospects for achieving SDG 16, Agenda 2063, and improved access to justice.

Reasons for self-representation

The findings from interviews and document analysis (e.g., the Law Society of Zimbabwe regarding Tariffs or Fees for Legal Practitioners (USD) With Effect from April 2021) suggest that litigants go unrepresented for a number of reasons. While the major reason cited for example, during interviews was about cost. During interviews, one magistrate's response to the question regarding why the majority of litigants were unrepresented was: *'Money is always the issue, and many people would hire lawyer if they could'*. This finding about legal costs confirmed previous research (e.g., Solo & Nsengaali, 2022; Rice, 2022). The cost barrier to access to justice compromises the JSC's core value of accessibility and principle of accessible justice for all through elimination of cost barriers.

However, other participants believed they were best qualified to present their issues in court, particularly in domestic violence and child maintenance cases. They often acted in person, believing their cases were straightforward. However, some were advised against representation due to cost-benefit analysis and ethical concerns, and some lawyers believed certain situations were simple enough for clients to manage themselves.

Finally, the study found that most unrepresented participants were aware of legal aid and representation but chose not to seek it due to past unsuccessful attempts. Self-representation was the only option available. Some participants were unaware of legal aid and wanted to learn more about it, as legal aid offices are only found in provincial towns and not in districts, making them physically inaccessible. The study highlights the need for more awareness and accessibility in legal aid services.

Costs of accessing justice

From the researchers' examination of legal documents (e.g., the General Tariff or Fees for Legal Practitioners (USD) With Effect From April 2021) available from the Council of the Law Society of Zimbabwe, the researchers established that legal practitioners are professionally and legally obliged to charge fees for legal work which are fair and reasonable in all circumstances. This is an important professional requirement which ensures that legal fees are fair and uniform for both service providers and clients.

The Law Society of Zimbabwe recommends tariffs for all legal work by practitioners, except for law-imposed tariffs or client-agreed rates. The tariffs document covers fees for legal practitioner and client in civil litigation, criminal and general non-litigious work, but does not cover party and party fees in civil litigation, conveyancing fees, collection commissions, and deceased estate administration fees. This aims to ensure uniformity and consistency in legal practices and services.

In Table 14.1, the researchers present some of the fees charged by lawyers for services as stipulated in the General Tariff or Fees for Legal Practitioners (USD) With Effect From April 2021) of the Law Society of Zimbabwe. The table outlines the fees charged for general professional services, including time spent by legal practitioners in performing their mandates, such as taking instructions, attending court, researching, preparing, drafting, dictation, and perusing letters and documents. The researchers focused on the time lawyers spent attending court trials. The charge for general services is per hour and depends on the lawyer's years of experience in the law field, as shown in Table 14.1.

Table 14.1 Fees for General Professional Services

	Years of experience	*Basic hourly ranges*
1	30 years and over	USD 310.00 – USD 350.00
2	20–29 years and 11 months	USD 270.00 – USD 310.00
3	15 to 19 years	USD 210.00 – USD 270.00
4	10–14 years	USD 150.00 – USD 210. 00
5	5–9 years	USD 120.00 – USD 150. 00
6	2–4 years	USD 90.00 – USD 120.00
7	0–1 year	USD 60.00 – USD 90.00
8	Unregistered law graduate whose name is recorded by the Law Society	USD 30.00 – USD 60.00

(*Source*: Law Society of Zimbabwe, 2021)

Apart from the rates applicable for general professional services, the tariffs document also includes separate fees for such services as preparing a sale agreement, a lease agreement, uncontested divorce, will, company formation, notarial work, shop licence, liquor licence, and a few others.

The applicable fees shown in the document regarding uncontested divorce are as shown here.

Uncontested divorce

The high costs of accessing justice in Zimbabwe cited earlier have led to challenges for many individuals in pursuing their cases to finality. Respondents, including unrepresented litigants, magistrates, and public prosecutors, agreed that all legal fees were unreasonable. Although nominal court fees were nominal, they were not as inhibitive as lawyers' fees. However, appeals fees were on the high side. Interviews revealed that poor women were the worst affected by these inhibitive costs. The results related to legal costs confirm previous research by Bellsmith et al. (2022) who discussed the relationship between poverty legal outcomes.

This compromises the JSC's founding principle of accessible justice for all through the elimination of cost barriers and Strategic Priority 4 of access to justice for all through the elimination of all barriers to justice.

Procedural and linguistics barriers

As observed from case law documents analysed by the researchers, unrepresented litigants had their cases dismissed on procedural grounds because of their failure to understand and apply required procedures in filling their appeals. From the two cases analysed, the unrepresented appellants at the High Court and the Constitutional Court respectively, had their appeals dismissed because both judges did not see any prospects of success of the appeals.

In *Mbatha v Ncube and Another*, for example, the applicant in the matter was a self-actress seeking the indulgence of this Court to be granted condonation for non-compliance with the Rules. On 29 March 2023, the applicant's application for direct access to the Supreme Court under Case No. CCZ

(with or without consent paper, with minimal negotiations and including appearance in court, where necessary)

(i) For Plaintiff USD 1,200.00
(ii) For Defendant USD 800.00

Figure 14.1 Fees for Uncontested Divorce

(*Source*: Law Society of Zimbabwe, 2021)

55/22 was struck off the roll due to her failure to effect proper service on the first respondent. The applicant's appeal was dismissed due to the applicant's failure to follow the court's rules, which stipulate that the applicant must not evict the first respondent from his property, as the case has been deadlocked since 2016. The rules state that:

> One cannot institute an action or application in the High Court, or any other court, without due observance of and compliance with the Rules of that court. The Rules inform a litigant of what is required of him to access the court concerned. If he fails to observe or comply with those Rules, he will inevitably be non-suited.
>
> (Justice Patel citing Justice Makarau, 2023)

The two cases highlighted the challenges faced by unrepresented individuals in court proceedings. Their continued appeals exhibited their inability to comprehend court procedures and unsubstantiated allegations of unfair treatment by lower courts. These cases highlight the procedural difficulties unrepresented litigants face in legal proceedings. If represented, lawyers would have provided appropriate advice and avoided costly appeals.

Research participants and observations of court trials revealed numerous procedural hurdles faced by unrepresented litigants, including difficulties in filling documents, linguistic inaccessibility of court records, and unavailability of interpreters. These issues often result in delays in proceedings and negatively impact the justice system's efficiency. Challenges include illiteracy, functional illiteracy in English, difficulty understanding legal language, and pressure to meet court times. These issues can lead to delays in proceedings and a negative impact on the justice system's efficiency.

With respect to inaccessibility of court records it was noted that most litigants are functionally illiterate in English, the language of record in courts and there is no guarantee for free translation services. The Court Acts do not guarantee public access to courts and court records in fluently spoken languages or accessible communication for persons with disabilities. They also do not provide access to interpreters or translation services, and the proceedings are in English, a language many people are functionally illiterate in (see Ndlovu, 2017, 2023a, 2023b). In view of the unavailability of qualified interpreters during the pre-trial stage and lawyer-client interactions, legal practitioners noted that the right to an interpreter is more fundamental during the foundational phase of a case than during the trial, but not guaranteed during pre-trial and lawyer-client interactions, potentially compromising the right to justice.

As regards court etiquette and procedures, the researchers observed that some unrepresented litigants had challenges understanding court etiquette, especially the use of address terms such as *Changamire* or *Mambo* (Your Honour or Your Worship). Others failed to understand the purpose of cross-examination, leading to failures in court proceedings. In one instance, when an unrepresented accused was asked to cross-examine an unrepresented complainant, the cross-examination became chaotic, making it challenging for the court interpreter. The interpreter had to go beyond her interpretation mandate and intervene in the ensuing conflict and said:

> *Zvisinei, hamufaniri kuitisana nharo. Chenyu kubvunzana nekupindurana chete Zviri kudare kuona chokwadi kana manyepo.* (Nevertheless, you two should not argue about issues here. Your responsibility is limited to asking and responding to questions only. It is the court's duty to decide on what is true and what is false.)

This intervention by the interpreter was necessitated by the fact that the cross-examination between the unrepresented accused and complainant degenerated into a street argument against the strict rules of courtroom etiquette or decorum. Besides, the litigants were also not clear about the issue(s) in dispute during the cross-examination. From that way of cross-examination, the court could not judge the accused and complainant thereby defeating the whole purpose of cross-examination.

In addition, some unrepresented litigants could not use court official terms correctly, which is a crucial politeness marker that can be manipulated. These markers are a result of courtroom conventions that require certain participants, such as interpreters, lawyers, and litigants, to show respect to the court. Courts may also use these politeness markers to assess the litigant's credibility and trustworthiness (Rigney, 1999; Hale, 2004). Just consider the following example and see how the litigant leaves out the term of address and how the interpreter includes it her interpretation:

Interpreter: *Wanzwisisa mhosva yauri kupomerwa?* (Have you understood the allegations being levelled against you by the state?)
Accused: *Hongu* (Yes)
Interpreter: Yes, Your Worship

Because the unrepresented accused person in the preceding interaction was appearing in court as a first-time offender, he was not aware of courtroom etiquette and the importance of showing respect to the court. As a result, he just responded to the questions asked without including the terms of address. However, from the observation of cases involving repeat offenders, such terms of address occurred more frequently in litigants' questions and answers.

Turning to Zimbabwe, literature on the nation's legal system reveals a landscape marked by both colonial legacies and contemporary challenges (Svongoro & Kadenge, 2015). Svongoro and Kadenge (2015) for example, discuss how historical inequities continue to influence access to justice, particularly for marginalised groups. Despite Zimbabwe's adoption of progressive legal frameworks intended to enhance access to justice, such as the Legal Aid Directorate established under the Judicial Service Act, empirical studies on their effectiveness remain scarce.

The preceding findings confirm previous research on the challenges faced by those without legal representation, highlighting the complexity of legal procedures, psychological stress, and the daunting nature of the adversarial system (e.g., Moorhead & Mark, 2005; Rice, 2022). In Zimbabwe, the lack of structured support systems exacerbates these issues, highlighting the need for targeted reforms.

Psychological and emotional stress and perceived bias and inequality

The emotional impact of self-representation on litigants emerged as a common issue in this study, with many experiencing intimidation and stress when facing opposing lawyers or navigating court processes. This can hinder their ability to advocate effectively. Unrepresented litigants often feel overwhelmed by the complexity of legal procedures and jargon, and the absence of accessible legal information and resources is a critical obstacle, making it difficult for them to prepare their cases effectively.

In addition to the preceding, interviews with most unrepresented litigants revealed that a perception of bias against unrepresented litigants was evident during trials. Some respondents indicated that their cases were not taken as seriously as those of represented parties. This perception extended to treatment by court personnel and the judiciary, with concerns raised about fairness, impartiality, and speedily administration of justice.

Judicial accommodations

During interviews with magistrates and public prosecutors, dominant narratives indicated that while some magistrates and public prosecutors made efforts to accommodate unrepresented litigants by simplifying language or explaining procedures, the researchers' observation revealed that such practices were not uniformly observed across all courtrooms. Variability in judicial approach significantly affected the litigants' ability to participate effectively in their cases.

Discussion of findings

The findings from this study highlight challenges faced by unrepresented litigants in Zimbabwe's courtrooms, including lack of legal knowledge or procedural guidance, emotional stress, and perceived systemic biases, which hinder their ability to identify disputes, understand litigation purposes, and reconcile law with social or moral justice (see Gamble & Mohr, 1998; Moorhead, 2003; Moorhead & Mark, 2005; Sande & Buhai, 2009; Hurter, 2016; Solo & Nsengaali, 2022). In the case of Zimbabwe, the study highlights the challenges in the court system, particularly in terms of judicial accommodations and efficiency, and suggests that further research is needed to address these gaps and ensure justice for all, regardless of representation status.

Towards transformative equality

As explained earlier in the theoretical section, Fraser (1995, 1999) emphasises the need for certain institutions (e.g., institutions of justice) to be reformed to address crises of injustice in contemporary societies. These reforms may include expanding gender justice and increasing participatory parity (e.g., in courts of law between represented and unrepresented litigant). In the context of this chapter, the researchers identified various accommodations that courts of law in Zimbabwe can adopt to increase access to justice by unrepresented litigants.

Zimbabwe's justice institutions can enhance access to justice for unrepresented litigants by establishing dedicated support services within court systems, such as help desks and legal clinics, staffed by legal professionals and volunteers. Public legal education initiatives can also be enhanced to improve legal literacy among the general population. Legal aid guides and online platforms can be developed to provide essential information on legal procedures and rights for all citizens.

Apart from support services and the development of legal resources, the justice system should create training programmes for magistrates, public prosecutors, and court personnel to accommodate unrepresented litigants, focusing on communication strategies, procedural fairness, and bias mitigation. Standardised guidelines should promote consistency in judicial accommodations, and free translation services should be provided to accommodate language preferences, including those illiterate in English. Qualified interpreters should be guaranteed at all stages of the legal process.

Furthermore, human rights organisations can advocate for legal reforms to simplify court procedures and increase legal aid availability, especially in self-representation areas. Alternative dispute resolution mechanisms can alleviate court system burdens. Academics and researchers can conduct longitudinal studies to monitor reforms' impact on unrepresented litigants and explore intersectionality of challenges faced by marginalised groups.

Rawl (2001) and Fraser (1999) emphasise the importance of justice as a fundamental human right. They highlight the significant gaps in access to justice for unrepresented litigants in Zimbabwe, urging all stakeholders to work together to dismantle these barriers (Fraser, 1999). Through targeted reforms, Zimbabwe can achieve an accessible, equitable, and efficient legal system through targeted reforms, ensuring alignment with international best practice and standards. This will enhance the country's prospects of achieving SDG 16, Aspirations 3 and 4 of Agenda 2063, and the effective realisation of JSC's core values, principles, and strategic priorities, leading to improved access to justice.

Conclusions

This chapter sought to examine the barriers faced by unrepresented litigants in Zimbabwe's justice system and whether the country's law and courtrooms adequately support their participation in the trial process. The findings presented in this chapter reveal significant challenges, including procedural complexities, lack of legal knowledge, language barriers, emotional stress, and perceived biases, which not only undermine the principle of fair trial but also strain the judicial system's efficiency. These procedural and linguistic obstacles also undermine the Judicial Service Commission's motto of 'delivering world-class justice' in Zimbabwe. Furthermore, the obstacles hinder Zimbabwe's progress towards fulfilling SDG 16's goal of access to justice, particularly Target 16.3 and Target 11.10 of Agenda 2063. They reduce the prospects of achieving the JSC's Strategic Plan priorities and aspirations in NDS1 of improved access to justice for all. The chapter, therefore, underscores the need for comprehensive reforms and initiatives to improve access to justice, ensuring that all individuals can navigate the legal system effectively and fairly, regardless of their legal representation.

References

Bellsmith, I., Goertzen, O., Neilsen, K., & Stinson, O. (2022, February 3). *Poverty and access to justice review of the literature research report 2022–2.* Report presented to the National Advisory Council on Poverty Vancouver. International Centre for Criminal Law Reform. https://icclr.org

Fraser, N. (1995). From redistribution to recognition? Dilemmas of justice in a 'post socialist' age. *New Left Review*, *212*, 68–93.

Fraser, N. (1997). *Justice interruptus: Critical reflections on the 'post-socialist' condition.* Routledge.

Fraser, N. (1999). Social justice in the age of identity politics: Redistribution, recognition, and participation. In L. Ray & A. Sayer (Eds.), *Culture and economy after the cultural turn* (pp. 25–52). Sage.

Gamble, H., & Mohr, R. (1998, September 4–6). *Litigants in person in the federal court of Australia and the administrative appeals tribunal: A research note.* Paper presented to Australian Institute of Judicial Administration 16th Annual Conference.

Hale, S. (2004). *The discourse of court interpreting: Discourse practices of the law, the witness and the interpreter.* John Benjamins.

Hunter, R. (1998). Litigants in person in contested cases in the family court. *Australian Journal of Family Law*, *12.*

Hurter, E. (2016). The litigant in person and the access to justice dilemma: *Quo vadis* South Africa. *The Comparative and International Law Journal of Southern Africa*, *49*(3), 428–454. https://www.jstor.org/stable/26367610

Knowlton, N. A., Cornett, L., Corina, D., Gerety, C. D., & Drobinske, L. J. (2016). *Cases without counsel: Research on experiences of self-representation in US family court.* Institute for the Advancement of the American Legal System, University of Denver.

Law Society of Zimbabwe. (2021). *General tariff or fees for legal practitioners (USD) with effect from April 2021.* Law Society of Zimbabwe.

The Legal Resources Foundation. (2018). *Justice delivery sector survey.* The Legal Resources Foundation.

Maja, I. (2007). *Constitutional framework for the protection of language rights of linguistic minorities in Zimbabwe.* Retrieved from https://zimlii.org/akn/zw/doc/book-chapter/2020-06-30/chapter-10-constitutional-framework-for-the-protection-of-language-rights-of-linguistic-minorities-in-zimbabwe/eng@2020-06-30

Matsikidze, R. (2014). *The civil procedure in the magistrates court of Zimbabwe: A denial of justice to self-actors?* [Unpublished M.Phil. thesis, University of Zimbabwe].
Mbatha v Ncube and Another (7 of 2023) [2023] ZWCC 7 (2023, June 26).
Moorhead, R. (2003). Access or aggravation? Litigants in person, McKenzie friends and lay representation. *Civil Justice Quarterly*, *22*, 133–155.
Moorhead, R., & Mark, S. (2005). Litigants in person: Unrepresented litigants in first instance proceedings. DCA Research Series 2/05. https://orca.cardiff.ac.uk/id/eprint/2956/1/1221.pdf.
Ndlovu, E. (2017). A critical analysis of the provisions of statutory instruments and policy documents relating to court interpreting in Zimbabwe: A case study of selected sections. *Zambezia*, *44*(ii), 1–19.
Ndlovu, E. (2023a). The right to an interpreter in the Zimbabwean justice system: The missing link. *Journal of African Languages and Literary Studies*, *4*(1), 17–45.
Ndlovu, E. (2023b). The open court principle in Zimbabwe: A language rights perspective. *Southern African Linguistics and Applied Language Studies*, *2023*, 1–14.
Rawls, J. (1999). *A theory of justice*. Harvard University Press.
Rawls, J. (2001). *Justice as fairness: A restatement*. Harvard University Press.
Rice, D. F. (2022). *What are the barriers experienced by self-represented litigants in civil court?* [Unpublished doctoral thesis, Walden University].
Rigney, A. C. (1999). Questioning in interpreted testimony. *Forensic Linguistics*, *6*(1), 83–108.
S v Bethe (665 of 2023) [2023] ZWHHC 567 (2023, December 14).
Sande, L., & Buhai, J. (2009). Access to justice for unrepresented litigants: A comparative perspective. *Loyola of Los Angeles Law Review*, *42*, 979. https://digitalcommons.lmu.edu/llr/vol42/iss4/5
Solo, K., & Nsengaali, P. G. (2022). Access to justice in Botswana. *Beijing Law Review*, *13*, 489–495. https://doi.org/10.4236/blr.2022.133030
Svongoro, P., & Kadenge, M. (2015). From language to society: An analysis of interpreting quality and the linguistic rights of the accused in selected Zimbabwean courtrooms. *Southern African Linguistics and Applied Language Studies, 33*(1), 47–62.
United Nations Office on Drugs and Crime. (UNODC). (2011). *Access to legal aid in criminal justice systems in Africa: Survey report*. United Nations.
Williams, K. (2011). *Litigants in person: A literature review*. Ministry of Justice.

15 The impact of litigants' socio-economic status on the delivery of justice

The plight of the poor and illiterate in Zimbabwe's rural magistrate courts

Josephat Mutangadura and Felistus Tafadzwa Makumbe

Introduction

The administration of justice in Zimbabwe, particularly in its rural magistrate courts, involves a distinct combination of socio-economic and legal obstacles that have a greater impact on individuals who are poor and illiterate. These courts play a crucial role in delivering justice to the extensive and varied rural areas of the country, frequently serving as the initial and sole interaction point with the legal system for rural inhabitants. Nevertheless, the difficult situation faced by the poor and illiterate individuals in these environments emphasises a harsh truth: one's socio-economic standing significantly influences one's experience and results within the legal system. This study examines the challenges disadvantaged and illiterate rural residents experience in seeking justice. By examining the underlying structural disparities that impact the delivery of justice, it seeks to provide actionable solutions for enhancing access to justice. The study demonstrates how disadvantaged and illiterate defendants are more susceptible in court due to lack of legal rights knowledge, inadequate legal counsel, and institutional prejudices. This study concludes that socio-economic factors affect justice delivery in rural Zimbabwe for various reasons, including socio-economic imbalances that must be addressed.

Background of the study

Poverty is a major factor in Zimbabwe's limited availability of legal assistance, as a significant portion of the population is below the poverty threshold. This lack of financial means makes it difficult for legal aid organisations to provide adequate support, leading to challenges for many Zimbabweans. The geographic distribution of Zimbabwe's population also complicates access to legal assistance, as many residents live in isolated regions distant from legal aid providers. Legal aid organisations primarily operate in urban areas, excluding those in rural areas. The absence of transit services, internet

DOI: 10.4324/9781003569435-20

connectivity, and physical infrastructure further exacerbates the situation, further hindering the ability of these organisations to extend their services to remote areas. Justice in Zimbabwe often faces discrepancies, particularly for poor and uneducated individuals accused of crimes. These individuals face numerous socio-economic obstacles, such as high costs of legal proceedings, court travel, and potential income loss. Illiteracy also exacerbates marginalisation, limiting their understanding of legal proceedings and the severity of accusations. These inequalities hinder their ability to effectively navigate the legal system, defend against charges, and obtain legal representation. The principle of impartiality and fairness is crucial in ensuring justice for all.

The difficulties encountered by marginalised individuals in obtaining justice in rural locations can be impacted by variables such as financial limitations, and inadequate understanding of the law and the workings of the judicial system (Koroma, 2023). The unequal access to legal services due to economic status can worsen the difficulties experienced by the poor individuals residing in rural areas. Another research conducted by Mack and Roach Anleu (2007) highlights the significance of judge craft in subordinate courts, as magistrates skilfully traverse adversarial norms and practices in order to attain valid decision-making. The study, therefore, explores the difficulties faced by magistrates in balancing procedural obligations with the need for equitable and impartial outcomes, particularly for those economically disadvantaged and with limited literacy.

The legal court system in Zimbabwe

Zimbabwe's court system operates within a hierarchical structure based on the principles of English common law, inherited from its colonial past. The judiciary is independent, and the courts handle both civil and criminal matters. Zimbabwe's legal system is based on a mixture of Roman-Dutch law and English common law. Appeals typically move up from the Magistrates' Courts to the High Court, and then to the Supreme Court. Constitutional matters are referred to the Constitutional Court. The court system recognises both statutory law (as applied in Magistrates' and higher courts) and customary law (as applied in Local Courts).

1. Constitutional Court

The Constitutional Court is the highest court in Zimbabwe for constitutional matters. It has the final say in interpreting the constitution and protecting citizens' rights under the constitution. It handles cases involving constitutional interpretation, disputes over presidential elections, and fundamental rights and freedoms. It also hears appeals in cases that involve constitutional matters. As the highest court for constitutional issues, it ensures that laws and government actions comply with the Constitution of Zimbabwe.

2. Supreme Court

The Supreme Court is the highest appellate court for non-constitutional matters. It handles appeals from the High Court and lower courts. It has jurisdiction over both civil and criminal matters. The Supreme Court ensures the consistent interpretation of the law across Zimbabwe and provides legal precedents for lower courts.

3. High Court

The High Court deals with serious criminal and civil cases and has original jurisdiction in most major cases. It handles serious criminal cases such as murder, rape, and high-value civil cases. The High Court also has jurisdiction over election petitions and certain administrative matters. It has divisions such as the Civil Division and Criminal Division, and there are regional branches of the High Court in different cities, including Harare and Bulawayo.

4. Labour Court

The Labour Court handles disputes related to employment, labour laws, and workers' rights. This court addresses matters such as unfair dismissal, disputes between employees and employers, and cases involving trade unions. The Labour Court ensures that Zimbabwean labour laws are upheld and provides a specialised venue for employment-related cases.

5. Administrative Court

The Administrative Court deals with cases involving administrative actions by government bodies. It hears appeals from decisions made by government bodies, such as those concerning licensing, land, and broadcasting. It acts as a check on administrative powers in Zimbabwe. The Administrative Court ensures that government decisions are lawful and made according to due process.

6. Magistrates' Courts

Magistrates' Courts handle the bulk of Zimbabwe's criminal and civil cases at a lower level. They handle less serious criminal cases (such as petty theft and traffic offences) and civil cases involving lower amounts of money. Magistrates' Courts are also involved in family law cases like divorce and child custody. Magistrates' Courts are spread across Zimbabwe and are the first point of contact for most legal matters.

7. Customary Law Courts (Local Courts)

These courts handle cases that are governed by customary law, particularly in rural areas. They deal with issues such as inheritance, marriage, and other family disputes within the framework of local customs and traditions. Customary Law Courts provide a legal platform that is sensitive to the cultural and traditional practices of local communities. They are normally presided over by traditional leaders within the communities.

Zimbabwe's unique historical, cultural, and socio-economic context mirrors global patterns but also presents unique challenges. Rural magistrate courts are crucial for poor and illiterate individuals, allowing for analysis of how socio-economic and literacy factors impact justice outcomes. Existing literature suggests a need for specific actions and changes to ensure fair and equal access to justice for all Zimbabweans.

Methodology

This is a qualitative study that drew its data from interviews and analysis of selected legal documents. The study used case studies of rural magistrate courts in two districts of Zimbabwe to examine socio-economic effects on justice delivery. This method provides for a detailed assessment of legal processes, accused challenges, and rural justice system functioning. Two magistrates, a human rights lawyer, and former convicts were interviewed through semi-structured questions. The magistrates assisted with identifying willing participants after explaining. The interviews sought to understand personal experiences, fairness, and difficulties in navigating the legal system. A review of court records and legal documents, specifically charge sheets and case records, revealed sentencing trends and patterns, as well as poor and illiterate defendant representation rates. The study received ethical approval from the appropriate institutional review boards. Prior to participation, all participants were told about the research's goal, and their consent was obtained. The study ensured the preservation of confidentiality and anonymity for all participants, particularly defendants, in order to safeguard their names and personal data. The qualitative data from interviews and courtroom observations is analysed using thematic analysis, allowing for the identification of common themes and patterns related to access to justice for the poor and illiterate.

Literature review

The intersection of socio-economic status, literacy, and access to justice is a critical area of inquiry within the realm of legal studies and social justice. This literature review explores existing research and theoretical frameworks that shed light on how these factors influence justice delivery, with a particular focus on rural settings similar to those in Zimbabwe.

Socio-economic status and access to justice

Research has consistently shown that socio-economic status significantly impacts an individual's access to the justice system, with low-income individuals often unable to afford legal representation, affecting the quality of defence and outcomes in legal proceedings (Sandefur, 2008). The economic burden of legal engagement, including travel costs and lost wages, disproportionately affects the poor, deterring them from seeking legal recourse. Fair trials in rural African magistrate courts are crucial as they intersect with socio-economic status, racial inequities, and institutionalised inequalities. Rural courts tend to have more bias, leading to greater intervention for African Americans compared to metropolitan courts (Leiber & Fox, 2005). Magnus and Donohue (2021) posit that poverty, limited transit, childcare, and self-help options also impede equitable access to justice in rural areas. These socio-economic challenges highlight the challenges faced by residents in rural African areas in accessing legal remedies. Magistrate roles in rural judicial systems include resolving access to justice inequities and achieving fairness (Statz, 2022). They affect rural court decisions. Ragusa (2012) found that rural Australian women seeking legal help for intimate partner violence face social inequalities such as anonymity and poor resource availability. These special barriers can inhibit women victims of assault from accessing equal legal proceedings. Entrenched legal system discrepancies also affect equitable access to impartial trials. Omori and Petersen (2020) note that judicial institutions affect racial and ethnic differences in custody, conviction, and sentencing. They indicate legal system structural concerns cause unequal treatment, especially in rural areas. Koroma (2023) notes that financial hurdles can prevent disadvantaged rural litigants from using formal justice institutions, forcing them to use customary venues. This shows the intricate interaction between rural African socio-economic conditions, institutional frameworks, and legal access.

The intersection of gender and legal representation significantly impacts the ability to achieve equitable trials. Chenwi (2022) highlights the African Court's role in promoting human rights and gender equality through women's rights protection. Feld and Schaefer (2010) argue that geographical factors, particularly in rural courts, can decrease fairness, emphasising the need to address discrepancies in legal results. Geographical variables can significantly impact the equity of judicial processes, especially in regions with limited resources.

Equity requires considering varied perspectives and life experiences in legal decision-making. Smaller rural courts may lack resources, influencing legal representation and outcomes (Zane et al., 2020). The sort of juvenile justice legal representation affects case results. Brady and Peck (2021) stress the relevance of courtroom participants in moulding juvenile justice by examining how different styles of legal representation affect juvenile court cases. For fairness, legal proceedings must address minors' specific requirements. Gaines (2007) also examines how African American males' socio-economic status influences judicial trust and psychological discomfort, demonstrating the link between socio-economic status and legal system attitudes. Moore (2013) emphasises how previous legal apartheid has left racial inequities in the judicial system, affecting fair trials. These findings imply that historical and institutional factors influence marginalised communities' justice views and relationships. Socio-economic position, institutional inequalities, gender dynamics, legal representation, and geographical limits affect fair trials in rural African magistrate courts. Addressing these issues and creating a fair judicial system accessible to all requires identifying and removing barriers to impartial legal processes in remote locations.

Literacy and legal outcomes

Literacy plays a pivotal role in justice delivery as it affects individuals' understanding of their legal rights, the charges against them, and the proceedings of the court. Studies have highlighted the disadvantage faced by illiterate accused, who are less likely to comprehend legal documents, communicate effectively with legal counsel, or participate meaningfully in their defence (United Nations Office on Drugs and Crime, 2016). This disadvantage extends to the accessibility of legal information and services, where literacy is a prerequisite for engaging with legal resources and support systems.

Legal aid for the poor and illiterate in Zimbabwe

Legal aid is universally acknowledged as a crucial component in the administration of justice. Many individuals in societies lack the financial means to seek legal advice or legal aid, making it crucial for them to exercise their rights. Around 80 percent of Africa's population, including Zimbabwe, lives in rural areas with limited access to legal services (Manase, 1992). The government alone is insufficient in providing satisfactory services, leading to Non-Governmental Organisations (NGOs) needing to enhance their services. NGOs have effectively promoted human rights in the Third World, relying on projects and collaborations with other developmental groups (Othman & von Riesen, 2001). The Legal Resources Foundation has contributed to education and guidance on legal entitlements, but many rural residents are unaware of their legal rights.

The International Commission of Jurists has partnered with various NGOs in developing countries to provide legal assistance to impoverished rural communities (Manase, 1992, p. 79). In Zimbabwe, the court assigns lawyers to individuals facing death-related offences who lack the financial means to hire legal representation. However, the Legal Resource Foundation (LRF) can also play a crucial role in providing legal aid. The National Assembly has enacted legislation on legal aid provision, and the Ministry of Justice and Legal Affairs has established a Directorate for Legal Aid. Other organisations, such as the Women Lawyers' Association and the Zimbabwe Law Society, can also play a significant role. Zimbabwe can implement a policy requiring private lawyers or advocates to handle at least 10 percent of their annual cases pro bono (Othman & von Riesen, 2001). The LRF collaborates with other NGOs, including Lawyers for Human Rights, to handle test cases, which may involve court interpretation or constitutional examination of legislation. The International Commission of Jurists (ICJ) has been organising a series of seminars across

Asia, Africa, and Latin America to promote the provision of legal services in rural areas, which are predominantly inhabited by the majority of the population. The objective is to explore strategies for ensuring that the rural impoverished population has access to fundamental legal services that are typically accessible to wealthier individuals. The purpose of these seminars is to convince practising lawyers, law teachers, and law students to educate grassroots development organisations on how the law may be utilised as a tool to assist the rural impoverished.

Currently, several organisations provide legal aid to the poor and illiterate in Zimbabwe, helping to bridge the gap in access to justice for these vulnerable populations. Key organisations include:

(i) Legal Resources Foundation (LRF): The Legal Resources Foundation (LRF) in Zimbabwe is dedicated to promoting human rights and access to justice by providing legal education, services, and advocacy. It aims to empower people with legal information and assist them in navigating the legal system, targeting the poor and marginalised in both urban and rural areas.

(ii) Zimbabwe Lawyers for Human Rights (ZLHR): The ZLHR safeguards and upholds human rights through litigation, legal advice, and representation, offering free legal assistance to those who have been violated, particularly the poor and those facing unfair legal proceedings in rural magistrate courts. They have gained popularity during political persecution, particularly in rural areas where opposition voices are often targeted.

(iii) World Vision, renowned for its humanitarian efforts, also supports vulnerable communities through legal aid projects, advocating for legal rights and providing legal education to empower community members.

(iv) Mercy Corps, an international organisation, operates in Zimbabwe to assist the most vulnerable through legal assistance programmes. It focuses on community development and provides resources for legal assistance.

(v) Catholic Relief Services (CRS): CRS partners with local organisations for capacity building and sustainable practices, often providing legal aid and advocacy to underserved communities through strategic partnerships.

Establishment of the Legal Resource Foundation

The Legal Resources Foundation, established in 1984, is a philanthropic trust that focuses on providing legal aid and education to impoverished individuals (Manase, 1992). It was established through a Trust Deed and began its activities on 1 July 1985. The foundation comprises 14 Trustees – including Chief Justice of Zimbabwe, Hon. E Dumbutshena, Dean of the Law Faculty at the University of Zimbabwe, Professor Reg Austin, Vice-Chancellor of the University of Zimbabwe, Professor Walter Kamba, High Court judge, Justice Ahmed Ebrahim, Bishop Mutume, Chairman of the Catholic Bishops'

Conference – social workers, educationists, and lawyers (Manase, 1992). The Foundation's aims and objectives included the following:

- to initiate and support projects that facilitate the development of legal resources in Zimbabwe;
- to establish and maintain a law library or libraries that are accessible to all individuals and organisations in Zimbabwe;
- to train paralegal personnel and provide them with necessary support;
- to promote public legal education;
- to contribute to legal research and legal publications;
- to assist in the training of law students, legal practitioners, persons holding judicial office, court staff and administrators;
- to support organisations which provide legal advice and assistance to the public;
- to initiate law reform; and
- to engage in or provide assistance for any related activities which, in the opinion of the Trustees, are likely to further the interests of law and justice in Zimbabwe.

(Manase, 1992, p. 180)

Global and regional perspectives

Comparative studies from regions with similar socio-economic and legal landscapes, such as rural India and sub-Saharan Africa, highlight the challenges faced by the poor and illiterate in accessing justice. These studies emphasise the need for legal aid, community legal education, and reforms to make the justice system more accessible and responsive to marginalised populations (Barendrecht, 2011). The intersection of poverty, lack of education, and the justice system creates a complex web of challenges that hinder access to fair legal processes. Shariah, a religious concept, is crucial in fostering socio-economic justice in Islamic cultures (Zauro et al., 2020). Addressing monetary obstacles is essential for marginalised individuals in Zimbabwe's rural magistrate courts (Koroma, 2023). The interconnectedness of environmental and social justice is also evident in Tehran, where the availability of green spaces in metropolitan areas is linked to socio-economic inequalities (Roodsari & Hoseini, 2021). A comprehensive perspective is needed to tackle the complex obstacles faced by impoverished individuals and the lack of education in seeking justice.

Socio-economic variables in legal and environmental frameworks can make systems fairer for everyone, including rural populations. To promote socio-economic equality in legal systems, youth justice delivery systems should move from punitive to more efficient, inclusive treatments that address young offenders' socio-economic conditions (Case & Haines, 2018). In Ukraine's administrative justice improvement, economic factors and legal procedures are interconnected, highlighting the need to understand how socio-economic conditions affect access to justice for impoverished and illiterate people

(Korniienko, 2024). It also shows the challenge of handling justice issues in quickly changing urban contexts, needing a strategy that incorporates the socio-economic effects of justice administration for different demographic groups (Sengupta & Sengupta, 2022). Restorative justice can benefit young people in court disputes by addressing socio-economic conditions that cause crime (Cassell, 2021). A holistic approach to rehabilitation can reduce recidivism and improve outcomes. Improving general practitioner recruitment in impoverished and rural areas requires addressing healthcare delivery socio-economic inequalities. Better legal outcomes can result from expanding justice access for economically disadvantaged and illiterate people.

The fourth industrial revolution in South Africa shows how technology affects socio-economic dynamics and justice delivery (Mtotywa et al., 2022). Understanding these developments is essential for adapting legal systems to rural marginalised communities. Colombia's resilience and transitional justice demonstrate how socio-economic factors affect post-conflict justice (Weber, 2021). Transitional justice can promote peace and stability by meeting war victims' socio-economic needs. Moral implications of the global basic structure as an issue of justice highlight systemic socio-economic justice ethics (Corvino, 2019). Socio-economic justice in post-transitional cultures like Tunisia is difficult, especially with disruptive reparations (Destrooper, 2023).

Understanding and negotiating complex socio-economic processes can create more efficient restitution procedures for marginalised groups. Prioritising socio-economic considerations in transitional justice procedures is crucial, as demonstrated by the shift in compensations for cholera victims in Haiti (Lemay-Hébert & Freedman, 2021). Adopting a comprehensive strategy for reparations can lead to more lasting solutions for communities impacted by violence and injustice. The post-apartheid era in South Africa's municipalities reveals socio-economic justice issues causing urban unrest (Ngcamu, 2019). This perspective is relevant to understanding the fundamental conflicts affecting justice and legal outcomes in rural Zimbabwe. Resilience-building tactics are crucial in addressing socio-economic disparities, as they help disadvantaged groups recover from challenges and establish fair legal systems (Diržytė et al., 2017). This approach addresses the specific needs of impoverished and lack of literacy groups, ensuring fair and just outcomes in legal systems.

Illiteracy and legal justice

Illiteracy significantly affects defendants' understanding of legal proceedings, rights, and court involvement. Studies show that defendants' perceptions of procedural fairness influence their adherence to court orders and outcomes (Dollar et al., 2018). Lack of literacy can lead to misconceptions and unjust treatment. Research on financial inclusion in underdeveloped nations also highlights the negative impact of illiteracy on accessing services (Hoque et al., 2015). Therefore, addressing illiteracy is crucial for ensuring fair treatment and promoting justice.

Likewise, rural defendants who cannot read may struggle with legal paperwork, legal counsel interactions, and court arguments, potentially worsening socio-economic inequalities and isolating marginalised individuals. Emotional communication is crucial in legal procedures, as illiterate defendants may struggle to understand information, leading to misunderstandings and misinterpretations (Song & Zhao, 2023). This can affect the fairness of the legal process. Legal representation is essential for equitable treatment in court proceedings, as illiterate defendants may struggle to comprehend their rights, engage in plea negotiations, or present a defence (Zane et al., 2020). This lack of understanding can hinder their meaningful participation in judicial proceedings and effective advocacy for themselves. Therefore, legal representation is crucial for ensuring fair treatment for all defendants. Illiteracy in rural areas hinders rural defendants' access to fair justice, hindering their ability to understand legal information, communicate with legal experts, and comprehend court proceedings. To overcome these challenges, customised measures like simplified legal documents, linguistic assistance, and adequate legal counsel are needed, ensuring that individuals with low literacy levels can navigate the legal system fairly.

Findings

The study uses primary and secondary sources. It interviewed magistrates, a human rights lawyer, and former convicts from rural courts. The study also uses accessible court records to reveal the number of convicts, cases, and years served.

Socio-economic background of rural cases

The study established that the poor often cannot afford legal representation, leaving them to navigate the complex legal system on their own. This can lead to less effective defence and poorer outcomes in court cases. Studies have shown that those with legal representation are more likely to receive favourable outcomes compared to those without (Manase, 1992). Magistrates interviewed confirmed that most rural cases never have legal representation unless they are high-profile cases.

Magistrate Respondent 1: *In all the time I have worked here, I have not seen many lawyers coming down to represent clients. In most cases, we deal with local rural kind of crimes like village fights, stock theft, etc.*

Magistrate 2: *On isolated cases, I have seen a lawyer come down to represent a client. Currently, only political crimes have sponsored human rights lawyers coming, even in the most remote court sittings. Otherwise, these offenders cannot afford to hire a lawyer.*

Court fees and bail

Bail applications are a basic right for any accused during the trial period. However, they require sufficient arguing to convince the magistrate to grant bail, which is why one needs legal representation.

Human Rights Lawyer: *Economic barriers, such as the inability to pay court fees or post bail, can lead to prolonged pre-trial detention. This not only affects the individual's livelihood but also impacts their ability to prepare an adequate defence. This is common with political detainees who may not find justice without representation.*

Human rights lawyers have become a common occurrence in cases involving political detainees since the feeling is that such charges are mostly trumped up to fix opposing voices and would never be fairly tried, hence the need for robust legal representation.

Former Convict 1: *I did not know I could seek for bail while my case was being tried. I only knew, once inside, serving my sentence.*
Former Convict 2: *I was only able to fight for my freedom after mixing with other convicts, and they advised that my case was simple, and I went back to court even more wise without a lawyer.*

The responses from former convicts indicate that they missed out on an opportunity to get bail granted because they had no representation due to their economic situation. They end up advising each other while in the holding cells in ways that are not always legally professional.

Transportation and accommodation costs

Another sticky issue in this study was accessibility. Rural populations often face significant travel distances to attend court, incurring transportation and accommodation costs that are prohibitive for many. This can lead to missed court appearances and subsequent legal penalties. All magistrates who were interviewed confirmed that some cases had to be decided in the absence of the accused for a number of reasons, but all were classified as absconding. Convicts, on the other hand, revealed they sometimes fail to attend court cases because of a lack of funds to travel or inaccessible locations due to poor road networks. Once the magistrate has concluded and sentenced a person, they now use the law to follow up and apprehend the convict who is not given a chance to explain the reason for their non-appearance.

Former convicts 2, 3, 6, and 7 all confirmed they were sentenced in absentia because they failed to travel to the courts on the appointed day. They gave varied reasons, ranging from lack of travel funds to failure to get any form of transport to make the long journey to the courts due to inaccessibility due to bad roads/weather in poorly developed rural areas. Even if magistrates understand this condition, they are bound by the law to make a final determination and close court cases.

Magistrate 2: *Unfortunately, court procedures consider this non-appearance as absconding. Hence, the judgment is still given in the absence of the accused.*

Illiteracy

Due to illiteracy, rural offenders face considerable obstacles in obtaining justice and guaranteeing just trials. Illiterate individuals encounter significant challenges in comprehending legal proceedings, navigating the judicial system, and adequately representing themselves in court. This part examines the consequences of illiteracy on rural prisoners, emphasising the obstacles they face and the consequences for the principles of justice and fairness.

Understanding legal rights

Illiterate offenders and convicts often lack awareness of their legal rights and the judicial process. This can lead to unintentional self-incrimination or failure to utilise available legal protections. All convicts interviewed acknowledged they never had any knowledge of their legal rights due to their level of education and the fact that some were first offenders.

Former Convict 12: *I never committed a crime in my life before, and did not bother to understand the law.*
Former Convict 8: *I cannot read and write; it is not possible for me to understand as well. I only relied on the magistrate explanations and convictions.*
Magistrate 4: *We try to explain to them about their rights, but you can see they are not comprehending all the legal explanations. Sometimes they just nod in acceptance. What can I do? I must proceed with the sentence.*
Human Rights Lawyer: *Legal literacy programmes are crucial in mitigating this gap (Legal Resource Foundation).*
Human Rights Lawyer: *we travel out into the countryside to give legal education under Legal Resource Foundation in view of this challenge. Unfortunately, we cannot be everywhere due to limited funding and time. The country is large (Nyika yakakura).*

Comprehending legal documents

The inability to read and understand legal documents severely hampers an individual's ability to effectively participate in their defence.

Human Rights Lawyer: *Misunderstandings in courtroom conversations can lead to unfavourable outcomes, such as wrongful convictions or harsher* *sentences. When the accused are put to their defence, they need to understand the nature and meaning of the accusation, also the implications.*

Magistrate 2: *We deal with these cases on a daily basis, a rural accused who is being charged with committing theft, for example, does not know the gravity of the offence. Stock theft is a serious offence in this country with a mandatory custodial sentence no less than 6 years, yet the accused may still think it's a civil matter.*

Magistrate 1: *Sometimes the accused does not understand genuinely, but some pretend not to understand so that they confuse the presiding magistrate. It is unfortunate that the outcome may not be the best under such circumstances.*

Due to their illiteracy, individuals lack the ability to comprehend the allegations brought against them or the legal documents they are given.

Human Rights Lawyer: *They fail to attend crucial court hearings because they misunderstand the summons and struggle to complete the necessary paperwork to seek legal assistance.*

During legal procedures, individuals are unable to comprehend the proceedings or effectively engage with their legal counsel, resulting in a conviction that may have been prevented with improved comprehension and legal representation.

Communication challenges

Zimbabwe is one of the countries with the highest literate rate. However, some who remain uneducated to a certain level remain vulnerable, and this is especially true when talking about legal language and representation.

Illiterate individuals in rural courts may struggle to communicate effectively with the presiding magistrate, understand legal advice, or follow court proceedings.

Human Rights Lawyer: *This communication gap can result in misrepresentation and inadequate defence strategies. The intersection of socio-economic background and illiteracy creates a compounded disadvantage in accessing justice.*

Former Convict 3: *Papers were served me in English, but because I could not get someone to read for me, I didn't know I was supposed to pay a fine. I failed to meet the deadline which resulted in me being given a custodial sentence. I only learnt later when I was already serving my sentence that I only needed to pay an affordable fine for my release.*

Data from document analysis

The information provided in this table was obtained from court records to assist in the analysis of the impact of socio-economic status and level of education on access to fair trials and justice in Zimbabwe's rural magistrate courts.

Table 15.1 helps illustrate the types of common offences, their corresponding incarceration lengths, and the demographic characteristics of the accused in rural Zimbabwe.

Explanation and insights

Table 15.1 provides a summary of the typical offences, which include theft, domestic abuse, assault, poaching, fraud, public disorder, and drug possession. It displays the aggregate number of perpetrators for each kind of offence, emphasising the frequency of each criminal act among the examined population. These offences are commonly observed in rural areas, where socio-economic variables influence criminality. The duration of imprisonment differs depending on the nature of the offence, with more serious crimes such as stock theft, poaching, and fraud leading to lengthier terms, while less severe offences such as common assault and public disorder generally result in shorter sentences. The age range of offenders varies significantly depending on the nature of the offence. For instance, theft and assault generally occur among individuals in the age range of 18–35 years, whereas fraud predominantly occurs among individuals aged 30–60 years.

It is worth mentioning that the table stats reveal intriguing topics about gender. The table illustrates the gender distribution of offenders, indicating

Table 15.1 Common Cases and Length of Jail Time

Offence	*Average length of incarceration*	*Age range (years)*	*Gender distribution (M/F)*	*Number of offenders*
Theft	1–10 years	18–45	30/10	40
Domestic violence	1 year	20–50	20/5	25
Assault	1–5 years	18–35	15/5	20
Poaching	2 years	25–55	10/2	12
Fraud	1–5 years	30–60	5/5	10
Public disorder	4 months	18–40	20/8	28
Drug possession	1 year	18–35	12/4	16

Notes:

Petty Theft: This includes minor thefts often driven by economic necessity. Both young men and women are typically involved, though men are more frequently charged.

Assault: Physical altercations, often resulting from personal disputes. This category shows a slightly higher representation of males, though females are also involved.

Public disorder: Includes offences like disturbing the peace or minor riots. The age range is broader, including younger individuals. Both genders are represented.

Domestic violence: This serious offence often results in longer incarceration. It involves primarily male perpetrators, but female offenders are also present.

Poaching is common in rural areas due to wildlife laws. It typically involves adults who rely on poaching for their livelihood, and more men are involved in this offence.

Trespassing is often linked to land disputes or economic desperation. This offence includes young and middle-aged individuals of both genders.

that males are predominantly engaged in the majority of offences. For example, when it comes to incidents of theft and public disruption, there is a substantial disparity in the proportion of males compared to girls. Nevertheless, gender disparity is less pronounced in crimes such as fraud. Finally, the figures indicate that there is a lower incidence of individuals engaging in these criminal activities in rural areas.

This data provides valuable insights into how socio-economic factors and literacy levels may influence involvement in different types of crimes and the resulting legal outcomes. It also highlights potential areas for targeted legal aid and educational programmes to reduce recidivism and improve justice delivery for marginalised groups.

Figure 15.1 depicts the breakdown of educational attainment among individuals involved in legal proceedings in Zimbabwe's rural magistrate courts.

1. No formal education: 24.2%
2. Primary education: 37.7%
3. Secondary education: 19.1%
4. Tertiary education: 0.9%

This chart emphasises that a significant proportion of offenders possess only a primary level of education or lack any formal education, therefore emphasising the connection between low educational achievement and an increased probability of engaging in criminal behaviour. The limited presence of higher education underscores the necessity for specific educational and legal measures to assist economically disadvantaged and uneducated individuals in effectively navigating the legal system.

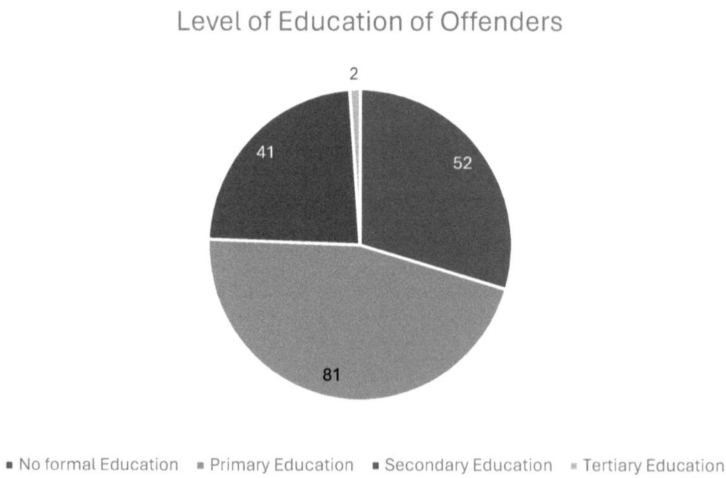

Figure 15.1 Level of Education of Offenders

Discussion

The countryside study revealed that the majority of rural offenders could have obtained bail if they had been literate enough to read and understand the procedures for their various rights. The study by Song and Zhao (2023) dwelt so much on this challenge that results from failure to comprehend legal rights. The inability to afford bail, combined with a lack of understanding of bail procedures, often results in unnecessary and extended pre-trial detention for the poor and illiterate. This affects their immediate freedom as well as their ability to prepare a robust defence.

Both socio-economic status and illiteracy influence court outcomes. Individuals from lower socio-economic backgrounds and those who are illiterate are more likely to receive harsher sentences and less favourable rulings, as pointed out earlier by Zane et al. (2020), with respect to accused rights. This is often due to inadequate legal representation, misunderstanding of legal processes, and the inability to present mitigating factors effectively. Whilst in the holding cells, they tend to advise each other on the laws and what each case entails. This can only be done if offenders are mixed with repeat offenders who are now using experience more than grounded literacy. Unfortunately, rural offenders are mostly isolated and first-time inmates. Their freedom relies more on their eloquence and level of literacy.

The number of people interviewed established that more accused persons end up in jail for petty offences because they fail to understand the procedure or cannot afford legal representation, which mirrors what Song and Zhao (2023) said regarding the consequences of misinterpretation and misconceptions of the law and legal rights. Data showing the correlation between socio-economic status, literacy levels, and legal outcomes can underscore the systemic nature of these issues. For instance, studies could reveal higher conviction rates and longer sentences for individuals from lower socio-economic backgrounds.

Post-conviction challenges

Post-conviction, the socio-economically disadvantaged and illiterate individuals face additional hurdles in appealing decisions or seeking freedom, largely due to their inability to navigate the legal system and lack of resources.

Recommendations

The study's primary recommendation is for the government to aid in the establishment of an easily accessible, impartial, and just justice delivery system in Zimbabwe that reflects the genuine essence of justice for all individuals. This can be achieved by rolling out countrywide education to make people learn and understand their rights and the various forms of legal assistance they can access even without paying anything. The location of rural magistrates' courts makes it impossible for all rural citizens to know and access basic legal aid, which results in most of them going to prison for offences that do not warrant such outcomes. The Legal Aid Foundation seemed to have done well at its inception but may have failed due to capacitation challenges. The government has a role to play in the capacitation of such noble establishments so that the legal system becomes friendly and not vindictive in all cases.

Conclusion

This study examined the socio-economic and literacy effects of rural magistrate courts in Zimbabwe serving deprived and illiterate citizens. It has highlighted the major challenges to fair and impartial justice. The study demonstrated legal system inequities that affect legal representation and judicial outcomes. Disparities are caused by economic, educational, and institutional factors. Results show the need for major reforms to address these inequalities immediately. A fairer justice system requires legal education, legal assistance, economic support, and regulatory and legislative improvements. Improving judicial infrastructure and training court personnel on socio-economic issues also promotes a more humane and knowledgeable approach to justice. The suggestions give policymakers, legal professionals, and civil society organisations a clear framework to help impoverished and illiterate rural offenders overcome socio-economic barriers. Enacting these policies requires cooperation, devotion, and the determination to ensure that justice is truly accessible for everyone, regardless of socio-economic status or literacy. Socio-economic issues affect justice delivery in rural Zimbabwe as a result of greater socio-economic imbalances that need attention and action.

Potential areas for future research

Although this study has yielded significant insights, it also underscores the need for additional research in certain areas. Subsequent research could investigate the effects of certain reforms on justice outcomes, the significance of legal representation for rural offenders with various challenges, and comparative examinations with other nations confronting comparable difficulties. Gaining insight into the intricacies of justice administration in rural settings is crucial for formulating efficient remedies and promoting the pursuit of legal fairness.

References

Barendrecht, M. (2011). Legal aid, accessible courts or legal information? Three access to justice strategies compared. *Global Jurist*, *11*(1), 6. https://doi.org/10.2202/1934-2640.1270

Brady, C., & Peck, J. (2021). Examining the type of legal representation and its influence on disaggregated dispositions in juvenile court. *Youth Violence and Juvenile Justice*, *19*(4), 359–383.

Case, S., & Haines, K. (2018). The future of youth justice. *Youth Justice*, *18*(2), 131–148.

Cassell, J. (2021). *Impacts of restorative justice on youth in conflict with the law: A narrative approach* [Thesis, Toronto Metropolitan University]. Retrieved May 20, 2024, from https://doi.org/10.32920/ryerson.14668365.v1

Chenwi, L. (2022). Women's representation and rights in the African court. *The Age of Human Rights Journal, 18*, 345–375.
Corvino, F. (2019). The moral implications of the global basic structure as a subject of justice. *Glocalism, 2*. https://doi.org/10.12893/gjcpi.2019.2.3
Destrooper, T. (2023). Disruptive reparations? Tunisia's victim regions and the collective reparations dilemma in transitional societies. *Journal of Peacebuilding & Development, 18*(2), 127–141.
Diržytė, A., Rakauskienė, O., & Servetkienė, V. (2017). Evaluation of resilience impact on socio-economic inequality. *Journal of Entrepreneurship and Sustainability Issues, 4*(4), 489–501.
Dollar, C. B., Ray, B., Hudson, M. K., & Hood, B. J. (2018). Examining changes in procedural justice and their influence on problem-solving court outcomes. *Behavioral Sciences & The Law, 36*(1), 32–45. https://doi.org/10.1002/bsl.2329
Feld, B., & Schaefer, S. (2010). The right to counsel in juvenile court. *Criminology & Public Policy, 9*(2), 327–356.
Gaines, J. (2007). Social correlates of psychological distress among adult African American males. *Journal of Black Studies, 37*(6), 827–858.
Hoque, N., Khan, M., & Mohammad, K. (2015). Poverty alleviation by Zakah in a transitional economy: A small business entrepreneurial framework. *Journal of Global Entrepreneurship Research, 5*(1). https://doi.org/10.1186/s40497-015-0025-8
Korniienko, M. (2024). Development of administrative proceedings in the context of economic globalisation. *Baltic Journal of Economic Studies, 10*(1), 136–144. https://doi.org/10.30525/2256-0742/2024-10-1-136-144
Koroma, S. (2023). Following the money: Understanding forum shopping and the 'justice marketplace' in Sierra Leone. *Social & Legal Studies, 33*(3), 328–350. https://doi.org/10.1177/09646639231195312
Leiber, M., & Fox, K. (2005). Race and the impact of detention on juvenile justice decision making. *Crime & Delinquency, 51*(4), 470–497.
Lemay-Hébert, N., & Freedman, R. (2021). Appraising the socio-economic turn in reparations: Transitional justice for cholera victims in Haiti. *International Journal of Transitional Justice, 15*(3), 533–552.
Mack, K., & Roach Anleu, S. (2007). 'Getting through the list': Judgecraft and legitimacy in the lower courts. *Social & Legal Studies, 16*(3), 341–361. https://doi.org/10.1177/0964663907079763
Magnus, A., & Donohue, F. (2021). Reimagining access to justice through the eyes of rural domestic violence survivors. *Theoretical Criminology, 26*(3), 434–455.
Manase, W. T. (1992). Legal services in rural areas: The Zimbabwean experience. *Third World Legal Studies, 11*(7), 179. http://scholar.valpo.edu/twls/vol11/iss1/7
Moore, W. (2013). The stare decision racial inequality: Supreme court race jurisprudence and the legacy of legal apartheid in the United States. *Critical Sociology, 40*(1), 67–88.
Mtotywa, M., Manqele, S., Manqele, T., Moitse, M., Seabi, M., & Mthethwa, N. (2022). The perceived societal impact of the fourth industrial revolution in South Africa. *International Journal of Research in Business and Social Science, 11*(9), 265–279, 2147–4478.
Ngcamu, B. (2019). Exploring service delivery protests in post-apartheid South African municipalities: A literature review. *The Journal for Transdisciplinary Research in Southern Africa, 15*(1). https://doi.org/10.4102/td.v15i1.643
Omori, M., & Petersen, N. (2020). Institutionalizing inequality in the courts: Decomposing racial and ethnic disparities in detention, conviction, and sentencing. *Criminology, 58*(4), 678–713.
Othman, H., & von Riesen, D. (2001). *Legal service to the poor people in Zimbabwe*. SIDA Valuation 10/39.
Ragusa, A. (2012). Rural Australian women's legal help-seeking for intimate partner violence. *Journal of Interpersonal Violence, 28*(4), 685–717.

Roodsari, E., & Hoseini, P. (2021). An assessment of the correlation between urban green space supply and socio-economic disparities of Tehran districts – Iran. *Environment Development and Sustainability, 24*(11), 12867–12882. https://doi.org/10.1007/s10668-021-01970-4

Sandefur, R. L. (2008). Access to civil justice and race, class, and gender inequality. *Annual Review of Sociology, 34*, 339–358.

Sengupta, U., & Sengupta, U. (2022). Sdg-11 and smart cities: Contradictions and overlaps between social and environmental justice research agendas. *Frontiers in Sociology, 7*. Retrieved June 20, 2024, from https://doi.org/10.3389/fsoc.2022.995603

Song, Y., & Zhao, T. (2023). Inferring influence of people's emotions at court on defendant's emotions using a prediction model. *Frontiers in Psychology, 14*, 1131724. https://doi.org/10.3389/fpsyg.2023.1131724

Statz, M. (2022). "It is here we are loved": Rural place attachment in active judging and access to justice. *Law & Social Inquiry, 49*(1), 247–277.

United Nations Office on Drugs and Crime. (2016). Global study on legal aid: Global report. *United Nations Office on Drugs and Crime*. Retrieved from https://www.unodc.org/documents/justice-and-prison-reform/LegalAid/Global_Study_on_Legal_Aid_-_FINAL.pdf

Weber, S. (2021). The personal and socio-economic dynamics of resilience and transitional justice in Colombia. In *Resilience, adaptive peacebuilding and transitional justice: How societies recover after collective violence* (pp. 187–209). Cambridge University Press. Retrieved May 20, 2024, from https://doi.org/10.1017/9781108919500.009

Zane, S., Singer, S., & Welsh, B. (2020). The right to a good defence: Investigating the influence of attorney type across urban counties for juveniles in criminal court. *Criminal Justice Policy Review, 32*(2), 162–192.

Zauro, N., Saad, R., & Sawandi, N. (2020). Enhancing socio-economic justice and financial inclusion in Nigeria. *Journal of Islamic Accounting and Business Research, 11*(3), 555–572.

Theme 5

Women in sexual assault cases

16 Rape myths in written judicial opinions from the Tanzanian Court of Appeal

Patricia Muraguri, Emmanuel Satia, and Simon Nganga

Introduction

The crime of rape is common in many societies throughout the world. A World Bank (2022) estimate from a study carried out in Tanzania in 2021 shows that 40 percent of all women aged 15 to 49 years had suffered physical violence, while 17 percent have suffered sexual assault, the total recorded rape incidents in Tanzania. Furthermore, according to a Legal and Human Rights Centre (LHRC) (2022) study, 81 percent of the 350 recorded instances of violence against minors throughout Tanzania's mainland were related to sexual violence. Twenty-five percent of the victims were younger than ten years old. According to the Tanzania Demographic and Health Survey and Malaria Indicator Survey 2010, by the age of 18, more than three in ten females had experienced sexual assault (NBS, 2011). The data serves to show that rape is a relatively prevalent crime in Tanzania.

This study intends to determine the existence of rape myths from written judicial opinions from the Tanzanian Court of Appeal and then examines the impact of victim empathy on the existence of rape myths. The concern with the rape myths arises from their potential to influence the judgment by setting official or social expectations on the behaviour, actions, or response of the victim to the alleged assault. The study establishes the ingredients of rape which set the standards of the official and social expectations and later presents the rape myths and how victim empathy features in rape myths.

Background of the study

Rape cases are tried in the Tanzania's legal system based on the English common law derived from the former British Coloniser. The sources of law include the Constitution, statutes, case law, received laws and the customary and Islamic law. Tanzania is also a signatory to International Laws (Treaties and Conventions) which become applicable after ratification. The Judiciary in Tanzania has four tiers: the Court of Appeal of the United Republic of Tanzania; the High Courts for Mainland Tanzania and Tanzania Zanzibar; and Magistrates Courts, which are at two levels, i.e. the Resident Magistrate

DOI: 10.4324/9781003569435-22

Courts and the District Court, both of which have concurrent jurisdiction. Primary Courts are the lowest in the judicial hierarchy. Rape is regarded as a criminal case and is initially tried at the Magistrates Courts. Appeals against the judgments are made to the High Court and they can also be made to the Court of Appeal where the appellant is dissatisfied with the ruling of the High Court.

The Tanzania Penal Code Cap. 16 R.E. 2022 provides for male and female sexual assault in separate subsections, whereby rape (which is sexual assault of a female) is provided for under subsection 130 (1)–(5), whereas sexual assault of male persons is provided for under subsection 154 (1)(a)–(c) as unnatural offences. Rape is described as a sexual assault committed by a male person against a female person in the Penal Code. Ehrlich (2001) contends that, given its adversarial character, the rape trial offers a special platform for looking at ways in which dominant ideas of sexual violence are propagated discursively, as well as ways they may be opposed and challenged. Unlike other cases, rape cases include emotional and personal engagement on the part of the magistrate or judge trying to make sense of the facts before them. The judge's knowledge of the norms of their community may serve to implicitly influence their opinion, though they may intertwine it with legal expressions. Research conducted by Feild (1978) concluded that extra-evidential factors had significant effects on rape trials. In a rape case, the beliefs (mostly incorrect) of the society are put forth in the reasoning process of the judicial opinion. According to the 2011 National Judicial Education Program (NJEP), sexual assault cases are special in that they are rife with a variety of strongly held preconceptions and beliefs that could compromise the court system and, therefore, provide a special difficulty for the court.

First proposed by Burt (1980), rape myths were defined as 'prejudicial, stereotyped, or false beliefs about rape, rape victims, and rapist'. Lonsway and Fitzgerald (1994) contended that while Burt's 1980 rape myth definition was descriptive, it was insufficient for research needs. Then Lonsway and Fitzgerald (1994) suggested that rape myths be described as 'Attitudes and beliefs that are generally false but are widely and persistently held and that serve to deny and justify male sexual aggression against women'.

Rape myths may be said to represent our conscious and unconscious view of the position of rape and its victims in our society (Prochuck, 2018). The reactions to rape vary depending on the society. Payne et al. (1999) note that rape myths include elements of victim blame, perpetrator absolution, and minimisation or rationalisation of sexual violence, and they perpetuate sexual violence against women. The society's first recourse is usually to determine that there was no culpability on the part of the victim. The victim's reactions and behaviour before the incidence and after the incidence are minutely examined to establish whether the victim attracted the offence to herself in the manner of dressing or verbal or non-verbal cues to the perpetrator. Where the victim is deemed to have fulfilled all the implicit and explicit criteria, victim empathy kicks in, and depending on the details of the assault, the victim is assigned a descriptor depending on how close their account relates to the 'ideal victim' standard (Muraguri & Satia, 2023).

Furthermore, setting off rape myths is society's view of the anticipated behaviour of a victim. A victim is required to show a certain degree of emotion; she should bear evidence of the assault in the form of injuries and damaged clothes. Further, she should show that she did her best to protect herself; she should, therefore, promptly report the assault and voluntarily provide specifics of the attack. In retrospect, research suggests that rape myths often focus on victim/survivors' behaviour, ignoring how fear, guilt, and shock can cause them to act counter-intuitively (Burrowes, 2013). Therefore, since these beliefs appear to influence juries and legal personnel, as well as police and evidence-gathering, they are likely to be an important part of rape trials and even influence the written judicial opinion of the case (Burrowes, 2013; Temkin & Krahe, 2008).

The presence of rape myths has been linked to lack of empathy for the victim on the part of those adjudicating rape or even in the society. Davis (1983) defines empathy as the capacity to be affected by the emotional states of others. Further, Bandes and Feigenson (2021) defined empathy as the capacity to comprehend the situation of another and their emotional responses to that situation. In courts, there has been a debate on whether empathy is a desirable attribute of judges, and Bandes and Feigenson (2021) note that the application of empathy in courts is beset with issues of selective application of empathy and empathy divides, which may disadvantage who are seen as 'other'. They note that these divides can impair the accuracy and fairness of legal proceedings. They further argue that empathy can be misdirected even when exercised with the best of intentions an in addition it is also subject to various biases such as the egocentric, affective, or similarity biases. In essence, those adjudicating the rape cases particularly in the court of origin of the case hear all the gruesome details of the assault and which may influence their perception of the sexual assault and its victim.

Studies have been carried out on how victim empathy can help to reduce sexual aggression and foster empathy towards survivors of sexual assault (O'Donohue et al., 2003; Foubert & Newberry, 2006). Victim empathy studies have shown that after empathy induction, rape myths acceptance reduces significantly (Patterson et al., 2022).

The purpose of this study is to investigate the rape myths present in written court opinions from the Court of Appeal in Tanzania in order to ascertain the contribution of victim empathy to the existence of rape myths and how the cultural expectations of sex help to support the negative attitudes on rape. The study is conducted within the context of Critical Discourse Analysis (CDA). CDA seeks to make clear the links among social institutions, social behaviours, and discourse techniques connections that can be invisible to the average individual (Fairclough, 1995).

Literature review

When judges adjudicate cases, they use not only legal knowledge but also knowledge about the world. The judges' knowledge about their culture is ingrained in their minds, and this informal knowledge based on their social group's point of view is often applied to reason out events in the real world. The judge's knowledge of the expectations of the public may serve to implicitly influence their opinion though they may intertwine it with legal expressions. The commonly accepted norms which at times exist in our subconscious minds may lead to attitudes and beliefs which are prejudicial and false. These are beliefs that may influence judges in the process of adjudicating cases, and they are revealed in the language used in framing thoughts and arguments in the decisions. These incorrect beliefs provide inaccurate portrayal of the victim, the perpetrator, and the violence of the act of rape.

Rape myths influence perception of what rape or is not in a community. They are reported to be the reason for victims refusing to report sexual assault. In this case we are assuming that Tanzania as a nation forms a community. Different ethnic groups can have their perceptions of what sexual assault entails but the general perception of what constitutes rape can be gathered from the values that are exhibited in organs such as the media and other key discussions or documents which reveal the general stance on rape. Some rape myths are also culturally specific therefore some which are found in regions like North America and Europe may not be found elsewhere.

Over years of study, the list of rape myths accumulated is extensive. Acceptance studies of rape myths have been conducted to demonstrate their presence. Different researchers have examined the degrees and kind of acceptability for rape myths. Researchers have looked at rape myth acceptability in non-Western civilisations (Kanekar & Kolsawalla, 1980) and Western ones (Suarez & Gadalla, 2010; Burt, 1980). Men's propensity to rape has been correlated with acceptance of rape myths (RMA). Higher rape myth acceptance scores, according to DeLisle et al. (2019), might point to a person's lack of empathy for victims of sexual assault. Barnett and Mann (2013) describe empathy as 'a cognitive and emotional understanding of another person's experience, resulting in an emotional response for the observer which is congruent with a view that others are worthy of compassion and respect and have intrinsic value'. Studies on empathy typically target criminals (Blake & Gannon, 2008; Brown & Walker, 2012; Levenson & Prescott, 2009). In a ruling, one may find different points of view including that of the appellant, the witnesses, the state counsel, and the judges. The many parties engaged might show empathy for the victim of rape or lack of empathy in the language used in presentation of their opinion or to defend their position on the part of the appellant.

Patterson et al. (2022) studied how empathy can aid in lowering the acceptance of male rape myths. Using a 22-item questionnaire, they evaluated pre-induction male rape myth acceptance of incorrect or prejudiced ideas about male rape. They created a fictitious narrative about a man who experienced sexual assault and sought to challenge rape stereotypes by inspiring empathy for the hypothetical victim. Scholarly experts and licenced practitioners focused on sexual assault trauma recovery examined the hypothetical narrative to confirm that it fairly represented the testimony of a genuine victim. The participants worked on an empathy writing project after listening to the fictitious narrative. The findings showed that for both male and female participants, empathy induction greatly lowered the acceptability of male rape myths.

The Attribution theory pioneered by Heider (1958) can be applied to the existence of rape myths to provide insight into how people assign blame and responsibility in sexual assault cases. Internal attributions occur where people attribute the cause of a rape to the victim's behaviour (e.g., clothing, alcohol consumption), which reinforces the rape myth that suggest victims are responsible for the assault. Conversely, external attributions occur if the perpetrator's actions are viewed as the cause, thereby emphasising that the responsibility lies with the offender, hence challenging the rape myths.

Methodology

This study used the qualitative approach in examining online written judgments from the Tanzania Court of Appeal. The opinions were from different regional Courts of Appeal namely Mbeya, Dar es Salaam, Arusha, Mwanza, and Mtwara to ensure representation of the regional courts in Tanzania. The Court of Appeal judgments were selected on the grounds that the case had received expert attention in the process of adjudication through the various judicial levels such that any prejudices or in this case, rape myths had been deflected. For this study, 30 judgments available online were collected from the sites https:/www.judiciary.go.tz, https://tanzlii.org, and https://africanlii.org, and permission was sought and granted from the court to study the judgments. Using purpose sampling, judgments with the parameter rape or unnatural offence were selected for use in this study and only the rape charge/count was considered in the analysis.

Out of the 30 decisions studied, 19 decisions were made between the year 2016 and 2019 while 11 were made between the years 2006 to 2010. Out of the 30 written judgments gathered, 11 of the appeals were dismissed and the judgment of the High Court was upheld while 15 of the appeals were allowed and the conviction was quashed. Among the 30 judgments, four were not considered for analysis since they dealt purely with matters of the law concerning defective charge sheet, defective notice of appeal, and the law on an appeal that had been summarily rejected by the High Court and reference to the person who experienced sexual assault is very minimal. Some cases which had a defective charge sheet were considered for analysis where the reference to the person who experienced sexual assault is considered substantial. In the cases collected, all the appellants are male, and the complainants are both male (3) and female (27).

Of the 26 cases studied, 15 cases were included in this study either because they contained elements of rape myths or because they served to explain issues referred to in the study. The charges of the 15 cases included rape (11), unnatural offence (2), gang rape (1), and incest (1). For the purposes of this study, sexual assault of both male and female persons is regarded as rape.

The language used in the judgments was examined and words, phrases, or sentences that either implicitly or explicitly exhibited the presence of rape myths were identified together with the rape myth to which it subscribed using the Critical Discourse analysis perspective as propounded by Fairclough (1992). Cases presented to the Court of Appeal will usually have been brought before at least two other courts, that is, the court of origin and the High Court. This implies that ample opportunity to deflect rape myths has been provided and the assumption would be that there would be no rape myths reflected in the judgments at this level.

Opinions from the Court of Appeal were considered in this analysis since they included descriptions of the assaults and the circumstances surrounding though they primarily deal with issues of the law. This study does not propose that the judgments reached are incorrect or faulty in any way.

Data analysis

Ingredients of rape

In order for an alleged sexual assault to be accepted as rape, it must bear the necessary official and social ingredients of rape. The official ingredients of rape according to the Penal Code are outlined in section 130 (4)(a)–(b).[1]

Penetration is one of the main requirements. For instance, in the judgment, *Issaya Renatus v Republic*, the appellant tried to argue that penetration was not proved through medical evidence, but the court maintained that the evidence was provided by the eyewitnesses of the assault. It is stated:

> In the present case, the most crucial witness was the victim (PW1) who categorically stated that the appellant penetrated her by inserting his manhood into her sexual organ.
>
> (p. 10)

Another requirement is consent. Consent is important since it distinguishes criminal sexual assault and non-criminal sex. Evidence has to prove that consent was not given by the complainant. In the *Issaya Renatus v Republic* case,

1 (4) For the purposes of proving the offence of rape (a) penetration although slight is sufficient to constitute the sexual intercourse necessary to the offence; and (b) evidence of resistance such as physical injuries to the body is not necessary to prove that sexual activity occurred without consent.

the complainant shouted for help, and this is indication that she did not consent to the sexual act. It is written that:

> As he did so, PW1 was repeatedly wailing to attract helping hands. Her screams were heard by two ladies, namely, Jesca 2 Boniface (PW2) and Violeth Philemon (PW3).

Eskridge (1995) argues that consent arises from a cultural script and reflects the ideology of traditional masculinity where the man exercises power over the woman. Further, sexual consent does not apply to sodomites, the child molesters, and the homewreckers. Sexual relations for those whose sexual orientation is homosexual is prohibited, and consent is not included as a criterion by the Tanzanian law.[2]

Although corroboration is not expressly stated in the Penal Code, it is also considered as an essential element in the evidence of a child. For example, in the case *Jackson Davis v Republic*, it was noted that corroboration of a child's evidence is essential, and they referred to the *Remigious Hyera v Republic* case where the court held that:

> It is settled law that the omission to conduct *voire dire* examination of a child of tender years brings such evidence to the level of unsworn evidence of a child which requires corroboration.

In the *Peter Abel Kirumi v Republic* case, it was noted that corroboration was necessary to establish the reliability and sufficiency of the victim's evidence. It is stated that:

> There was, so to speak, a dire need for an independent account to corroborate her story which, unfortunately, was not featured by the prosecution.

Another ingredient is threats. Threats are considered to be an essential element of rape, as revealed in the case *Musa Mwaikunda v Republic* where it is stated that:

> *threatening was not alleged* in the particulars of offence *the effect was that an essential element of the offence of attempted rape missed in the case against the appellant*. . . . the complainant did not say anywhere in her evidence that she was threatened by the appellant.

2 154. (1) Any person who (a) has carnal knowledge of any person against the order of nature; (b) has carnal knowledge of an animal; or (c) permits a male person to have carnal knowledge of him or her against the order of nature, commits an offence, and is liable to imprisonment for life and in any case to imprisonment for a term of not less than thirty years.

Threats may include threat against life or any other material aspect. In the *Dalali s/o Mwalongo v Republic* case, the appellant who is the father of the complainant threatens to throw her out of the house and even to kill her. It is written that the complainant said:

> I didn't tell anybody because the accused has (sic) been threatening to kill me.

The social ingredients of rape are additions to the official ingredients. The victims of rape should also prove that they were not responsible for their victimisation by wearing clothes that are in tandem with societal expectations, ensuring that they are in a safe space and in event of an attempt ensuring that they alert others by shouting or other means.

Rape myths

Various rape myths were identified in the judgments were examined and identified. The definition of rape is itself an indication of the presence of rape myths as it reflects the ideology of traditional masculinity. It recognises the sexual assault of a male on a female as rape and specifies that the assault is done using the male sexual organ where the woman is the object of the assault. Other sexual assault acts such as male-on-male assault or female-on-female assault, assault using objects or other body parts such as the hands are referred to as unnatural offences in subsection 154 (1)(a)–(c). It holds on to the traditional roles of sex being between consenting males and females. Other sexual acts are adjudicated using other subsections. This may have the effect of minimising the experience of victims who are assaulted in ways other than the one described in subsection 130 (2)(a)–(e).

The woman was lying/women cry rape for revenge

It is commonly believed that a woman may claim to have been raped as a form of revenge against a man. In *Shaban Amiri v Republic*, the complainant was considered to be untruthful, and it is stated thus:

> but worse still PW1 exposed herself as a liar in her evidence in court ***and by her conduct after the alleged incident of rape*** if ever it took place. (emphasis added)

In order to understand this statement, it is important to examine her conduct after the rape:

(i) She did not immediately report the incidence;
(ii) She did not confess immediately about the incident to her mother;

> When PW3 (her mother) asked her why she was not walking properly she replied that she was experiencing pains in her legs.
>
> (p. 7)

(ii) Late reporting of the incident.

> She never reported this incident to anybody until November 2001, when she was taken to hospital, examined, and found to be pregnant.

The complainant's testimony is considered doubtful due to lack of immediate disclosure of the incident to others. Empathy for the complainant is also diminished due to this, and it is explicitly stated that she was lying.

Complainants who immediately report the incident are viewed as truthful, for example, in *Omary Kulwa v Republic* it is stated thus:

> PW 1 immediately reported the incident to his mother, PW 2. He named the appellant as the culprit.
>
> (p. 3)

In this case, the complainant could positively identify the alleged perpetrator and also reported the assault immediately. The impact of this myth is victim blaming. The burden of proof of rape is placed upon the complainant and the criteria is set and it includes the following terms and conditions:

(i) Immediate reporting
(ii) Be as detailed as possible
(iii) Clearly identify the assailant

Lisak et al. (2010) reviewed the six most methodologically sound studies of false allegations and findings revealed that 5.9 percent of the cases were false allegations. This means that the number of false allegations was too minimal to be generalised to all rape victims.

The rape victim should exhibit victim characteristics after the rape

Section 234 (3) of the CPA provides that variance in time when alleged offence was committed may be regarded as immaterial if proceedings are instituted within time.[3] In the case *Issaya Renatus v Republic*, the appellant's third ground of appeal stated that there was a variance between the time of the occurrence of the assault as alleged in the charge sheet (10:00 hrs), with the

3 Variance between the charge and the evidence adduced in support of it with respect to the time at which the alleged offence was committed is not material and the charge need not be amended for such variance if it is proved that the proceedings were in fact instituted within time/if any, limited by law for the institution thereof.

time which was alleged by the prosecution witnesses in their respective testimonies (12:00 hrs). The court held that:

> The proceedings giving rise to this appeal were instituted within time and, in any event, the variance did not in any way, detract from the material account.

Immediate reporting is considered to be a sign of the validity of the assault. In the *Peter Abel Kirumi v Republic* case, the reliability of the complainant's evidence is questioned due to the fact that she did not report the first sexual assault immediately. It is stated thus:

> Nasma who withheld the details of the first occurrence for ten days.

Victim characteristics that are expected of a bona fide victim include shouting for help and exhibiting psychological trauma while remaining lucid enough to narrate all the minor details of the assault.

In the *Edson Simon Mwombeki v Republic* case, the defence claimed that the complainant did not behave like a typical rape victim since:

> Mr. Nasimire added that if PW1 was raped, it is ***unimaginable*** that on the following day she had managed to travel to Magu. (emphasis added)

The supposition here is that she should have been so traumatised such that she could not perform her daily tasks. The word 'unimaginable' is intended by the defence to create a sense that the victim was not sufficiently traumatised to prove that she was raped.

Further, in *Peter Abel Kirumi v Republic*, the complainant's testimony is not regarded as reliable since she delayed in reporting the initial incident and her character is assessed as follows:

> it is beyond question that Nasma was not quite the salt of the earth in her account on the alleged episode.
>
> (p. 11)

The idiom 'the salt of the earth', which is typically used to indicate that the person is honest and reliable is used in this case preceded by 'not' to avoid outrightly stating that she was lying. When there is delayed reporting of the assault, questions about the validity of the complaint surface. Among the rare victims who do report, those who experience stranger rape often report somewhat near to the date of attack, whereas those who experience non-stranger rape often hesitate. There are many reasons for this delay in non-stranger rape; the victim may not instantly identify the attack as rape. Along with the dread of loss of privacy and the criminal justice system, one may also be afraid of reprisal, of being disbelieved or blamed. Denial or suppression may cause the victim to fail to report the crime on time; alternatively, the victim may have psychogenic amnesia that is, loss of recollection of either part or all of an attack (Schafran, 1993; Kilpatrick et al., 2007).

'Real' rape and ideal victim

'Real rape' is a psychological picture of what a rape act should constitute. This picture is created by a person's or institution's beliefs of what consensual sex is as opposed to any other sexual act between a man and a woman. It is assumed that the assailant is a stranger. Some rape cases may come close to the expectation of real rape though the existence of 'real' rape is too ideal. The *Imani Charles Chimango v Republic* case, to an extent relates to the expectations of real rape. The appellant was a stranger to the complainant, and it is noted that 'the victim did not know the appellant prior to the incident'. It is also stated that she eloquently described her experience:

> She narrated ***eloquently*** how she was taken to the second accused's house and how she was undressed by the second accused under intimidation and forced to sex.

The adverb 'eloquently' was used to intensify their opinion of the believability of her narration. In most of the cases presented in court, the complainant knew the appellant and Ehrlich (2001) notes that the 'real' rape myth has been extensively challenged after research proved that the perpetrators of most rapes are people known to the victim.

Only loose women are victimised

It is assumed that a woman who places herself in a morally compromising situation should expect to be raped. For instance, in the *Sprian Justine Tarimo v Republic* case, the integrity of the complainant is questioned, and it is even insinuated that she was a loose woman who had several sexual affairs. Previous sexual experience is used to imply that she was a loose woman thus could not have been a sexually assaulted. It is stated that:

> she 'had ***undisputed sex*** on several prior occasions with, to mention only one, the appellant'

It is further stated that:

> What would one have expected from a 20-plus year old woman who had had undisputed sex on several prior occasions with, to mention only one, the appellant?

The rhetorical question 'What would one have expected from a 20-plus-year-old woman who had had undisputed sex on several prior occasions with, to mention only one, the appellant?' invites the listener or reader of the judgment to make a conclusion that the complainant was of the age to engage in sex and her previous sex encounters confirmed this. Ehrlich (2001) notes that defence attorney's use of presupposition in selected propositions can create negative ideological frames about the witness. In this case, the morpheme *un-* is added to the word 'disputed' to intensify the matter that she had previous sex encounters therefore lessening the believably of the claim that she was raped. The censorship of the victim is very overt, and this leads to victim blaming.

In the *Peter Abel Kirumi v Republic* case, the complainant did not shout for help or report the incident immediately and as per the particulars of the case further, she put herself in a compromising situation by massaging a married man while the wife was absent and staying up late into the night. It is stated thus in the judgment:

> From the foregoing particulars, it is beyond question that Nasma **was not quite the salt of the earth** in her account on the alleged episode.

The woman did not resist the assailant (sufficiently) and did not shout for help

The common expectation is that a sexual assault victim will raise alarm and when it does not happen the woman is regarded as a liar. In *Omary Kijuu v Republic*, the appellant raises the issue that the complainant did not raise an alarm.

> He also wondered why PW1 did not raise an alarm.
>
> (p. 11)

An alarm is important since it establishes corroboration. In many of the cases, the issue of corroboration is brought up. Corroboration is a necessary ingredient to prove rape. In *Omary Kijuu v Republic*, it is stated thus:

> it has long been the practice of the courts to look for and required corroboration in sexual offences.
>
> (pp. 5–6)

Rape is sex

In some of the judgments, rape is described using terms which are used for consensual sex these are for instance, sexual intercourse, fack (fuck*), sexual want, sexual relationship, sex, love affairs, make love. In *Eliah Bariki v Republic*, the appellant was appealing against a conviction in the case of sexual assault against an eight-year-old girl. The facts of the case are stated that the appellant had 'sexual intercourse' with the eight-year-old girl. It is stated thus:

> Eliah Bariki had sexual intercourse with one RF, a girl aged 8 years.
> (p. 2)

The language used does not express the seriousness of the act since the phrase 'sexual intercourse' presupposes that the act was consensual. The sexual act on an 8-year-old girl can even be life-threatening, so it cannot be described as sexual intercourse; it should be stated that it was an assault. The impact here is that the woman is viewed as an object of man's pleasure. The fact that sex is an act that occurs between consenting males and females is ideologically used to perpetuate the idea that any sex is enjoyable with the assumption that it is natural for a woman to want sex/receive sexual advances.

In *Peter Abel Kirumi v Republic*, the alleged sexual assault is described from page 1 of the judgment using consensual sex terms. For example, it is stated that:

> the appellant had **sexual intercourse** with a certain Nasma Said who was then aged sixteen.
> (16)

The complainant is not even referred to using formal terminology for alleged complainants but is referred to as 'a certain Nasma Said'. It implies that the opinion of the allegations of the complainant is that they are untrue, and the act was essentially wanted by the complainant.

In *Nurdin Wailu v Republic*, it is stated that the appellant 'made five "rounds" throughout the night'. The description used for the number of times that the complainant was raped is 'rounds' which is a sporting term. The implication is that the action of raping the complainant was a form of sport and since sports are mainly for enjoyment, it was enjoyable.

The victim did not give clear specific (candid) details of the rape

The expectation about rape is that a victim should give details about the assault and take every opportunity to talk about it. When a victim is not that forward with details it is assumed that the assault likely may not have happened. For example, in the case *Jamal Ally@Salum v Republic* it is written about the appellant that:

> He wondered why when **PW1 was asked about the rape in his presence and others, she had said nothing.**

While some researchers have observed that rape survivors will largely keep quiet about their experiences, Ahrens (2006) contends that silence is symbolic of weakness in our culture. Sexual violence, thus, is related to inequality. Because of age or other societal considerations, sexual assault offenders can target those they see as less strong or helpless. Some have said that rape actively reinforces women's weakness and 'keeps women in their place' (e.g., Brownmiller, 1975; MacKinnon, 1987).

In the *Jamal Ally@Salum v Republic* case, the judges disagreed with the appellant and sided with the evidence provided by the complainant, and they stated that:

> the victim (PW1) gave a detailed account on how she was lured to the bush, where she was threatened, forcefully raped and forced to endure much pain. . . . the evidence of the victim is overwhelming.
>
> (p. 13)

The complainant, despite their age, is required to give specific details of the assault. For instance, in the case *Alfeo Valentino v Republic*, prosecution witness 2 (PW2), a nine-year-old girl, testified about what the appellant did to PW1 she said:

> While Grace (PW1) was being done by the accused I was in another room with the other man.

She uses the phrase 'being done' instead of the explicit names for the sexual act; thus, it was concluded that the act of rape was not executed. The complainants who specify what was done minutely are considered credible.

Women ask to be raped by how they act

In the narration of the assault in the *Peter Abel Kirumi v Republic* case, the details are that the complainant agreed to massage the appellant, who was semi naked, and when the appellant sexually assaulted her, she did not shout for help or refuse to comply when he undressed her. It is stated that:

> the appellant called and asked her to massage him. . . . she massaged him, the appellant, who was clad in a pair of boxer shorts only, ... The appellant then went out of the house and returned home around 1.00 p.m. . . . Nasma was sitting in the living room. . . . the appellant pointedly told PW1 that he wanted to have sexual intercourse with her. . . . the appellant undressed her and, . . . he inserted his manhood into her vagina . . . she, however, did not disclose to anyone.

The testimony of the complainant went against all cultural expectations of propriety in several aspects:

(i) Agreeing to massage a semi-naked man while his wife is away
(ii) Staying up late (1 p.m.) when the wife is away

(iii) Remaining quiet while being assaulted
(iv) Lack of disclosure of the assault

The cultural script is very straightforward and does not account for victim paralysis and trauma. Therefore, based on the preceding facts in her testimony, the conclusion will be that she asked to be sexually assaulted due to her behaviour.

Rape myths and victim empathy

Lee (2014) notes that empathy is necessary for objective adjudication of cases and that it helps to enhance impartiality. The existence of rape myths is an indicator of diminished empathy for the victim of sexual assault. For instance, in the *Peter Abel Kirumi v Republic* case, several rape myths are observed, including rape is sex; only loose women are victimised; she did not exhibit victim characteristics; she did not resist; she was raped due to her actions. All these rape myths appear in cases where a 14-year-old girl was the complainant. As Muraguri and Satia (2023) observed, the complainant's alleged assault is graded along a hierarchy, and this can be observed in the type of descriptor assigned to them in the judgment. In *Peter Abel Kirumi v Republic*, the complainant is referred to constantly by her proper name, which places her account on the lower levels of the hierarchy and as noted in the judgment, her actions receive censorship because they seem to stray far from the expected victim standards.

It has been observed that the appellants seem to uphold rape myths as indicated in their grounds of appeal. As shown in the preceding analysis, in the cases *JamalAlly@Salum v Republic* and *Issaya Renatus v Republic*, their grounds of appeal included issues of variance of time. The claim in the Issaya Renatus case was that the variance in time between the time indicated in the charge sheet and the time stated by prosecution witnesses was an indication that it was unsafe to rely on the charge sheet to convict him. Their grounds of appeal reveal that these appellants do not empathise with the alleged victim of the alleged sexual assault.

Empathy for the complainant is not a guarantee that the appellant's appeal shall be denied, it may be an expression of the perspective taken with regard to the events described. For instance, in the *Jackson Davis v Republic* case, the complainant is referred to as a victim and the decision not to retry the case was based on empathy. A defence of the decision taken is included in the judgment since the account of the complainant arouses empathy.

It is stated thus:

> The sodomy was committed on the ***victim*** when the ***victim*** was nine years old. We are doubtful whether it will be in the best interest of the victim who is now aged 14 to put salt on the old wound and trauma the small boy suffered mentally and physically when the appellant sodomised him.

The use of the term 'victim' while referring to the complainant can be regarded as acknowledgement of the probable occurrence of the assault.

Empathy is expressed not only for the victim but also for the appellant. It is stated that:

> much water has passed under the bridge since the trial was conducted. On the other hand, ***the appellant has been in prison, initially in remand and after conviction, in jail from time he*** was arrested to date.
>
> (emphasis added)

Therefore, empathy is more apparent where the complainant is viewed as a bonafide victim, but where there are doubts as to the victim's status, empathy levels diminish. Empathy is greater for complainants whose sexual assault account closely adheres to the 'real' rape standards.

Conclusion

Rape myths as observed in the study can be implicitly or explicitly expressed in courts. The courts need to resort to consultation with experts in other specialisations so as to understand victim response in instances of assault and probably in retelling of the assault. We propose further that empathy enhancement for judges should be conducted to orient them with victim behaviour in cases of trauma such as rape and also to highlight the importance of experts. Future research can consider creating a scale for determining the extent of rape myths in written judgments to help judges to self-assess their opinions to eliminate rape myths.

References

Ahrens, C. E. (2006). Being silenced: The impact of negative social reactions on the disclosure of rape. *American Journal of Community Psychology*, *38*(3–4), 263–274. https://doi.org/10.1007/s10464-006-9069-9

Bandes, S. A., & Feigenson, N. 2021. Empathy and remote legal proceedings. *Southwestern Law Review*, *20*, 51 (Symposium on Courts in the COVID-19 Era). https://ssrn.com/abstract=3892880

Barnett, G. D., & Mann, R. E. (2013). Cognition, empathy, and sexual offending source. *Trauma, Violence & Abuse*, *14*(1), 22–33. https://www.jstor.org/stable/10.2307/26638297

Blake, E., & Gannon, T. (2008). Social perception deficits, cognitive distortions and empathy deficits in sex offenders. *Trauma, Violence & Abuse*, *9*, 34–55.

Brown, S., & Walker, K. (2012). Empathy and sexual offending: A review of the literature. *Sexual Abuse: A Journal of Research and Treatment*, *24*(1), 3–21. https://doi.org/10.1177/1079063211402397

Brownmiller, S. (1975). *Against our will: Men, women, and rape*. Simon & Schuster.

Burrowes, N. (2013). *Responding to the challenge of rape myths in court*. NB Research. http://www.nb-research.co.uk/index.php/projects-2/

Burt, M. R. (1980). Cultural myths and supports for rape. *Journal of Personality and Social Psychology*, *38*, 217–230.

Davis, M. (1983). Measuring individual differences in empathy: Evidence for a multidimensional approach. *Journal of Personality and Social Psychology*, *44*, 113–126. https://doi.org/10.1037/0022-3514.44.1.113
DeLisle, A., Walsh, H. C., Holtz, P. M., Callahan, J., & Neumann, C. S. 2019. Rape myth acceptance, male gender role norms, attitudes towards women, and psychopathic traits in a military sample. *Personality and Individual Differences*, *144*, 125–131. https://doi.org/10.1016/j.paid.2019.03.005
Ehrlich, S. (2001). *Representing rape: Language and sexual consent.* Routledge.
Eskridge, W. N. (1995). The many faces of sexual consent. *William & Mary Law Review*, *37*, 47. https://scholarship.law.wm.edu/wmlr/vol37/iss1/7
Fairclough, N. (1992). *Discourse and social change.* Polity.
Feild, H. (1978). Juror background characteristics and attitudes toward rape: Correlates of jurors' decision in rape trials. *Law and Human Behavior*, *2*, 73–93.
Foubert, J. D., & Newberry, J. T. (2006). Effects of two versions of an empathy-based rape prevention program on fraternity men's survivor empathy, attitudes, and behavioral intent to commit rape or sexual assault. *Journal of College Student Development*, *47*(2), 133–148. https://doi.org/10.1353/csd.2006.0016
Heider, F. (1958). *The psychology of interpersonal relations.* Wiley.
Kanekar, S., & Kolsawalla, M. B. (1980). Responsibility of a rape victim in relation to her respectability, attractiveness, and provocativeness. *The Journal of Social Psychology*, *112*, 153–154. https://doi.org/10.1080/00224545.1980.9924310
Kilpatrick, D. et al. (2007). *Drug-facilitated, incapacitated and forcible rape: A national study.* http://www.ncjrs.gov/pdffiles1/nij/grants/219181.pdf
Lee, R. K. (2014). Judging judges: Empathy as the litmus test for impartiality. *University of Cincinnati Law Review*, *82*.
Legal and Human Rights Centre (LHRC). (2022). *Tanzania human rights report.* LHRC.
Levenson, J. S., & Prescott, D. (2009). Treatment experiences of civilly committed sex offenders: A consumer satisfaction survey. *Sexual Abuse: A Journal of Research and Treatment*, *21*, 6–20.
Lisak, D., Gardinier, L., Nicksa, S. C., & Cote, A. M. (2010). False allegations of sexual assault: An analysis of ten years of reported cases. *Violence Against Women*, *16*(12), 1318–1334. https://doi.org/10.1177/1077801210387747
Lonsway, K. A., & Fitzgerald, L. F. (1994). Rape myths: In review. *Psychology of Women Quarterly*, *18*, 133–164.
MacKinnon, C. A. (1987). *Feminism unmodified: Discourses on life and law.* Harvard University Press.
Muraguri, P., & Satia, E. (2023). Ranking of descriptors for complainants based on perceived victimhood: A case of written opinions in the Tanzanian court of appeal. In *Language, crime and courts in contemporary Africa and beyond.* African Sun Media.
National Judicial Education Program. (2011). *Judges tell: What I wish I had known before I presided in an adult victim sexual assault case.* National Judicial Education Program.
NBS (National Bureau of Statistics). (2011). *Violence against children national survey, 2011: Part of the Tanzania household demographic survey.* NBS.
O'Donohue, W., Yeater, E. A., & Fanetti, M. (2003). Rape prevention with college males: The roles of rape myth acceptance, victim empathy, and outcome expectancies. *Journal of Interpersonal Violence, 18*(5), 513–531. https://doi.org/10.1177/0886260503251071
Patterson, T. P., Fiene, S. L., & Cole, B. P. (2022). No less of a man: Inducing empathy to reduce male rape myth acceptance. *Journal of Interpersonal Violence*, *37*(19–20), NP18152–NP18174.
Payne, D. L., Lonsway, K. A., Fitzgerald, L. F. (1999). Rape myth acceptance: Exploration of its structure and its measurement using the Illinois rape myth acceptance scale. *Journal of Research in Personality*, *33*(1), 27–68.

Prochuck, A. (2018). *We are here: Women's experiences of the barriers to reporting sexual assault.* West Coast LEAF. http://www.westcoastleaf.org/wp-content/uploads/2018/10/West-Coast-Leaf-dismantling-web-final.pdf
Schafran, L. H. (1993). Is the law male: Let me count the ways. *Chicago-Kent Law Review*, *69*, 397. https://scholarship.kentlaw.iit.edu/cklawreview/vol69/iss2/9
Suarez, E., & Gadalla, T. M. (2010). Stop blaming the victim: A meta-analysis on rape myths. *Journal of Interpersonal Violence*, *25*, 2010–2035.
Temkin, J., & Krahe, B. (2008). *Sexual assault and the justice gap: A question of attitude.* Hart Publishing.
World Bank. (2022). *Tanzania GBV assessment.* World Bank.

17 Ethical journalism practice in Zvinoyera, zvinotyisa uye zvinoda kufumurwa's coverage of allegations of abuse of women and children against Madzibaba Ishmael

Witness Roya

Introduction

Radio remains 'Africa's medium of choice in the global age' (Mano, 2012, p. 102) because, among other things, it is accessible to poor and semi-literate people (Englund, 2019). Zvinoyera is simulcast on the Zimbabwean commercial radio station, Star FM and its YouTube and Facebook platforms. Before the advent of social media, no radio programme known to me exposed abuses of women the way Zvinoyera did through the Madzibaba Ishmael exposé, which shows that despite initial 'moral panics',[1] technology has its positives. Flanked by her son and brother-in-law, Memory Mukanairi appeared on Zvinoyera in February 2024 where she disclosed that her daughter had mysteriously died and had been buried by her former churchmates without her knowledge. These revelations opened floodgates for more allegations against GJP leader, Ishmael Chokurongerwa, popularly known as 'Madzibaba Ishmael', which included running a cult at his Lily Farm in Nyabira, Murewa (which he called Canaan ostensibly because it would be the only place left after the 'imminent' end of the world). Women and underaged girls were allegedly subjected to hard labour and forced marriages at the behest of Madzibaba Ishmael who was deified by GJP congregants.

Ethics are moral principles which guide human behaviour; they enable people to choose between what is right and wrong (Firmstone, 2023). Every profession has its ethics. Ward (2020) defines media ethics as principles which foster responsible gathering and production of information. Principles of ethical journalism include seeking consent from subjects, protecting sources, disclosing conflict of interest, seeking objectivity and truth and accuracy (Ricchiardi, 2024). Ricchiardi adds that these principles foster responsible journalism which operates in the interests of the public. Zvinoyera exposed a host of

1 A term which was coined by Cohen in 1972 to describe how society tends to (often unnecessarily) resist new ideas and phenomenon fearing that they will corrupt social values.

DOI: 10.4324/9781003569435-23

undesirable behaviours which include contravention of laws governing registration of births and deaths and abuse of underaged girls and women. Other mainstream media outlets such as The Herald and Newsday subsequently followed up on the story and the police, which had dragged its feet, sprang to action, arresting Madzibaba Ishmael and his seven accomplices (Masinga, 2024). The study aims to (i) establish Zvinoyera's portrayal of Madzibaba Ishmael's relationship with his female congregants, (ii) assess the extent to which the show fulfilled ethical journalism principles, and (iii) find out what can be done to prevent abuse of congregants by religious leaders.

In the next section, the background of the study sheds light on the impact of the media in exposing immoral and illegal practices and the police's complicity in such activities. Thereafter, a review of literature on ethics and media coverage of issues related to the abuse of religious followers, especially women and girls in Zimbabwe's African indigenous churches is done within the realms of law and ethics. This precedes discussion of intersectionality, the study's theoretical framework, which is followed by the methodology, an outline of research tools that were employed and justification for their selection and utilisation. Subsequently, discussion and analysis of findings, respectively usher the reader to the study's recommendations and, ultimately, the conclusion which provides a synopsis of the study.

Background

Patriarchy has its provenance in biblical times where social values prioritised men over women (Wood, 2019). Despite progression in terms of social values and technology, for many years, women remained marginalised through their exclusion from voting, relegation to less significant jobs, allocation of less income than men for the same jobs, among other things. Classical philosophers like Plato and Aristotle considered women to be intellectually weaker than men. De Beauvoir (1949) famously noted that society ascribes inferior status to women by projecting men as representative of human beings. She lamented the fact that she was often identified as Sartre's lover though she was an accomplished scholar in her own right.

Since religion had been a vital cog for colonialism, Africans' realisation of the need to leverage their worldview with positive Christian aspects (Musoni, 2022) birthed what came to be known as African Independent Churches, African Indigenous Churches, African instituted churches, African initiated churches, and African international churches 'abbreviated as AICs' (Musoni, 2021a, p. 1). Inspired by John the Baptist, Shonhiwa Masedze, better known as 'Johanne Masowe', pioneered this trend in Zimbabwe when he established the Johanne Masowe Chishanu Churches (John of the Wilderness Churches which congregate on Friday) (Mukonyora, 2007, p. 18). Other AICs include the Ezekiel Guti led Zimbabwe Assemblies of God (Africa) Forward in Faith (ZAOGA FIF), Nehemiah Mutendi's Zion Christian Church (ZCC), and the African Apostolic Church (AAC) led by Paul Mwazha (Musoni & Gundani,

2016, p. 3). Though 'Zimbabwe is a secular state' (Bertelsmann Stiftung, 2022, p. 7), AICs have a significant following in the country (Musoni, 2021a).

Critics of AICs, especially apostolic churches, accuse their leaders of running cultic organisations where women, including minors, are, among other forms of ill-treatment, denied access to medical attention, subjected to virginity testing, forcibly married off, at times to old men, sexually abused and exposed to diseases as they are regarded as an 'apostolic diet of wives' for male congregants (Machingura, 2011, p. 185). AIC members, especially leaders who have hogged the limelight for negative reasons on numerous occasions, have added traction to these allegations. On the 13th of November 2021, Goodness and Mercy Ministries leader Tapiwa Freddy, popularly known as 'T Freddy' was accused of raping a female congregant, Rutendo Makuti (Ndoro, 2021). In January 2024, Walter Magaya, Prophetic Healing and Deliverance (PHD) ministries founder was, for the third time in a decade, embroiled in a sex scandal when he was accused of raping a 14-year-old girl, Amanda Moyo, who he had adopted (Mavhimira & Dube, 2023). Madzibaba Ismael's arrest in February 2024 marked his second incarceration in less than a decade, on charges which included facilitation of child marriages (O'Reilly, 2024).

Worryingly, it seems as though, due to their well-documented relationship with the ZANU PF government, prominent AIC leaders commit crimes with impunity because they are protected by the police and state media (Tarusarira & Humbe, 2022). However, privately owned newspapers such as the Zimbabwe Independent sometimes expose church leaders' scandals. In 2023, the paper ran a story in which Yolanda Makaya claimed to have sought refuge in a foreign country after Passion Java, a self-styled prophet who she accused of impregnating her, sent people to force her to terminate the pregnancy. However, it is members of the apostolic church, famed for their white garments, who appear to be the biggest beneficiary of government links (Musoni, 2019). On the 19th of January 2011, then Zimbabwean president Robert Mugabe controversially released Godfrey Nzira from prison after Nzira had served only seven of his 42-year jail sentence following his conviction on seven counts of rape and one of indecent assault involving female congregants (Nyangani, 2023).

Bhobhi Makaza, another JMCC member was granted presidential amnesty by President Emmerson Mnangagwa in 2023, just four years into his 18-year jail sentence for raping his 11-year-old niece (Mangwaya, 2023). To add insult to injury, Makaza was rewarded with a Toyota Aqua vehicle by controversial ZANU PF benefactor Wicknell Chivayo after Makaza likened Mnangagwa to honey ('huchi' in Shona) in an interview with news reporters following his release from prison (Mangwaya, 2024). 'Huchi' has since gained usage in informal Shona parlance where it is used as an expression of approval, and Makaza attracts admirers wherever he goes. Chivayo himself was once arrested on charges of fraud in 2018, though he was later acquitted (ZW News, 2023).

Literature review

Since Dillon-Malone published his seminal work on origins of Johanne Masowe in 1976, AICs have attracted a groundswell of scholarship (Kgatle, 2019; Musoni, 2021a). Many researchers who study white garment churches, however, focus on JMCC at the expense of Johanne Marange Apostolic Church (JMAC) (Madziyire, 2013; Mukonyora, 2015; Musevenzi, 2017). This could be because JMCC was established before JMAC so the former may be regarded as more authentic than the latter. Scholars have called for more studies on child marriages and the denial of access to education and medical facilities to female members across apostolic churches (Bengesai et al., 2021, p. 1).

AICs have an unenviable reputation of condoning suppression of female voices in the church. Apparently, this is a colonial relic, as in 1984, Brandel-Syrier argued that women had always actively participated in AICs whilst 'in Europe we still have a long way to go' (p. 13). Mukonyora (2015) blames Western historians for downplaying African women's participation in churches. Obare (2021) concurs that AICs recognised men and women, but the colonial administration recorded activities of male leaders whilst 'the women remained nameless and faceless with their efforts diminished' (p. 3).

Zimbabwean talk shows have done commendably in handling women and children's issues. Radio Zimbabwe's Nguva Yevanhukadzi (women's issues) has been aired for decades. Zvakanangana Nemadzimai on Zimbabwe Broadcasting Corporation (television) was introduced in 1997 before its rebranding to Nguva yemhuri (Family time) and, ultimately, Mai Chisamba Show (Hove, 2007). These programmes, however, hardly resulted in the apprehension of culprits since they avoided saying names of suspects. Zvinoyera somewhat flouted ethical principles by revealing the name of the complainant in a way that is convincing and exposes the culprit, a rarity from a Zimbabwean talk show.

Theoretical framework: intersectionality

Intersectionality, which undergirds this study, emerged as a reaction to feminism's tendency to advance white women's interests to the exclusion of non-white women. Crenshaw (1989) who used intersection as a metaphor for the convergence of race, gender, and class in the marginalisation of vulnerable groups, particularly women, popularised this theory. hooks (2015) concurs that black women are at the receiving end of multiple forms of segregation. Though white women are oppressed by male whites, they racially oppress non-white people whilst black men oppress black women.

Crenshaw (1991) clarifies that gender and race are not the only factors that affect women. She adds that women who experience several forms of marginalisation understand segregation more than those who suffer less, so only considering sex and race 'marginalises those who are multiply burdened and obscures claims that cannot be understood as resulting from discrete sources of discrimination' (Crenshaw, 1991, p. 40). Intersectionality was selected for this study because it recognises that women 'do not necessarily share the same experiences or form a homogenous grouping' (Pelak, 2010, p. 63).

Though Crenshaw (1989) initially applied intersectionality to legal matters, such as workplace-related and domestic abuse, it has since found resonance in different social contexts. Leath et al. (2023, p. 157) note that different forms 'of oppression leave individuals and communities erased from the public view and leave their needs veiled from public understandings, buried under a heap of social locations seen through prejudiced lenses'. hooks (2015) avers that, unlike feminism, intersectionality recognises experiences of women from different groups Davis (1989, p. 3) opines that those who overcome marginalisation must assist others: 'We must always attempt to lift as we climb'.

When lines between protectors and predators are blurred

Media shows like Zvinotyisa have a duty to expose undesirable behaviour. Instead of protecting women and children as vulnerable groups, leaders of white garment churches have become somewhat synonymous with violation of rights of female congregants. Polygamy reflects the institutionalisation of patriarchy through social background (upbringing), culture (tradition), and religion (churches). As highlighted earlier, establishment of the first AICs was strongly influenced by African tradition and the Bible. Women who are raised in polygynous families within AICs 'potentially experience a triple form of oppression: in the home, church and society' (Masoga & Shokane, 2016, p. 89). Virginity is regarded as a symbol of purity and faithfulness in African cultures and churches, which, unfortunately, often results in the trampling of rights of female members. Nhamoyebonde (2015) lamented JMCC's 'Recovery', an 'operation' which forced young virgins into marriages with older men. Female Student Network Trust (FSNT) assistant advocacy officer, Molyne Mukomawasha, a former JMCC congregant revealed 'gross human rights violations' like 'mandatory virginity testing for young girls by older women using fingers. Those who were found not to be virgins were forcefully given away into marriages with older men' (Kubatana.net, 2021). In JMAC, girls who are found to be virgins are congratulated whilst those who fail the test are shamed (Machingura, 2011; Mutseta, 2018). Female members are biologically disadvantaged because, unlike their male counterparts, their conduct can be easily 'judged' through pregnancy, giving birth among other means yet corresponding tests for males hardly exist (Chisale & Moyo, 2016, p. 89). Sadly, many women and girls are socialised into acquiescing in violation of their rights. Writing about the Batswana culture, Selokela (2005, p. iv) revealed that young girls were indoctrinated that their virginity is the pride of their future husbands and women have an obligation to fulfil men's sexual urges.

Abuse of women and girls in religious formations in Zimbabwe, especially white garment churches, also has a political dynamic because of the close relationship between government leaders and the leadership of these churches (Bengesai et al., 2021). Apparently, religious leaders condone the government's suppression of dissenting voices (Bertelsmann Stiftung, 2022, p. 7) so that the latter 'turns a blind eye' on their abuse of women and children to the frustration of victims who are often reprimanded by their perpetrators for reporting to the police. As a result, many cases are unreported (Amnesty International, 2021; Malaba, 2024) – the power of unity among stakeholders.

Abuses of women and girls in some countries are perpetuated by a lack of political will among their leaders. Though many countries have ratified the Convention of the Rights of the Child,[2] child marriages are still practised in South Asia and sub-Saharan Africa (Bengesai et al., 2021). Since ethics is moralistic, lacking the coercive aspect of laws, media exposure of errant behaviour and calls for authorities and stakeholders to act decidedly to seek justice for abused women and children often get ignored. Some governments contradict legislative advice. The Zimbabwean government only enacted the Marriages Act, six years after the constitutional court ruled that existing marriage laws were anachronistic. In fact, the enactment of the law was triggered by public uproar and pressure from the media following a spate of deaths of underaged pregnant girls. To her credit, Sithembiso Nyoni, then Minister of Women's Affairs, Community, Small and Medium Enterprises, investigated circumstances surrounding the death of a 14-year-old girl who died whilst giving birth at an apostolic church in Marange and her recommendations influenced President Emmerson Mnangagwa to sign the Marriage Act (Chapter 5:17) on the 27th of May 2022. This law, among other things, criminalises marriage of children who are below 18. Other stakeholders have also made commendable efforts.

In 2019, Andby Makururu leader of a JMCC church and founder of a civic group, Ruvheneko Rwenyenyedzi Trust (RRT) broke ranks when he revealed that institutionalised rape is pervasive in apostolic churches and led multi-denominational campaigns against child marriages (Nyangani, 2019). That Nyangani, a reporter at The Standard, a Zimbabwean private newspaper which often accuses the government of protecting leaders of apostolic churches who violate rights of women and girls' rights, covered Makururu's noble efforts demonstrated objective reporting by the paper. In addition, though in 2023 Zim Eye described Makururu as 'ZANU PF linked', in 2021, alongside The Standard's sister paper, Newsday (Nyangani, 2021), the online paper characterised the religious leader as a 'child rights defender'. In fact, a random

2 Adopted by a General Assembly resolution 44/25 of 20 November 1989, the United Nations Convention on the Rights of the Child (UCRC) recognizes anyone below the age of 18 to be a child and deserves access to basic human rights such as health, shelter, education, protection from violence, freedom of thought and religion among others (Convention on the Rights of the Child, 1989).

Google search for Makururu reveals positive stories from papers that are usually dismissive of apostolic sect leaders. These include reports in The Standard (2019) and Post on Sunday (Masekesa, 2021). Through stories of survivors of abuse, the media empowers women and girls in similar situations. Tambu Moyo's acquisition of sewing skills at Simukai Child Protection Program rescued her from an abusive husband who had married her when she was just 16 years of age and he was 43 (Malaba, 2024).

Methodology

Most of the studies on white garment churches (Madziyire, 2013; Mukonyora, 2015; Musevenzi, 2017) overgeneralise them, yet the emergence of numerous breakaway sects since the establishment of JMCC in 1932 is testament to differences between members. Caution, must, therefore be taken to avoid stereotyping JMCC churches. This chapter approached the GJP as a church which has typical white garment church features, as its peculiarities.

Zvinoyera episode which was uploaded on the Star FM YouTube channel on the 6th of March 2024 was purposively sampled for a few reasons. It influenced other victims to speak out, leading to the arrest of the culprit. With over three decades of broadcasting experience, the presenter, Tilder, has carved a niche for sensitive issues and the interactive nature of Zvinoyera which is available through livestream, YouTube, Facebook among other platforms that allow listeners to participate through these platforms.

Studies on white garment churches (Selokela, 2005; Mukonyora, 2007; Masoga & Shokane, 2016; Mutseta, 2018) tend to use gendered lenses, since they largely concentrate on violation of rights of female congregates as if male members are immune to such violations or their violations do not matter. Intersectionality facilitated recognition of unique challenges faced by women under study due to their gender, race, education, age and class, among other factors. A thematic analysis as the next section indicates, was done to explain findings of the study in line with the main aim to show how Zvinoyera ethically covered allegations against Madzibaba Ishmael.

Findings and discussion

Key issues were organised into subheadings though sometimes there is overlap. For instance, 'A law unto himself' and 'Child abuse' reveal how the patriarchal nature of religion, tradition, society, and lack of education contributed towards the success of Madzibaba Ishmael's activities. The study confirmed the hypothesis that Madzibaba Ishmael's victims, church members, and police officers were complicit in his criminal activities due to their reluctance to expose him. Thematic analysis yielded the following subheadings:

Zvinoyera as a platform for diverse views and its framing of allegations against 'Madzibaba' Ishmael

Consistent with its reputation for mundane issues, Zvinoyera starts off with a disclaimer, the signature tune which includes the words 'shocking, strange, bizarre', a loose translation of the show's Shona title, 'Zvinoyera, zvinoshamisa uye zvinotyisa'.

Apparently to set her guests at ease, Tilder employs colloquial language to introduce her three guests; the mother of the deceased woman who she calls 'mama', the younger brother of the father of the deceased (bam'nin, a contraction of 'babamunini', uncle). She further lightens the mood by jokingly asking the brother of the deceased if he wants to be referred to as 'tsano', (Shona urban lingo for brother-in-law) which he affirms, and she complies throughout the interaction. (In the analysis, I will use these names as proper nouns to identify the three guests.)

Tilder is often accused of interrupting guests, but, in this episode, she allowed the three relatives to express themselves by providing less interjections and responding in a supportive way which clarifies for the audience who the guests sought assistance from. For instance, when she asks how members of JMCC are buried, Bam'nin explains that they are wrapped in a cloth. The trio discloses that they witnessed a strange spectacle. Bam'nin and Mama underline their shock at seeing many newly dug graves. Tilder empathises with her guests through exclamations of disbelief such as 'zvakaoma' (it's strange), 'ey!', 'unbelievable' and 'huye bodo' and 'nikisi'. At some point she likens the events to folktales, 'zvinoita kunge ngano'. She repeatedly asks if what she is hearing is real. It is indisputable, thus far, that the show is living to its claims of presenting weird issues. The content cannot be made up, it is reality broadcasting in its prosaic sense.

The way Mama mimics Madzibaba Ishmael reveals his inconsiderateness in a hilarious way. For example, when Tilder asks whether a member of the church can ask after running out of some provisions, Mama responds in 'Madzibaba Ishmael's' brutal tone, 'gutai zvamapiwa' (be content with what you are given) and 'hamukumbidzane' (you don't lend things to each other). 'Ndomutemo wangu' (that's my rule); 'vangazondipandukira' (they may turn against me) is the justification that 'Madzibaba Ishmael' gives for outlawing education, national identity documents, visits to clinics and hospitals, and listening to the radio. Mama answers the presenter's question on how they conduct church services using the royal 'we' when she again simulates the GJP leader: 'takatonamata kare' (we have already prayed so we are now waiting for the arrival of Canaan).

Tilder expands the public sphere by reading readers' comments, which show that they are basically as baffled as she is so they, like the presenter, ask if what they have heard is real. They advise the family to report the matter to the Police General Headquarters (PGHQ), engage law enforcement agents, among other things. Other readers recall that Madzibaba Ishmael and his followers physically assaulted police officers a decade ago, which Tilder confirms with Mama. The presenter advises Mama to state services which she can offer instead of relying on handouts which do not last, to which the latter reveals that she wants to start a poultry project. By affording relatives of the deceased the opportunity to discuss their experiences, interpreting these statements, asking them follow up questions, including comments from Zvinoyera fans, the show facilitated discussions from diverse perspectives. However, Tilder could have enhanced the show's interactivity by opening lines and engaging representatives from the police and the government.

A law unto himself

The status of AIC leaders is almost cultlike. Though they are aggrieved by Madzibaba Ishmael's deeds, the three guests refer to him as 'mukuru' (the elder, leader) and at some point, Mama calls him 'Mambo' (Lord), apparently because she used to address him as such during her time in Nyabira. A brother of Professor Itai Muwati who died in mysterious circumstances at Lily Farm disclosed that Madzibaba Ishmael calls himself 'God'. This arrogance sharply contrasts with the JMCC founder's rejection of being referred to as 'the Secret Messiah' (Musoni, 2021b, p. 4). Consistent with his lofty status, Mama states that Madzibaba Ishmael and his inner circle live in large brick houses whilst the rest of the GJP members live in plastic makeshift shelters.

White garment churches are known for their preference of outlying areas, especially for praying. Apparently, Madzibaba Ishmael used the seclusion of Lily Farm as cover for his sinister deeds. Mama reveals that there are no headmen in sight; she never saw one when she lived at the farm. Conducting burials without informing the headman or police demonstrates Madzibaba Ishmael's arrogance.

Ishmael's activities may have gone unnoticed because those who were close to him feared him. Bam'nin and Mama reveal that police officers stationed at Nyabire Police Station reiterated that it is risky to confront Madzibaba Ishmael and his followers, with the former adding that it would take the whole police camp to fight them. Bam'nin complains that many followers of Ishmael barged into the police station yet only two relatives of the deceased were allowed. As Tsano indicates in the section with the subheading, 'Child abuse', the police turned a blind eye on blatant contraventions of laws at Lily Farm.

'Charismatic figure'

Madzibaba Ishamel's charismatic nature is indisputable, as Mama and Bam'nin reveal. Many of his followers surrendered their daughters' bride price to him and many more heeded his call to resettle in their rural areas whilst he served his prison term and followed him to Nyabira upon his release. Mama adds that, like other GJP congregants who include her late daughter and her husband who sold their house before moving to Nyabira, she believed that Madzibaba Ishmael was anointed 'taiti ane mweya mutsvene waMwari'. Mama concedes that though she spent just four months at Lily Farm before her expulsion, Madzibaba Ishmael has many followers 'vanoona zvichivaitira' (used to the lifestyle) who have been there for years whilst others leave one at a time, 'vamwe vanobuda one one'. Bam'nin speculates that the GJP leader used his extraterrestrial powers to cast a spell on his followers, 'vanhu ava vakatoputirwa'. One can also question if that is the case, how is it that some people like Mama leave the sect.

The impact of Ishmael's dishonesty on his followers

Churches are expected to inculcate honesty. However, it appears as though Madzibaba Ishmael's dishonesty spirals downwards to his followers. Just as Bam'nin reveals that members of GJP use cell phones despite Madzibaba Ishmael's discouragement, Mama's revelation that he secretively listens to the radio 'anoterera kabisira' suggests that they are taking a leaf from his book. Just as Ishmael is evasive when anyone, including the police, look for him, his followers have mastered the art of lying as they simply said the father of the deceased was not around, 'mukuwasha ainzi akafamba' when relatives arrived at Lily Farm. The police also realised that claims by members of the church's statement that a representative had reported the death were false, as the police had no such record.

Conceptualisation of family relations

Bam'nin's revelation that the family reported the church for burying their relative without informing them to the police and his accompanying Mama and Tsano to Zvinoyera demonstrates their unity. He also supports Mama's plea for assistance when he reveals that at some point she worked as a maid but the $20 that she earned was not enough to sustain her family of four children who she lives with in an unfinished house.

He uses terms like 'mai vemunhu' (mother of the deceased) and 'muridzi wemwana' (the owner/parent of the child). In Shona culture, a child cannot be buried without informing the parent, especially the mother. Both Bam'nin and Mama explain the irony that Madzibaba Ishmael's concept of family often estranges his followers from their relatives. Bam'nin says his brother now claims that his only relatives are his fellow apostolic sect members, 'mukoma ari kuti hatisisiri hama dzake, hama dzake aamapositori' and further explains that when the police summoned his brother to the police camp, his churchmates accompanied him in numbers 'because they are now his family'. Mama confirms that that GJP church members regard her husband as a blood relative, 'ndeweropa redu' (we carry the same blood in our veins) and 'taaropa rimwe' (we are now of the same blood). It is surprising that the congregants believe that fallacy because GJP members cannot replace biological relatives. This is shown when in a clear sign of neglect, Tsano reveals that children of the deceased woman were seen wandering. In contrast, Mama discloses that during her time in Nyabira, whenever she called her children who had refused to relocate, opting to stay with relatives in Harare, they expressed happiness with how they were being looked after. By offering Mama, Bam'nin, and Tsano a platform to speak, Zvinoyera fulfilled a few principles of ethical journalism: consulting verifiable sources and truth and accuracy through Tilder's interaction with Mama, Bam'nin, and Tsano and protection of subjects by publicising allegations of abuse against Madzibaba Ishmael.

Indoctrination of victims

Mama reveals that female members of the GJP church are supposed to bow down before any man who they meet, and failure to do so attracts expulsion from the church, which implies that men are superior to women. The church's patriarchal nature is also reflected by Mama's husband's decision to sell their house in which she stayed with their children to punish her for her expulsion by Madzibaba Ishmael. As highlighted earlier, Madzibaba Ishmael interfered in marriages. Mama's expulsion was based on the GJP leader's unproven allegations that she had killed two children, one of them belonging to her co-wife and the other, her daughter's, and her husband offered no resistance to her departure. Mama further says Madzibaba Ishmael can use the slightest misunderstanding between a couple to excommunicate the wife. Instead of building relationships, Madzibaba Ishmael's church destroyed families and made lives of women who stayed at his farm worse than that of women elsewhere.

Furthermore, Madzibaba Ishmael receives the lion's share and gives small rations to the workers, women and children. Despite their hard work, women are not guaranteed food, a basic right, and supply of vegetables and sugar is erratic. Menstruating women are made to use unhygienic methods of preventing blood flow such as cloths instead of sanitary pads. Mama discloses that women make their requests for everything, including undergarments, to Madzibaba Ismael through their husbands. Not only is this dehumanising to both spouses but Mama adds that Madzibaba Ishmael is so unresponsive that he hardly delivers, which prompts Tilder to ask whether many women end up wearing tattered undergarments, which Mama confirms. This is consistent with Tsano's description of tattered clothes worn by children in the next section. Though girls and women generally struggle to get decent clothing and other necessities, failure to get sanitary pads affects most of them as a textual analysis of Tilder's guests show. As intersectionality theory notes, females who have privileged backgrounds, unlike their poor counterparts, have access to their needs, which makes them better off than even some males, though that is rare among Zimbabweans.

Child abuse

The Zvinoyera episode under study exposed various illegal activities at the farm: marrying off girls who are barely in their teens and their subjection to hard labour whilst nursing babies, depriving medical care to women who fell ill during pregnancy, and burial of those who died at childbirth without their parents' knowledge (see discussion under 'child abuse'). To Tilder's credit, in fulfilment of ethical journalism, no minor nor person of any age was named on Zvinoyera.

Children's rights are violated as they are denied access to educational and medical institutions. Bamn'in uses words like 'havana zivo yehupenyu' (they live a hopeless life) and 'matambudziko' (it's sad) whilst Tsano describes the clothing of children who he came across as heartrending. Both Bam'nin and Tsano agree that GJP condones child abuse through child marriage and child labour. Bam'nin states that girls as young as 12 enter marriages: 'kamwe kasikana kandakaona kanogona kuva netwelve years'. Tsano estimates that girls are married from 13–15 years of age and despite their youthfulness, these children fulfil adult chores such as carrying maize meal sacks 'vanotsiga hupfu hwavo nehudiki hwavo'. That the deceased woman who was barely 27 left a nine-year-old son presents a high likelihood that she got married before she reached 18.

Violation of human rights

Madzibaba Ishmael's order for members of the church to sell their houses and move to makeshift shelter violated their basic human rights to shelter. That he also instructed husbands to sleep with all their wives on a single bed dehumanised them: 'isu madzimai nemurume tainzi tirare muimba one hupenyu hwese . . . tairara pamubhedha hwani' (me, my co-wife and our husband slept in the same room all the time). As Mama unconsciously reveals through her remark that GJP members do not participate in political activities like voting, destroying and discarding their forms of identification as instructed by their leader disenfranchises them. Clearly, Madzibaba Ishmael enforces a media and education blackout so that he maintains a stranglehold on his followers. To show how successful he was in achieving this, towards the end of the programme, Tilder states that the weird practices that have been exposed by her show are taking place in Nyabira, a place which is very close to Harare 'pedyo pedyo neHarare'. As Bam'nin states, deaths whose circumstances are dubious, judging by their frequency and flouting of cultural and legal protocol which require notification of authorities, lend credence to doubts; despite all this, most of Madzibaba Ishmael's followers defend him.

From a cultural and human rights perspective, burial of Mama's daughter in a shallow grave, without her relatives, was a show of disrespect from Madzibaba Ishmael and his followers. As shown in the previous section, in the African tradition, burial of a loved one unites relatives, as they regard death as a loss to all relatives. Conditions of living at Nyabire are so appalling that Bam'nin reckons that a woman can be raped because of the heights of the grass at places resided by Ishmael's followers. In addition, families disintegrate in the name of religion and prohibition of sharing of commodities among residents of Lily Farm violates freedom of association. Madzibaba Ismael's followers are also stripped of dignity by having a man sleeping with his two wives on one bed as previously highlighted.

Conclusion and recommendations

Zvinoyera exposes injustices and abuse of human rights issues which are shunned by many mainstream media channels because they are 'not newsworthy'. The episode under study reminded listeners that, like other human beings, religious leaders are not perfect. Zvinoyera revealed Madzibaba Ishmael's violation of freedoms of expression, association and flouting of basic human rights like the right to education, shelter, and health. Due to indoctrination by Madzibaba Ishmael, victims aided their oppression through compliance to his questionable orders like surrendering their possessions to him and following him to Nyabire. Churches ought to instil discipline and a sense of dignity instead of immoral behaviour such as two wives sharing a bed with their husband, dehumanising women by making them toil for Madzibaba Ishmael and relying on him for intimate clothing such as underwear. Madzibaba Ishmael had become a law unto himself, as he did not answer to anyone. Police officers at Nyabira Police Station clearly colluded with the GJP founder though fear appears to be a contributory factor, in which case, the police should always seek back-up manpower when dealing with dangerous people. Church leaders who abuse their influence should be handed deterrent custodial sentences. Civic groups, the government, the media, and people who once followed religious leaders who are accused of abuse should work together to expose their evil acts. This helps to discourage practices like marrying young girls and chauvinism, and the government should make education and health accessible to create awareness towards abuses and reduce avoidable deaths, respectively.

Tilder should bring representatives from the police, women's groups, and the GJP church and open phone lines to increase channels of communication with her audience. Perhaps she could consider hosting a live audience in the studio as well. Religion should allow all members, regardless of gender, age, and class, access to basic human rights such as health (medical facilities), education, and freedom of association. Women and girls who are the most affected groups as observed in the study, also ought to be allowed to choose partners for marriage.

References

Amnesty International. (2021). *Treated like furniture: Gender-based violence and COVID-19 response in Southern Africa*. https://www.amnesty.org.zw/2021/08/zimbabwean-authorities-must-take-decisive-action-to-prohibit-and-end-child-marriage/

Baloyi, E. (2022). Pioneering gendered African theology: A historical perspective of Mary-Anne Elizabeth Plaatjies-Van Huffel. *Studia Historiae Ecclesiasticae*, *48*(2), 12. https://doi.org/10.25159/2412-4265/10585

Bengesai, A. V., Amusa, L. B., & Makonye, F. (2021). The impact of girl child marriage on the completion of the first cycle of secondary education in Zimbabwe: A propensity score analysis. *PLOS One*, *16*(6), e0252413. https://doi.org/10.1371/journal.pone.0252413

Bertelsmann Stiftung. (2022). *Bertelsmann Stiftung transformation index 2022 country report*. Bertelsmann Stiftung. https://bti-project.org/fileadmin/api/content/en/downloads/reports/country_report_2022_ZWE.pdf

Brandel-Syrier, M. (1984). The role of women in African Independent Churches. *Missionalia: Southern African Journal of Mission Studies (Southern African Missiological Society (SAMS))*, 12(1), 13–18.

Chisale, S. S., & Moyo, H. (2016). Church discipline as virginity testing: Shaping adolescent girls' sexuality in the Evangelical Lutheran Churches in Africa. *Alternation*, *23*(2), 89–104.

Cohen, S. (1972). *Folk devils and moral panics*. Routledge.

Convention on the Rights of the Child. (1989). *Treaty no. 27531* (United Nations Treaty Series, 1577, pp. 3–178). Retrieved July 3, 2020, from https://treaties.un.org/doc/Treaties/1990/09/19900902%2003-14%20AM/Ch_IV_11p.pdf

Crenshaw, K. (1989). Demarginalizing the intersection of race and sex: A Black feminist critique of antidiscrimination doctrine, feminist theory and antiracist policies. *University of Chicago Legal Forum*, *1*, 139–167.

Crenshaw, K. (1991). Mapping the margins: Intersectionality, identity politics, and violence against women of color. *Stanford Law Review*, *43*(6), 1241–1299. https://doi.org/10.2307/1229039

Davis, A. Y. (1989). *Women, culture and politics*. Random House.

De Beauvoir, S. (1989). *The second sex*. Vintage Books. (Original work published 1949)

Dillon-Malone, C. M. (1976). *The Korsten basketmakers: A study of the Masowe Apostles, an indigenous African religious movement*. Manchester University Press.

Englund, H. (2019, March 26). Radio as a political medium in Africa. In *Oxford research encyclopedia of politics*. Retrieved September 23, 2024, from https://oxfordre.com/politics/view/10.1093/acrefore/9780190228637.001.0001/acrefore-9780190228637-e-814

Firmstone, J. (2023). *The shaping of news: A framework for analysis*. Springer International Publishing. https://doi.org/10.1007/978-3-031-21963-4

hooks, b. (2015). *Feminism is for everybody: Passionate politics* (2nd ed.). Routledge.

Hove, U. (2007). Mai Chisamba becomes independent producer. *The Herald*. https://allafrica.com/stories/200702170024.html

Kgatle, M. S. (2019). A remarkable woman in African independent churches: Examining Christina Nku's leadership in St John's Apostolic faith mission. *Studia Historiae Ecclesiasticae*, *45*(1). https://doi.org/10.25159/2412-4265/3323

Kubatana.net. (2021). *I have witnessed gross human rights violations against girls in the name of religion*. https://kubatana.net/2021/08/21/i-have-witnessed-gross-human-rights-violations-against-girls-in-the-name-of-religion

Leath, J. S. Hadebe, N., Symmonds, N., & Perkins, A. K. (2023). Black feminism, womanism, and intersectionality discourse: A theo-ethical roundtable. *Journal of Moral Theology*, *12*(Special Issue 1). https://jmt.scholasticahq.com/issue/7228-vol-12-issue-special-issue-1-2023

Machingura, F. (2011). A diet of wives as the lifestyle of the Vapostori sects: The polygamy debate in the face of HIV and AIDS in Zimbabwe. *Africana*, *5*(2), 185–221.

Madziyire, N. M. (2013). *Perceptions of the link between religion and the feminization of poverty: A case of the Johanne Marange Apostolic Faith of Seke area in Zimbabwe* [PhD thesis, University of South Africa]. http://hdl.handle.net/10500/13764

Malaba, B. (2024). *The ties between the Zimbabwean state and a church*. Center for Collaborative Investigative Journalism (CCIJ). https://www.zammagazine.com/investigations/1807-the-ties-between-the-zimbabwean-state-and-a-church-government-turns-a-blind-eye-to-religious-sect-s-child-marriages

Mangwaya, M. (2024). *Murewa rape victim's unending ordeal.* https://www.newsday.co.zw/local-news/article/200027387/murewa-rape-victims-unending-ordeal-as-zanu-pf-fetes-tormentor

Mangwaya. (2023). *News in depth: After Mnangagwa amnesty, Murewa convicted rapist returns to broken home.* https://www.newsday.co.zw/thestandard/news/article/200012715/news-in-depth-after-mnangagwa-amnesty-murewa-convicted-rapist-returns-to-broken-home

Mano, W. (2012). Why radio is Africa's medium of choice in the global age. In D. Ligaga, D. Moyo, & L. Gunner (Ed.), *Radio in Africa: Cultures, publics and communities* (pp. 102–117). Johannesburg Wits University Press.

Masekesa. (2021). *Madzibaba Andby wants dialogue with Noah Taguta over child marriages.* https://postonsunday.co.zw/2021/08/11/madzibaba-andby-wants-dialogue-with-noah-taguta-over-child-marriages/

Masinga, M. (2024). *No relief for Madzibaba Ishmael, accomplices.* https://www.hmetro.co.zw/no-relief-for-madzibaba-ishmael-accomplices/#:~:text=Madzibaba%20Ishmael%20and%20his%20accomplices%20are%20facing%20charges

Masoga, M. A., & Shokane, A. L. (2016). Women in polygynous marriages and African initiated Churches: Selected narratives in Greater Tzaneen, South Africa. *Agenda, 30*(2), 1. https://doi.org/10.1080/10130950.2016.1259868

Mavhimira, B., & Dube, S. (2023). *My life is in danger . . . Passion Java's pregnant mistress calls for help.* https://www.newsday.co.zw/thestandard/standard-style/article/200007650/my-life-is-in-dangerpassion-javas-pregnant-mistress-calls-for-help

Mukonyora, I. (2007). *Wandering a gendered wilderness: Suffering and healing in an African initiated Church.* Peter Lang Publishing Group.

Mukonyora, I. (2015). Four ways into an African sacred wilderness: A study of Johane Masowe's teaching. *Religion, 45*(2), 209–220. https://doi.10.1080/0048721X.2014.992107

Musevenzi., J. (2017). The African independent Apostolic Church's doctrine under threat: The emerging power of faith-based organisations' interventions and the Johanne Marange Apostolic Church in Zimbabwe. *Journal for the Study of Religion*, *30*(2), 178–206. http://dx.doi.org/10.17159/2413-3027/2017/v30n2a8

Musoni, P. (2019). White garment churches (Vapositori) and ZANU-PF party politics in Zimbabwe: True marriage or marriage of convenience during and post-Mugabe era. *HTS Theological Studies*, *75*(1), 1–7. https://dx.doi.org/10.4102/hts.v75i1.5412

Musoni, P. (2021a). Spiritualised political theology in a polarised political environment: A Pentecostal movement's response to party politics in Zimbabwe. *HTS Teologiese Studies/Theological Studies*, *77*(4), a6312. https://doi.org/10.4102/hts.v77i4.6312

Musoni, P. (2021b). African spirituality in the Johane Masowe Chishanu religious movement in Zimbabwe: A Christian church-sect dichotomy. *HTS Teologiese Studies/Theological Studies*, *77*(4), a6317. https://doi.org/10.4102/hts.v77i4.6317

Musoni, P. (2022). Johane Masowe Chishanu Church theology and spirituality: A transition from the written Bible to holy spirit utterances. *Studia Historiae*, *48*(3). Ecclesiasticae. https://doi.org/10.25159/2412-4265/7907

Musoni, P., & Gundani, H. (2016). Easter celebrations with a difference: A critical study of the Johane Masowe Chishanu Yenyenyedzi approach to the event. *Studia Historiae Ecclesiasticae*, *42*(1), 22–35. https://doi.org/10.25159/2412-4265/422

Mutseta, A. (2018). Christian polygamous marriages in Zimbabwe, women's experiences and the dual scourge of HIV/aids and poverty: The case of 'Apostles'/Vapostori of Marange. *International Journal of Sciences: Basic and Applied Research (IJSBAR)*, *39*(2), 186–207.

Ndoro, N. (2021). Rape accused Prophet T Freddy arrested then granted free bail. *Nehanda*. https://nehandaradio.com/2021/11/18/rape-accused-prophet-t-freddy-arrested-then-granted-free-bail/#google_vignette

Nhamoyebonde, L. (2015). *Johane Masowe Yechishanu victims neglected: Focus put on police assault*. Genderlinks. https://genderlinks.org.za/casestudies/johane-masowe-yechishanu-victims-neglected-focus-put-on-police-assault-2015-05-23/

Nyangani, K. (2019). Madzibaba Andby moves to curb rape culture in churches. *The Standard*. https://www.thestandard.co.zw/2019/12/01/madzibaba-andby-moves-curb-rape-culture-churches

Nyangani, K. (2021). *Vapostori withdraw children from schools over vaccination*. https://www.newsday.co.zw/southerneye/news/article/13404/vapostori-withdraw-children-from-schools-over-vaccination

Nyangani, K. (2023). Revisiting Madzibaba Nzira's legacy 13 years after. *Newsday*. https://www.newsday.co.zw/local-news/article/200020689/revisiting-madzibaba-nziras-legacy-13-years-after

Obare, A. (2021). *The role of women in African indigenous Churches: A case study of the Ruwe Holy Ghost Church in East Africa*. The Social Science Research Network (SSRN). http://dx.doi.org/10.2139/ssrn.4255629

O'Reilly. (2024). Zimbabwe police charge self-proclaimed prophet Ishmael and rescue 251 children. *BBC*. https://www.bbc.co.uk/news/world-africa-68564667.amp

Pelak, C. F. (2010). Women and gender in South African soccer: A brief history. *Soccer and Society*, *11*(1), 63–78. https://10.1080/14660970903331342

Ricchiardi, S. (2024). Journalism in the public interest. *International Journalists Network*. https://ijnet.org/en/resource/journalism-public-interest#:~:text=Pubic%20service%20journalism%20comes%20in%20various%20forms.%20In%20one%20example

Selokela, O. N. (2005). *African women overcoming patriarchy: A study of women. In Apostolic faith mission (AFM) Church. In Rustenburg, South Africa* [Master of theology in religion and theology thesis, University of KwaZulu-Natal].

The Standard. (2019). *Madzibaba Andby helps drug abusers*. https://bulawayo24.com/index-id-news-sc-national-byo-167067.html

Tarusarira, J., & Humbe, B. P. (2022). The ambivalence of African independent/initiated Churches in colonial and postcolonial politics. In W. S. Goldstein & J.-P. Reed (Eds.), *Religion in rebellions, revolutions, and social movements* (pp. 158–172). Routledge.

Ward, S. J. A. (2020). Introduction: Media ethics in a global age. In *Ethics and the media: An introduction. Cambridge applied ethics* (pp. 1–8). Cambridge University Press.

Wood, H. (2019). Gender inequality: The problem of harmful, patriarchal, traditional and cultural gender practices in the church. *HTS Teologiese Studies/Theological Studies*, *75*(1). https://www.10.4102/hts.v75i1.5177

Zim Eye. (2021). *Vapostori withdraw children from school over vaccination*. https://www.zimeye.net/2021/05/29/vapostori-withdraw-children-from-school-over-vaccination/

Zim Eye. (2023). *Vote ED and get 15 more years on earth: Madzibaba Andby*. https://www.zimeye.net/2023/03/19/vote-ed-and-get-15-more-years-on-earth-madzibaba-andby/

ZW News. (2023). Shock as Wicknell Chivayo wins US$22 million damages against ZPC. *ZW News*. https://zwnews.com/shock-as-wicknell-chivayo-wins-us22-million-damages-against-zpc/

Index

Note: page numbers in **bold** indicate a table on the corresponding page.

Able Child Africa: Disability-inclusive Child Safeguarding Guidelines 115–116
academic: institutions 150, 237, 239; literature 65, 120; performance 36, 158; professionals 64, 230, 251
access to justice: accommodation 2, 5, 13; for children 14, 17, 20–21, 26; definition of 14; for the hearing impaired 202, 205–208, 210, 213–214; limited 5, 87, 120, 213; migrant workers 167–168; persons with disabilities 79–80, 84, 87, 89–90; *see also* girls with disabilities; poor-illiterate 230, 232, 257, 260–261; right of 79–80, 83–86; unrepresented litigants 237, 251
accommodation: for children 13, 79; costs 264; hearing impaired 131–132, 136; judicial 250–251; persons with disabilities 80, 83–84, 88, 91, 115, 117; *see also* girls with disabilities; procedural 211, 236, 244
accuracy: child testimony 35, 39; interpretation 126, 141; witness 98, 109
accused person: evidence/testimony 24–25, 33, 105, 109–110, 118, 178; *see also* child witness; rights of 16, 19–20, 117, 165n1, 196, 209–210
ACRWC *see* African Charter on the Rights and Welfare of the Child
Adjei, Stephen B. (et al 2024) 203, 206
adjourn 105–106, 110, 177, 230
African Apostolic Church (AAC) 45, 294
African Charter on the Rights and Welfare of the Child (ACRWC) 37, 42, 61, 76, 159
African Charter to Human and People's Rights 116, 124
African churches 294
African Independent Churches 294
African Indigenous Churches 294
African Initiated Churches (AICs): perpetuate crimes against children 44–45, 50–51, 295; political affiliations 45, 52; religious inspiration/affiliations 294–297
African Sign Languages Resource Centre 151
age: appropriate accommodations 79, 84, 115; children under eighteen (18) 14, 46, 51, 61, 114–115, 298n2; of consent 51, 299; discrimination 15, 17, 50, 118, 299, 304–305; of offenders 267, 287–288; threshold for criminal liability 61
albinism 185
Albright, Madeleine 219
alcohol consumption 95, 98–99, 103–106, 241
Allen, Colin 157
Alternative and Augmented Communication (AAC) 90
Ame, Robert K. 64, 68
American Sign Language (ASL) 132, 151, 206
amnesty 295
anxiety 30, 34, 38, 179, 181
Apostolic Church (AAC) 45, 294
appeals: courts of 96, 255–256, 276; fees/costs 247; outcomes 279; procedural/linguistic barriers 247–248
applied linguistics 6–7
Ashagre, Aschalew 89

ASL *see* American Sign Language
assault (other than sexual) 109, 258, 267; *see also* domestic violence
audism 89, 134

Bada, Xochitl 171
Bahdi, Reem 83
bail 68–69, 103, 264, 269
Baillie, J. 191
Banda, Kamuzu (President of Malawi) 221
Bandes, Susan A. 277
Barnett, Georgia D. 278
Bartels, Lorana 189
Bateson, Gregory 187
Batterbury, Sarah 203
Bauman, Dirksen 131, 134
Bayley, Robert 158
Bellsmith, Ireland (et al 2022) 247
Berk-Seligson, Susan 189
Berzins McCoy, Marina 223
Beyond FM (radio station) 115
bias: judicial 177; perception of 250; societal and systemic 95, 108, 170, 250
bilingual 113, 140, 170, 242
Blake, Nicolas 194–195
Blood, Kelsie 172
Botswana 224, 239, 242
Boucher, Anna 171
Brady, Caitlin 258
braille 87, 91
Brennan, Mary 136
Bressman, Mark 153
British Sign Language (BSL) 132, 143
Brown, Richard 136
Brunson, Jeremy L. 132
BSL *see* British Sign Language
Buhai, Sande L 240–241
bureaucratic delays 37–38
Burt, Martha R. 276
Byrne, Bronagh (et al 2021) 157, 205

Cardno, Carol 154
Catholic Relief Services (CRS): 260
CC Act (2022) *see* Children's Code Act
CCPJA *see* Child Care, Protection and Justice Act
CDA *see* Critical Discourse Analysis
Chadwick, John (Justice) 85
Chanda, Vincent M. 150–151
Chibwe, Juliet 158
Chichewa (national language of Malawi) 29, 209, 221–222, 231, 233
Chichiri Maximum Prison 67
child: abuse 24, 55–56, 304; law 61, 68, 70; marriages 45, 50–51, 295–296, 298, 304; rights 44, 46, 298; victimisation 45–46, 50–51, 53, 55
Child Care, Protection and Justice Act (CCPJA) 30, 42, 62, 73, 76
child detention cases: *Frackson Case* 62, 68, 70–71; *Kaudzu Case* 69–71; *Moyo Case* 67, 69–71; *Police Cell Case* 68, 70–71
Child Justice Court 68
child terminology cases: *Nkhonjera Case* 67, 70; *Prisons Case* 66–68, 70–72; *Republic v MC* 66–67, 69–71
child witness: cross-examination procedures 22–26; definition of 13–14; perception of 20–21; protection 7, 15, 17, 26, 36; rights 15–16; testimony 7, 20–22, 25–26, 33–35–36
children: access to justice 14, 17, 21, 26; agency 45; best interests of 13, 15, 37, 45–46, 51, 53, 56, 61–63, 66–70, 72; communication challenges 23, 25, 31–32; competence test 21; conflicts with the law 18–20, 26, 30, 60–62, 64, 67–68; conviction terminology 62, 64–67, 70; defendant 63, 66, 70; definition 13–14; in detention 60, 68–70; with disabilities 50–51, 53, 117, 127; with disabilities 50–51, 53, 117, 127, 150; emotional distress 33–34, 37; intimidation of 24, 32; in the legal system 7, 38, 61; limited understanding of justice system 33, 65; miscarriage of justice 61, 64, 71; as most vulnerable 13; protection of 7, 15, 17, 30, 34, 37, 42, 299; rights of 32, 37, 46, 62, 68; silent victims 7, 44, 53, 56; stress/trauma 22; third party influence 20–21; treatment of within the legal system 62, 66; *see also* detention; victimisation 45–46, 49–51, 55; vulnerabilities 25, 34, 36; welfare inspector 20, 23; welfare ministry 56
Children's Code Act (CC Act) 2022: child-friendly environment provisions 22–23, 25–26; definition of child 14; efficacy 19; guarantees legal representation 20; provisions for child witness/protection 15–19, 21–22

Children's Court (Zimbabwe) 96
Children's Court (Zambia) 18
Chilomwe (language of Malawi) 29, 222, 233
Chilwa Approved School 67
Chirwa, Dennis K (Zambia): *Mumba v The People* (1984) 15
Chisena (language of Malawi) 221–222, 233
Chitha, Mateo 63
Chitonga (language of Malawi) 221, 233
Chitumbuka (language of Malawi) 29, 221–222, 233
Chiyao (language of Malawi) 29, 221
ChiYawo (language of Malawi) 222, 233
Choruma, Tsitsi 134
civic society organisations (CSOs) 237, 239
civil procedure/rules 80, 87, 241, 243
Civil Procedure Rules (CPR): excludes persons with disabilities 88–89, 91; High Court proceedings 84–85; litigation costs 89; needed reforms 91–92; summons signing/service of 86–88
climate change 44, 47–48
coercion 62, 98, 106–107, 111
colonisation 1
Coltart, David 133
Committee on the Rights of Persons with Disabilities 89, 94; *see also* CRPD
common law: British 103, 167; English 29, 88, 228, 236, 255, 275; litigants 241–242
communication: barriers 115, 122, 133, 136–137, 139, 142, 155, 205, 211; breakdown 158, 178; *see also* misinterpretation; misunderstanding; challenges 96, 102, 105, 108–109, 115, 125, 127, 132, 135, 138, 142, 184, 204; disorders 113–114, 117–118, 120–123, 125–126; gap 122–123, 137, 140, 173, 219, 266; style variations 29; verbal/non-verbal 113, 276
communities: hostile 3; marginalised 258, 262; *see also* Deaf; rural 45, 55–56, 175, 259
Compo, Nadja (et al 2011) 99, 110
comprehension: of legal language 184, 205, 207, 211, 266; limited in children 32–33; migrant workers 165, 177–180
conceptual framework 61, 69, 135
confession: admissibility 99; becomes political slogan 50; coerced 108; false 102, 107; intoxicated suspect/witness 95–99, 108, 110
confidentiality 120, 140–141, 175, 179, 191, 257
conflict resolution 1
Constitution of Kenya/Kenya Constitution 186, 193–194, 196
Constitution of the Republic of Malawi: discrimination and inequality 225; MSL as a language 203–204, 207–210, 212–214; right of access to justice 79–80, 119–120; rights of children 30; structure 29
Constitution of the Republic of South Africa 166
Constitution of Zimbabwe: Amendment (N0. 20) 96–97, 100, 103, 130, 137; right to representation 140, 236, 238
Constitutional Court: South Africa 166; Zambia 17; Zimbabwe 96, 243, 247, 255, 298
constraints: financial 138, 174, 186, 236; resource 105, 174
Convention on the Elimination of All Forms of Discrimination against Women (CEDAW) 225
Convention on the Rights of Persons with Disabilities (CRPD): human right to dignity 81–83, 159, 225; prohibits discrimination 84, 87, 89–91, 213; right of access to justice 79–80, 83, 86, 115–116, 149, 203, 205–207, 211, 225
Convention on the Rights of the Child (CRC): guarantees best interests of the child 37, 53–56, 62–63, 298n2; prohibits discrimination 46, 50–51, 53, 61, 72, 225
conviction: based on confessions 99; challenges 66–67, 70, 269; imprisonment 120–121; wrongful 5, 109, 122, 126–127, 169, 172, 176–177, 179, 265
Correctional Development (CD) 166
corrections officers 60
corroboration 21, 281, 286
corruption 51, 53–54, 56
Council of Europe 47
court clerks 228–229
court fees 89, 236, 247, 264

court interpreters: misinterpretation/inaccurate interpretation 32, 159, 161; necessity of 33, 35, 170; obstacles 176; selecting 229, 231–232; training 52, 117, 143, 169, 173, 180, 198, 229, 232–233
court marshals 229–230
Court of Appeal/Supreme Court (Zambia) 17–19
court proceedings: children in conflict 18–20, 26, 30, 60, 62, 64, 67–68; criminal 96–97, 100, 105, 166, 237; participation 21, 31–32, 70, 83, 88; right to communicate 165–166, 170
courtroom: environment/infrastructure 22–23, 26, 34, 60; etiquette 249; interactions 4, 188; internal security 97, 229; interpretation, concept of 220, 227–229, 233; interpreters 219, 228–232; languages 5, 23, 158, 161, 189–190
CP&EC *see* Criminal Procedure and Evidence Code
CPEC *see* Criminal Procedure and Evidence Code
CRADLE (Children's Foundations) 186
Crasborn, Onno (et al 2009) 161
credibility: child witness 20, 33–34, 36, 38; compromised by parent 123; of intoxicated witness 8, 95, 97–99, 104–105, 108–111; unrepresented litigant 249
Crenshaw, Kimberlie 296–297
criminal: acts 50, 62–63, 97, 267–268, 299; court 96–97, 100, 105, 166, 237; law 44, 62, 103, 172
Criminal Investigation Department (CID) 107
criminal justice system: addressing communication disorders 113–114, 119, 157, 204, 207–211, 213–214; children within 13, 62, 65; credibility of testimony 36; interpreters 131, 136, 139; right to access 90
Criminal Procedure and Evidence Act (CPEA) Zimbabwe 97, 100, 103
Criminal Procedure and Evidence Code, Malawi (CP&EC/CPEC) 30, 42, 64, 76, 121, 207, 210–211, 213–214
criminal proceedings: child witness protection 13, 16; intoxicated witness 98; legal representation for children 19, 60–61, 64, 66, 69, 72; terminology 60, 66; translators/interpreters 165, 238
criminology 97
Critical Discourse Analysis (CDA) theory 187–188, 277
Critical Language Policy Framework 208
Critical Theory 87, 206–207
cross-examination: controls 24–26; memory impairment 126; purpose of 248–249; speech/hearing impaired 88; use of language 189; witness 7, 16, 22, 32
CRPD *see* Convention on the Rights of Persons with Disabilities; United Nations Convention on the Rights of Persons with Disabilities
cult 293
cultural: lag 63–64, 68, 71; sensitivity 36, 39, 166; stigma and taboos 35–36
cultural norms 2, 29, 35
customary law 44, 51, 79, 84, 96, 228, 255–257

damage 4, 113, 277
Darity, William A. 184
data collection 65, 99, 119, 190–191, 207, 244
De Beauvoir, Simone 294
De Meulder, Maartje (et al 2019) 130, 132, 140, 203
Deaf Bill of Rights 143
Deaf community: access to justice 205–208; communication challenges 125, 127, 132, 134–135, 138, 142, 204–205, 210; culture 131, 138, 142, 159; deaf citizens 130, 133, 136, 139, 142–143; deaf interpreters 141–142, 158, 161; *see also* Sign Language interpreters; LHRs 203, 205, 207, 210, 212–214; limited access to services 134–136, 143; linguistic/cultural minority 149, 158, 160–161, 202, 212; main distinctions of d/Deaf 202, 205–207; recognition of MSL as national language 209–213; signers 132, 136, 142; vulnerability 203–204
death penalty 66–67, 70–71, 259
defilement *see* sexual offences
Degener, Theresia 82
DeLisle, Alexa (et al 2019) 278
Demessie, Elizabeth 203

Demographic and Health Survey: Malawi 114; Tanzania 275
Department of Justice (DoJ) 166
Department of Social Development (DSD) Zimbabwe 55
Derrida, Jacques 134
detention 97, 121, 154, 209, 264, 269; *see also* children in detention
Dhanda, Amita 86
dialect 113, 151, 176
Dignan, Cameron (et al 2020) 131
dignity 62, 80–83, 92, 115–116, 226, 305
Dillon-Malone, Clive Mary 296
Dingfelder Stone, John Henry 219
Disability Act (Zambia) 154, 159
Disability Act 2012 (Malawi) 80, 119–120, 124, 207–212, 214; *see also* Persons with Disabilities Act
Disability Alliance 81
discrimination: against children 13–15, 46, 50–51, 53, 55; dual-layered 116; linguistic 1–2, 4, 6, 8, 80, 190; *see also* GCDs
divorce 231, 240, 247, 256
Docrat, Zakeera (et al 2017/2021) 165, 189, 197, 206
document: analysis 95, 100, 103, 119, 149, 154, 160, 207, 243, 245, 266; case law 100, 243, 247; policy 69, 149
domestic violence 245, 258, **267**
domination 45, 56, 99, 188, 194, 207
Donohue, Frank 258
Dotter, F. 134
drug possession 267
drunk/drunken suspects 98, 100, 105–106, 109
Dudzai, Cornelius (et al 2023) 49
duty bearers (Malawi) 60–61, 65, 70–72
Dzuwa (the sun) 115

Eades, Diana 204–205
ECHR *see* European Convention on Human Rights
education: access to 150, 296, 304; for d/Deaf 150, 203; legal 7, 169, 251, 260–261, 265, 270; levels 268
Ehrlich, Susan 9, 276, 285–286
Emond, Alan (et al 2015) 206
emotional strain 34, 179, 242
Encyclopedia Britannica 153
English as official language 28–29, 31, 149, 220–221, 230
Entman, Robert M. 187
epilepsy 115, 117
equity 110, 139, 176, 180, 258
Eskridge 281
Eskridge, William N. 281
ethics: courtroom 179; in journalism 293–294, 296, 299, 304; research 101, 107
ethnic: differences 258; groups 28–29, 185, 278
ethnicity 118, 158, 189
European Convention on Human Rights (ECHR) 48, 85, 172
European Council (EC): guidelines for child-friendly courtroom 22
European Union (EU) 47
Evans, Jacqueline 98–99
evidence: gathering 139, 277; lack of 53–54, 56; presentation of 7–8, 65, 88–89, 99, 104; tempering 55

Facebook (social media) 293, 299
Fair Work Ombudsman 296
Fairclough, Norman 188, 280
fairness: of legal proceedings 37, 95, 105, 110, 158, 251, 258; perceptions of 165, 170; safeguards 178, 180, 220, 244
false: allegations 283, 302; beliefs 276, 278; confession 98, 102, 107; induced admissions 62, 102
family court 240–241
fear 30, 34–36, 51, 110, 133, 141, 166, 174, 186, 204, 205, 230, 277
Feigenson, Neal 277
Feild, Hubert 276
Feld, Barry C. 258
Female Student Network Trust (FSNT) 297
Ferreira, Pedro M. (et al 2019) 153
FGDs *see* Focus Group Discussions
Figueroa, Iris 171
financial resources 91, 167, 174, 180, 243
Fineman, Martha 187, 223
Fitzgerald, Louise F. 276
Flynn, Eilionóir 83, 86–87, 90, 120
Focus Group Discussions (FGDs) 46, 119, 190–191, 193, 195–198, 220
foreign language speakers: disadvantaged persons 191, 193; migrant workers

165–166, 172, 187; prejudices 2–3; vulnerability 185–188, 194–195, 197
forensic linguistics 6–9, 95, 205
framing theory 187, 197
Fraser, Nancy: Social Justice Theory 118, 126; Transformative Equality 244, 251; Transformative Justice Approach 6
fraud 20, 267–268, 295
frustration 34, 54, 135, 137, 194, 298

Gaines, Jonathan 258
Gándara, Patricia 220
GDCs *see* girls with communication disorders
gender: accommodations 84; discrimination 81, 118, 296, 299, 305; disparity 268, 296; equality 225, 258; justice 244, 251; of offenders **267**; studies 7, 9
Ghana, West Africa 64, 203, 206
Gibbons, John 113, 125–126
Giladi, Paul 189
Gill, Paul 191
girls with communication disorders (GCDs): barriers to justice 116–117, 119; disparaging terminology 118; inequalities 127–128; legal provisions 120–121; parent/guardian assistance 123; policy recommendations 126–128; rights of 124; use of interpretation services 117, 122–123, 126; *see also* Sign Language; violence against 114–115
GJP (Gorejena Penyeranyika) sect/cult: leader 293, 300–302, 305; members 293, 301–304
Glasser, Abraham (et al 2021) 133
Gleeson, Shannon 171
Global Corruption Barometer (GCB) 54
Gloppen, Siri 49, 225, 230
Gómez, M. Cecilla 220
González, Rosann (et al 2012) 197
Gor, George 63
guardian ad litem 85–86, 91
Gudjonsson, Gisli H. 98, 100–102, 107
Guidelines on Justice in Matters Involving Child Victims and Witnesses of Crime 2005 32, 34, 36
Guild, Alexis 171
guilt/guilty 4, 16, 21, 51, 56, 66, 70, 97, 102, 115, 120, 277
Gulliver, Mike 203

Hage, Sally M.: Social Justice Theory 101–102, 106
handcuff (gagging) 136
Handmer, John 48
hardships 4, 34, 47, 52
Haualand, Hilde 132, 140, 157, 160–161
Haworth, Kate 184
Hayes, Brittany 133
health: mental 30, 175, 181; physical 95; services 86, 116, 131, 134–135, 184, 223, 262, 305
hearing: court 16, 100, 187, 197, 230, 266; favorable treatment 141, 143; impairment 44, 52–53, 88, 113, 117, 134, 142, 150, 209
Heider, Fritz 279
Heikkil, Mikaela 48
Helbling, Jürg (et al 2015) 186
heritage 4, 161, 168
High Court: appeals 247–248, 256; interpreter 229; jurisdiction 17–19, 256, 276; Malawi 29, 65, 68, 79–80, 84, 231; Tanzania 275–276, 279; Zimbabwe 96, 255–256
HIV/AIDS 52, 115, 185, 224
Hollely, Karen 23–24
Hollingsworth, Kathryn 62
hooks, bell 296–297
HRM *see* Human Rights Model
human rights: abuses 5, 45, 55, 305; law 3, 47, 79; lawyers 173–174, 177–178, 257, 263; personal liberty 62, 154; right to be heard 15–16, 22, 32, 114, 156, 170, 211
Human Rights Model (HRM) 80–82
Hurter, Estelle 241–242

ICCPR *see* International Covenant on Civil and Political Rights
illiterate (and poor): access to justice 8, 225–226, 228, 230, 233, 261–263; accused and witnesses 104, 224, 230, 232–233; children 70; communication challenges 1–2, 123, 139, 219–220, 266; deaf persons 139; functionally 248, 251; legal obstacles 254, 257, 259–260, 269–270
impairments: hearing and speech 44, 50, 52–53, 88–89, 91; visual 68, 82, 87, 91, 134

impartiality 122, 126, 141, 165, 168, 173, 179, 250, 255, 289
imprisonment 64, 67–68, 120–121, 124, 267, 281n2
inclusive: accommodations 72, 84–85, 124–125, 168; justice 90–92
India 226, 261
indigenous: churches 294; language 8, 131, 149, 152, 155, 159, 166, 173, 198, 221–222
Individual Model 81
indoctrination 303, 305
Industrial Relations Court (IRC) 29
inequality 5, 47, 102, 204, 214, 225, 250, 288
injury 4, 85, 295
injustice: within the legal system 4–7; migrant worker 167, 177, 179; procedural 71; social 45, 47; substantial 196, 236, 244, 251; towards hearing impairment 117, 119, 126, 155, 157
Integrated Household Survey 224
International Convention on the Protection of the Rights of All Migrant Workers and Members of Their Families 171
International Covenant on Civil and Political Rights (ICCPR) 81, 115, 204, 225
International Covenant on Economic Social and Cultural Rights (ICESCR) 81, 225
International Labour Organisation 172
International Organisation for Migration (IOM) 185
interpreter: burnout/stress 175; caseloads 34–35; ethical/professional challenges 174; financial resources 174, 180; language complexities 176; obstacles 34, 167, 169, 176, 179, 181; public expectations 227
interrogation: methods 102; police 15, 98, 140, 142, 204
intoxication: communication challenges 105; suspects 96, 97, 103, 105–106; witness 8, 95, 97–99, 102–105, 108–111
Issa, Misheck 223

Jakaza, Tafadzwa Ngonidzaishe 114
JMAC *see* Johane Marange Apostolic Church
Johane Marange Apostolic Church (JMAC) 45, 49, 296–297
Johanne Masowe Chishanu Churches (JMCC) 294–301
Johnston, Trevor 158
journalism 293–294, 303–304
JSC *see* Judiciary Service Commission
judge craft 255
judges: corrupt 54; courtroom appearance 23; Englis-speaking 231; misinterpretation 32
judgments: court 65, 67, 99; written 279, 290
judicial officers 26, 37, 60, 67, 70, 90, 119, 124, 172, 229
Judicial Service Commission 96, 237–238, 252
Judiciary Service Commission (JSC) 228, 239, 245, 247, 251–252
jurisdiction 18; comparisons 98
jury/juror 66–67, 99, 232
juvenile delinquents 16, 62
Juveniles Court (Zambia) 18

Kadenge, Maxwell 249
Kalaluka, Likando 159–160
Kamwendo, Gregory 222
Kanyongolo, Fidelis Edge 49, 219, 225, 227, 229–230
Kaschula, Russell H. 165
Kashoki, Mubanga E. 151
Kayambazinthu, Edrinnie 221
KELIN Kenya (KELIN) 186
Kelly, Jane Francis (et al 2022) 155
Kenny, Maureen 101
Kenya: access to legal services 186, 191, 193; foreign language speakers 185–186, 195–197; International Commission of Jurists 186; official languages 150, 198; vulnerable groups 187, 190
Kerigan, Fergus (et al 2012) 14
key participants' interviews (KII) 119
Key, J.J.A. 24
Kishindo, Pascal 219, 221
Kiswahili (language of Kenya) 185, 193, 195–196, 198
Kituo cha Sheria (legal aid) 186
Knowlton, Natalie Ann (et al 2016) 240
Koroma, Simeon 258
Kotze, Ernst 176
Kozinski, Wyatt 98
Krausneker, Verena 131

Kress, Gunther 188
Kretzer, Michael 222–223
Kuenburg, Alexa (et al 2016) 206
Kumwenda, Joshua 222–223
Kunaka, Derrick: *Joseph Mulenga, Albert Joseph Phiri v The People* 24
Kusters, Annelies 136

Labour Court (Zimbabwe) 256
Ladd, Patty 203
land rights 48
Lane, Harlan (et al 1996) 140
language: activists 1–2, 9; application 2, 60, 113, 125, 128, 189, 207; barriers 3, 32, 34, 165, 167, 176, 197, 227, 231, 252; child appropriate 24, 32, 63, 66–70, 72; colloquial/slang 233, 300; comprehension 113; *see also* linguistic; impact 34, 167, 176, 178; less-heard languages 5, 8; mother tongue 70, 160, 202, 222; plain 72, 91; policies 131, 135, 206–207, 212, 219–220, 222; production 113; proficiency 170, 196; *see also* SL; seventy three (73) 152; sexually explicit 2, 4, 8; use of idiot/imbecile 118, 124–125
language policy and planning (LPP) 220
language rights (LRs): activists 2; are human rights 190; for hearing impaired 130, 139, 160, 168–169, 202; *see also* MSL; SL; regarding children 70; unrepresented litigant 238
Laster, Kathy 227
law enforcement: agencies 15, 91, 107, 140, 149, 153, 155–157, 160–161; bribery 51, 54; *see also* police pay–offs; corruption 51–53, 56; interviews 106; need for training 84, 91, 109–110; personnel 117, 132, 136, 140, 161, 300; rights violations 46, 49, 60, 65
Law Society of Kenya 186
Law Society of Zimbabwe 117, 243, 245–246; General Tariff or Fees for Legal Practitioners 246
Laws of Malawi 42, 76, 80, 94, 118, 228
Lawson, Anna 90, 120
lawyer: communication skills 23; lack of training 87; legal fees 14, 19, 224, 236, 245, **246**, 246–247; questioning techniques 4, 32
Lawyers for Human Rights 259–260
leadership 1, 298
Lee, Jieun 157
Lee, Joann (et al 2019) 190
Lee, Rebecca K. 289
legal: capacity 84–87, 90–91, 116; language 7, 15, 31, 33, 184, 204, 232–233, 248, 266; rights 124, 130, 141, 177, 211, 254, 259–260, 265, 269; services 15–16, 19–20, 87, 167, 186, 220, 240, 255, 259–260; standard 28
Legal Act (Malawi) 210, 213
legal aid: availability 20, 198, 224, 238–239; schemes 14; services 20, 111, 167, 170–172, 210, 224, 239, 246
Legal Aid Act 20, 207–208, 211, 213–214
Legal Aid Botswana 242
Legal and Human Rights Centre (LHRC) 275
legal documents: analysis 100, 105, 203–205, 243, 246, 257; comprehension 259, 265–266; language 31, 167–168, 208, 210, 212, 214; relevant 103–104, 207; violations 207–208
Legal Language Services 232
legal proceedings: accommodations for PWDs 84–85, 89; age-appropriate language/communication 28, 32, 72, 79, 265; child-friendly 36–39, 62–67, 69; cost of litigation 89, 91, 241, 255; fairness 158, 170, 277; understanding of 255, 262
legal professionals: alternative language use and training 126, 142, 180–181, 184, 194; linguistic knowledge 6–7, 9, 36–37, 39, 60, 167, 169; misinterpretation 32–33
legal remedies 80, 120, 258
legal representation: affordability 8, 19, 236, 257, 269; equitable treatment/fairness 258–259, 263–264; global perspectives 240; guarantee of 19–20, 64, 84, 238, 240; *see also* legal aid; inadequate/unattainable 87, 176–177, 236
Legal Resources Foundation (LRF) 238–239, 245, 259–260
LHRs *see* Linguistic Human Rights
Lily Farm 293, 301–302, 304
Limantė, Agnė 3, 47–48
limited English proficiency (LEP) 1–2

linguistic: assimilation 212; barriers 3, 8, 28, 34–36, 177; challenges 4, 39, 165; comprehension 4; crucial aspects 66; discrimination 1–2, 4, 6, 80, 190; diversity 149, 152, 160, 167, 169, 176, 213; justice 165, 170, 190; rights 80, 131, 142, 149, 160–161, 169, 205–206, 211; variation 157–158, 161; vulnerability 185
Linguistic Human Rights (LHRs): for the deaf 205, 207, 212–213; includes right to a fair trial 211; recognition 203, 210–211
Lininger, Tom 188
Lisak, David 283
literacy: adult 226; campaigns 152; lack of; *see also* illiteracy 262–263, 266, 268–268; legal 251, 265; and legal outcomes 242, 259
litigants: intoxicated 95; language barriers 196–197, 202, 211, 227; socio-economic status 254
litigants, unrepresented: access to justice 8, 236; definition 237; economic barriers 242, 246; prevalence 245; procedural barriers 243, 247; rights of 244–245; support services 251
litigation: capacity 85–86; cost of 89; guardian 88; public interest 186, 226, 233
Lonsway, Kimberly A. 276
Lucas, Ceil (et al 2003) 157–158

Mabilo, T.J. 174
Macioce, Fabio 47
Mack, Kathy 255
Madzibaba Ishmael (Chokurongerwa, Ismael): allegations of child abuse/rape 299–300; arrest of 294–295; child abuse 303–304; cult leader 293, 301; dishonesty 302; human rights violations 304; indoctrination of victims 303, 305; self-proclaimed status/charisma 301–302
Magaya, Walter 295
magistrates: appointment of 65–66, 68; corrupt 54; interviews 100, 103, 106, 108, 229–231, 244, 250; perceptions of 109; suitability for children's cases *(Kashuga Case/Prisons Case)* 68–70, 72; support for 29, 251; training and support 29, 69, 127, 172
Magistrates Court: Malawi 26, 65, 71; South Africa 166, 172; Tanzania 275–276; Zambia 18–19; Zimbabwe 96, 106, 238, 255–256, 269
Magnus, Amy 258
Magwero, Zambia 150–151
Makanje, Gift 189
Makaza, Bobby/Bhobhi (AIC member/rapist) 50, 295
Makururu, Andby 298–299
Makwavarara, Zifikile 206
Malan, Koos 189
Malaria Indicator Survey 275
Malawi: case law 65, 118; colonial period 221; criminal justice system 61, 126–127; language issues 125, 208; multiparty period 221; one-party-period 221; primary languages 28–29, 221–222, 233
Malawi Congress Party (MCP) 221
Malawi Disability Act 2012 120, 207, 209
Malawi National Social Support Programme 224, 227
Malawi News Agency 115
Malawi Penal Code 61, 114, 118, 120, 124–125
Malawi School Certificate of Education (MSCE) 119, 222
Malawi Sign Language (MSL): interpreters 212; legal aid service 210; legal documents 208–209; legal recognition 204–205, 207, 210–211, 213–214; legal status 202–203, 206, 210
Malgieri, Gianclaudio 47
maltreatment 49, 62
Malunga, Bernadette (et al 2017) 124
Malunga, Tiyera 150
Mambwe, Kelvin 152
Manica Post (newspaper/Zimbabwe) 100, 109
Mann, Ruth E. 278
marginalisation: communicatively challenged 119, 134, 155, 160–161, 202, 205; socio-economic 226, 239, 255, 296–297
marginalised groups 1, 4–5, 136, 185, 249, 251, 262, 268
Marinos, Voula (et al 2009) 88
Maritim, Rebecca 190
marriage: annulment 231; forced 56, 293; *see also* child marriages; laws 51, 56, 256; *see also* family law
Martin, Angela K. 185

Masedze, Shonhiwa (Johanne Masowe) 294, 296
Matende, Tawanda (et al 2023) 133–134, 138, 202
Matiki, Alfred J. 220—222
Matsikidze, Rodgers 243
medical: attention 45, 50, 295–296, 304–305; documentation 38, 118, 280; impairment 80–81, 86, 155, 184; professionals 33, 46, 51–52, 135
Medical Model 81, 83
memory: effects of intoxication 95, 97–99, 104–106, 108–109, 111; loss 126
mental: capacity 85–86; disability 115, 118, 120–121; health 175, 181
Mercy Corps 260
Merriam Webster 185
methodology (research): document analysis 207, 243, 257; in-depth interviews 190, 257; *see also* FGDs; purposive sampling 119, 135, 191, 279; use of case law 65; written judgments 279, 290
migrant worker: deportation 166, 171; emotional distress 178; equity disparities 176, 180; hurdles 166–167, 170, 176, 179; interpreters for 170, 173; lack of documentation 166; support networks 181
Mikkelson, Holly 176
Miller, Katrina R. 131–133
Ministry of Gender, Community Development and Social Welfare 226
minority: group 2, 157–158, 160, 202, 206, 224; *see also* Deaf community; language 4, 131, 134, 139, 160, 203, 238, 242
Miranda rights 209, 211
misinterpretation 28, 32–33, 158, 169, 178, 263, 269
misunderstanding 33, 158, 168, 172, 177, 179, 184, 263, 266, 269, 303
Miti, Lazarus 133
Mnangagwa, Emmerson 50, 295, 298
Monds, Loren A. (et al 2021) 97
Monson, Rebecca 48
Moore, Wendy 258
Moraa, Terry 63
Mozambique 173–174, 239
Mpasha, Lekau Eleazar 170, 178
Mpemba Staff Development Institute 229
Msipa, Dianah 117
Mtata, Kenneth 52
Mugari, Victor (et al 2019) 133–134, 138
Müller, Karen 23–24
murder: conviction of minor *(Republic v MC; Blackson Nkhonjera v Republic; Evans Moyo v Attorney)* 66–67, 69–71
Murray, J.J. 131
Musami Arupe Jesuit School of the Deaf 46
Mustaniemi-Laakso, Maija 48
Mutele, Tshilidzi Constance 170, 178
Mutevedzi, Munamato (Judge) 104
Mwazha, Paul 294
Mweri, Jefwa 202
Mzuzu High Court 229, 231
Mzuzu University 229, 232–233

Nairobi, Kenya 191
Napier, Jemina 136, 140
National Adult Literacy and Education Strategic Plan 226
National Disability Policy (NDP) 142
National Institute of Justice 172
National Judicial Education Program (NJEP) 276
National Prosecutions Authority 19
Ndlovu, Eventhough 206, 232
Nemukuyu, Daniel 54
New Zealand Sign Language Act 2006 206
Nganga, Simon 204
NGO *see* Non-Governmental Organisation
Ngulube, Anderson 22
Ngure, Eunice 204
Nguyen-Trung, Kien (et al 2019) 184–185
Nifosi-Sutton, Ingrid 47
Niklas, Jędrzej 46
Nkhata Bay District Magistrate Court 229, 232
Nkhata, Chipo (et al 2016) 90
Nkhata, Mwiza Jo 87, 120–121
Non-Governmental Organisation (NGO) 52, 171, 181, 259
Nsengaali, Pitlagano Godfrey 242–243
Nyakudya, Dorothy 114
Nyasa Times (Malawi) 115, 233
Nyirenda, Andrew K.C. 224–226
Nyoni, Sithembiso 298
Nzira, Godfrey 295

Obare, Alice 296
obligations 72, 79, 116, 118, 127, 155, 181, 213, 223, 225, 297
offence: criminal 13, 62, 155; predominately male **267**, 268; *see also* sexual assault; sexual 21, 286
offender 121, 131, 249, 261, 263, 265, 268–270, 279, 288
official language: English as 28–29, 31, 70, 149, 159, 185, 220–222, 228; MSL 209–211
Ogburn, William F. 63
Omori, Marisi 258
opponent 14, 22, 24
oppress 81–82, 296–297, 305
Organisation for Economic Co-operation and Development (OECD) 14
Ortoleva, Stephanie 85, 90
Otchere, F. (et al 2020) 227
outcome: case/trial 35, 95, 132, 178, 188, 195; educational 134, 155

Palmer, Francesca T. (et al 2013) 108
Pangsapa, Piya 171
Pariotti, Elena 184–185
Park, Julie (et al 2015) 206
patriarchy 294, 297
Patterson, Tristan P. (et al 2022) 278
Payne, Diana L. (et al 1999) 276
PEACE model 100, 102, 107
Pearse, John 100, 102, 107
Peck, Jennifer 258
People With Disabilities (PWDs): accommodations 79–80; communication challenges 88; communication disorders 113, 117, 123, 127; deafblind women 89; definition 124; hearing/speech impairment 88, 117, 132, 150, 209; intellectual disabilities 85, 88–90, 125; intellectual disabilities 85–86, 88–91, 117, 125; limited access to justice 5, 22; right to justice 79–80, 83–86, 121, 142
perception: cultural 64, 68, 99; influence 29, 37, 168, 278; traditional 17, 20
perpetrator: alleged 13–14, 22, 26, 283; identification process 26, 276
personal liberty 154
personnel: court 109, 227, 250–251, 270; legal 84, 140–141, 261, 277; police 54, 107, 136; shortage 36
persons with disabilities: access to justice 22, 79–80, 84, 90, 93, 115, 120; discrimination against 90; financial burden 80, 89, 91; fundamental freedoms 81–83; legal capacity 84, 90–91; litigation guardian 85, 88; rights of 117, 121, 142
Persons with Disability Act 2024 79, 84
Petersen, Nick 258
Petherbridge, Danielle 189
poaching 267
police: coercion 62, 98, 106–107, 111; interviewing techniques 96, 100, 102; pay-offs 53; rogue 54; services 96, 130–131, 135–136, 143; statements 7; stations 54, 100, 102, 107, 110, 117, 121, 123, 135–143, 238, 301; training 84, 109–111, 121–123, 126–127, 136, 138
Police Deaf Network Unit (PDNU) 143
Police General Headquarters (PGHQ) 300
Police Link Officer for the Deaf (PLOD) 142–143
Police Suspect Interviewing (Gudjonsson & Pearse) 101–102
policymakers 2, 9, 72, 203, 239, 270
political: interference 49–50, 56; party 50; rights 15, 82
poor and illiterate *see* illiterate (and poor)
post-conviction 269
poverty 13–14, 16, 19, 45, 47, 56, 224, 247, 254, 258, 261
power: abuse of 184, 188, 194, 281, 298; distribution of 47, 61, 89, 118, 131
Powers, Ráchael 133
prejudice 2, 6, 167, 169, 179, 243, 254, 278–279, 297, 160161
primary languages 28–29, 167, 190
prison: inappropriate for children 64–66, 68–70; officers 105, 191; release from 50, 66, 68, 295
procedural: inefficiencies 38–39; justice 65
Procedural Justice Theory 64
procedure: civil 80, 87, 241, 243; court appearance, timely 19, 38, 62, 113; improper 71; violations *(Frackson, Chikalamba and Jabes v Republic)* 62, 68, 70–71
Professional Counselling Services 181
Prophetic Healing and Deliverance (PHD) 295

prosecutors: obstacles 70; public 51, 100, 104, 106, 109, 244, 247, 250–251; rogue 54
protection: of children 15, 30; equal 115, 204; order 97, 100, 105, 109; of vulnerable groups 47, 204, 212, 219
psychology 35, 97, 108–109, 184
public disorder 267
Public Law Institute (PLI) 186
PWDs *see* People With Disabilities

Quadri, Nasreen (et al 2023) 190

race: protection from discrimination 15, 81, 118, 225, 227, 296, 299
radio 152, 221, 293, 296, 300, 302
Ragusa, Angela 258
Ralarala, Monwabisi K. 127, 211
Ranosa-Madrunio (2013), Marilu 189
rape: allegations 283, 295; case law 281; child *(Republic v Limbikani Cosmas Mpokosa; Eliah Bariki v Republic)* 33, 286–287; consent/ lack of 51, 280–281; corroboration 281, 286; definition 276; *Eliah Bariki v Republic* 286–278; incest 50, 52, 295; is sex 286; judical 4, 9; literature 278; myths 9, 275–279, 282; *see also* rape myth acceptance; *Omary Kijuu v Republic* 286; penetration 33, 280; *see also* sexual intercourse; *Peter Abel Kirumi v Republic* 281, 284, 286–289; real rape 285, 290; reporting 125, 283–284, 298; scandals 295; statistics 275; statutory 50–52; terminology *(Nurdin Wailu v Republic)* 287; threats 281–282; trauma 279, 284, 289–290; trials 4, 276–277; victim 276, 278, 283–284, 289
rape myth acceptance (RMA) 278, 280
Rawl, John: Theory of Justice 241, 244, 251
Reagan, Timothy 202–203
recall 34, 98–99
reformatory 66–68, 70–71
reforms 39, 55, 60, 110–111, 243, 250–252, 261, 270
refugee: advocates 187; communication barriers 193–195; ensuring fair treatment 197–198; experiences 191, 193; vulnerability 185–187, 189
Reid technique 100, 102, 107
reliability 20, 34, 95, 97–98, 108–110, 126, 174, 281, 284
religious: background 118; leaders 294, 298, 305; organisations 56; sect/ cults 49, 55–56, 293; violence 293; worldviews 294
research: data analysis techniques 102, 135, 243, 257, 279; data collection techniques 65, 99, 119, 190, 207, 244; document analysis 95, 100, 103, 119, 149, 154, 160, 207, 243, 245, 266; rationale 114; thematic analysis 101, 257, 299; theoretical framework 101, 244
resources: access to 118, 181; availability 238, 258; legal 251, 259, 261; limitations 69, 88, 174
restorative justice 262
Ricchiardi, Sherry 293
Rice, Darwin F. 241
Richards, Kelly 189
Roach Anleu, Sharyn 255
rule of law 5, 55, 97, 226, 236
Russell, Deb 131
Ruvheneko Rwenyenyedzi Trust (RRT) 298

Sabatello, Maya 158
safety homes *see* reformatory
Sall, Adjaratou Oumar 131
Sathe, Satyaranjan P. 226
Satia, Emmanuel 190, 193, 289
Schaefer, Shelly 258
Schembri, Adam 158
Schoultz, Isabel (et al 2023) 172
second language speakers 4, 197
segregation 296
Self-incrimination 242, 265
self-representation 240–241, 244–245, 250–251
Senegalese sign language (SSL) 131
sentence: custodial 266, 305; imposed 50, 67–68, 209; rehearing 67, 70
sexual: abuse 52, 116–117, 193, 295, 298, 301; consent 281; intercourse 29, 50–51, 120, 280n1, 286–288; orientation 118, 281; violence 114, 116–117, 275–276
sexual assault: evidence 38, 277; *see also* rape; trauma 32, 34, 290; victims 4, 125, 278; *see also* GCD; witnesses 28, 30–35, 38–39; against women 4, 8, 273

sexual offences: defilement 21, 33, 67, 115, 120; incest 22, 280; indecent assault 21, 29, 295; against order of nature 21, 281n2; sodomy 24, 190, 281, 289; victims of 4, 30, 125, 278
shame 4, 35–36, 297, 301
Shariah 261
sign language: homegrown 52–53; learning 116; system 4
Sign Language (SL): alternative communication 91, 126; definition of 153; interpreters 89, 131, 135–136, 138–143; meaning making 150, 152–153; minoritised minority language 131; *see also* minority language; teachers (Zambia) 152, 161; in Zambia 149
Sign Language Interpretation Services (SLIS) 132, 140
Sign Language recognition (SLR) 153
Sigurdsson, Jon F. 98
Silungwe, Annel (Zambia): *Benard Chisha v The People* (1980) 20–21
Simukai Child Protection Program 299
skills: communication 4, 23; interpretation 180, 229–230, 233; language 31–32, 166–167, 176–177; sign language 142
Skinner, Robert 136, 140
SLIS *see* Sign Language Interpretation Services
social: exclusion 3–4, 116, 160–161; inclusion 2–4, 7; justice 7, 101–102, 104, 114, 118–119, 124, 172, 204, 207, 257; suffering 4; values 293n1, 294
Social Model 81–82
sociolinguistics 152, 159, 229
Solo, Kholisani 242–243
Song, Lichao 188
Song, Yun 269
Soto, Hernando de 219
South Africa (SA): 1944 Magistrates' Courts Act 172; guarantee of representation 236; language policy 168; official languages (11) 167–168
South African Constitution 166, 169, 230
South African Development Community (SADC) 55–56
South African Human Rights Commission 170
South African Sign Language (SASL) 206
speech impairment 44, 50, 52–53, 88–89
spoken language 4, 89, 134, 152–153, 158, 161, 175, 202–203, 213
St Paul Musami Mission Hospital 46
Staff Development Institute (SDI) 229
Stalford, Helen 62
Star FM (radio station) 293, 299
stereotypes 133, 136, 279
stigma 35–36, 38, 72, 110–111, 160–161
Stone, Marcus 25
subordinate courts 18, 29, 80, 255
summons 87–88, 91, 229, 266
Supreme Court of Appeal 29, 64–65, 68, 80, 120, 166
suspects: criminal 60, 64; inebriated/intoxicated 97–98, 100–109
Svongoro, Paul (et al 2023) 117, 127, 211, 249

Tallroth, Paulina 131
Tambulukani, Geoffrey 151
Tanzania: Court of Appeal 275; legal system 275; regional courts of appeal 279
Tanzania Demographic and Health Survey 275
Tanzania Penal Code 276
Taylor, Veronica L. 227
technology 175, 211, 262, 293–294
Tereškinas, Artūras 3, 47–48
terminology: appropriate 63, 66–67, 72; d/Deaf 202; inappropriate 69, 72; legal 125, 168, 174, 179–180
testimony: completeness of 28, 32, 88; credibility 98–99, 104, 106, 108–111, 283–284, 288–289; redundant 21
Third World 259
threats 4, 52, 184, 282
Tollefson, James W. 206, 212
tradition 4, 48, 297, 299, 304; *see also* culture
training: civil service 229; insufficient 34, 137–138, 174, 179; mandatory/specialised 26, 28–29, 35–37, 39, 136, 154, 157, 159, 161; sign language 122–123, 136, 149–150, 154–156, 179
Transparency International (TI) 186

transportation 264
trauma: psychological 28, 33–35, 37–38, 284; reducing 17, 22, 26, 30; sexual assault 32, 34, 279, 289–290
Trovato, Sara 131, 212
truth 21, 125, 189, 254, 283, 293, 303
Tsakare resettlement 46, 52–54

UDHR *see* Universal Declaration of Human Rights
UNCRC *see* Convention on the Rights of the Child
UNCRPD *see* Convention on the Rights of Persons with Disabilities
underprivileged 2, 8, 53
uneducated 3, 5, 8, 255, 266, 268
UNHRC *see* Human Rights Committee
Union of Physically Impaired Against Segregation (UPIAS) 81
United Nations (UN): Economic and Social Council Resolution Guidelines for Action on Children in the Criminal Justice System 31, 42; Guidelines on Justice in Matters involving Child Victims and Witnesses of Crime 2005 30–31, 36–37, 42; Human Rights Committee 227; Human Rights Office of the High Commissioner 1, 6; International Principles on Access to Justice 90; Office on Drugs and Crime (UNODC) 104, 237, 239; Standard Minimum Rules for the Administration of Juvenile Justice 1985 31, 43, 61, 76
Universal Declaration of Human Rights (UDHR) 81, 115
University of Malawi 127
University of Zambia (UNZA) 150, 152, 155–157
UNZA *see* University of Zambia
US Courts 99, 240
Usadolo, Sam E. 176

Van den Bos, Kees 118
Van Dijk, Teun 188
Van Leeuwen, Theo 188
Veritas, Zim 96
vernacular language 108, 220–222, 225, 233
victim: behaviour 118, 277, 290; empathy 275–277, 289; of sexual violence 114, 116–117, 275–276, 288; *see also* rape
Villanueva, Virna Sayson 189
vindictive 21, 270
virginity 295, 297
visual impairment 87, 91
vocabulary 23–24, 32–33, 125–126, 153, 178
von Agris, Ulrich (et al 2008) 153
vulnerability: concepts of 3, 233–234; *see also* discrimination; etymology of 223; linguistic 204; *see also* communication barriers; theory 187, 195, 223
vulnerable groups *see by listing* (i.e. migrant workers; Deaf); rape victims

Wakumelo, N.M. 150, 155–153
Ward, Stephen J. 293
Wazakili, Maragret 211
Weller, Penelope 87
white garment churches 296–297, 299
Widyawati, Anis 171
Wilcox, Sherman (et al 2012) 159
Williams, Kim 237, 241
Wily, Liz Alden 48–49
witness: communicative disorders 113, 121; *see also* MSL; SL; Deaf; intoxicated 8, 95, 97–99, 102–105, 108–111; poor-illiterate 219–220, 224, 230, 232–233; protection 13, 15–16, 104; questioning 7, 102; vulnerable 104, 189
Wodak, Ruth 188
women: abuse of 295–297; black/of color 296; crimes against 275; reporting rape 282–283
Women Lawyers' Association 259
Woodward, James C. 202
World Bank 222, 275
World Federation of the Deaf (WFD) 202
World Vision 260

Yamada, Shoko 223
YouTube (social media) 293, 299

Zambia: Constitution 1996 13, 15–16, 19; court structure 17–18; justice delivery system 15–16; Legal Aid Board 16, 19–20; national language of 149; safeguarding of child rights 13, 15–17; *see also* CC Act; Supreme Court 17
Zambia Institute on Special Education (ZAMISE) 150, 152, 155–157

Zambia National Association of the Deaf (ZNAD) 150–151
Zambian Sign Language (ZAMSL) 151
ZAMISE *see* Zambia Institute on Special Education
Zane, Steven (et al 2020) 269
ZANU PF (Zimbabwe African National Union–Patriotic Front) 45, 50, 52, 295, 298
Zhao, Kaili 172
Zhao, Tianyi 269
Zietlow, Rebecca 83
Zimba, Yvonne 159
Zimbabwe: case law (president) 44, 100, 108, 243; child victimisation 51; children viewed as property 44; courts system 96, 255; informa pauperis (IP) 239; justice system 117; legal system 46, 103; marriage laws 51; newspapers 100; provinces (Masonland East/Central) 45–46, 50–52, 56; radio talk shows 296; recommendations for improving the judicial system 269–270; social workers 55; Statutory Instrument (SI) 2 51
Zimbabwe African National Union–Patriotic Front (ZANU–PF) 45, 50, 52, 295, 298
Zimbabwe Council of Churches (ZCC) 52, 294
Zimbabwe Human Rights Commission (ZHRC) 56
Zimbabwe Lawyers for Human Rights (ZLHR) 260
Zimbabwe Republic Police (ZRP) 97, 142
Zimbabwean Sign Language 133
ZNAD *see* Zambia National Association of the Deaf
Zvinoyera (radio): ethical journalism 293; exposure of abuse 294

FSC
www.fsc.org
MIX
Papier | Fördert gute Waldnutzung
FSC® C083411

Kolibri 360 GmbH
Ferdinand-Jühlke-Straße 7
99095 Erfurt, Deutschland
produktsicherheit@kolibri360.de